D0401913

SAME DATE
OF RANK

SAME DATE OF RANK

Grads at the top and bottom
from West Point, Annapolis, and
the Air Force Academy

Lt. Col. C. J. Hoppin, USAF Ret.

Copyright © 2009 by Lt. Col. C. J. Hoppin, USAF Ret.

Library of Congress Control Number: 2008912139
ISBN: Hardcover   978-1-4363-9896-1
                 Softcover   978-1-4363-9895-4
                 Ebook   978-1-4535-2441-1

All rights reserved. No part of this book may be reproduced or transmitted in any form or by any means, electronic or mechanical, including photocopying, recording, or by any information storage and retrieval system, without permission in writing from the copyright owner.

This book was printed in the United States of America.

Design by Jim Hoppin
Photos courtesy of family archives and USMA, USNA and USAFA

To order additional copies of this book, contact:
Xlibris Corporation
1-888-795-4274
www.Xlibris.com
Orders@Xlibris.com
42602

Contents

Preface

The happy home crowd nearly filled Michie Stadium's 39,929 seats that sunny May 22 morning as West Point's Class of 1985 prepared to graduate. Tradition and pageantry drove the schedule of music, marches, and speeches by dignitaries who included Superintendent Lt. Gen. Willard W. Scott Jr. and U.S. Army Secretary John O. Marsh. The 1,010 young men and women who were about to become the 187th class to join the Long Gray Line basked in warm greetings from their families and friends.

My wife, Barbara, and I were there from our home in Northern New Jersey to commend Bill Kowal, who had been dating our daughter, Patti, long enough to invite us to the celebrations that marked the end of his Academy years. These included a number of special events, starting with the athletes' "A Club" dance a few nights earlier at the Thayer Hotel. William E. Kowal was a strapping Pennsylvanian who had played varsity soccer for the Army Black Knights and, like many cadets, had met up with young ladies from nearby communities during too-seldom breaks from the rigors of cadet life.

In typical military fashion, the graduation day's agenda had been carefully planned with a detailed Operations Plan that dictated to the minute who did what, when, where, and how. The schedule moved slowly for the guests as we patiently waited in the sun-filled bleachers for our senior cadets to be recognized.

First to receive his coveted diploma from Secretary Marsh was Lawrence M. Young from Massapequa, NY. By tradition, soon-to-be Second Lieutenant Young was the first to be called to the stage at the fifty-yard line in front of his classmates. First in the class, with a cumulative academic grade point average exceeding 4.0, meant that Young also had first choice of the 1,010 initial job assignments the Army would provide him and his classmates.

Young was followed by Pennsylvanian Leslie A. Lewis, who ranked second. Next were the 48 other members who made up the top five percent of the class. These grads were called up in order of their class rank achievement. Next, General Scott began calling cadets up to the stage in alphabetical order, starting with Derric L. Abrecht. Graduates lined up on both sides of the stage to receive their diplomas from General Scott on one side and the Commandant of Cadets BGen Peter J. Boylan and Academic Dean BGen Frederick Smith on the other. Two very methodical queues brought the graduates to the stage.

Each new name brought cheers from somewhere in the stadium as the people who knew the cadet saluted his or her walk across the stage. Like some college graduations, this was not an occasion when guests held their applause to the end of the event. So as each of the graduates had their moments in the sun, the crowd reacted with a lusty cheer or whistle from neighboring sections throughout the stadium. Sometimes, someone would shout a nickname above the din, or the graduate would leap and offer a high five to the next classmate.

Suddenly, in the midst of the grads whose last name began with the letter *C,* the routine litany of announced names and localized cheers was sharply interrupted. With the name of one Martin Robert Clark, *all* of his fellow classmates rose from their chairs on the stadium floor to cheer this seemingly anonymous cadet.

"Who's that?" asked voices in the crowd. "What's that all about?" They wanted to know as questions buzzed around the stadium.

"Last in the class," someone offered in reply. "He's last in the class."

"Ah, that's it, he's last in the class," the buzz continued.

That explained the cheers, which by now had died down as quickly as they had begun. Then the momentary silence was broken by a single voice.

"It really is *something* to be *last* in the class!"

And that's how this book was conceived. Who was Martin Clark, and how did he become last in the Class of 1985 at the United States Military Academy? And what did he do next? What happened to number one Lawrence M. Young? And what happened to the others who were at the top and bottom in their classes at our nation's military academies?

Although they all start out differently, each graduate of West Point, Annapolis, and the Air Force Academy ends graduation day with the same date of rank as a brand-new "butter bar" or Second Lieutenant or Ensign in the U.S. Army, Navy, Air Force, or Marine Corps. Their class rank determines their first job since they choose their initial assignments in the order in which they graduate. Their graduation and officer commissioning ceremony signal important milestones. They also launch postgraduate military service and civilian careers that impact country and, evermore, the global community.

The academies' class rank system reminds me of the old joke about what you call the person who's last in their class at a medical or law school.

The answer is very simple: "Doctor" or "Lawyer." At the academies, *all* of the graduates are called "Lieutenant" or "Ensign." So despite considerable emphasis on class standings while at the academies, the graduates begin their military careers with the same date of rank.

American taxpayers foot the bill for costly tuition, room and board, special training, and salary that these cadets and midshipmen receive at the U.S. service academies. This book explores the return on those investments as it reports the achievements and adversities of a select group of graduates of all three schools. It also describes the class rank of several more notable graduates, illustrating my hypothesis that class rank is not necessarily a predictor of fame and fortune.

Most of the people in the book actually selected themselves. They were among several dozen who responded to my survey distributed to graduates at the top and bottom of their classes by the three academies' alumni associations: the Association of Graduates at West Point and the Air Force Academy and the Alumni Association at the Naval Academy. West Point has had more than 62,000 grads, Navy's exceed 73,000, and the newer Air Force Academy has 38,000 alumni.

Grads range from an Army infantryman who was last in his class but first to be promoted to General to an Admiral who was first but surprised to become the only number one in the history of the Naval Academy to achieve the Navy's highest position as Chief of Naval Operations. Others include an African-American basketball player who graduated last in his Air Force Academy class and rose to be the deputy director of Equal Opportunity Employment in the U.S. Department of Defense. The men and women at or near the top and bottom of their classes whom I interviewed defy simple classification, but are all achievers. They include Soldiers, Sailors, Marines, Airmen, combat-and-support pilots, astronauts, computer engineers, organizational and financial wizards, fathers, mothers, grandparents, and great-grandparents.

These men and women cross cultures and generations, but share an important heritage through their educational preparation. They are active citizen patriots who contribute to the fabric of the American society they swore to protect when they were commissioned as officers in the United States military. It has been my distinct pleasure to get to know these people over the past few years, and I believe you will enjoy meeting them too.

Christopher J. Hoppin
Lt.Col., USAFR Ret.

Peaks Island, Maine

Introduction

The Academies, Their Students and Class Rank

Throughout history, many citizens of the United States of America have questioned their military. I was introduced to this questioning as the son of a career U.S. Air Force officer born in the Bronx, NY, but raised in military communities in Ohio, Indiana, and Japan. When my family transferred to Westover Air Force Base in Western Massachusetts in 1957, as I began my sophomore year at Cathedral High School, I learned that not everyone understood what my father did for a living. "He's in the Air Force; does he fly?" was a common query. My Father, John E. Hoppin, was also born in the Bronx and enlisted in the Army Air Corps before World War II without a high school diploma. He was commissioned through the Officer Candidate School program and served as an administrative, special services, and personnel officer for twenty years.

In the broader American society and history, many earlier questions about the military stemmed from past European links between soldiers and aristocrats that early Americans found unsettling at best. American colonists established individual state militias but resisted a national standing army. Eventually, the Founding Fathers created the Marines and the Continental Army and Navy for the common good. However, many leaders of those forces were imported from overseas.

After the Revolutionary War, the absence of homegrown and educated military leaders led men such as George Washington, John Adams, and Alexander Hamilton to call for an institution to train military officers. Thomas Jefferson was persuaded to support the school because he believed that officers trained for military engineering could also build civil projects like roads and bridges. This combination of military needs and the potential for civic works led the U.S. government to establish the Military Academy for the Army in 1802 during the Jefferson presidency.

Fortress West Point, fifty miles up the western banks of the Hudson River from New York City, was chosen as its home. The United States Military Academy (USMA) is the current host organization, but American military forces have been posted to West Point since 1778, making it the oldest U.S. Army post in continued operation. The site of Fort Clinton, originally called Fort Arnold after Benedict Arnold, occupies a natural bend in the wide river. The area played a key part in the American Revolutionary War. In addition to the natural hills and cliffs above the river, a flat plain above was ideal for a military facility. It also housed large man-made structures, including 1,700 feet of iron chain with one-hundred-plus-pound links that stretched across the river as a barrier to enemy shipping. The Hudson River defines the eastern edge of the campus and punctuates its geography with an exclamation.

The Hudson Highlands rise 170 feet above the river in a magnificent setting. The challenging terrain in the surrounding hills provides cadets ample opportunities to study and practice Army field maneuvers. Visitors approach the Academy through the community of Highland Falls, NY, an almost quaint collection of businesses and homes in a quiet village setting. Shops, motels, and the Federal Credit Union announce the Academy's presence. A modern Visitors Center and the West Point Museum offer pleasant welcomes. Just inside the main gate stands the Thayer Hotel, named for Colonel Sylvanus Thayer, ranked third of 15 men in the Class of 1808 and fondly called "the Father of the Academy."

In 1825, President John Quincy Adams urged Congress to establish a Naval Academy "for the formation of scientific and accomplished officers." His proposal, however, was not adopted for twenty years. When the Naval Academy's founders were looking for a suitable location, it was reported that Secretary of the Navy George Bancroft decided to move the naval school to "the healthy and secluded" location of Annapolis, a beautiful port city and the capital of Maryland. He wanted to rescue midshipmen from "the temptations and distractions that necessarily connect with a large and populous city." The Philadelphia Naval Asylum School was its predecessor. Other small naval schools in New York City, Norfolk, VA; and Boston, MA, also existed in the early days of the USA. Bancroft established the Naval School in 1845, without Congressional funding, on a ten-acre Army post named Fort Severn in Annapolis. Five years later, the Naval School became the United States Naval Academy (USNA) to produce officers for the U.S. Navy and the U.S. Marine Corps.

Maryland's capital, the city of Annapolis, dates from 1649, nearly two centuries before the USNA was established. That longevity and history permeate every corner of the Yard as the Naval Academy shares the city with an older neighboring college, St. John's College. With roots to 1696, it is a liberal arts college with 450 men and women students on a thirty-two-acre campus one block west of the Yard. St. John's and the city shops, homes, and restaurants directly link Annapolis, like folded hands, with the Naval Academy campus. Shared walls and alleys on land match up like the Severn River and Chesapeake Bay waters of the harbor, jetties, and marinas.

The Naval Academy Chapel's green copper dome towers over the Yard, the main part of the campus. The Chapel's lower level holds a precious part of America's history. It includes a vaulted crypt with the remains of John Paul Jones, the Revolutionary War naval hero whose words, "I have not yet begun to fight," still inspire. Called the Cathedral of the Navy, the chapel and other near-century-old buildings make the Naval Academy a National Historical Site.

The U.S. Air Force is the youngest service and traces its roots to a 1908 contract between the Army Signal Corps' Aeronautical Division and the Wright brothers. Civil and military aviation worked together in peace and war, developing planes that were bigger and faster and capable of carrying larger payloads in longer distances. In 1926, Congress established the U.S. Army Air Corps. Four years later, the Corps dedicated Randolph Field, near San Antonio, TX, as its Training Center in ceremonies that included a flyover of 233 aircraft. Dubbed "West Point of the Air," Randolph served as a model for later pilot-cadet training programs throughout the country. The school prepared pilots but relied on officer training from sources such as the USMA and the USNA and Reserve Officer Training Corps (ROTC) units at civilian colleges and universities.

Separated from the Army and officially launched on September 18, 1947, the Air Force took steps to create its own officer training academy in 1949. However, global and political conflicts delayed establishment of the United States Air Force Academy (USAFA) until 1954. A distinguished group of citizens, including famed aviator Charles A. Lindbergh, reviewed proposed locations. The finalists included Colorado Springs, CO; Alton, IL; and Lake Geneva, WI. Choosing the Colorado site was helped by its location just east of the Rampart Range of the Rocky Mountains, sixty miles south of Denver. The academy's grounds are well protected by open areas in all directions, and the weather is ideal for flying.

Prominent displays range from replicas of class crests on the Chapel wall to a memorial wall listing the names of graduates who have perished in combat. The courtyard also provides homes to F-105 Thunderchief, F-4 Phantom, F-15 Eagle, and F-16 Fighting Falcon aircraft. The golf course is named for former President Dwight Eisenhower, an avid golfer and a West Point Class of 1915 graduate. He signed Public Law 325, the legislation establishing the Air Force Academy, on April 1, 1954. Nearby, the youngest service academy memorial cemetery has already recorded its first burials. Like its sister schools, the Air Force Academy has an inspiring Chapel that offers a profound statement of human designs to try to complement nature's magnificent setting. The Chapel's spires are actually made of aluminum; and the building itself houses services for all faiths, including Protestant, Catholic, Jewish, Buddhist, and Muslim. Many cadets find peace and quiet there; the doors are always open, and no one can bother them inside.

Cadets and Midshipmen

Although students at West Point and the Air Force Academy are called cadets, Naval Academy students are midshipmen. The origins of those labels speak of the history of their services and schools. The French words *cade*, referring to the junior member of a family, and *capde*, or *Captain*, provide the origins for the English word. In Spain, cadets were young volunteer officers while in England, cadets were young men who served in India. The word derives from the Latin term for head: *caput, capit*, and *capitellum*. Students in military training have always been called cadets, referring to younger branches of noble families whose armored shields included a section called a cadency. Naval cadets were called midshipmen because, while serving on triple-deck English warships in the 17th Century, they relayed messages between officers on the quarterdeck and those of the forecastle. In English naval service, midshipmen were the second rank attained by a combat officer after service as a beginner. Then, with three and a half years in this rank and by passing an examination, they were eligible for promotion to the rank of lieutenant.

Naval Academy midshipmen, both male and female, are sometimes called "mids" or "middies"; but they don't like either term. West Point and Air Force Academy cadets call their U.S. Naval Academy peers "squids." In the mid-20th Century, unidentified or "John Doe" midshipmen were called Joe Gish or WT Door, for the watertight doors found on all ships. Each Annapolis class includes a percentage of grads who become Second Lieutenants in the U.S. Marine Corps, which is officially part of the U.S. Navy Department. Navy and Marine Corps officers who did *not* graduate from Annapolis refer to the Naval Academy as "the trade school." Others sometimes call it "Canoe U." In the past, Navy midshipmen referred to unidentified West Pointers as "Dumb John." Today, both Navy and Air Force cadets call the West Pointers "grunts" or "kaydets." Their school is called "Hudson High" by the Air Force or "Woop" by Navy midshipmen as a shortened version of "WooPoo." The others return the favors by calling the Air Force cadets "zoomies." That reflects at least two possible definitions: "Zoom" as aircraft actions in flight or, more likely, inhabitants of "the Blue Zoo," which is one of the terms the Air Force Academy cadets sometimes call their campus. The "Zoo" designation may derive from the sense some cadets experience as the inhabitants of a major Colorado tourist attraction.

Each academy uses the four-class system to describe what are traditionally freshmen, sophomores, juniors, and seniors at civilian schools. For example, West Point uses the Cadet Leader Development System to develop leaders throughout the four years. At West Point, first-year rookies are plebes. Sophomores are called Yearlings or Yuks, then Cows as juniors, and Firsties as seniors. Naval Academy midshipmen are also plebes as freshmen, Youngsters as sophomores or Third classmen and women, then simply Second classmen and women as Juniors, and also Firsties as seniors. Air Force cadets are "basics" or "doolies" when they begin. Some upperclassmen call them "maggots," the lowest form of life with the potential to fly. The term "doolie" originated with the Academy's first Class of 1959 in their Basic Cadet Training program. It derives from the Greek word *doulos,* or subject, but is not widely used by cadets themselves. They are also called "four degrees"; and then they advance as Third-, Second-, and First-class cadets called "three degree," "two degree," and Firsties. All of the academies promote their cadets and midshipmen on graduation day when they share the "hats off" celebration with the new graduates.

Labels for cadets and midshipmen reflect their services too. Previously, each of the four U.S. military branches had its own distinct way of describing its members. The Army had its soldiers and officers, the Navy had sailors and officers, and the Air Force had airmen and officers. Only the Marines, as Jim Bradley reported in his Iwo Jima flag-raising book, *Flags of Our Fathers,* called *all* of its members Marines, including both men and women. "Alone among the U.S. military services, the Marines have bestowed their name on their enlisted ranks" (Bradley 2000, 71). By the beginning of the 21st Century, all of the services had adopted the Marine Corps practice, now proudly calling *all* of their members Soldiers, Sailors, Airmen, and Marines.

Special language always sets any organization apart from other societies, especially in the military. Such jargon is not a recent phenomenon. President Dwight D. Eisenhower described outstanding West Point students as "tenth boners" in his engaging autobiography, *At*

Ease (Eisenhower 1967, 22). Eisenhower ranked 61st among 164 graduates in the Class of 1915.[1]

United States Military Academy in West Point, New York

                                                              General
George S. Patton, who was 46th out of 103 members of the Class of 1909, sent a note to his son, George, at West Point during World War II. The legendary commander wrote, "Be particularly *spooney* [well-groomed], so *spooney* that you not only get by but attract attention. Why do you suppose I pay so much attention to being well dressed? Have your clothes well pressed; when I was boning [working to advance academically] I always had one uniform that I never sat down in" (Puryear 2000, 97).

Naval Academy midshipmen—including Arizona U.S. Senator John S. McCain III, who was sixth from the bottom among 900 grads in the Class of 1958—strove to have "good grease" to work the military side of their school's rating successfully (McCain 1999, 130). Another Naval Academy grad told me that the technical term was "Aptitude for the Service." A West Pointer told me the cadets at the top of the class were called "hives" because they were always busy as bees.

Euphemisms abound in the service academies just as they do in any other special group. For example, cadets and midshipmen have always been in danger of failing to maintain high-enough grades to remain at their schools. At West Point, when cadets were forced to take makeup exams or be told to leave, they were "turned out." The day of reckoning when poor performing cadets were told they had failed and would depart

---

[1]   Chapter 21 includes a selection of famous academy grads and their class ranks.

was called Foundation Day (Puryear 1983, 10). The Naval Academy equivalent borrowed the seafaring term for wastewater. A midshipman who was dismissed was said to have "bilged out" (McCain 1999, 142).

New cadets and midshipmen learn these labels and an abundance of other details, traditions, customs, and history in the pocket-sized fact books they receive upon arrival. Officially called "Fourth Class Knowledge," the books become constant companions since part of every cadet and midshipman's training is their virtual memorization. Reciting their contents upon demand by upperclassmen and women is an important part of initial cadet and midshipman training. In the year 2000, West Point's leather-bound *Bugle Notes* crammed 320 pages full of information, from the score of the first Army-Navy game in 1890 (Navy won, 24 to 0) to the number of lights in Cullum Hall (340). Navy's hardcover *Reef Points* book was a bit larger but had fewer pages, numbering 248. The Air Force book, called *Contrails*, was covered in card paper stock and contained hundreds of pages of needed information. Each of the books lists greetings from superintendents and deans and other senior officials. They also describe their academy's history, traditions, and facilities while listing endless details of past sports heroics and present service facts like uniforms, insignia, and equipment. New books are edited for each entering class, which quickly grasps their significance as a "bible."

Today's fourth-class cadets and midshipmen read and memorize their handbooks whenever they can, sometimes while standing at parade rest in formation or sitting in the privacy of their rooms. The book's knowledge must be assimilated totally. That requirement adds to the pressure the new students feel during their plebe summer or basic cadet training. Upperclassmen and women quiz new students constantly as they help train officer candidates to assess situations and respond quickly and accurately. Failure to respond promptly and correctly may lead to verbal abuse bordering upon harassment. Incorrect responses can also lead to more pressure and possibly punishment with demerits that affect privileges. Learning and reciting Fourth Class Knowledge also introduces new cadets and midshipmen to the concept of class rank.

Class Rank

Unlike those who complete studies at virtually all other colleges and universities, graduates of the service academies are guaranteed employment when they conclude successfully. In fact, the required five years of military service provide "payment" for these misnamed "free" educations. Their employers, the military branches that sponsor their academies, line up literally hundreds of entry-level jobs each year for new second lieutenants and ensigns. Like any first job, these Initial Active Duty assignments include some positions that are more desirable than others. Class rank or a similar order of merit provides an equitable means of eliminating favoritism and politics in the process of obtaining these first jobs.

West Point was the first academy to adopt the class rank system. Its General Order of Merit was used to determine which grads would enter the various branches of the U.S. Army at the time: engineers, cavalry, artillery, and infantry. In March of 1816, Secretary of War William H. Crawford created a Board of Visitors to oversee the school, along with the Academic Board. The latter was charged with assuring that graduates successfully passed final examinations. "The Academic Board would rank the cadets in order of general merit; the cadet's position in the ranking would determine the corps to which he would be assigned" (Ambrose 1999, 56). Although several publications later questioned whether this plan was put into effect, it is clear that it was adopted no later than 1819. That year, Sylvanus Thayer, famed for his tremendous work as West Point's Superintendent from 1817 to 1833, created the merit ranking system. Thayer established the merit roll to compute each cadet's performance throughout his four years. Ambrose called it simply "the most complete, and impersonal system imaginable" (Ibid., 73).

Each day, cadets were graded for their activities in all parts of their lives at West Point. Each cadet received a grade in each class every day, and class rankings were posted each week. Scores ranged from 3.0 for perfect to 0 for failure. The higher the total, the higher the class rank that was recorded. Behavior outside the classroom also contributed to or detracted from the overall score. Demerits were assigned for misbehavior or rule infractions and could reduce class rank. Cadets were subject to dismissal if they accumulated a certain number of demerits in a single year. Keen competition resulted, and cadets appreciated the system because it removed favoritism and was "scrupulously fair" (Ibid., 75). "Competition permeated cadets' experiences and competition became a virtuous endeavor for all cadets. As a result, social class, birth, wealth, manners and position counted for nothing" (Ibid., 131). Thayer also provided public recognition of the top five cadets in each class; they were listed in the official Army Register.

At the same time, during the early 19th Century, colleges and universities were focused on the "whole man" concept to measure individual success. They considered both academic grades and character issues to take the measure of success. However, following the Civil War, in 1869, Harvard University began to rank students solely by academic achievement. Character and performance outside the classroom no longer mattered (Ibid., 280). When he became the youngest-ever West Point Superintendent (at age 39) in 1919, Douglas MacArthur rejected this narrow definition. To MacArthur, who was first in his Class of 1903, the "whole man" was just as important as academic prowess. As a result, he counted such issues as leadership, military bearing, athletic performance, and extracurricular participation in class rank considerations. Cadets also received ratings by their peers and tactical officers.

This combination of academic, military, and physical rankings provides overall class rank of today's academy students. Grades appear in the 4.0 system widely used by educators, with 4.0 the equivalent of an A and below 2.0 an F, or failure. At the academies, two points (4.0 to 2.0) separate the top from the bottom passing grades. Awards and recognition are very public. At the Air Force Academy, for example, cadets on the Dean's List for a grade point average of 3.0 or higher in the previous semester wear the silver star Dean's Pin. Those with a Military Performance Average of 3.0 wear the silver wreath Commandant's Pin while the lightning bolt Athletic Pin signifies a 3.0 Physical Education Average. Cadets who achieve all three simultaneously wear a special combined "Supt's [pronounced 'soups'] Pin" award on their uniform's left pocket.

Class rank of West Point graduates was illustrated publicly for many years in the *Biographical Register of the Officers and Graduates of the United States Military Academy* produced by Brevet MGen George W. Cullum, who was third among 43 graduates of the Class of 1833. The Cullum Register provided an official roster of class rank through a series of consecutive numbers through the Class of 1977. The Class of 1978 was the first to be listed alphabetically. The Naval Academy's Register of Alumni listed graduates by class rank until the early 1990s and then alphabetically with a code that displayed class rank. The Air Force Academy's Registers of Graduates used class rank or Order of Merit from its first directory in 1965 through 1979 and then switched to alphabetic lists with the Class of 1980.

Same Date of Rank lists the class ranks to illustrate the relative class standing of all graduates included in the book. Although some of the featured grads objected to this policy, I was able to convince them that the class rank identification supported the book's thesis that class rank was not always an indicator of future success.

Although academic rankings predominate, military performance and demerits for rule infractions or just plain bad behavior are major contributors to class rank. Demerits are meted out as punishment and can only be erased by marching "tours," mindless pacing that wastes time—a precious commodity. Although upperclassmen and women and staff members can assign demerits, the primary judge and jury in all disputes about them is the cadets' and midshipmen's commanding officer. West Point Tactical Officers, Air Force's Air Officer Commanding (AOC), and Navy's Company Officers serve as their military commanders working in the dormitories. They are assigned to specific companies or squadrons comprised of 100 to 120 cadets or midshipmen and are responsible for all aspects of cadet life for their students. These officers are key members of the staff at the academies assigned to the office of the Commandant of Cadets or Midshipmen who is responsible for all military training. The Commandants might be called the military's alter ego to the Academic Dean.

One graduate of the Air Force Academy from the 1980s who returned ten years later as an AOC reported, "I think I had a better perspective as an AOC. If I caught a cadet intentionally trying to get away with something, such as sleeping through [and missing] a parade, I hammered him with a 30-30-2 hit [thirty demerits, thirty tours, two months' restrictions]. The cadet squadron commander might have recommended *only* a 5-5-0, and I laughed. Why should ninety-nine cadets get up in the morning and stand out on the parade field either sweating or freezing while this one lone cadet sleeps in? On the other hand, I would often give cadets the benefit of the doubt. For example, parking tickets were the rage when I was there. Some AOCs took great pleasure in handing out parking tickets. If you got more than two, you lost your car privileges for the rest of the semester. Often, upperclassmen would loan their cars to underclassmen who would park in the wrong spot, and the upperclassmen would end up with the parking ticket through no fault of their own. However, the higher-ups decided that you were responsible for your own car, and you should take the hit for the ticket no matter who parked it. I didn't exactly agree and would occasionally make those hits disappear."

Institutional changes in response to serious issues of sexual assaults at the Air Force Academy in 2003 led to a considerable number of changes in discipline practices. The changes were intended to mirror punishments available in the active-duty Air Force under the Uniform Code of Military Justice and other regulations. However, cadets still receive demerits and march tours for select violations.

Although West Pointers at the bottom of their classes have been called "the goat" for many years, no one knows its origins. James S. Robbins, professor of international relations at the National Defense University in Washington DC, wrote about 19th Century West Point grads at the bottom in his 2006 book, *Last in Their Class*. In his introduction, Robbins noted that BGen John C. Tidball, 11th out of 38 men in the Class of 1848, described "the Immortals"—those at the bottom of the class—when he was Commandant of Cadets in 1864 (Robbins 2006, xi).

In 1880, General William Tecumseh Sherman visited West Point for graduation exercises in his role as General in Chief of the U.S. Army. Sherman, who was sixth out of 42 in the Class of 1840, was the fourth West Pointer to hold the Army's senior post. He spoke fondly about "the Immortals" at the bottom of the class.

Over the years, as inter-service rivalry grew, labels for the last members of the class also evolved. Goats have been official mascots for the Naval Academy since 1893. Robbins also said he doubted "a causal connection" between the "goat" term and the mascot for the U.S. Naval Academy though "it may have reinforced it." So far, the Naval Academy has not reciprocated by calling its lasts "the mules" for West Point's mascot. Instead, the last in the Naval Class was called "the anchorman" and later, "the anchor."

In its early history, the Naval Academy used a system of drawing "preference numbers" by lot to enable seniors to select their initial active duty jobs. Of course, physical exams and fitness contributed to the process, as did the need to fill a combination of new assignments for sea and shore duty as well as commissions into the U.S. Marine Corps. Class rank has determined preference numbers for many years.

The Air Force Academy called its last cadet "Tail-end Charlie," a name steeped in the history of American military air power. During World War II, U.S. Army Air Forces' heavy bombers flew in tight formations to improve bombing accuracy and defend against enemy fighter attacks. Massive groups of B-24 Liberators and B-17 Flying Fortresses, sometimes totaling to hundreds of aircrafts, would assemble in the skies to attack targets. The first or lead aircraft's bombardier determined when and where to release his bombs, and the remaining aircraft followed that lead immediately. In his epic description of South Dakota U.S. Senator George McGovern's B-24 bomb group, historian-author Stephen E. Ambrose described Tail-end Charlie as "the last plane in the squadron [over the target], the most vulnerable if German fighters attacked, and the hardest position to hold. Usually new pilots and crews got that assignment" (Ambrose, 159).

For many years, goats, anchors, and Charlies received a dollar from each of their classmates on graduation day. With contributions from hundreds of classmates at the academies, that was a sizeable amount or bonus for graduating last. The tradition is believed to have come from the practice of newly-commissioned lieutenants paying a dollar to the first person to proffer them a salute.

Tail-end Charlie lives on in the Air Force Academy's library, which sits in the midst of Fairchild Hall. That long building houses most of the school's classrooms and is named for former Air Force Vice Chief of Staff

General Muir S. Fairchild.[2] The library's three floors offer a full view across the terrazzo of the Chapel and Harmon Hall with the Rockies forming a breathtaking Hollywood backdrop.

When I visited the Air Force Academy in 2000, archivist Duane Reed was teaching Air Force history in an inner sanctum conference room lined with huge amounts of history, such as books, photos, *Stalag* Prisoner-of-War uniforms from World War II, and military plans from the 1990 Gulf War. Reed also kept another engraved trophy. But this one was wrapped in a shawl and tucked away in a storage closet, far from the eyes of tourists and other visitors. It's a large sterling silver Revere bowl, eight inches high and fourteen inches across, on a four-inch-high base. The base has a large plaque on one side that reads, "TAIL-END CHARLIE'S SILVER." Created in the mid-1970s, the bowl seems to have been used only once. Although its base holds a dozen blank silver plates ready for engraving, only one has been completed. It reads, "The Spirit of 1976," in silent testimony to the end of a tradition. Inside the bowl is a four-inch-by-seven-inch card with this message:

> Until 1977, cadets were graduated by order of merit. The last cadet to graduate was the lowest man in the order of merit and referred to as "Tail-end Charlie." After receiving his diploma, each cadet put a silver dollar in this silver bowl and it was all given to "Tail-end Charlie." Beginning with the Class of 1978, cadets graduated in alphabetical order by squadron and there was no longer a "Tail-end Charlie."

Archivist Reed, who retired in 2004, explained, "Like our sister academies, we are honored with graduation speakers each year who are either the President of the United States, Secretary of Defense, Secretary of the Air Force, or the uniformed Chief of Staff." Reed relayed a story about Tail-end Charlies told to him by Retired Air Force Lt.Gen. Albert P. Clark, USAFA superintendent from 1970 until his retirement four years later. Clark was ranked 106th out of 275 men in West Point's Class of 1936. I spoke with General Clark in 2004, and he recalled one year when the class "Charlie" friskily asked the visiting Air Force Chief of Staff General

---

[2]   Fairchild was *not* a graduate of a service academy, and he entered military service in the State of Washington's National Guard in 1916. This book provides the class ranks for virtually *all* academy graduates when they are first mentioned. People included *without* an academy noted are *not* academy graduates.

John P. McConnell to exchange hats with him. McConnell went along with the gag. He was 74th out of 261 members in West Point's Class of 1932 and served as USAF Chief of Staff from 1965 to 1969. However, the next year, General John "Jack" D. Ryan was the visiting Chief of Staff for graduation, General Clark recalled. Ryan ranked 65th out of 300 grads in his West Point Class of 1938. That year's "Charlie" asked General Ryan to swap *his* hat, but Ryan replied, "No, I'm not going to do that, because I don't reward mediocrity." That remark was widely used in the eventual demise of the Tail-end Charlie tradition a few years later. (Clark and Reed Interviews.)

That experience and numerous reports of near-bottom cadets who were vying to be absolutely last—and *almost or did* fail to graduate on time—caused all the academies to drop the recognition officially in the 1970s. That was just about the time that all three academies began to accept female students. In her 1981 book about the introduction of women to the Air Force Academy, *Bring Me Men and Women,* Judith Hicks Stiehm described the process at Colorado Springs, West Point, and Annapolis. In a reflection of the emerging recognition of women's rights, equal opportunities for all citizens, and all-volunteer military service requirements, all three academies were directed to integrate their schools in a bill passed by the U.S. Congress on October 7, 1975. Stiehm reported that the Air Force Academy officials were determined to make the integration of women work successfully. She reported that West Point focused more on maintaining standards while the Naval Academy called integration a "nonevent," and women were "slipped as unobtrusively as possible into the academy" (Stiehm 1981, 6).

In 1976 and 1977, the Air Force Academy's Military Order of Merit (MOM) program rated cadets using six criteria. Three were objective measurements: grades in military studies, wing training experiences, and numbers of demerits for mistakes or transgressions. Three were more subjective: performance reports by cadet leaders, ratings by the Air Officer Commanders, and "peer" ratings. Peers could mean either squadron or dormitory colleagues. For men, the two were the same; but for women, they were mostly different. Therefore, it was decided to omit any dormitory-based ratings either by peers or the special female Air Training Officers who were assigned to the Air Force Academy to assist the integration.

As a result, the "separate but equal" treatment of women was exacerbated during this period, especially as it related to MOM. Since MOM was a factor in the cadets' overall class rank, it would appear that this difficulty might have contributed to the loss of the Tail-end Charlie designation at the Air Force Academy in the mid-1970s. West Point and

Annapolis have also de-emphasized the notoriety of their lasts in class. Like USAFA, they cited gamesmanship that sometimes resulted in students who were trying to be last actually failing to graduate.

In 1977, the West Point Study Group, convened by its Board of Visitors, addressed several institutional issues. The Group's Recommendation No. 31 stated, "Eliminate all orders of merit which establish relative ranking of cadets from first to last." The Superintendent, then Lt.Gen. Andrew J. Goodpaster, found that the graduate order of merit (or General Order of Merit as it was called at the time) had some negative ramifications; and he ultimately decided that it should be eliminated. General Goodpaster had ranked second among 456 in the Class of 1939. West Point historian Dr. Stephen B. Grove quoted Goodpaster, "I hated to give up the Order of Merit, but it had been overused and misused to the point where becoming the goat was the goal whereas the real goal should have been the learning process and the kind of education the graduates received." (Grove Interview.)

United States Naval Academy in Annapolis, Maryland

Sometimes the contrasts between the first and last graduate in a class are even more profound than the numbers they registered. For example, Retired Navy Captain Philip J. Ryan, who ranked 437th among 691 graduates in his Class of 1950 at the Naval Academy, told me the story of Charles Dobony, who was second in his class. Dobony was from Buffalo, NY, and, like some before him, went to Annapolis after attending a civilian college. In his case, Dobony had *graduated* from MIT after concerned citizens from his hometown had helped pay for his education. He was commissioned a Navy Ensign through the V-12 Navy College Training Program, a special World War II commissioning program with over 125,000 officer candidates at 131 colleges and universities.

Dobony entered Annapolis in 1946 as a lowly plebe and graduated four years later at the outbreak of the Korean War. He was enjoying a weekend during flight school at Pensacola, FL. On that fateful February day, he was horseback riding with friends when he ran into a wire and was thrown from the horse, suffering a concussion and a compound leg fracture. He woke up in the hospital to the news from the doctor that the leg had to be amputated. Knowing full well that this drastic action would eliminate him for Navy duty, including flight training, he asked the doctor to delay for twenty-four hours. The next day, the doctor returned, checked his patient, and said the leg had to be amputated. Again, the young Ensign begged for delay, and the doctor reluctantly agreed. The third day, the doctor returned; and Dobony was delirious, experiencing a raging fever from gangrene. The leg had to come off. But it was too late. Dobony died less than a year after his graduation day.

Last in that Class of 1950 was a man who walked across the stage cheered by the anchorman accolades. He also collected a dollar from each of his 690 classmates. He served his commitment, completed his active duty, and returned to his hometown as a quiet civilian citizen. He surfaced in 1990 for the fortieth reunion of his class. He called Ryan and explained that he was unable to attend the reunion but wanted to pass on the anchor belt buckle to the true anchorman. It seems the graduating anchor had appealed the results of a test after the final list of merit had been published and had actually moved up thirty spots in class rank. Now, forty years later, he wanted to switch the recognition to the man who actually deserved it. Unfortunately, he refused to restore the $690 along with the buckle, denying that he had received it. As a result, Ryan refused to accept the anchor on behalf of his heretofore unknown classmate. (Ryan Interviews.)

Perhaps the most famous last in *any* class was George Armstrong Custer of West Point's Class of June 1861. He was a fearless cavalry leader who had eleven horses shot out from under him in combat. Custer rose quickly through the ranks and was a general officer at the age of twenty-three. He died with his two-hundred-man force at Little Big Horn in Montana on June 25, 1876. Custer's last-in-class rank deserved clarification. West Point graduated two classes in 1861, one in May and the other in June. Henry A. DuPont was first, and Sheldon Sturgeon was last among the 44 in the contingent that graduated on May 6. Patrick Henry O'Rorke was first, and Custer was last among the 33 who graduated on June 24. The class register also listed 72 other cadets as non-graduates. Many quit the school to fight for the Union or Confederacy in the Civil War. Although Custer may have actually ranked above one or more of those non-graduates, he was surely last in 1861.

"Class rank was always very important," explained retired U.S. Navy RADM Jeffrey C. Metzel Jr. of Huntington Beach, CA. He was "right in the middle," as he said—430th out of 821 in the Naval Academy's Class of 1947. "Class ranks established your precedence, and you stayed in that step until that guy was promoted or left the Navy." Another Naval Academy grad, retired Commander Frank Cleary of Ramsey, NJ, recalled that the rank order precedence was sometimes carried to an extreme. Francis P. Cleary was another Annapolis graduate near the middle, 319th out of 789 in the Class of 1962. He said the Navy's practice of one ship's crew rendering honors to another approaching ship in the open seas was affected by class rank. All officers were listed in order of precedence in the "Blue Book" then published annually by the Bureau of Naval Personnel. "Believe it or not," Cleary explained, "when an approaching ship was captained by an officer of equal rank, the officer of the deck would scramble to see who was senior or junior based upon the order of precedence that originated with class rank." The junior officer, of course, saluted first.

The early stages of this book's research revealed considerable differences among first and last graduates surveyed. All the USAFA grads received the survey letter at the same time. However, at first, only the top among the graduates replied. They ranged from Captains still on active duty assignments to retired general officers. The first of the USAFA grads to reply sent letters and resumes and e-mails crammed with achievements. These were dutifully filed as I prepared for interviews. Firsts from West Point and Annapolis followed suit, replying promptly with detailed resumes full of their significant achievements.

The first graduate to reply who had been *last* in his class, sent a very moving e-mail that reached me late one Friday night. Its poignancy prompted me to consider how to reply and to face, for the first time, that *some* might view a down or dark side to this book. This revelation resulted from the fact that I had always focused on the premise that last in the class was and is still an *achievement*. In fact, the "doctor" and "lawyer" jokes in the preface were key parts of my survey requests.

This chilling response reminded me that I was possibly opening old wounds that may not have healed completely.

The e-mail began starkly:

> I got your letter and it stirred a few emotions. Very few people outside of USAFA know that I graduated dead last in my class. I believe that I have told my wife, but I know I have never mentioned it to my kids.

My first reaction was, OK, so he kept it a secret although the Tail-end Charlie dollar-bill business at graduation would have tended to make it very public. Perhaps I was over-reacting and so was the grad. Then I continued to read from the screen of my PC:

> I assume you realize (but why would you?) that I was last not because I was particularly stupid, but because I was dropped 50 places in the graduation order of merit by order of the superintendent for disciplinary violations.

Although I object to the "stupid" designation for obvious reasons, the disciplinary violations were intriguing. The confession continued,

> I and another cadet (now a Colonel, USAF, retired) were arrested in Denver in January of our senior year on charges of being drunk and disorderly and resisting arrest. We were almost expelled, but finally were stripped of all rank (basic class shoulder boards), confined to quarters and given a hundred tours each.

Any academy cadet, graduate, or parent would recognize the severity of this punishment. And any civilian college student would see immediately the difference between their status and that of service academy students. During their senior year, cadets and midshipmen can almost taste the fruits of graduation. First-class privileges make the academies tolerable in a "light at the end of the tunnel" way. These privileges relieve the tedium and tension that they experienced as underclassmen and women. The ability to leave the campus on liberty is a cherished relief. In many ways, the beautiful campuses are prison-like with absolutely no privacy since they restrict the ability of cadets and midshipmen to relax.

Discipline tours are terrible reminders of powerful authority that still controls members of the senior class. Calling them "tours" attempts to make light of these costly exercises. And they are costly since they take away cadets' most valuable commodity: *time*. Each tour lasts an hour and consists of mind-numbing marches up and down a courtyard. The similarity to the pacing of a caged animal or prisoner is intended to remind the marcher that he or she has transgressed and must pay for the transgression. Although cadets attempt to make light of the experience, the punishment succeeds because it's most unpleasant.

United States Air Force Academy in Colorado Springs, Colorado

During their four years, virtually all cadets and midshipmen accumulate demerits for transgressions, and nearly all will march tours. Air Force cadets who accumulate one hundred tours are called Centurions in a jovial reference to the officers of the Roman Army who commanded companies of one hundred men. West Point calls its one hundred tour recorders century men or century women. Retired U.S. Air Force Lt.Col. George Bumiller, who ranked 866th among his 961 classmates in the USAFA Class of 1986, said he logged his one-hundred-plus tours for a range of transgressions. He returned to Colorado Springs for two years as Air Officer Commanding of his former squadron, Squadron IX. He said his cadets were surprised to learn that this outstanding junior officer, veteran global transport pilot, award-winning flight instructor, and happily married father of three darling children had been such a "troublemaker" as a cadet. (Bumiller Interview.)

The "last in the class" e-mail continued with the painful consequences of deeds long ago:

> I was kicked off the track team.

Again, the poignancy of the comment shocked me. Sports are important outlets at the academies. Many of the book's subjects were varsity athletes, and several more well-known grads are described in Chapter 21. Intercollegiate sports provide opportunities for athletic competition of course. They also provide a social environment that helps the academies to be more tolerable and less onerous for the cadet and midshipmen students. So our transgressor lost his organized sports outlet and was deprived of teammates who could have supported him.

Next, the most publicly degrading penalty:

> We were the only first classmen who carried rifles during parades.

Despite the pageantry that they create, cadets and midshipmen tend to abhor parades. They take time away from other activities like studying and sleeping, and they can be most uncomfortable marathons in the hot sun or chilling cold. They are also very visible demonstrations of academy organization, full of tradition and history. Underclassmen and women carry rifles; seniors have earned the privilege to lead. Firstie seniors who carried rifles would be obviously enduring penalty. And the public humiliation of that penalty took place at least once a week in their last semester of college life.

Finally, the e-mail reported the ultimate consequence of the transgression:

> Each of us was dropped 50 places in the General Order of Merit. Since I was already in the bottom 50, I wound up last.

He concluded by thinking out loud,

> I really want to think about how you would use any information that I would give you. As a starting point, could you describe how I would be portrayed in your book if I were to give you no personal information about myself?

And then he signed off with his name and the fact that he was a retired Colonel in the Air National Guard of his state. The writer had confirmed the premise of the book. He had succeeded! Now my question was, *how* could I convince him to participate?

So I wrote back,

> Heartfelt letter. Thanks for sharing it. I was near last in my Class of 1964 at Holy Cross College in Worcester, MA. Air Force ROTC saved me; that's where I did well. My book is not about who or why folks were first or last but what happened next. You have obviously succeeded just from reading what you wrote to me: wife, kids, full Colonel rank. And that's why I want you to be in this book. Recall what I wrote in my survey request? The doctors and lawyers who were last in their classes are still called

Doctor and Lawyer. You folks were all prepared and served as lieutenants and ensigns. No doubt you served well. As radio personality Paul Harvey said, we want the rest of the story. My focus will be on what happened after graduation. The entire premise of the book is that all grads were prepared to succeed. And did. Please share your story.

He never replied.

Fortunately, several other grads stepped forward with their stories that began with their class rank. Eventually, I heard from three dozen at or near the top and a half dozen from the bottom of their classes. I communicated with many for a diverse and balanced representation from all three academies, service branches, eras, and experience. I also tracked down the senior officials and the first and last graduates from that West Point Class of 1985 who triggered this book.

The Superintendent, Lt.Gen. Willard W. Scott Jr., who had graduated 23rd among 301 members of the Class of 1948, retired in 1986. The Commandant of Cadets—BGen Peter J. Boylan Jr., who was 54th among 534 in the Class of 1961—retired as a Major General in 1992. Academic Dean BGen Frederick A. Smith Jr., who ranked 22nd among 474 classmates in 1944, retired later that year of 1985. Larry Young, who was first in the class, went to the Infantry Officer Basic School and Ranger School at Fort Benning, GA. Then he moved to Vicenza, Italy, in an airborne assignment and was a light infantry officer at Fort Drum, NY. He left active duty in 1990 and graduated from Yale Law School. He worked in a firm before moving to the finance industry as legal counsel and became director of legal counsel for Credit Suisse First Boston in New York City. Marty Clark, who was the goat who triggered this book, served in the artillery, including a stint in Korea, and then resigned in 1992. He later worked in the pharmaceutical industry.

Our friend Bill Kowal, who graduated 825th, first served as a graduate assistant soccer coach at West Point until he went to the Field Artillery Officer Basic Course at Fort Sill, OK, and then to the Airborne School at Fort Benning, GA. After more than three years in Germany as a field artillery officer, he transferred to the Transportation Corps for more schooling and duty at Fort Eustis, VA. He deployed to Saudi Arabia and received the Bronze Star Medal for his work in support of Operation Desert Storm. He returned to the USA and left the Army in 1992. He went to work for Airborne Express, which later merged with DHL, where he was named a Senior Vice President for Operations in 2007.

Respecting the privacy of all graduates, I "networked" through countless sources to identify more people who could and would speak with me. I would contact class members who I could identify and ask them to approach their classmates. In each case, I identified myself as a writer who was a retired Air Force public affairs officer, an Air Force Academy Admissions Liaison Officer, and father of a 1990 USAFA grad who was trying to tell stories about a remarkable group of Americans. I restated my purpose to describe the accomplishments of graduates of our nation's academies who became contributors to our society no matter where they had graduated in their classes. I also added that I was near last in my own college class. And finally, I promised to write about grads using their own words as authorized biographies.

When I asked one Air Force Academy grad, Major Michael D. Millen, for his class rank, he first said he remembered being "in the 600s" among his 993 classmates in 1990. He checked and later promptly reported, "Try 840th out of 993." He added, "I should have remembered that when we picked UPT [flight training] bases and dates [by order of merit], *I was like the short fat kid on the playground—last one left!*" (Millen Interview)

Among the many remarkable responses was that of retired U.S. Army Colonel Ralph H. Graves, a former District Engineer for the Army's Corps of Engineers in Seattle, WA. Colonel Graves ranked first among 833 graduates in his West Point Class of 1974, continuing a family tradition perhaps unique among all three service academies. His father and grandfather, Ernest Graves Jr. and Ernest Graves, ranked second in their respective West Point classes of 1944 and 1905. His great-grandfather, Rogers Birnie, ranked first in the Class of 1872.

Ralph answered my questions about his family's success.

"I went to West Point because I admired the Army careers of my father and grandfather. After plebe year, I realized I had a shot at finishing first academically and raising the family average. My Dad encouraged me to do my best, as his father had encouraged him. It wasn't all tedious 'grubbing for tenths,' (of a grade point) and I think I came away from the Military Academy with as good an education as my prep school classmates who went to places like Harvard and MIT." (Graves Interview.)

The following chapters describe former cadets and midshipmen who worked their ways through West Point, Annapolis, and the Air Force Academy. The day *before* they graduated, they were ranked *differently*—at the top and bottom of their classes. However, on Graduation Day, they pinned on their golden bars as Second Lieutenants or Ensigns, with the *same date of rank*, prepared to succeed.

Chapter 1

And the Last Shall Be First

John D. Crowley Jr., USMA '42

In 1942, West Point's new Second Lieutenants were eager to leave the plains above the Hudson River for the war that had begun when the Japanese attacked Pearl Harbor in December of their First Class year. Perhaps no one was as eager as Jack Crowley, who was about to graduate last in his class of 374 men. However, that graduation day was to be Jack's last time at the bottom. The combination of heroic and skillful combat duty plus working successfully in the right places at the right times would lead him to be the first man in his class to reach the rank of general officer.

John Denis Crowley Jr. was born August 8, 1916, in Cambridge, MA, the second child of Gertrude McHough and John Denis Crowley. His sisters, Corine and Gertrude, and brothers, Robert and Edward, formed a strict Roman Catholic family in the 1920s and 1930s; but Jack always had a bit of a rebel in him while attending Cambridge Latin High School. Fortunately, his athletic gifts carried him through high school successfully, as he played both varsity football and hockey. However, his father insisted that studies for the priesthood would "straighten him out." In a slight compromise, he enrolled Jack with the Jesuits at Boston College instead of a seminary. Jack took his happy-go-lucky attitude to college and enjoyed himself, often playing practical jokes. However, one of those jokes—impersonating a priest—went awry, and he was expelled.

Rather than disappoint his strict parents, Jack announced that he was leaving BC and enlisting in the Army because, as he told them, "there's a war coming, and I want to do my duty for the country." His football skills on the Army post team attracted the attention of several West Pointers who promptly recruited him for the Army team. When Jack reported for plebe summer on the first of July in 1938, he was less than two months from his twenty-second birthday, the cutoff date for his class. He was the oldest man to enroll in the class although other classmates who were turnbacks from earlier classes were older.

Jack found himself on a campus little changed from the days of Lee and Eisenhower and Patton. Its gray granite gothic architecture matched the gorgeous multi-terraced terrain above the wide and winding Hudson. Fortress-like buildings announced serious study there then as they do now. The land and locale offer ready opportunities for the study and practice of land warfare. West Point and adjacent Camp Buckner now include 16,000 acres of campus, military post, and maneuver woods named for storied battles and campaigns in America's wars. And a new 6,700-yard golf course slopes through the hills. Golfers hear the click of rifle fire and the boom of artillery when they play their eighteen. Tight fairways lined by heavy woods swallow errant drives. In the winter, neighboring ski slopes provide both recreation and training for four thousand cadets.

Throughout its history, West Point's campus grounds have marked history. Preparations and memories show through the parade grounds and sports fields. The Plain, or parade grounds, that lead to Washington Hall's Cadet Mess are next to Doubleday Field, the Army baseball team's home field. It's named for retired U.S. Army Colonel Abner Doubleday, who ranked 24th among 56 men in the USMA Class of 1842 and the man credited with inventing the national pastime. The Cadet Chapel rises above the barracks and academic areas while the church and synagogue for Catholic and Jewish worship welcome those believers nearby. The outdoor running track is down below, closer to the river near the Eisenhower Hall social center.

Relics of war and peace include scores of cannon from past conflicts. Statues and monuments speak volumes for West Point's history and the history of the United States of America. They mark the American Revolution with President George Washington and Polish patriot Thaddeus Kosciuszko and march forward to the 21st Century. The cemetery, which abuts the Old Cadet Chapel, includes heroes of every age and era. Many buried there are family members connected in genealogy as well as through the Long Gray Line.

In 1938, Jack Crowley arrived and quickly adjusted to plebe summer with help from his football teammates. He found a new home that he enjoyed. He worked hard, and he played hard, both on and off the sports field. However, he severely injured his knee during the team's first game against Rutgers University. That effectively ended his football career and *almost* led to his premature departure from West Point. A lengthy stay in the Academy's infirmary brought him back, but his grades suffered. By the end of his plebe year, he was last in the class and would remain at or near the bottom for the next three years. Classmate John Baker, the man who introduced me to Jack, described him as a "hail fellow, well met" and one of those happy guys to be around. Several other classmates used the same description as I learned more about this unusual man.

West Pointers' references to goats at the bottom of the class contrasted to hives, as in busy bee hives, at the top of the class. Years ago, prior to the Army-Navy football classic each fall, the goats and hives played each other in a spirited intramural football game. The game's tradition predicted that, if the goats won, Army would beat their inter-service rival. Classmate Pete Russell, who was a member of I Company with Jack, remembers that Jack coached the 1941 goats' team, which lost. Then the Army team lost to Navy, 14-6, at Philadelphia a week before the attack on Pearl Harbor. Peter T. Russell, who entered the infantry after graduating 304th, served thirty years on active duty and retired as a Colonel in 1972.

His yearbook noted that "Jack graced the D List" (opposite the Dean's List) throughout his West Point career. In fact, as he approached graduation, he was in danger of being "found" or thrown out, but was able to score high enough in a final electrical engineering exam to graduate, albeit last.

Finally, on May 29, 1942, Army Chief of Staff General George C. Marshall presented the first of 374 diplomas to James H. Hottenroth of the Bronx, NY. He entered the Army as a civil engineer and would later graduate first in his class at the California Institute of Technology in Pasadena when he received his MS in civil engineering in 1950. Hottenroth served as an Army civil engineer and retired as a Colonel in Albuquerque, NM, in 1969. He later served his adopted state in its Environmental Health Service for nearly twenty years and died in 1999. Second in the class was James H. Hayes, who is profiled in the next chapter.

Cadet First Class John D. Crowley Jr.

Brigadier General John D. Crowley Jr.

Jack Crowley's brother, Edward, entered West Point a few weeks later as a member of the Class of 1946. Ed would graduate 754th out of a much larger class of 875 men that year and enter the infantry. His prowess on the Army hockey team led him to the U.S. Hockey Team in the 1948 Olympics in London. After combat in Korea and studies in Madrid, he returned to the USMA for two tours as a Spanish teacher. He was also a decorated combat advisor in Vietnam and retired as a Lieutenant Colonel in 1970. He died in 1995.

After graduation, Jack first moved south to Fort Benning, GA, for basic infantry officer training. Several of his classmates went with him to Georgia, including Californian John R. Deane Jr. who was also called Jack. Jack Deane, who ranked in the middle of the class at 191, was a highly decorated combat arms officer who retired as a General in 1977. He also described Jack Crowley as a happy fellow but recounted a time when that easy-going nature was abruptly challenged during his post-graduation training at Fort Benning. "Jack Crowley was in excellent physical condition, and that served him well," Jack Deane recalled. "At Benning in the middle of a hot summer, we had an instructor who was a 'mean muscleman' and cast aspersions on us as a group of West Pointers," he continued. "Jack took him on in a pushup challenge and bore him into the ground. We were amazed and very pleased."

During his Fort Benning training, Jack managed to take time out to marry Mary Elizabeth "Betty" Foley from Newton, MA. They had met on a blind date during Jack's senior year and were married in the Fort Benning Post Chapel on August 1, 1942. They honeymooned during a trip across country to Fort Ord, CA, where Jack was sent for advanced training. En route, they visited the Grand Canyon where Jack insisted that the newlyweds ride the famed mules down to the canyon floor. As a veteran horseman, Jack fared better than his bride in the comfort of that experience, leading to hilarious family tales retold in the future.

While training at Fort Benning, Jack had befriended two Philippine Army classmates who would provide the first of many unusual twists in his career. When the young officers transferred to Northern California, Jack was introduced to more members of the Philippine Army who had come to the USA from their war-torn country. One early California morning in January of 1943, Jack and his unit were preparing for a major field exercise at the sprawling Fort Ord complex. They were picked for a river crossing by an engineering group. As a Second Lieutenant seven months out of West Point, Jack was the junior member of the Battalion's S-3 or Operations Staff. Unfortunately, his battalion commander and executive officer were unavailable and nowhere to be found early that morning. So Jack had to assume command. The crossing went off without a hitch, prompting the group's commander to commend the battalion for such a great job in crossing the river.

That commendation led the division commander to select Jack for the next opening at Command and General Staff College at Fort Leavenworth, KS. At Leavenworth, Jack was a new First Lieutenant—one year out of West Point—on an equal footing in the Army's graduate school of leadership with Captains, Majors, and Lieutenant Colonels many years his senior. And he ranked high, achieving the status of an honor graduate.

"That changed my life," Jack said simply.

When he returned to Fort Ord, Jack worked for a while with the Philippine infantry and then was appointed the Assistant G-3 (General Officer Staff for Operations) of the Second Armored Division in the Second Army Corps. As the war progressed in the European Theater, then MGen Matthew B. Ridgway led the 82nd Airborne Division on D-Day. After his landing at Sainte-Merè-Église, Ridgway needed a headquarters staff in Europe to support his moves toward Germany. He recruited the Second Army Corps team from California that included Jack Crowley. Ridgway had ranked 55th out of 138 in West Point's Class of 1917 and was one of the Army's foremost leaders. The new Major Crowley became Assistant G-3 of the 18th Airborne Corps and deployed overseas in July 1944.

In mid-April 1945, General Ridgway sent Crowley and German-speaking U.S. Army Captain Frank "Brandy" M. Brandstetter on a special secret mission. Displaying a white flag of truce, they rode in a jeep without weapons behind enemy lines into the Ruhr Valley. The two officers and their driver finally reached a Nazi field headquarters. They were able to convince a German general staff officer that his forces were surrounded and that he should surrender to them, prompting the sudden collapse of the Ruhr Pocket.

A half century later, the modest West Point goat admitted that he was both lucky and brave. "We did what we had to do," he said simply. Ridgway promoted both men and nominated them for the Distinguished Service Cross, the nation's second highest combat award. They were awarded Silver Stars for their action. A few weeks later, Ridgway sent Jack to Belgium during the Battle of the Bulge. He had received a battlefield promotion to Lieutenant Colonel less than three years after graduating from West Point and was leading a reconnaissance team. Avoiding capture behind enemy lines, Jack was able to help BGen Anthony McAuliffe. McAuliffe, who was 28th among 283 in West Point's 1919 class, was the 101st Artillery Commander who successfully defended Bastogne after replying "Nuts" to a German general's demand for surrender.

At the end of the hostilities in Europe, Crowley returned to the USA and was named aide-de-camp to the Commanding General of the First Army, headquartered on Governors Island in New York City. That was General Courtney H. Hodges, who had been a member of West Point's Class of 1908 but had not graduated. Jack also stayed in touch with General Ridgway, who was in New York as the senior U.S. delegate to the Inter-American Defense Board and the U.S. representative on the Military Staff Committee at the United Nations.

Nearing the end of his three-year New York assignment, Jack was scheduled to go back to Fort Leavenworth for the advanced senior officer school when fate once again intervened. General Ridgway wanted his former aide to accompany him south on his new assignment to Panama as commander-in-chief of the Caribbean Command. The general claimed that Crowley's on-the-job training in Europe and New York had provided enough graduate school officer training and suggested that he skip the Fort Leavenworth course.

Meanwhile, Jack's West Point classmate, Lt.Col. Edward J. Aileo, had been assigned to assist career management among his classmates and other officers. Ed was an infantryman who ranked sixteen spots above Crowley in the Class of 1942, making him number 357 out of their 374 classmates. Ed had received the Purple Heart for his wounds and earned the Bronze Star Medal in combat in Italy. He suggested that Jack heed the call for special French language training at the Sorbonne University in Paris as a path back to West Point and an opportunity to work for the legendary Charles Barrett. Colonel Charles J. Barrett, who was first out of 101 men in the West Point Class of 1922, was a scholar-athlete who competed in the Pentathlon during the 1928 Olympics in Amsterdam. Barrett earned the Silver Star during World War II as an artillery officer in the 84th Division. He was professor of foreign languages at West Point from 1947 until his death in 1963.

By 1948, Betty and Jack had added two sons to the family: John in 1943 and Chris four years later. The four Crowleys journeyed to Paris in 1948 where Jack quickly determined that his new European assignment was light-years away from his last visit to the continent. Life in Paris and at the Sorbonne offered lots of freedoms to the young family, and they enjoyed themselves for two years. They were also able to hire an immigrant couple from Vietnam to help at home with cooking and housekeeping. French language lessons were an added bonus. They set the stage for the time, a few years later, when Jack would work in Saigon and speak French to his hosts with an accent they recognized.

Back at West Point a year later, Jack taught plebe French for three years, and he reported that no one asked about his class rank. In fact, he said it was a topic that rarely surfaced unless he was among his classmates.

One of those classmates is the man who introduced me to Jack and other members of USMA '42, Kentuckian Colonel John Baker, who eventually retired to Maine. I met John at a Maine Officers Association Lobster Bake one fine summer day at Two Lights Park in Cape Elizabeth. When I described this book, he immediately encouraged me to call his classmate, Jack Crowley, as he remarked, "We are all proud of the fact that he went from last in the class to be the first man to make general." John went into the Artillery Branch after graduating 61st and "missed serving in combat engineers by two spots," he explained. He spent the war years in antiaircraft defense units, guarding aircraft plants in Southern California. He returned to West Point in the Mechanics Department, which loaned him to other departments to teach Chemistry, Electricity, and Physics. After the war, he went to Yale Law School and became a member of the Army's JAGC (Judge Advocate General's Corps). He was the Staff JAG for the Army's Third Infantry Division in Korea and returned again to his Alma Mater to teach law from 1953 to 1957. After a series of JAG assignments in the USA and overseas, he retired from the Army in 1970. Then he served as a Magistrate in the U.S. Canal Zone in Panama until 1982 when he and his wife, Jean, retired to Castine, ME.

As the Cold War was developing in the early 1950s, the North Atlantic Treaty Organization (NATO) and the Supreme Headquarters Allied Powers Europe (SHAPE) staffed senior positions with a variety of officers from the armed forces of member countries. In 1952, SHAPE's Director of Logistics was a French general who required an American deputy, preferably one who spoke French. Jack was invited to be his assistant. However, West Point's Colonel Barrett suggested that he should *not* go back to France to become a translator, but that he should consider becoming a logistician.

"I couldn't even *spell* 'logistician,'" Jack chuckled. "My West Point friends were all kidding me."

Among those friends was a West Point Tactical Officer named Robert Besson who introduced Jack to his older brother, Frank. Robert had graduated 207th among 298 in the Class of 1937. The senior Besson had graduated seventh among 262 in the Class of 1932 and had become the youngest general officer in the Army. Jack explained that Frank had achieved that rank through a lot of hard work in logistics and transportation. "You should transfer to the transportation business," urged Frank Benson. "We'll teach you how to spell 'logistics,' and we'll put you to *work*!"

And work he did. First the family moved to Fort Eustis, VA, where Jack not only learned to spell 'logistics' but also became one of the Army's key troubleshooters and problem solvers in the often bewildering world of moving people and material efficiently. He transferred from the infantry to the Transportation Corps in 1952 as Director of Transportation Training for the Army's Transportation School. Later he was Director of Transportation and Deputy Director of Instruction. One of his many achievements there was planning and developing the School's first aviation maintenance training facilities.

"Once again, that changed my whole life," Jack reported. "I went from being an infantry officer who spoke French to a manager who could help others succeed in their missions by getting troops and what they needed to the right place at the right time." He later followed General Besson to Paris in 1955. Jack finally joined SHAPE when he was named Chief of Emergency Defense Plans for the allied command, and a year later, he was promoted to full Colonel.

In 1959, way ahead of his classmates, he was sent for senior officer training to the National War College at Fort McNair in Washington DC. He was chosen as the class leader to make the graduation speech in 1960. That school led to command of the Army's Transportation Research Command back at Fort Eustis. Next, he was Project Manager for Bell Iroquois (UH-1) Helicopters' development project for the Army Materiel Command. The Huey would become the U.S. military's most widely used aircraft, with more than five thousand used in Vietnam for missions ranging from air-to-ground combat support to medical evacuation.

Jack was finally assigned to the Pentagon at the Army's headquarters as Director of Transportation and Installations for the Army Material Command in 1963. He was in charge of more than one hundred Army ports and terminals as well as the administrative fleet of vehicles, aircraft, rail equipment, and boats. He also led the Army's land acquisition and property disposal programs. He modestly admitted to success in those high-visibility posts.

In 1963, twenty-one years after graduating last from West Point, Jack Crowley was the first member of his Class of 1942 to pin on a star as a general officer.

What was his reaction to that speedy progress from last to first? "I was a late starter," he laughed. "I never cared much for academics, and I was project oriented. Give me a job to do, and I'll do it. Plus, I never got bogged down with an assignment in the Pentagon." When discussing the issue of graduates who aspired for General Officer or Flag Rank, Jack's classmate, retired Army Colonel John Baker, repeated this comment from a younger four-star general he knew: "The promotion system was as perfect as human beings could make it." John said he asked the general to explain his comment, and he simply repeated it. With a chuckle and slight Down-East accent, John concluded, "*That's* what the guys who *make* it think, but *not* what the guys who *don't* make it think."

In May of 1966, *Fortune* magazine described the West Point Class of 1942 as the "backbone class" of the U.S. Army's officer corps. Class members are justifiably proud to be the first to enter World War II, and many also served in the Korean War and Vietnam conflict. In addition to Jack Crowley and Jack Deane, 37 other men reached general officer rank. The 374 men of the class received six Distinguished Service Crosses, the nation's second highest award for bravery, and 64 Silver Stars for gallantry in action. More than a third of the men were wounded in combat as they received a total of 134 Purple Heart medals. And 74 men, nearly 20 percent of the class, were killed in action.

After pinning on his star at the Pentagon, Jack was sent to the Military Assistance Command, Vietnam (MACV) during the buildup of forces in the early stages of the Vietnam War. However, once again, fate played its hand in an unusual twist. Jack was hit with a sudden medical disability that led to a discharge and early retirement in 1969. The Crowleys moved to San Francisco where Jack managed to overcome his illness and became General Manager of the San Francisco Public Utility Company. Later he served for two years as Special Assistant to Ed Daly, Chairman of the Board of World Airways, renowned for its transport services to and from Vietnam. He was also a commissioner of the National Park Service from 1986 to 1994 when he fully retired.

Jack and Betty enjoyed their retirement with golf and a time-share home at Lake Tahoe. They continued to travel, visiting family and friends around the world. They journeyed to New Mexico and other states as well as overseas to England, France, and Belgium where the language still served them well.

Repeating a description shared by virtually all who met him, his classmate Jack Deane said, "Jack was popular, very outgoing and a guy who could maneuver in many circles." To prove the point, he explained, "After we retired, I recall we were playing golf with a couple of local civilians at a private golf course in San Francisco that bordered the Presidio Military Reservation. We were standing at this tee that backed up against government property when one of our foursome said, 'It's too bad the club can't make a deal with the government to acquire twenty or thirty feet of land to make this an easier tee.' Jack replied, 'Good idea. I'll look into it.'" Jack Deane cited that exchange as an example of Jack Crowley's positive outlook. "He had confidence that he could get almost anything done through creative thinking, good associations, and an ability to suggest solutions that were pleasing to all parties," he concluded.

Jack and Betty's son, John, was born in Grass Valley, CA, in 1943. He graduated from Princeton University in New Jersey, received his Master's from the University of Michigan, and was a Fulbright Scholar in England. Later he earned a PhD in history from Johns Hopkins University in Baltimore. John and his former wife, Mary Noffinger, had two children, Amy and Adam. He married Marian Binckley of Toronto, Canada, in 1990 and teaches Early American History at Dalhousie University in Halifax, Nova Scotia. He was awarded a Guggenheim Fellowship in 2002.

Christopher Crowley was born in Pinehurst, NC, in 1946. He attended Duke University in Durham, NC, for two and a half years before enlisting in the U.S. Army during the Vietnam War. After helicopter training in Mineral Wells, TX, and Savannah, GA, then Chief Warrant Officer Christopher Crowley deployed to Cu Chi in South Vietnam in January 1970. Chris flew Bell Iroquois (UH-1) Huey helicopters that his father had helped develop as project manager in the Pentagon a decade earlier.

Chris was a "Dust off" Army aero-medical evacuation pilot in Vietnam for more than a year. Jack proudly reported that Chris was involved in rescuing more than two thousand people in 1,600 missions, often flying five times per day. Chris—who lives in Pleasant Hill, CA, and works in the automotive industry—is equally proud of his father. "We were able to meet up briefly in Vietnam just before my Dad retired from the Army," Chris reported, "and that was very special." Chris and his former wife, Marie Maionchi, had two sons, Christopher and Timothy. He married Donna Vellone of San Francisco in 2001.

During the last few years of his life, Jack Crowley suffered quietly from the debilitation of prostate cancer. He passed away peacefully with his wife and family members at his side on Sunday, July 25, 2004, just before his eighty-eighth birthday. His ashes were placed in an urn at the Columbarian near the Presidio of San Francisco.

Society and its component parts provide many labels that reveal identities and sometimes provide the stories behind them. Boston's Jack Crowley, the son, became the West Point cadet and class goat. Then he became a lieutenant and a husband and a father. Still later, he became a general and a grandfather. Perhaps his finest description comes from his son, Chris, who reported simply after his death, "My father and I were very close; he was my best friend."

Chapter 2

Poetic Patriarch

James H. Hayes, USMA '42

John Baker also suggested that I contact his classmate Jim Hayes. I told Jim that I wanted to publish biographies of men and women who had served the USA in uniform after graduating from the military academies, the sometimes underappreciated national resources. With his historical perspective of a then-87-year-old man, Jim replied with poetry. He promptly quoted from Rudyard Kipling's epic "Tommy," reciting the first two lines of the final verse:

> For it's Tommy this, an' Tommy that, an' "Chuck him out, the brute!"
> But it's "Saviour of 'is country," when the guns begin to shoot.

That 1890s poem was the first of many cited by this career soldier and computer systems analyst who displays an uncanny ability to bring poetry to many situations.

He said the verse's point was first driven home to him in the winter of 1940. "I was on Christmas Leave from West Point and had taken a girl to the movies and had worn my uniform," he recalled. "In those days, I had very few civilian clothes simply because I had no money. My date and I stood in the lobby waiting for the usher to show us to our seats when a rather bossy and elderly lady peremptorily ordered me to take her to a seat. I tried to explain that I was not an usher and that I was, instead, a cadet from West Point on Christmas leave. The woman, rather than admitting her mistake, or accepting my explanation, merely became infuriated. She told me that I should be grateful that I was in the Academy and that, in any case, she and other citizens paid for my upkeep. The following Christmas was different, of course, because by then the Japanese had attacked Pearl Harbor," he recalled in 2003.

"It's somewhat like the present when the U.S. military is once again in favor due to the attacks of September 11, 2001." He suggested, "Even the old biddy who thought I was an usher might have been less acerbic today."

The Hayes family has served their country in uniform throughout virtually all of the century that has passed since Kipling wrote the verse. In 1898, Jim's father was a U.S. Navy seaman during the Spanish-American War. James H. Hayes would serve in World War II and the Korean War after graduating second in his class of 374 in 1942 at the U.S. Military Academy. His son, James Jr., would graduate 91st out of 944 in the West Point Class of 1973. His other children served as well; and his grandson, James H. Hayes III, would complete his studies ranked 29th out of 948 classmates in the Class of 2002 at the U.S. Air Force Academy.

Asked about his success and his offspring in uniforms, Jim proudly and modestly commented, "We've had a *run!*" When asked what his father, the sailor, might think of the run, Jim replied, "My father was an orphan who never got beyond the third grade, and the Navy was his family until my mother and I came along. He was always very proud that his son became an officer, and it made no difference to him that I hadn't gone into the Navy. He was very proud of the accomplishments of his family."

The run that began with the Spanish-American War continued during World War I when Edward Daniel Hayes served as a Chief Boatswains Mate aboard the USS *Scorpion* overseas in Turkey. His ship's port was in Constantinople before it became Istanbul. And he spent the war interned in Turkey since that country was allied with Germany, which was in conflict with the USA and its allies. While U.S. crew members were restricted to Constantinople for three years, several sailors, including Jim's Dad, courted and married local girls. His mother, Katina Duka, was a Christian Greek living in Muslim Turkey. She gave birth to Jim on September 14, 1916, but they both remained in Turkey for another five years.

Meanwhile, Ed and his *Scorpion* shipmates returned to the USA in 1920. Jim and his mother followed a year later. By then, the five-year-old spoke mostly Greek. He would learn his English quickly. More than seventy-five years later, Jim produced a detailed 200-page autobiography for his family called *The Valiant Die Once.* He borrowed its title from William Shakespeare's *Julius Caesar,* act 2, scene 2.

Cowards die many times before their deaths;
The Valiant never taste of death but once,
Of all the wonders that I yet have heard,
It seems to me most strange that men should fear,
Seeing that death, a necessary end,
Will come when it will come.

Jim believes that Shakespeare's words for Caesar describe an essential philosophy for a soldier. "All of us go through life in perpetual concern about what has happened, what is happening, and what will happen," he wrote. "Unhappily, men have little control over the events which govern either the present or the future. Therefore, most people live in a sort of low-level apprehension and fear. Long ago, I became a true realist and realized that I had to do the best of which I was capable, and then I had to accept what fate dealt to me."

As a young boy, fate dealt Jim a hard life as the only child of a stern task master and loving mother. He grew up poor in South Philadelphia in a tough neighborhood and remembers a lonely childhood. He was fascinated with the military, and his father encouraged him. He also excelled in school and cited a number of key teachers who inspired and guided his early progress in the classroom. He started at South Philadelphia High School a month before the stock market crash of 1929 and worked very hard to excel in all his classes, including French and the sciences. Although he enjoyed Boy Scouts and sports, especially baseball, he was relatively small at five feet and one hundred pounds.

One long-lasting lesson taught by his sailor father, by then an unemployed Philadelphia Navy Yard worker, was how to tie knots. As he put it, "My father knew literally hundreds of knots and lashings, and he taught me quite a few. I can still tie many knots like the bowline on a bight, the carrick bend, the timber hitch, and the fisherman's bend, along with many variations. In addition, I can still execute splices as well as a variety of lashings."

Encouraged by his teachers to work on the school magazine, *The Southerner*, he first wrote a sports column and eventually became its editor-in-chief as a young junior. He cites the experience as a key part of his leadership development that would serve him well when he entered the Army. "I learned several important lessons," he recalled. "These included the importance of supervision and attention to detail plus delegation and the need for quality control." He learned these truths at the age of fourteen.

Jim would graduate near the top of this class from South Philadelphia High at the age of sixteen. Although he was interested in the military and possibly attending West Point or Annapolis, he and his family thought they lacked the proper political connections to pursue a nomination. He won a one-year scholarship to Drexel Institute of Technology, now Drexel University, and started there as a chemical engineering major in June 1933. He was shocked at the difficulty, and as he said, "It became evident, in short order, that I was not studying correctly. I figured out that I must raise my grades or lose my scholarship." He correctly blamed poor study habits but explained how he worked through his difficulties with many hours' extra study in the library. Eventually, he began tutoring other students in mathematics to supplement his meager scholarship funds, which were renewed each year. He also worked in a chemistry lab as part of Drexel's work-study program. He completed his five years to graduate with a BS degree in Chemical Engineering with honors in 1938.

During his junior year at Drexel, Jim saw the clouds of war in Europe and decided to join Army ROTC. He also decided to apply to West Point to pursue a regular Army commission, so he joined the Pennsylvania National Guard to obtain a nomination. He won one of the six National Guard appointments to the Class of 1942.

When he entered the U.S. Military Academy on July 1, 1938, Jim Hayes was a college graduate just a few weeks shy of his twenty-second birthday. That maturity and his academic experience would serve him well. He thrived in the rigorous environment of West Point, usually ranked near the top of his class. With his Drexel degree in chemistry, he now concentrated on math studies. He also sharpened his analytical skills. And he enhanced his French language to the point of fluency. "That French language actually helped me survive the war," he said bluntly. He also competed on the gymnastics team, working the rings. Those exercises would help him later to maximize the use of his lithe five-feet-eight frame's 125 pounds when he was carrying a 65-pound pack as an infantryman.

Jim also enjoyed his military training in the field, especially one specific episode that he delighted in recounting many years later. During the summer of 1941, just before his senior year, Jim spent two weeks with the 29th Division off campus at Camp Hill training as an infantry platoon leader. He was also introduced to the cavalry. "The whole thing reminds one of a Graustarkian comic opera, after Graustark, the imaginary kingdom in novels by G. B. McCutcheon (1866-1928)," he explained with obvious relish. "The class divided into two halves, each comprising an oversized cavalry troop with a few men loaned from the famous Tenth Cavalry composed of black soldiers. That regiment had a distinguished record of fighting in the Indian Wars and had been assigned to West Point to train cadets in cavalry tactics," he reported. "I like to think that

I led what might have been the *last* cavalry charge in the history of the United States Army!

"Our side enjoyed the services of a trooper named Benifield, the Tenth Cavalry bugler. Benifield towered over everyone at six feet eight and had to have a special large horse or his legs would have scraped the ground as he rode. On the last day, I commanded a platoon, and Benifield was assigned to me because we had a key role to play in our mock battle. In addition to other talents, Benifield was what I would call the first rapper. He woke us up each morning with his bugle and would shout verse in the rapper style. These were humorous and extremely vulgar but were in every sense of the word rapping as we now know the form today.

"Our troop advanced towards a creek when our forward scouts reported that the other half of our class [the second troop] had taken defensive positions behind it. My commander decided to flank them with my platoon. Benifield's bugle call would announce that I was in position and signal the charge for the entire troop. According to our plan, I found myself leading about forty men and horses across a field while simultaneously trying to use a small copse of woods as cover to prevent the second troop from observing our maneuver. The opposing commander had, of course, stationed security on his flanks. One of his security team was a classmate named George Sherman. When I saw that he had seen us, I turned to my second in command and said something like, 'It's *George!*'

"Benifield, riding to my left, thought I said '*charge!*' and immediately sounded the bugle call for the charge! None of the cadets had reckoned on the fact that the horses had been in the cavalry far longer than we. At the sound of the bugle, the horses went wild! With minor exceptions, none of us were good riders, so we found ourselves incapable of controlling them and became passengers. The charge picked up speed. The horses lowered their necks, threw their ears back, distended their nostrils, and thoroughly enjoyed the exhilaration of the charge! In an instant, a stone fence appeared, and we jumped over it only to encounter another fence and then another! Then abruptly the horses realized that they would run into an almost vertical hill unless they made an abrupt left turn.

"By now, the horses were really foaming at their mouths and became totally uncontrollable. Nevertheless, they had the presence of mind with some persuasion and rein action by the cadets to get onto the road, which lead directly into the left flank of the second troop. Despite my best efforts at control, I found myself at the mercy of the horses running helter-skelter toward the others. Now, because of the coordinated action of the remainder of our troop, the others found themselves incapable of much action. Behind me was my platoon, holding on to their horses for dear life; and to the left of me was Benifield, still blowing the charge!

"One of the second troop moved his horse out into the middle of the road in such a way that I could not avoid it. The impact threw me and my horse to the ground, and the rest of the platoon began to pile up on us because they could not move around the pile comprised of me, my opponent, and our horses. The ensuing pile appeared as a mass of hooves, arms, legs, cadets, and a huge figure blowing the charge! Several cadets were injured as well as several horses. The equivalent of cadet emergency response and veterinarian emergency response soon appeared on the scene to transport the injured to the appropriate hospital.

"I picked myself up and could see my entire military career dissolving before my eyes before it even got started. Instead, we had a critique by Captain Peter Haines, later a general officer who commanded an armored division. His remarks stunned me: 'The charge was in the finest spirit of the cavalry. Cadet Hayes understood the value of shock action and should be commended for prompt and forceful decision!'"

A few days later, back in the classroom as a Firstie or senior, life was considerably calmer. Jim continued to prosper and finally, during his final year, was named a Cadet Instructor in mathematics. Although a considerable honor, he could no longer compete in class rank because the new duties excused him from certain classes. As a result—just like Confederate General Robert E. Lee, who was also an instructor and ranked second in the Class of 1829—Jim was runner-up on graduation day. Ironically, he received an engraved silver saber as the top student in mathematics. It was called the Robert E. Lee Award. Lee also had been first in math in his 1829 class.

Jim and his Dad at graduation

On May 29, 1942, the first man to walk across the stage and receive his diploma from U.S. Army Chief of Staff General George C. Marshall was James H. Hottenroth of the Bronx, NY. After distinguished careers in the military as a civil engineer and working in the Environmental Health Service, he died in 2002. Last in the class was John D. Crowley, who was profiled in the previous chapter.

Runner-up Jim Hayes said he remembered very little of Marshall's graduation speech except the sentence, "I promise you that you will land on the shores of France." Jim said simply, "Most of us did." After graduation, Jim Hayes spent a few days with his proud parents in Philadelphia and immediately reported to basic infantry officer training at Fort Benning, GA. Thirteen weeks later, he was a platoon leader in Company G, 317th Infantry Regiment in the Eightieth Division in Camp Forrest, TN. For the next two years, he would hone his skills in the Blue Ridge Mountains of Eastern Tennessee. Jim describes the work in the hollows or valleys as physical and mental endurance. "The practice turned groups of men into regiments and groups of regiments into divisions prepared to meet the best that Hitler and Tojo could field," he said proudly. He progressed through a series of increased responsibilities and was promoted to Captain in July of 1943 and Major in early 1944. He also completed battalion commander's school back at Fort Benning and was assigned as the 317th Regiment's S-2, or Intelligence Officer.

Eventually, Jim fulfilled General Marshall's graduation prediction. In July of 1944, he and his regiment landed at Omaha Beach on one of the huge causeways constructed shortly after the D-Day invasion. From there, they moved inland to an assembly before heading south to the Avranche battle zone. The infantry poet described the stark scene. "All of us immediately noticed that the assembly area had a peculiar and unforgettable odor—dead men who had begun to decay. Once smelled, the stench of a decaying body is never forgotten. In the next ten months, that stench stayed in my nostrils as if it would never go away. Those first dead bodies reminded me of something odd. Dead men's eyes are open unlike Hollywood's where the dead die gracefully." Two days after arriving in France, his unit was in combat. "That first operation, though minor and insignificant, showed that combat differed markedly from maneuvers," he explained. "For one thing, maneuver casualties returned to duty the following day. In combat, the dead and wounded stayed dead and wounded."

Sixty years later, he articulated the subjects of the enemy and death. "The enemy is simply that: an evil creature devoid of humanity and devoid of any desires other than to kill you," he reported succinctly. "The exaggerated cinema reactions of remorse to killing an enemy are, to me at least, false and misleading," he continued. "I suspect they were mostly written by people who probably never actually engaged in combat and had friends killed or themselves shot." That observation led him to explain his philosophy about death, "As we began combat, I suppose all of us had come to grips with the possibility of killing and being killed. Truth to tell, I didn't dwell on my own death too much because I felt, fatalistically, that I would have little control over the timing and manner of my own demise. Anent the possibility of killing another human being, my reactions seemed the acme of realism: either kill the enemy or he'll kill you."

He continued to explain ever so eloquently, "Ascribing the pejorative epithet *enemy* to all those who fought us neatly erased any psychological reaction from my mind. When I knew for the first time that I had killed an enemy, I had no reaction other than one of having saved my own life. I never regretted killing those who had killed or wounded several of my soldiers. Later, when I knew I had killed some more, either directly or indirectly, I felt elation that they could not inflict damage on me or my unit. In my estimation, the more of them we killed, the sooner the war would end and *all* the killing would cease."

Soon after landing, Jim moved into an area south of Normandy and north of Avranche. A fierce battle had raged there when the Germans tried to close the gap created by the successful moves of the allies' D-Day forces. "As we drove south," Jim recalled, "flashes of light from thousands of artillery pieces lit the sky as if huge lightning bolts were striking the battle area. We continued south through the countryside and through many small, demolished, and deserted towns. Fingers of bricks grasped for the darkened sky as if praying for the right to continue to allow their town to continue to exist. The smell of death reached into our nostrils. Dead horses, dead men, and ruined equipment littered the roadside. We could occasionally see a dead man grinning in the moonlight. I felt like I had entered into a part of Dante's *Inferno*."

As an S-2, or Intelligence Officer, Jim was charged with learning as much as he could about the enemy to help guide the plans for the allied army's advance. He reported that this process included searching the dead bodies of enemy soldiers for their personal papers called "soldbuch." Sometimes these artifacts would yield important clues to enemy actions. And at other times, he put his French language to good use to solicit help from the civilians who watched one army advance and the other recede.

He remembered one incident outside the city of Châlons. "As I searched a dead German major, I looked up and saw a pretty French girl watching me. Of course, I immediately spoke to her in French. As the conversation continued, I finally asked her if I might visit her that evening because we had not received orders to move out and we had a reasonable expectation of the regiment's staying in the assembly area through the night with an early morning departure to continue the pursuit. She demurred for a moment and then told me to ask her father, who just then drove up on his bike. His reaction dripped with suspicion as he asked me why I wanted to visit his daughter. I told him that I simply wanted to chat with her and to get the reaction to the events of the day from our ally. When I visited that evening, I don't think I had a chance to say more than a half-dozen words to this young lady. Her father talked incessantly, and her mother kept a sharp eye on her daughter. I remember even now where the family lived in Châlon. Later, after the war ended, I drove through that city and stopped by the house at 13 Rue Arquebusque. The grandmother who answered the door told me simply that Marie had married a GI and was in America. I was not surprised since she was quite the prettiest young lady I had seen in France."

Jim's grasp of the French language would have a more critical use during the important crossing of the Moselle River on the night of the eleventh and twelfth of September 1944. The 317th Infantry had been unable to cross the river since difficult terrain and heavy German artillery on the eastern side were preventing access to bridges. Looking for a shallow location to ford the 30-meter-wide Moselle, local resistance partisans brought Jim to a French parish priest who was a history buff. In animated conversation, the cleric claimed that centuries earlier, Roman legions had crossed the Moselle River near the northern end of Scarpone Island. Jim's rediscovery of the ford helped more than two thousand allied soldiers cross successfully during World War II. Later he learned that his Third Army commander, Lt.Gen. George S. Patton, had scouted the region after World War I with the same interest. Jim said his discovery "revealed the wisdom of teaching Army cadets history as well as another language to interact with the local populace," and he believes the action saved hundreds of casualties. The river crossing in the Lorraine Campaign has been described in textbooks used at the U.S. Army's Infantry School at Fort Benning and at the Command and General Staff College at Fort Leavenworth, KS.

Jim was named commander of the Second Battalion on September 22, 1944, and continued to move his troops east. At one point, on the outskirts of Sivry, a German machine gun began to fire, leading to what he calls "a classic case of being 'pinned down.' Fortunately, he explained, "the cabbage patch in which we found ourselves offered cover. The patch had deep furrows and gave enough protection from the machine gun fire to prevent getting hit. Finally, in anger and frustration, I stood up and began to fire my sub-machine gun at the machine gun and ultimately threw a hand grenade into it to knock out the gun and crew." As a result, he received a Silver Star for Gallantry in Action. He also received the Combat Infantry Badge, two Bronze Star medals, and a Purple Heart Medal as a result of a near miss by a sniper during another enemy engagement. Throughout the war, Jim was wounded four times and also suffered a bout of pneumonia.

He bluntly recounted the endless tolls of injury, death, and destruction during wartime. While describing his role in the Battle of the Bulge during the winter of 1944 and 1945 and then later in intense battles crossing the Seille River, Jim said, "My duties kept me too busy, which, I suppose, acted in a therapeutic manner. Life, after all, had to go on; and combat was a jealous mistress." Jim philosophically referred to Shakespeare's "Valiant Death" and many other poets when he talked about how his friends died and he survived. "Our 317th Regiment used up fifteen battalion commanders during the war for a casualty rate of 500 percent. It could hardly be classified as a safe job," he said sharply. "After finally crossing the Rhine River near the end of the war, so far as I could tell, only about half a dozen of the original group of officers remained in the regiment, and a couple of them were chaplains or medics. Only one other officer and I had actually been battlefield commanders. We discussed this situation and wondered whether we would see the end of the war or whether a particular bullet would have our number on it." Fortunately, both men survived.

He vividly recalled V-E Day, when peace came to the European Theater, on May 9, 1945. "At first, we didn't celebrate the news of the German surrender like they did in New York or London or Paris," he recalled. "We had no champagne, no pretty girls to kiss, and no way to express our joy. Our celebration finally amounted to *turning on the lights!* We had lived under blackout conditions for almost a year, so when we finally realized that peace had come, we took the curtains off the windows of our command post and drove the jeep down the road with the lights on."

Five months later, he was promoted to Lieutenant Colonel and went home to Philadelphia for R&R (Rest & Recuperation). Then he returned to Germany as part of the occupation forces, assuming command of the Tenth Constabulary Squadron at Kitzingen, Germany. He was charged with two conflicting missions of training soldiers for war and the peacekeeping occupation, later called nation-building, of war-torn Germany. During his first inspection tour, he met Earlene L. Flory, an American Red Cross representative who helped manage the recreation center for his troops. Jim said simply, "I saw a woman who I quickly recognized as being unusually beautiful as well as being a woman of courage and conviction, with great compassion and a love for children."

In less than three months, they would begin a marriage that has thrived for more than sixty years.

Earlene was born in Michigan's Upper Peninsula in the town of Ishpeming on November 15, 1919. After graduating from high school, she worked as a private secretary for fifteen dollars a week. "But I always wanted to fly," she recalled stubbornly, "I just couldn't afford flying lessons!" When World War II started, she went to work in the famed Ford Motor aircraft factory at Willow Run near Detroit. She tested flight instruments and installed them in B-24 bombers, which came off the assembly line every hour. "It was good enough pay that I finally earned enough money to begin flying lessons," she explained happily. She learned how to fly biplanes out of a cow pasture just outside of Lincoln Park.

After she soloed, Earlene joined Jackie Cochran and Nancy Love and a select group of young women in the WASP program. "Women Airforce [as it was called then] Service Pilots flew wherever they needed us, ferrying planes and transporting officials to free up pilots, who were men, for combat overseas," she explained proudly. She flew dozens of different aircraft, logging over five hundred hours. Thirty-nine WASPs died in the line of duty during the war (Yellin 2004, 159). When the WASPs were grounded in December 1944, Earlene looked around for another opportunity to fly. And she carefully cherished her silver flying wings, which would play another important role many years later.

"After the WASP disbanded, we had heard that the Red Cross needed pilots to fly their officials," she explained. "So some of us signed up to go overseas to England. I never *flew* again, but I sure *drove* every kind of *truck* they had," she laughed. "We went from camp to camp making donuts and serving coffee." After the war, Earlene wound up in occupied Western Germany. "I was stationed at Kitzingen and met Jim Hayes in October, and we were married in January," she reported with a smile. "I guess I figured I was getting to the point that I was getting along in age, and I'd better settle down," she chuckled. She was twenty-seven.

When they first met, Jim and Earlene were almost adversaries. *He* was charged with creating a combat-ready force, and *she* was trying to provide her clients with an environment for their relaxation. "Our courtship began on a fairly rocky foundation because Earlene saw me as an unnecessarily strong disciplinarian," Jim recalled. Earlene remembered that Jim was a very energetic person who didn't kid around. "He was very direct and to the point." She reported that he was very persistent. "When he sets his mind on something, he doesn't deviate."

Despite the distractions of their diverse environs, the romance quickly blossomed, and the couple grew closer. Explaining the whirlwind romance, Jim mentioned that World War II interrupted relationships and delayed romance for many young people at the time. "We were attracted to each other and decided to get married," he said directly. However, Germany in early 1947 offered very few outlets to shop for wedding niceties. Fortunately, one of Earlene's friends was a paratrooper and gave her a parachute. The staff of the Red Cross Club used its silk to create her wedding dress. Jim picked up a veil in Switzerland while on a mission to Zurich. Earlene's maid of honor and bridesmaids wore colorful traditional Lithuanian folk dresses borrowed from the women of a nearby displaced persons camp. The men in the wedding party wore their U.S. Army uniforms, including freshly starched shirts and ties. French champagne magically appeared, courtesy of Jim's combat driver who had helped to liberate a German champagne factory in Wiesbaden.

"This was the first American wedding to occur in our area after the first group of American families arrived as part of the German Occupation," Jim explained, "so it was a big deal." Their wedding anniversary recorded two dates—the seventeenth and the eighteenth of January 1947. That combined both U.S. Army bureaucracy and German hospitality. First they were married by the German *burgermeister*, or mayor, who had the proper authority to issue a license. The next day, the religious ceremony was celebrated by a Lutheran chaplain. They honeymooned for a week in Berchtesgarden, the German mountain resort. Jim reported, "We had a wonderful honeymoon and have lived happily ever after."

The newlyweds sailed back to the USA where they met each other's families, and Jim introduced his new bride to Army life outside the Red Cross canteen. They were assigned to West Point where the Army placed Jim in an unusual academic experiment. During World War II, both West Point and Annapolis released their regular instructors for wartime service and recruited a number of senior civilian academicians as teachers. Once the war ended, both schools sought combat veterans who could bring their military experience to the classroom. Jim was assigned to West Point's mathematics department. But he was told to first obtain a master's degree in mathematics. His Catch-22 was to gain the credential in less than one year. Earlene and Jim journeyed 150 miles north to Ithaca, NY, where Jim pursued his advanced degree at Cornell University.

The combat veteran described his return to the classroom philosophically: "I had not touched a math textbook for five years and had been embroiled in battles that were far removed from academic pursuits. Plus, when I entered grad school, I found myself competing with a group of young students who had been studying all during the war years. The mental effort involved in learning advanced mathematics while trying to revive my knowledge of algebra, trigonometry, and calculus was exhausting. When I first started my graduate work, I struggled with the concepts of mathematics and labored under the initial impression that mathematics was something that had been created by nature. In effect, some great cosmic force had created mathematics. Fortunately, I gained an immediate but huge insight: *Man invented mathematics.* Therefore, mathematics is subject to change just as any other scientific theory. Mathematics contains many inherent problems, which man is trying to resolve but cannot with the present theories. Therefore, new types of mathematical theories must be invented and used, provided that they form a coherent and logical system. Thus mathematics is like a game: it has rules and its players have to abide by the rule to play the game properly. However, when situations arise in the game for which there are no rules that lead to solutions, then new rules must be devised, tested, and finally adopted. Sometimes the rules work for long periods of time and then a new problem is encountered for which the rules do not work and new rules must be found. The process will continue as long as there are mathematicians."

With his quick master's degree in hand, Jim returned to his Alma Mater and worked there for three years teaching math. He was a natural teacher and loved it. Earlene liked it too. And although she didn't share West Point graduation experiences with other wives who had met their partners as cadets, she eventually made special connections through her own offspring.

On August 30, 1950, their first son, James H. Hayes Jr., was born at the Academy. He was raised as an Army brat in communities ranging from England and Germany to Virginia, South Carolina, and California. He graduated from Taft High School in Woodland Hills, CA, and entered San Fernando State College in 1968, intending to become a doctor. However, anti-Vietnam War turmoil on the campus, now the University of California-Northridge, prompted him to reconsider. In the middle of his first year, Jim decided to apply to West Point. He was accepted and returned to his birthplace in 1969 for plebe summer as a member of the Class of 1973. He successfully combined academics with gymnastics just like his father. He received his BS degree in applied science with an electrical engineering concentration.

As fitting reminders of history, graduates of all three service academies carry long shiny sabers at their graduation exercises. Jim Senior's Robert E. Lee saber, awarded in 1942, mysteriously disappeared when the family was stationed in Germany in the 1950s. At his graduation in 1973, Jim Junior presented his father his own saber, replacing the one his Dad had earned thirty-one years earlier. Earlene and Jim remembered the presentation as a very moving one. Jim Junior had engraved the names of both father and son on the saber that he presented to his Dad.

Jim Hayes Jr. spent twenty-three years in the U.S. Army Corps of Engineers. His career included an assignment in Germany, where he met his wife, Terri, just like his Dad. Terri Callahan, of Hadley, MA, was directly commissioned in the U.S. Army after she graduated from Salem State College near Boston. She was assigned to Aschaffenburg in West Germany in 1978 as a quartermaster officer. That's where she met her future husband, just like her in-laws. Government bureaucracy also required two weddings, official and church. After Jim Junior retired as a Lieutenant Colonel in 1996, he was a U.S. government contractor and later worked for the U.S. State Department. He and Terri reside in Springfield, VA, and have two children: James H. Hayes III, known in the family as Jamie, and Colin Andrew. Colin graduated from West Springfield High School, VA, in 2003 and entered the U.S. Marine Corps where he became a member of the elite Marine Reconnaissance teams. Unfortunately, as a Marine Lance Corporal during duty in Iraq, he experienced what his grandfather called "the agony of a commander who loses a man to enemy fire." Colin served four tours of duty in Iraq.

Both his grandfather and father were not surprised when Jamie applied for the Air Force Academy. They said he had always wanted to fly and become an astronaut. "For as long as I can remember," confirmed Jamie, called James outside the family. He also said that he has been helped along the way by the military roots of his remarkable family. James was a good student athlete at West Springfield High, not far from the nation's capitol. Like his father and grandfather, he was a successful gymnast. He was recruited by all three service academies plus several civilian schools, including Penn State, Temple, and University of Massachusetts. As he left for his recruiting trip to Colorado, Terri told her son, "Jamie, don't let them dazzle you." When he came home, she remembered that he said, "Mom, they *dazzled* me, I'm going *there!*" James graduated in the USAFA Class of 2002 and then completed the Euro-NATO Joint Jet Pilot Training program at Sheppard AFB, TX. Later he flew the B-1B Lancer bomber on missions in Afghanistan and Iraq and then transitioned to the B-2 Stealth bomber.

Jim and his Grandson Jamie

In June 1950, with the outbreak of the Korean War, Lt.Col. Jim Hayes was eager to leave academia and return to his primary career of soldiering. He was named Chief of the Plans and Estimates Division for Eighth Army headquarters first at Taegu and then Seoul. He arrived in South Korea in December 1950 with the job to predict when and where the Chinese Army would attack United Nations' forces. This new enemy was both huge in numbers and unknown in tactics. Jim's first assignment was to learn as much as he could and predict their offense. "I quickly realized that I would need to analyze tactical reports in our files and look for patterns," the mathematician explained succinctly. "So I read hundred of pages of patrol reports, sightings, conjectures, after-action reports, and prisoner interrogations. I finally began to discern patterns of fourteen very specific steps on the battlefield that predicted attack." He was able to convince the U.N. commanders when and where attacks were likely to occur and believed this intelligence saved literally thousands of lives during the war. Of the experience, Jim said simply, "If there is a Valhalla, I think I might have earned a ticket with my work in Korea."

He returned to the USA at the end of 1952 to attend the Army's Command and General Staff College at Fort Leavenworth. Jim and Earlene's second son, Edward Allen, was born there on Mother's Day, May 11, 1952. He would eventually fly commercial aircraft as a Captain for American Airlines based out of Los Angeles.

After Jim completed the Fort Leavenworth class in the top 10 percent of his class, he reported to the Pentagon for his first "head shed" job. In a natural fit, he was the deputy chief of the office that assigned infantry officers to new posts. He was surprised to discover that 30,000 personnel files were being handled manually. So he set out to automate the system using the new tool called a computer. "I ran into pretty stiff resistance from my staff about technology," he recalled, "so at one point, I finally told them that any officer who did not use computerized lists would be described on his efficiency report as resisting change, lacking in foresight, and unable to formulate new plans." That worked rather quickly and led to his next assignment as chief of plans and the decision to introduce computers throughout the entire personnel system.

But again he ran into resistance, this time from a senior general officer who had been a cavalryman. "Of course, I told him my 'George, charge!' story," he laughed. "And thankfully, he no longer wore spurs! However, the general objected to what he called 'the use of machines' to assign officers or for anything else connected with their personnel files. Fortunately," Jim explained. "I discovered that the general was a poker player who rather fancied himself an expert at the game." Jim had begun to dabble in card tricks and used one to make his point successfully. "I had 'shaved' the edges of the aces in the deck so I could select and produce them by feel when face down," he explained. "I used them in a briefing to select aces when I wanted them. Naturally, the general was curious and that allowed me to explain that a computer could be programmed to select various categories and exclude others. Next, I explained, the assignment officer could spend more time analyzing records and selecting those most qualified for assignments. By the time the briefing had ended, the general had enthusiastically endorsed the use of computers."

Jim reports his second project in the personnel field was not so readily adopted. Long concerned with the problem of periodic officer efficiency reports and the variations between "hard" and "easy" ratings officers, he studied several hundred reports and computed a system to rate the raters. "This would allow a 'correction factor' to smooth out the differences," he said. "It wasn't adopted right away, but later it helped the Army and the other services to 'smooth out' the real value of a rating."

During the Pentagon assignment, the Hayes' third son, Keith Flory, arrived on March 4, 1954, in the post hospital at Fort Belvoir, VA. He served as a military policeman in the U.S. Army and later graduated from California State University-Northridge. A radio news director in Barstow, CA, Keith and his wife, Katie, have a son named Scott.

After living in Virginia, the five members of the Hayes family next moved to Europe. First Jim was assigned as a U.S. exchange officer at the British Joint Services Staff College at Latimer, England. During the six-month course, Earlene chose to join a Scottish dancing group to become more involved in the social life of the college. Jim said he confirmed that dancing was not one of his strengths, to say the least. "Scottish dancing, at the time, was more graceful and lilting than the heavy-heeled steps which I associate with square dancing," he explained. "I'm inept at both. Earlene got the gifts in that category," he continued, "and I did not!" She added, "Jim is not a very good dancer, but we enjoyed it anyway."

At the end of his course in England, Jim made arrangements to retrace his wartime itinerary en route to his new assignment in Heidelberg, Germany. He wanted to take the family to his old battlefields to reminisce and see how they had changed in the past decade. The solemnity of the return was broken by the famed Moselle and Seille rivers. Europe was in the midst of a drought when they revisited them. They were considerably narrower than the war stories recalled. However, Jim's wartime experiences really hit home in the towns of Sivry and Moivron, the scenes of bloody battles. Since neither town had been rebuilt completely at the time, much of the war's devastation still showed. "Bullet holes reminded us that a few millimeters here or there were the differences between life and death during those battles," he reported thoughtfully. "This return to those pitiful towns emphasized to us all the more the madness of war, which makes men fight and die to hold insignificant towns whose only importance is that they happened to be in the path of hostile armies."

As chief planner for the Seventh Army's personnel department, Jim worked on several major issues involving unit transfers and deployments in the mid-1950s. The Hayes clan also enjoyed their time in Europe as tourists and expanded their family once again. Their daughter, Heather Lynn, was born on July 17, 1956, in the 30th U.S. Army Hospital in Heidelberg, Germany. She would eventually graduate from California Lutheran University and be commissioned a Second Lieutenant in the U.S. Army through Army ROTC. After serving in the Army's Ordnance Corps in Aberdeen Proving Grounds, MD, Heather began teaching high school history in Los Angeles.

In 1958, the Hayes family returned to the USA; and Jim went to the Army War College in Carlisle Barracks, PA. Next he was named commander of the First Infantry Regiment, the Army's oldest unit, part of the Second Division stationed at Fort Benning. After he trained his regiment in Georgia and deployed them to Korea, Jim returned to the USA as the Commandant of cadets at the Citadel, the private military school in South Carolina. "I found to my amusement that Citadel cadets were not too different from my West Point classmates," he recalled. "There was little they could do that I had not already seen done before at West Point with one exception." One evening, he and Earlene walked by the cadet barracks and smelled freshly cooked pizza. "I decided to investigate," he reported. "I found out that one of the cadets had a thriving business buying and selling pizzas at a rather large markup. We broke up this lucrative business about the time the senior cadet who ran it was about to graduate. If anyone took it over, I presume they found a way to suppress the odor of freshly cooked pizza being sold to hungry cadets."

After two years at the Citadel, Jim returned to the Pentagon in the summer of 1963. He was an Army advisor for the so-called civilian "Whiz Kids" in the Department of Defense. "All of these young men were PhDs with large egos, and all but one or two of them had never served a day in the military," he explained. "None of them had any combat experience, but all of them were convinced that they knew more about the military than their military counterparts. It was a challenging assignment and contributed to my decision to retire from active duty."

Based upon his experience, performance ratings, and steady early promotions, Jim seemed to be on track for promotion to general. However, a combination of Catch-22 factors involving age and assignments intervened. During the Kennedy years, Jim said rumors began to circulate that, in the future, anyone older than forty-five would not be considered for promotion to General Officer. "Well, of course, at the time I was forty-six and had been a colonel since I was thirty-nine," he noted. "When I was thirty-nine and forty, Army promotion policies made me too young to be considered for promotion to general." So he retired in 1965 and went to work for the famed think tank RAND Corporation.

Like fellow West Pointer President Dwight D. Eisenhower, Jim Hayes took up painting in his retirement. He favored mostly watercolors and landscapes, but at least one portrait of his younger grandson as a baseball player was good enough to frame. He credited the genes of a grandfather from Turkey, who was reported to have painted the holy church and mosque of St. Sophia in what was then Constantinople. He added quickly, "But that's another story."

RAND Corporation, Jim Hayes's post-military employer, was established in 1948 as the original government think tank. It provided a range of research-oriented programs from early computing to the planning, programming, and budgeting system adopted by the U.S. government in the 1960s. Jim's arrival coincided with renewed attention to the military's personnel policies, especially issues of overseas assignments. He believed his studies gained wide acceptance in the Department of Defense. "My Personnel studies resulted in some changes which were beneficial to the lives of officers who followed me," he said proudly. "In fact, as a civilian at RAND, I may have had more impact on our national strategy and policies than I would have had as a General Officer."

When Jim discussed his favorite poems, he cited many that deal with courage and dedication and service—no doubt because they mirror his life in the military. When asked to suggest one to discuss the love of his life, he cited this sonnet from Elizabeth Barrett Browning:

> How do I love thee? Let me count the ways.
> I love thee to the depth and breadth and height
> My soul can reach, when feeling out of sight
> For the ends of Being and ideal Grace.
> I love thee to the level of everyday's
> Most quiet need, by sun and candle-light.
> I love thee freely, as men strive for Right;
> I love thee purely, as they turn from Praise.
> I love thee with the passion put to use
> In my old griefs, and with my childhood's faith.
>
> I love thee with a love I seemed to lose
> With my lost saints,—I love thee with the breath,
> Smiles, tears, of all my life!—and, if God choose,
> I shall but love thee better after death.

Jim and Earlene continued to actively support West Point and the country they have served for so long. When asked to describe the differences between watching her son, Jim, graduate from West Point in 1973 and her grandson, Jamie, graduate from the Air Force Academy in 2002, Earlene focused on fashion for a moment. "Actually," she reported, "the graduation ceremonies were very similar. They marched in to the stadiums very smartly and were perfect and orderly. It was really amazing. The differences were in the uniforms." Another difference is the conclusion, she recalled. "The Air Force boys [Please note that grandmothers have *special* permission to call new lieutenants 'boys.'] put twenty-dollar bills in their hats because the kids collect them after they toss 'em and get the money." (For the record, graduates of West Point and Annapolis now do the same.)

When James H. Hayes III talked about his military family and his roots, he also mentioned the special connections with his Grandmother Earlene.

At the completion of Basic Cadet Training, Air Force Academy cadets receive their shoulder boards after the Acceptance Parade. In the spring semester a few months later, they are officially "recognized" as full-fledged cadets with special insignia. They begin to wear unique emblems on their flight caps. The *silver* "prop and wings" insignia copy the badges worn by pioneering U.S. Army Air Corps flight officers many years ago. World War II WASP pilots, like Earlene, wore them as well. The original insignia was silver *and gold*. The Air Force Academy encourages cadets who have family members who served in the Army Air Corps to wear those unique *gold-and-silver* emblems on their flight caps to represent their heritage. Jamie proudly wore his grandmother's flight wings in an unusual link to the past.

Terri said, "Jamie's graduation was spectacular and so amazing. It was a perfect day, and I guess because we're such a military family that it was extra special." James H. Hayes III remembered his 2002 graduation day. "It was pretty incredible, one of the best days of my life. It was pretty emotional day for all of us but especially the three of us as grads," the most recent Hayes academy grad recalled in 2003. He presented his father with his engraved saber just has his Dad had done for his father twenty-nine years earlier. Jamie's father administered the oath of office and commissioned him. His mother and grandfather pinned on his Second Lieutenant bars as his grandmother beamed.

The poets smiled, too.

A similar scene took place two years later at a special gathering when Jamie completed his Euro-NATO Flight School training in Texas. The commander called Jamie to the stage and announced that his

Grandmother, Earlene Hayes, would pin on his flight wings, adding, "She received *her* wings in *May 1944*." Grandfather Jim reported later, "There was a gasp in the room and then a spontaneous ovation, particularly by the women in the audience. The applause lasted during the entire time that Earlene was pinning on the wings on Jamie's tunic. As she exited from the stage, the Major General from the Italian Air Force, who had given the graduation speech, stopped her and kissed her hand! I have to admit that I had a tear or two of happiness in my eyes to see her finally being recognized for the pioneer that she was," Jim continued. "It was a great evening, and both Jamie and his Grandmother spent the rest of it on cloud nine!"

Unfortunately, life's relentless calendar caught up with Jim and Earlene in 2008. Liver ailments claimed him March 6th and her loving heart failed September 24th. Both were interred with full military honors in the Columbarium at West Point.

Everyone who knew Jim Hayes remarked on his incredible memory. His recall was almost legendary. They also described a nice guy with few faults. When pressed to disclose a weaknesses, they might mention a singing voice that would benefit from coaching, to be kind. "He sometimes tried to sing that poem they turned into a song," Earlene said fondly. "*The Road to Mandalay* sounded better when he recited it rather than trying to sing it," she concluded.

Jim agreed, with a sigh and a smile.

Chapter 3

The Plebe Was a Combat Lieutenant

William B. DeGraf, USMA '50

The youngest man to win a battlefield commission during World War II was not just another plebe when he arrived at West Point on July 1, 1946. When 20-year-old Bill DeGraf removed his First Lieutenant bars and turned in his U.S. Army officer's uniform for the gray of a USMA cadet, he was finally able to fulfill a lifelong dream to attend the U.S. Military Academy. He had successfully reached West Point after two failed physical exams and frontline combat as a decorated and wounded infantryman in the European Theater of Operations. Four years later, he would graduate first in his Class of 1950 as the top-ranked cadet academically and also command the First Regiment, which included 1,200 cadets, half the Corps of Cadets. Then he married his young sweetheart and returned to combat to lead a platoon in the Korean War where he was again decorated for bravery. He came back home and later served his country in a third war as he remained in uniform for another quarter century.

However, when Bill first reached West Point on that blistering-hot first of July in 1946, he was one of 45 former officers, including an ex-Prisoner of War from the U.S. Army Air Corps, among his 922 classmates. Upperclassmen reacted one of three ways to the new cadets' previous status, Bill explained. "Some took advantage of it and were not going to let you off easy while others were uncomfortable when they disciplined someone who had been in combat," he answered when asked to recall. But, the majority didn't know or even care about the new plebe's past. "It was *interesting*," he understated quietly a half century later. "Interesting" is a word Bill DeGraf uses often, with slight inflections in his voice that indicate varying levels of significance. "I wasn't paying too much attention to the upperclassmen because I was anxious to get going since I had been waiting so long to begin."

Like thousands of other ex-GIs, Bill came back from Europe after World War II to follow his dreams and to meet a girl who had written to him. After a couple of stops at the special USMA prep school programs at Amherst College in Massachusetts and Fort Benning, GA, he returned home to California to separate from active duty. He had accumulated enough points from wartime duty to complete his service and be demobilized.[3]

So Bill collected a mustering-out bonus of $300, which represented almost two months' pay. He remained a First Lieutenant in the inactive U.S. Army Reserve for almost two years. And although he wasn't paid as a Lieutenant, that reserve time would eventually accrue to his Army retirement pension many years later. He would earn it in a variety of "interesting" experiences.

William Bradford DeGraf was born in San Francisco on January 10, 1926. His mother, Margaret Sharp, had married his father, Gerald DeGraf, on Washington's Birthday, February 22, in 1925. A younger brother, Donnell Rankin, arrived in 1928. Dad was an electronic appliance wholesaler, and Mom was a homemaker. Gerald had been a Lieutenant in the California National Guard, so young Bill was introduced to military life at an early age. He remembered that his father was in the first California guard unit called to active duty after the Japanese attack on Pearl Harbor on December 7, 1941. "He was guarding the Golden Gate Bridge *that night*," Bill reported proudly. Bill couldn't wait to join Junior ROTC at Polytechnic High School in San Francisco, and he discovered he was good at it. He happily donned the ROTC uniform for weekly parades and participated in battalion reviews from time to time in the parking lot of Kezar Stadium at the southeast edge of Golden Gate Park.

Poly High in San Francisco's Haight-Ashbury District had 2,000 students, including around 250 Junior ROTC cadets who drilled regularly. They studied rifle marksmanship and map reading, and Bill proudly reported, "I could fieldstrip the M-1 rifle before the regular Army had it!" Bill was a member of the school's championship rifle team for four years. The young cadets provided opposition for the adult drilling guardsmen

---

[3] Demobilization released those who had been in combat the longest first by assigning points to the degree of "suffering" which each individual had endured. Points were awarded for months in the service, overseas, in combat, for the number of wounds received, decorations received, etc. (Hayes Interview.)

and generally learned soldiering by on-the-job training in the field. Ten local schools provided enough cadets to produce two regiments, and Bill was the city's Cadet Brigade Commander. His ROTC training would prove to be critical later since a turn of events kept him from ever attending basic training, the Army's intense introduction to military life for ordinary civilians.

After graduating at the top of his class from Poly in June 1943, Bill enlisted in the U.S. Army Reserve. Even though the country was at war and the Selective Service System was drafting young men, the Army recognized the need for new cadres of educated officers. The Reserve and National Guard offered opportunities for part-time soldiers to participate in military training while completing their full-time educations. When he had graduated from high school, Bill had every intention of entering Stanford University in Palo Alto, CA, in the fall of 1943.

But the U.S. Army had other plans and quickly changed his course. They placed him in the Army Specialized Training Reserve Program, intended to provide the Army with a steady source of engineers during the war years. That program first sent him for a semester to the University of Utah where he was based in "the world's biggest dormitory room" for 1,080 men in the field house at the Salt Lake City campus. He was introduced to college courses and motivated by both the desire to excel and the fact that, by successfully completing one college semester, he could skip West Point's entrance exam.

When he arrived in Utah, Bill called his parents, who told him he had received his appointment from West Point to enter in the following summer of 1944. Unfortunately, a bad case of sinusitis caused him to fail his entrance physical examination. Next, the Army moved him to Pasadena Junior College in Southern California for more studies.

As part of the war effort, three schools provided training for soldiers scheduled to attend West Point: Cornell University in New York, Lafayette College in Pennsylvania, and Amherst College in Massachusetts. In March of 1944, the Army called Bill to active duty and sent him to Cornell where he enjoyed both the curriculum and the setting in the Finger Lakes region of central New York State. There Bill continued to soak up his engineering studies while adding some other favorites like studying the Portuguese language and geomorphology, the study of land and formation of the earth. However, his idyllic student life ended abruptly that summer when the Army told him to report to Company A of the 397th Infantry Battalion of the 100th Infantry Division at Fort Bragg, NC. While training with his unit, Bill continued his pursuit of a West Point appointment, taking the U.S. Senate's entrance exam. That would eventually lead to another nomination.

But first, his unit deployed overseas in late September, just three months after the Normandy invasion. Bill landed in Marseille in Southern France to be part of the Seventh Army forces, heading through the Rhone Valley toward Germany. His unit trucked north and east in a quiet sector in early November and tasted combat for the first time. "We were trying to push forward and break through so the First French Army could capture Strasbourg," he recalled. "And the fighting was pretty intense." He started out as one of two forward scouts as his unit moved across the Vosges Mountains in the Alsace region. On the first day, Bill saw the other scout killed ten feet from him as their unit took heavy losses. In bloody fighting, Bill was promoted from scout to squad leader. He and his company felt the ripple effect of the Battle of the Bulge to the north as the German Army tried to prolong its inevitable defeat.

Promoted again then to Staff Sergeant, Bill's company commander told him he had received another nomination to West Point. After a few delays by skirmishes in the field, he was told to report back to his division headquarters for another physical. Coming off three days without rest, Bill was exhausted. The examining doctor asked him to read an eye chart, and when Bill replied, "What eye chart?" he had failed again. So he was sent back to his company, realizing that he had lost still another chance at a West Point appointment. A short time later, in the battle of Rimling, the Seventh Army shifted to anchor the line caused by Patton's Third Army's move north. That's when his company commander nominated Bill for a battlefield commission.[4]

On January 17, 1945, Bill DeGraf received his battlefield commission as a Second Lieutenant in the U.S. Army. It was exactly one week after his nineteenth birthday, and the National Order of Battlefield Commissions believed he was the youngest person to receive such a commission in World War II. Bill was among a half-dozen Army enlisted leaders in his division selected then to fill vacancies created by combat losses. He remembered that the senior officers broke into footlockers in the rear areas and found a gold second lieutenant bar for each new lieutenant. Then they sent the new officers to a replacement depot, called a "repple depple" in military

---

[4]   From 1845 through 1918, enlisted soldiers commissioned for outstanding leadership in combat were called Brevet Officers. Six thousand noncommissioned officers earned battlefield commissions in World War I. World War II saw approximately 25,500 receive battlefield commissions, approved by the War Department, the forerunner of the U.S. Department of Defense.

parlance, for new assignments. After a five-day officers' training, the new lieutenants joined new units, moving east toward Berlin.

Bill was now a platoon leader in Company F of the 143rd Infantry Battalion in the 36th Division. "We were up against the Siegfried Line," he explained, "and a few days later, the company commander called me in and said, 'I want you to take a night patrol through the line to see if we can find out where the enemy is.' He told me to pick out three good people, which I did, and then a regimental communications officer came along with us. We were working our way through the line when, all of a sudden, the Germans hurled a couple of hand grenades at us, causing considerable damage. We picked up our buddies who were hurt and quickly retreated back to safety, carrying our wounded."

Bill said he didn't even realize he had been hit himself until they reached the aid station, and blood was running down his right arm. Fortunately, he fully recovered and was awarded the Purple Heart Medal along with the Combat Infantry Badge and three Bronze Star medals.

When the Germans surrendered on May 8, 1945, the 36th Division was tapped to transfer to the Pacific Theater where the fighting still raged. But, by now, Bill had received his *third* nomination to West Point. And this time, he had passed the physical. Although his eyesight was 20-70, an enterprising ophthalmologist encouraged him to exercise his eyes, then a relatively new practice. Bill followed that advice and eventually was able to improve his vision to reach 20-20. In August 1945, after returning to the USA and a quick trip home to San Francisco, Lieutenant DeGraf reported to the West Point Prep School at Amherst College. He studied there until he entered USMA eleven months later. In his spare time, he took flight instruction and learned to fly. "We first flew off snow skies in Western Massachusetts, and it was fun!" he recalled. Eventually, he would complete the necessary requirements for a pilot's license in California. And it would come in handy.

While he had been in Europe, Bill had corresponded with several folks back home in Northern California. His mother's sister, Evelyn Sharp, taught at Petaluma High and served as that school's yearbook advisor. Robin Wilde was a 15-year-old yearbook staffer, and Bill's Aunt Evelyn encouraged the pretty high school junior to write to her nephew. Robin said, "It was an easy thing for me to do because I always liked to write letters." So one day in the winter of 1944, a letter with a new return address appeared at mail call for the soldier on the front lines. As he tore it open, Bill discovered "she was a great correspondent." He said happily, "And she still is!" Robin and Bill wrote back and forth until he returned to San Francisco.

Back home, Bill's parents had arranged a party to celebrate the safe return of their older son. Aunt Evelyn called Robin and asked her to attend. "I wasn't too sure about going," she thought, "because I was a relative youngster and a rising senior in high school." Robin said she agreed to go. "And I enjoyed myself even though he was an older man." She remembered that he was a *nice* older man and *very* polite. "He was blond and fit and trim, just an ordinary guy."

After that first meeting, she recalled years later that her mother, Gwyneth, had asked her what she thought about her correspondent now that she had finally met him. "I said to my Mother, 'Ah, he's all right.' And my Mother replied simply, 'Mark my words, young lady. You're going to see that man again.'"

Bill liked the girl behind the letters, and the feeling was mutual. However, she was entering the University of California-Berkeley, and he was entering West Point in New York. Many more letters were to be written and read during the next years of the burgeoning bicoastal relationship.

During his Beast Barracks in the summer of 1946, Bill was first paired with another former lieutenant named Charles O. Eshelman from Pennsylvania. They would swap places, ranking first or second in the class academically, for all four years. In the middle of the 20th Century, West Pointers took the same classes in a rigid engineering-oriented curriculum. These included physics, chemistry, engineering mechanics or principles, and mathematics that included solid geometry, trigonometry, calculus, differential equations, and statistics.

Class grades were posted each week in the divisions or barracks' entranceways called "sally ports," named for the area where cadets would "sally forth" outside. The term dates to times of medieval castles. Cadets' options in course selection were limited to choosing one of five languages: French, German, Spanish, Russian, or Portuguese. Those who had taken a special U.S. History course were also allowed to take U.S. Diplomatic History. When asked how he achieved the number one ranking, Bill replied humbly and succinctly, "good luck." He also has an incredible memory, recalling details and names from the distant past as if it were yesterday. He modestly admits his memory was "a big help" when studying.

Outside the classroom, he continued his shooting on the rifle team, enjoying competitions among marksmen from the Naval Academy and another perennial power—the University of Maryland. More than fifty years later, Bill recalled a regional meet where both West Point and Maryland fired an identical 1,418 total score to a tie after regular competition. They matched again when they fired while standing, and then West Point fired a couple of points better in the kneeling position to take the national championship for 1950. He remembered that the

Maryland team's score was good enough to be runner-up in the east and take second place in the entire nation behind his West Point team.

Bill also joined the photo club and worked on the cadet magazine, the *Pointer*, as its business manager, becoming introduced to the world of advertising space sales. He and another cadet from the Class of 1949 also established the West Point model railroad club in 1948 with help from the Army's Transportation Corps. That cadet was Richard C. Bowman, who was 69th of the 574 graduates in 1949. He would retire as an Air Force Major General in 1975. Bill built several HO gauge model railroad sets that he continued to operate decades later.

During their summer vacation in 1947, Bill arranged charter flights with some other cadets from the West Coast to return to California for the holidays. In one of his many letters to Robin, Bill had suggested that she fly back east with him as stewardess on their charter flight. She wrote back with a laugh and replied, "Sure, why not?" Bill explained with a laugh, "*She* was kidding, but I was *not!*"

Robin tells the story a half century later like it was yesterday. "I had a summer *job* working at a department store and was getting ready to return to *college* in the fall," she explained rather emphatically. "I met up with Bill for a farewell party the day before he was due to return east on the charter flight. He had that pilot's license and flew a small plane to pick me up in Petaluma," she continued. "We flew back to Bay Meadows Airport, south of San Francisco, about a half-hour flight. We were to have lunch with Bill's parents before going dancing that night.

"At the restaurant, Bill's mother took me aside privately and asked, 'Young lady, where are your things? You're flying back *east* tomorrow!'

"I was shocked and told her I had only been joking about going east. I was committed to resume my job. She said, 'I think we had better explain this to my husband and son.'"

In a quick aside as she tells the tale, Robin said, "I *wish* you had known Bill's parents, they were the *best* folks, they were *wonderful!*"

When Bill's mother and Robin returned to the table, the younger woman quietly remarked, "Gentlemen, I am terribly sorry, but there's been a misunderstanding. This was a *joke*. I'm returning to Petaluma. I have *no* intention of going east tomorrow!

"Bill's Dad reached into his pocket, took out a bunch of coins, and suggested, 'Robin, why don't you go call your mother and ask her? You can't lose anything by trying.'"

Robin continued, "I figured that would solve it. I'd call Mommy, and she'd say no. My mother was a teacher on school vacation; and my sister, Georgia, lived in Rochester, New York. I had *already* told Mom about the flight and Bill's earlier request as a *joke*.

"So I called my Mother right away and told her they were expecting me to leave the next day. There was a pause on the line. Then she asked, 'Do you think *I* could go too?'

"I turned and asked Bill if she could go along, and he said, 'Of course! There are plenty of seats on the plane.'

"We drove back up to Petaluma, and I packed in thirty minutes for the entire summer," she reported proudly. "*Then*, we drove back to San Francisco to go to dinner and dancing."

The next day, Robin and her mother, Gwyneth, returned east with the West Pointers. Later Bill convinced Robin to stay for the summer. She took a waitress job at the Thayer Hotel on the West Point campus. Although she eventually returned west to her U.C. Berkeley classes in the fall, more letters flew back and forth across the country. Robin completed another year's studies before coming back to West Point the following year. During their Christmas holidays of 1948, the couple became engaged, and Robin transferred to New York University in New York City. Throughout these times, Robin was becoming more familiar with Army life, West Point, and the members of the Class of 1950 and their "drags" as partners were then called.

Robin and Bill at the West Point Ring Dance

Bill and Charles Eshelman and his other classmates continued to trade places in class standing. However, on branch selection night in the spring of 1950, Bill DeGraf stood at the top. He chose to return to the infantry, only the third West Point number one to do so until then. Since West

Point was established as the first engineering school in the USA, most top graduates either entered the engineering branch or selected graduate school. Many of the latter returned later to their Alma Mater as teachers. Bill's choice was so rare that it prompted the Army engineers to send an officer to visit him to be sure he had not been pressured into selecting infantry. Bill said he had been an infantryman all his life and "that's where the soldiers are," so it was a natural choice for him. Times have changed since then with several more top men opting for the infantry.

Graduation Day for the Class of 1950 was exactly six years after D-Day, June 6. The members listened eagerly as Secretary of the Army Frank Pace Jr. spoke to the 670 grads, their families, and their friends in the field house on a pleasant late spring day. As Bill recalled it, "Then we picked up our diplomas and tossed our hats in the air! Next we went back to our rooms to change into our lieutenant's uniforms and started having *weddings!*"

Admissions and undergraduate rules at all three academies prohibit married cadets and midshipmen, so graduation days lead to numerous wedding celebrations.

After they attended and participated in the weddings of several other couples for four days, Bill and Robin were married outdoors at Camp Buckner on June 10. Bill's brother, Donnell, was Best Man; and four classmates served as ushers. Theirs was the last wedding of the cycle. The newlyweds left for a driving honeymoon that would take them to Niagara Falls and eventually back to California. However, fate would intervene a few days later.

Like many other academy grads, Bill talked about the special bonds that connect all service academy classmates. Many couples result from blind dates with roommates or siblings. And the closeness of the grads' duty assignments and travels contribute to a network of old friends perhaps unique among colleges and universities. This closeness exhibits itself in later years when connections and reunions of old friendly couples sometimes lead to second marriages among other old friends who are widows and widowers of classmates. Bill mentioned several couples from the Class of 1950 who bring real meaning to the phrase "extended family."

Bill's first roommate, Charles Eshelman, graduated second in the class. Even though Bill and Robin and several others told me they would prefer *not* to list their classmates' class ranks, I listed the ranks of all the academy grads included because I believe it illustrates my thesis. Charles would spend 25 years on active duty in the Corps of Engineers before retiring as a Colonel in 1975. Third in the class was James M. Thompson, a Rhodes Scholar who was a member of the 1952 U.S. Olympics Team and also served a full career in the Army as a Civil Engineer, retiring as a

Lieutenant General in 1983. Eighth in the class was Frank Borman, who joined the U.S. Air Force after graduation and entered pilot training to later explore space as a NASA astronaut. He commanded *Gemini 7* in 1965 in the first rendezvous of two spacecraft and the first manned lunar orbital mission, *Apollo 8*, in 1968. He retired from the Air Force as a Colonel in 1970 and later served as president of Eastern Airlines. He received the Congressional Space Medal of Honor in 1978.

Bill, who also served as his class scribe or alumni reporter, proudly claimed that his Class of 1950, was the only one of any of the three academies to have had three sitting Chiefs of Staff at one time. In the 1980s, Fidel "Eddie" Valdez Ramos, who had ranked 63rd in the class, was Chief of Staff of the Armed Forces of his native Philippines. He later became the twelfth President of the Republic of the Philippines. New Yorker John A. Wickham Jr., 149th, would be the Army Chief of Staff and retire in 1987. North Carolinian Charles A. Gabriel, who ranked 283th, would be the eleventh Chief of Staff of the U.S. Air Force. Four other men from the class would become four-star generals: Paul F. Gorman Jr. of New York who ranked 135th and Wallace H. Nutting of Massachusetts who was at 247th. Oklahoman Bennie L. Davis, who became an USAF General, ranked 473rd. South Dakotan Volney F. Warner, who ranked 480th, wrote the original plan for what eventually became Operation Desert Storm in the Gulf War. The class included sixty-four men who became general officers. Last in the class was New Yorker James R. Wheaton Jr. He served in the infantry and earned Bronze Star medals in combat in both Korea and Vietnam. He retired as a Lieutenant Colonel in 1971 to become a businessman.

New Jerseyan Joseph P. Buccolo, who ranked 522nd and would later track history for the class, reported that nearly two-thirds of the class (420 men) remained on active duty for more than twenty years. Joe, who entered the Army's Signal Corps at graduation, served in a range of military assignments in the USA and overseas until he retired as a Lieutenant Colonel in 1970. He then worked in the telecommunications industry for enterprises including New York Telephone, Mobil Oil Corporation, and American Airlines. Joe explained that 381 classmates, or 57 percent of the class, obtained Master's degrees and 28 completed PhDs. Their combat experience was extensive and costly. Bill and 165 others had already served in World War II; and more than half the class, 369 men, would serve in the Korean War while 301 fought in the Vietnam War. They recorded eleven Distinguished Service Crosses, the nation's second highest awards for bravery, and ninety-eight Silver Stars in combat among numerous other decorations. The Korean War claimed forty-one classmates, and seven men died in the Vietnam War.

As Bill DeGraf contrasted the West Point of the mid-20th Century with the academy fifty years later, he said, "We were all engineers and focused pretty much on that field. Today is much different and much better, I believe. Despite the fact that many of us old-timers object, I think today's cadet is really outstanding in many ways more so than when we were there." When asked about the introduction of female cadets 25 years after he graduated, Bill said, "They have added greatly to the academy. They have made the men work harder. I believe men's grades have gone up because they don't want to be shown up by the women." Pressed on the question of physical conditioning and standards, he replied, "The women's physical requirements today are more difficult than they were for men in my day."

As he was graduating, Bill chose an unusual infantry assignment. He wanted to go explore another part of the world. He thought that he and Robin could drive to the West Coast, enjoy a honeymoon across country visiting friends, and eventually end up living in Japan. His best friend was New Yorker Robert "Bob" R. Werner. He was an engineer who ranked 79th in the class and also had a Far East assignment. Bob and his wife, Leila Mae, and the DeGrafs thought they could continue to work together in Japan. However, once again, the Army and global politics had other plans.

West Point's classes of 1948 and 1949 had gone to "Ground General School" in Fort Riley, KS, right after their graduations. Following their four-year study at West Point, the Army learned that an extra year's schooling in Kansas was not productive. Therefore, Army Chief of Staff General J. Lawton Collins decided that the new lieutenants in Bill's class would go directly to work with troops in the field. Collins ranked 34th of 139 in the April USMA Class of 1917. Most of the top grads were headed for European assignments. Another large group was destined for special schools in the USA, including the 25 percent headed for duty such as pilot training in the U.S. Air Force in the days before the Air Force Academy produced its own new officer pilot trainees. The rest were headed for the Far East, in less desirable posts, that didn't include spouses. However, Bill had been able to find an infantry position in Northern Japan that enabled Robin to accompany him. He was to be assigned to the Seventh Division in Hokkaido.

Sunday, June 25, 1950, newlyweds Bill and Robin DeGraf spent the day touring Niagara Falls. After dinner, they returned to their hotel room to hear the reports of the massive North Korean invasion of South Korea. Plans for their move to Japan were questioned and eventually would be suspended. They continued their drive to California, stopping en route visiting friends, but understood that—once again—they would be separated. When they arrived in San Francisco, a friend of

Bill's parents—Bishop Karl Morgan Block, the Episcopal Bishop of California—offered the young couple a special wedding present. He was off to a meeting in St. Louis and loaned the DeGrafs his four-story townhouse in San Francisco's North Beach district overlooking the Bay. The bishop thought the younger DeGrafs might enjoy his residence before Bill departed for his second war. And enjoy it they did, entertaining classmates and other friends passing through San Francisco.

Eventually, Robin drove Bill forty miles northeast to Camp Stoneman in Pittsburg, CA, where he caught a train for the trip north to McChord Air Force Base, southeast of Seattle, WA. There he switched to an aircraft bound for Japan. Among his fellow passengers was his classmate, Second Lieutenant James R. Wheaton Jr.

The first and last men of West Point's Class of 1950 were on the same flight, heading off to war.

After a refueling stop at the Shemya Air Force Base in Alaska, the military aircraft landed at Tachikawa Air Base, just outside Tokyo. As the men awoke groggily from the long flight and its time zone changes, they went to Camp Drake, another post near Japan's capitol. There they fired live ammunition at stationary targets in a few hours' practice on the firing range. A quick train ride to the port of Sasebo took them to a boat ride across the Korean Straits to the southeast port city of Pusan. There they were able to fire their carbines once again before joining their units in combat.

When asked about the sudden transition of being thrust into combat a few weeks after graduation, Bill reported, "At least, I had had *some* experience."

When Bill arrived in Pusan in August of 1950, the North Korean Army had totally dominated the entire peninsula. They had crossed the Pusan Perimeter at the Naktong River on August 4th and were threatening to push the Republic of Korea (South Korea) army and their American-led United Nations' allies right into the sea.

He remembered one specific classmate who had been a cadet sergeant and had not directly led cadets at West Point, much less commanded troops in combat. Bill said they handed Will Hill Tankersley a platoon and added, "By the way, half your platoon are Koreans who don't speak English. And tomorrow we're going to attack!" Bill said that Will's character and training kicked in, and he was one of the successful ones. Tankersley, who had ranked 34th from the bottom of the Class of 1950, would serve on active duty and in the Army reserve, retire as an Army Reserve Major General, and later serve as a Deputy Assistant Secretary of Defense.

Bill was a new platoon leader in Company M of the 21st Infantry in the 24th Infantry Division. His battalion included four other classmates, beginning a pattern of fraternity that would continue throughout his career. "I never served without a classmate nearby," he would report proudly a half century later. His heavy weapons company was equipped with machine guns, recoilless rifles, and mortars. The company was charged with helping to defend the perimeter in a holding action. Bill's platoon had few veterans and four 75mm recoilless rifles, relatively light weapons that could be moved in small trucks. Usually, the recoilless rifles fought tanks or destroyed pillboxes, providing extra firepower to the company's regular rifle platoons. However, Bill and his team were shorthanded and improvising. They provided indirect fire using the 75mm "reckless" as a substitute for artillery. The action was effective as they hit enemy troops about 3,000 meters away. His division was waiting for the larger United Nations force that would land north and west of them at Inchon, west of the capitol of Seoul. On September 15, thousands of troops on 261 ships came ashore to turn the tide of the Korean War.

When asked to compare, Bill said his first few weeks in Korea contrasted considerably with his previous taste of combat in Germany. "We had quite a bit of support in Europe, and we were in the early stages of war in Korea, so we were improvising more," he said. "We just didn't have the firepower at first. Enemy intelligence and airpower support were lacking too." However, Bill and his platoon moved rapidly north to meet the landing forces and pushed the North Korean forces over the 38th parallel. He remembered General Douglas MacArthur's decision to keep moving north. They pressed on to Pyongyang, the north's capitol city, and recalled going through the "Narrow Necks" and Haiju where he believed "we should have stopped." They almost reached the Yalu River on the west coast within a few miles of China and Manchuria.

"My platoon was fairly busy because whenever we had contact, the scouts or forward platoon would call for some recoilless rifles because we could fire rapidly," he recalled. "That meant we were *always* the second platoon in a column"—he laughs—"while the regular rifle platoons would circulate from first to other positions behind us. We could set up and fire in a minute, and that made us very popular."

He remembered a rustic Thanksgiving dinner with his troops up near Sinuiju in North Korea but then smiles when he told about his travels in December. "My company commander knew that the store manager of the PX [Post Exchange] at Camp Drake back in Tokyo was a family friend," he explained. "So he collected some money, loaned me a jeep, and told me to go down to Kimpo Airfield and hitch a flight to Japan for a shopping expedition." By this time, the battalion had withdrawn from North Korea, and the troops were short on comfort supplies. "They had run out of coffee, and we were eating pancakes with no baking powder for meals three times a day. Chow lines were grim." He quickly added, however, "Now, *my* platoon was OK since my wife and parents were mailing over great packages that ranged from mock turtle soup to special marmalades and cookies. But the *other* troops were hurting. So I flew over and loaded up with coffee, playing cards, transoceanic radios, batteries, candy, writing paper . . . It was quite a stash," he recalled. But then, he had to find a return flight. "And that was not so easy!" Luckily, "Santa" was able to get back and fill up his jeep sleigh and return to the battalion before Christmas.

Food was one contrast to his earlier experience in Europe; lodgings were another. "In both places, you're basically living in holes in the ground," he explained. "But in Europe, you were moving through more towns. The battalion commander in Germany was *cute*, you might say," he continued. "We'd work our way through some fights and come up on a hill on the edge of a town, and the CO would say, 'OK, we'll stop here.' But then, troops would all say, 'Wait, let's move into town.' And then the commander would reply, 'OK, if you *really* want to, we'll move into the town.' We would get into town and put squads into houses and put guards outside and then go look for fresh eggs and potatoes and onions. In Korea, most of the time, we were out climbing through mountains. But occasionally, you'd come to a village and find these little hootches [huts], and even though they had these clever little heating stoves for heat, there were slim pickings for food."

By this time, in frequent contact with the enemy, Bill had picked up another Combat Infantry Badge and two more Bronze Star medals. He had also been moved over to lead an 81mm mortar platoon. That meant he was no longer second in the line of march. His company covered the withdrawal south of Seoul, and then Bill moved north again. He spent New Year's Day of 1951 astride the 38th parallel. Some of his classmates still heading rifle platoons called him a rear-echelon soldier because he was now 200 meters behind them. However, he managed to scrounge up some panoramic sights and an aiming circle from an artillery unit, and he was able to commence firing quickly. That made him popular with the riflemen. In February, the Ninth Corps commander tapped the young lieutenant to work in G-3 Plans, an unusual assignment for a junior officer. The commander, MGen Bryant Moore, had been West Point's Superintendent during Bill's cadet days and had ranked 104th among 151 grads in the August Class of 1917. Unfortunately, Bill worked for him for only a short time until General Moore died in a helicopter accident a few weeks later.

Although Bill helped to plan the relief of Chipyong-ni and other projects, he officially worked as a rear-echelon soldier until he was transferred back to the States. On their first wedding anniversary, Bill called Robin and said he was heading home. He left Korea on June 10 not knowing that he would eventually return to that country and still another one in Southeast Asia for more combat duty.

Bill came back to the USA to teach in the Army leader's course at Camp Roberts in California where he and Robin had the first of their four children. Gwyneth was born in 1952 and later went to Bryn Mawr College in Pennsylvania and law school at New York University. A member of the New York Bar, she teaches high school English in New York. Bradford arrived a year later in Indiana and lives in California where he produces computer graphics for cinematographers, including graphics for the U.S. Army's National Training Center. Scot, born in 1956 at West Point, is a computer guru and teacher in Washington DC. He and his wife, Linda, have three children: Denali, Colin, and Galen. Leslie, born in 1958 at Fort Knox, KY, is a quality control executive in the food industry in California. She has two children: Jesse and Kathryn.

Bill's duties at Camp Roberts introduced him to the combination of staff jobs and military training that would describe his military career outside of the battlefield. When he reported for work, the man in the next desk was another classmate, Robert M. Chambers, who had ranked 541st in the class. Bob was a company mate at West Point and usher in Bill and Robin's wedding. Bill was assistant operations officer for a couple of years until he returned to the classroom. This time, it was the world of the Big Ten at Purdue University in Indiana, and the subject was nuclear physics with a minor in electrical engineering.

"I was sent there by West Point's Department of Electricity because that's what they wanted me to teach," Bill explained. After the structure of military training, he found the civilian students *interesting* with a real contrast between math and physics classmates. The math folks, he said, did the minimum to get by. He recalled a Vector and Tensor Analysis class where the math professor spent more time teaching calculus than he did the main subject. However, he contrasted that with his physics classmates who were more into the subject and did not operate under time constraints. "They were just more interested in doing experiments than solving problems," he explained. "We had a pretty-advanced-for-the-time cyclotron for atom smashing. When it was unavailable, the physics students would say, 'don't worry, work on something else, and it will be ready next year.' I would say, 'I've got to do it *now*.'"

He and Robin returned in 1954 to West Point where Bill joined the Department of Electricity. He taught both electrical engineering, or "juice" as it's known to cadets, and nuclear physics. Both DeGrafs said it seemed "a bit strange" when they chaperoned dances where the Firsties or seniors were plebes the year Bill had graduated. He taught the top sections and, when asked about number ones or goats in his classes, replied, "The people who came out at the tops of their classes were in my classes at one point, but to me, they were all just cadets." He and Robin enjoyed the West Point tour but lamented that their speedy assignment progress had put them there much sooner than their friends and classmates. "We were a bit early to be assigned back at the Point," he said. "Six years later, there were dozens of classmates of mine stationed there. That would have been more fun."

Although Bill, like all number one graduates interviewed for this book, exuded modesty on the subject of class rank, he did tell a mythical tale of firsts and lasts when I pressed him. "It was an old story that you're in a classroom at the board presenting an answer and drop your chalk. In the last [class rank academic] section, some guy picks it up and hands it to you. In a first section, some guy puts his foot on it and grinds it into the ground. That's a *story*, of course; I can assure you it didn't happen," he added quickly.

After West Point, the DeGrafs headed for Kentucky and the Army's advanced armor course. There Bill was finally introduced to the full spectrum of armor warfare after combat in two wars. Then the six DeGrafs moved to West Germany where Bill finally was able to introduce his family to the joys of overseas living. First they were in Worms where Bill was an S-3 or Operations Chief of an Armored Infantry Battalion in his old unit, the Seventh Army. When asked to contrast his return to Europe, he replied, "It was a lot different than the first time. We didn't have a lot of money, but we played tourists with the best of them," he recalled. "We took the kids skiing, went to the Passion Play at Oberammergau, and saw the tulips in Holland. We went back to see the waterworks show at Hildesheim near Strasburg, and it was great. Grandparents came over from California, and we really enjoyed ourselves," he reported. Among the tourist sights was one former battleground.

In 1961, the DeGrafs returned to the USA so Bill could attend the Army's Command and General Staff College at Fort Leavenworth, KS. After that year, they moved to Washington DC for the first time. Bill was stationed in the Office of the Deputy Chief of Staff for Operations on the Army Staff at the Pentagon. After a year as a student at the Army War College, Bill returned to another wartime country when he was assigned to command an Armored Rifle Battalion at Camp Kaiser in South Korea. "Interestingly," he recalled years later, "I was located just a few miles from where I spent New Year's Day in 1951. Going to Kaiser, we would drive right by the area where I had put in mortars during the war. What was *more interesting*"—he emphasized—"was the transition we saw in Korea as a developing country. In my first tour, transportation was oxcarts and A frames on the backs of Koreans who walked an awful lot. By the time I was there in the sixties, they had a lot of motor scooters and busses jammed with people and animals riding on paved roads instead of dirt strips."

When Lt.Col. DeGraf arrived in Korea in 1966, the Vietnam War was heating up. "We were very slim in the battalion," Bill explained, "serving as a feeder outfit for the war down there." He remembered that his battalion had an authorization of 32 officers, but only 16 were assigned. His Sergeant Major filled the role of battalion executive, and several other key posts were filled by junior officers or noncoms. However, he remembered that the Selective Service draft provided troops who had completed a year or two of college in a range of specialties. "They were able to adapt, and we got the job done," he said. "We were able to build them up, and they became platoon *leaders*," he reported proudly. "We were the Corps' reserve, and we were able to train effectively."

After a division headquarters assignment, Bill returned to the Pentagon to work for the Defense Department under Defense Secretary Robert S. McNamara. He was part of a Systems Analysis team with people he called terribly bright. "My boss was Ivan Selin, 26-year-old with two doctorates and fluency in six languages, and we were studying nuclear weapons. It was *interesting*," he said once again, "because *now* I was taking my Army experience and working with the Navy and the Air Force on some very new programs." Selin eventually founded American Management Systems, a major consultancy, and was later Chairman of the Nuclear Regulatory Commission.

Bill left the Pentagon in August of 1969 to go off to his third war, in Vietnam. Robin stayed in their home in Fairfax County, VA. As a 43-year-old full Colonel, he assumed command of 2,000 troops in the First Brigade of the First Infantry Division—the famed Big Red One. Stationed in the old Michelin rubber plantation in the Field Force's area north and west of Saigon, his unit was part of the team securing the approaches to the capital. Once again asked to contrast Vietnam with his earlier combat assignments, he replied, "Well, actually, it wasn't as scary as the first two because now combat was less intense. But we had a lot of people and a lot of area to worry about." He continued, "We had to learn how to fight a new war that was entirely different from what we had done in the past. In my view, you had to figure out how to *win* the war, and there isn't a whole lot of guidance on that. For example, you did things like collect all the rice in the region and store it. That way you could control the rice, and it didn't flow out to the enemy. You had to try to stop his movement. It was called harassment and interdiction.

"When I got there, combat elements of battalions moved out as a group, and then they plodded back the next day, having missed the enemy that had simply avoided confronting them," he explained. "So we started breaking down into smaller units by sending out a U.S. squad and a Vietnamese squad of ten to fourteen men apiece. They would go out and try to stop the enemy's movement and then come back in after three or four days. These were spoiling movements, the same thing they were doing to us. We went after the enemy's leadership just like they were doing in Afghanistan in 2002 and Iraq more recently. We opened up the roads so we could travel safely. It was a different kind of war with no front line, and you had to keep everybody alert at all times. You had to keep the morale up. Before I arrived," he continued, "some of my platoons had spent six months at forward fire bases. So we began to rotate them. Every day, I would send a chopper out. They would pick up a platoon and bring another one back in. The troops would get 24 hours back with us and get cleaned up with hot showers and haircuts. They would grill some steaks and have some beer. Then they would check their weapons and go back on the hunt." Commanding three battalions that each had twelve platoons, Bill was able to rotate his troops every thirty or forty days.

Asked to contrast the men he led in the '60s with their predecessors in the '40s and '50s, he said, "The troops were much like we had in World War II and Korea. They were draftees over there doing their duty, and they did what was required of them. They didn't volunteer, and they groused when they needed to."

When he assessed the results of the first six months of his third war, Bill replied, "We controlled the area, and we reduced the enemy's infrastructure. We kept the enemy on the defensive, and we didn't have a single case when the enemy attacked any of my elements in the time I was there," he said proudly. "And we kept our own casualties down, which was very important because we didn't want a war of attrition out there." Summing up, he said, "In my opinion, I thought I had accomplished the mission that I had been given. Unfortunately, my division commander didn't agree with me. He wanted to see lots of headlines."

After six months with U.S. forces, Bill was sent down to the Mekong Delta in the area of My Tho. He led 125 American advisors who were helping 5,000 Vietnamese troops in the Seventh ARVN (Army of the Republic of Vietnam) Division.

In his epic description of the pivotal battles of the Ia Drang Valley early (November 1965) in the Vietnam War, *We Were Soldiers Once . . . and Young,* retired U.S. Army Lt.Gen. Harold "Hal" G. Moore described what he called the stupidity of the six-month assignment policy.

Even more devastating to the morale and effectiveness of every American unit in combat was the six-month limit on battalions and brigade command. This was ticket-punching: A career officer had to have troop-command time for promotion. The six-month rule meant that twice as many officers got that important punch. It also meant that just about the time when a commander learned the terrain and the troops and the tricks and got good at the job—if he was going to get good—he was gone. The soldiers paid the price. (Moore and Galloway 1992, 441)

Moore, who commanded the First Battalion of the Seventh Cavalry during the costly Ia Drang battles, graduated 641th among his 851 classmates in West Point's Class of 1945. Actor Mel Gibson played his role in the movie named for the book.

Reacting to Moore's claim, Bill said he both agreed and disagreed with the six months' policy. "On one hand, the Army needed to cycle commanders through combat to have a wider pool of senior leaders with combat experience," he said. "A lot depended on the area. I don't believe our soldiers suffered because, as a brigade commander, we owned the area, and we had things under control. My replacement didn't have a problem holding the area so our transition didn't hurt our soldiers or our mission." He added that he was also better prepared for the second half of his tour as a senior advisor to the Vietnamese.

At that time in early 1970, My Tho was the home of the president of the Republic of Vietnam. "As a result," Bill explained, "the Seventh ARVN didn't seem to do too much more than hang around the compound." Also in the area was a former U.S. Army post complete with barracks and all the facilities that Americans had come to expect. Bill said that his commander, a Major General, wanted him to move the Seventh ARVN to the base and put them on the offensive. The new Vietnamese division commander had been a sergeant in the French paratroopers during the 1950s Indochina War and was now a Colonel. "I was working to advise him in the command of *his* Vietnamese division," Bill explained. "However, *my* American commander wanted me to run *his* division like it was ours. It was *fascinating.*" (That was another word Bill used when "interesting" was not strong enough.) "So I talked to the former paratrooper and asked him what it would take to move his troops to the base," he continued. "He said he would do it if I could get him a radio tower, which I did. Then we were able to work together effectively. Eventually," he recalled, "you would have some engagements once or twice a day or once or twice a week. The enemy was on a pretty ragged edge by that time, and we kept whittling them down."

Bill said he was able to accommodate the needs of both the Americans and the Vietnamese. "I think we had a very good method of working together," he explained. "My boss would give me some orders, and I would write a memo to the Vietnamese commander and say 'Here are some suggestions' or 'I'm getting some pressure from my boss to do this and I would really appreciate it if we could do it.' And I would slip the note to him and walk away. We would never talk about it. Most of the time, he would do something. Sometimes he did more, and sometimes he did nothing. But that was his choice. I brought him assets like helicopters and jeeps, but we operated in two different fields. We went out to visit the regiments and down to the battalions to visit the troops." In a stark reminder of the fate of many of the South Vietnamese soldiers who remained in the country after the Americans departed, Bill reported that his former colleague committed suicide when the South Vietnamese surrendered.

Bill noted one other difference between his duty in Vietnam and his earlier combat tours. The Vietnam experience included an R & R (Rest & Recuperation) vacation with Robin in Hawaii and a quick trip to Hong Kong where he also met up with his parents.

The DeGrafs enjoyed some Hawaiian R & R.

Like virtually all U.S. Army personnel assigned to Vietnam, Bill returned home after exactly one year overseas. With Robin and the family still in Virginia, he asked for another assignment in the nation's capitol. He was named to a study group on the faculty of the National War College in Fort McNair, VA. He led a team studying senior military education. After two years, he joined the National Security Council staff where he worked on nuclear weapons problems for another two years. On August 31, 1974, Bill retired as a Colonel.

He joined a high-technology research and engineering company called Science Applications International Corporation or SAIC. Successfully applying his Army experience to the civilian workforce, Bill was promoted to Assistant Vice President and Division manager of the company's Training Systems and Analysis Division in McLean, VA. While at SAIC, Bill served as project manager for the development of the U.S. Army's National Training Center at Fort Irwin, CA. After he retired from SAIC in 1987, he stayed active with a number of volunteer activities, including the alumni club and the West Point Association of Graduates or AOG.

The AOG's alumni magazine, *Assembly*, included Bill DeGraf's biography to mark the Class of 1950's reunion in 2000. Classmate and author Louis V. Genuario reminisced by writing the following exchange in 1946 between new plebe cadet Bill DeGraf (basic cadets were called "dumb smack" then) and numerous upperclassmen:

"You, man. Halt! Who are you?"
"New Cadet DeGraf, sir!"
"Mr. DeGraf, pop your chest up, shoulders back, chin in, elbows in, butt in, eyes front—"
"Where are you from, Mr. DeGraf?"
"San Francisco, sir!"
"Have you had any previous military experience, Mr. DeGraf?"
"Yes, sir!"
"Where and when, Mr. DeGraf?"
"Sir, I received my first commission on the battlefields of Europe in January, 1945!"
[Long pause.] "Post! [Dismissed!] Dumb smack!"

Genuario goes on to write, "Bill had a relatively easy time as a cadet because he knew the answer to every question, and he was always in control of his emotions . . . The upperclassmen left him alone to concentrate on more fertile fields—the rest of us" (Genuario, 50).

Bill doesn't deny the charge.

Chapter 4

Perseverance

Frank J. Scolpino, USNA '53

Persevere is one word to describe Frank Scolpino. Stubborn might be another. And leader is certainly a third. He was a Depression-era kid born in Englewood, NJ, on April 9, 1928, and the last of three sons of Frank and Philomena Scolpino. They named him Frank Junior, and he followed big brothers Bob and Tony everywhere, paying his dues as the littlest and learning how to follow. The military academies teach leadership by first molding followers. Frank learned those lessons from the very beginning. He also learned the value of hard work, extra effort, and teamwork that served him well throughout life.

His dad, Frank Senior, was a milkman in the comfortable and diverse Bergen County community of Teaneck. He rose daily in the dark at 4:00 AM for Sheffield Dairies to make his rounds, occasionally accompanied by his youngest son. Sometimes he would let little Frankie take the reins of the horse-drawn milk wagon. And they would talk of the old days in Brooklyn, or their ancestors' lives in Italy. But his Dad always made it clear that hard work was the key to success. That lesson was well learned.

Frank and Philomena set strong examples for their boys. Bob and Tony played with their little brother and taught him the little things about life and sports: like treating others the same, fairly and with respect, and like taking off your shoes when playing soccer so you can kick without using your toes. All three understood the value of work but still managed to enjoy themselves and play sports.

World War II called the older boys into the Navy. Tony enlisted and served on the USS *Hancock* in the Pacific Theater. Their father by now had traded in his milk route for a job with the John Hancock Insurance Company. Like many Americans at home in that Greatest Generation, the Scolpinos supported the war effort with their family and with their sons and offered financial support by buying War Bonds. The Hancock connection helped them sell a lot of bonds. Bob started out as a pilot but was grounded for eyesight problems and became an aviation maintenance technician. Later he served in a California helicopter squadron.

Frank Junior was a dynamo despite his small size at five and a half feet tall and weighing less than 140 pounds. By the time he was in high school, Frank was also playing varsity sports, and his teammates had recognized that elusive quality called leadership. They elected him Captain of the Teaneck Highwaymen football, wrestling, and soccer teams. His success on the playing fields attracted the attention of a few colleges, including the West Pointers some forty-five miles up the Hudson. Frank wrestled against West Point plebes, and his football team had played the West Point plebe team during the war-shortened 1944 season. As team captain, Frank was selected to attend the ceremonies when West Point's Felix Anthony "Doc" Blanchard received his Heisman Trophy in 1945.

However, Frank didn't care much for studies and found academics tedious. He was also told he was too small to play college football for West Point. And he was eager to go into Naval aviation just like his hero big brothers. So he enlisted in the U.S. Navy right after graduation in July 1946 and went to boot camp at Bainbridge, MD. Sports helped him with the physical training. His Teaneck High academics helped him qualify for his first choice of Naval aviation just like his brothers who, by then, were back home in the postwar Garden State.

Frank's first assignment was to gunnery school at Jacksonville, FL. Next he was off to Memphis, TN, as an Aviation Machinist Mate. Then he transferred to Seattle, WA, where he served as a member of an air-land-and-sea emergency rescue unit. That December, the unit climbed up into the Cascades to check for survivors of a Marine Corps aircraft crash. Huge ten-foot drifts didn't stop the dozen sailors who spent nearly two weeks trying to reach the crash site. An Army ski team came up and relieved them—amazed that Frank's untrained group had been successful, surviving in the bitter cold.

He also qualified for combat air crewman duty. At the same time, he grew a bit and managed to play football as a fullback for the station team. His coach was charged to recommend enlisted men for Fleet Appointments to the Naval Academy, and five Seattle-based sailors took the 1947 test. Only Frank passed the mental test, and only Frank failed the physical exam.

"No one could believe it," he recalled. "They gave me a whole series of tests to see why I flunked the physical. I was a little guy who weighed about 150 pounds, but I felt like a pincushion with all those shots they gave me. But I finally was given the go ahead and moved back East to Bainbridge for the Naval Academy Prep School in the summer of 1947." While playing football and wrestling and running track, Frank also ran the base's photo lab. His performance was recognized with the Hambsch Award—a wristwatch he proudly wore throughout his life.

Finally, in June 1948, he received his appointment to Annapolis for the Naval Academy Class of 1952. When he arrived, Frank moved into a huge dormitory named for the school's founder, Navy Secretary George Bancroft. Bancroft Hall, the largest building on the Yard, later housed all four thousand midshipmen under one roof and also contains the dining hall and meeting rooms. Six cannons guard its steps, and two ceremonial bells signal its events. The huge gray structure, called "Mother B" by midshipmen, also contains Memorial Hall, an imposing large room with memorials to grads who have given their lives for service to their country. It reveres grads with a series of plaques that contain class crests with lists of grads who died in an operational loss on duty. The ballroom's walls hold every manner of plaque, painting, sculpture, and photo in memory of the many of the academy's seventy-three thousand graduates, especially those seventy-three graduates awarded the Medal of Honor. Those names include sixty-nine from the Navy and four Marines. The Hall is used for commissioning swearing-ins and retirements and other official and social events. A flag with the last words of Captain James Lawrence, "Don't give up the ship," dominates the western wall. Its two magnificent chandeliers spotlight the frescoes of famous naval battles painted on the ceiling.

Outside, the Yard itself now compactly houses all the Naval Academy's facilities and modern classrooms, plus the imposing library named for World War II Fleet Admiral Chester W. Nimitz, who ranked seventh out of thirty in the Class of 1905. Like its sister academies, Navy has named its buildings for heroes in naval history, such as the Rickover Engineering complex named for the nuclear navy pioneer Admiral Hyman Rickover, Class of 1922, who ranked 106th among his 539 classmates. One classroom building is named for the perhaps lesser-known graduate Albert A. Michelson, ninth of 34 in the Class of 1873. He made initial experiments into the speed of light, and the line he used is marked with metal disks on the grounds of the Yard. Michelson was the first American to receive a Nobel Prize.

Frank was introduced quickly to the Naval Academy's mission to produce officers for the U.S. Navy and U.S. Marine Corps, and he was never far from the waters of the Severn River and Chesapeake Bay visible virtually from every campus vantage. The academy's sailing program tells tall tales of naval training. It ranges from beginner's lessons to advanced intercollegiate dinghy and global, open-ocean racing. All midshipmen participate in sailing during their four years at the academy, which has a fleet of more than 250 boats, from dinghies and knockabouts to sloops and patrol craft. Those interested in becoming Marines go to Parris Island, NC, for special training to introduce them to the rigors of that branch of service.

Two years older than many of his classmates, Frank was the veteran who worked very hard at his military training and played very hard at sports. He earned the respect of the coach as a little guy with guts enough to give his all. He played Naval Academy football for two years. However, his academics were weak because he spent so much time on football in addition to wrestling and soccer. The combination resulted in a series of academic problems that eventually led him to repeat his sophomore or Youngster year and put him in the Class of 1953. Of course, years later, his classmates would say that was a good move, reporting "he saw the error of his ways and left '52 to join us!" Frank would be known as a "turnback," the word used by all three academies to describe midshipmen and cadets who repeat a year and then join a later class.

Frank explained simply, "My problems with academics were that I was a varsity athlete. I played ball and earned four letters in four sports. Those were the letters I concentrated on, not the academic ones. It took a lot of time and a lot of it impacted my ability to study. As a small football fullback, I played against the biggest guys they had, and I was beat up pretty badly. I also ended up with three concussions." Despite the setbacks, he proudly recalled that his football team of 150-pound players won the Eastern League Championship during his second sophomore year. "I had cauliflower ears from wrestling," he continued. "The guys called me 'the skinny little Guinea with the ravioli eyes.' However, sports taught me a lot about teamwork and taught me a lot about initiative and gave me even more respect for hard work that, as they say, never hurt anybody. I also earned respect from a lot of other guys who were at Annapolis because I never let my small size get in my way." Later they would call him Scoop, and he would incorporate that moniker into his e-mail address in the 21st Century.

Frank didn't realize how close he was to flunking out of the class in his final year until just prior to graduation when his company officer told him he was last in the class. "I was really surprised," he said. "But I enjoyed the notoriety." In fact, the three-foot plywood anchor they gave him at graduation still hangs in the Scolpino's den.

Frank with the anchor at graduation

Years later, the only questions heard about being the Class of '53's anchorman dealt with money. "We had 925 guys in our class, and if they had paid me a buck apiece, that would have been a nice piece of change," Frank lamented. "But for some reason that year, we just didn't collect the funds. Who knows why?" he asked a bit wistfully. "I have no idea. I could have paid for my new Pontiac!"

First among those 925 new Ensigns and Marine Corps Lieutenants on June 5, 1953, was Carlisle A. H. Trost from Valmeyer, IL. Trost would later become the only Naval Academy graduate at the top of his class to become Chief of Naval Operations. He is profiled in the next chapter. Of Carl Trost, Frank said, "He's Alpha, and I'm Omega. We played soccer together. So of course, I knew he was someone special. Since we have graduated, I've seen him quite a few times at reunions. I've got all good things to say about Trost. He's real fine. He's really one of those gentlemen. He's a good leader." Another classmate and soccer teammate was Kim Bassett, who recalled that Scolpino was injured seriously enough to end his football career, so he simply showed up to play soccer. "We were amazed at his athleticism and his ability to switch sports," Kim reported. "Carl and I were warming the bench, and here comes this little guy from the football team who makes the varsity soccer team two weeks after he joins us. We thought he was a neophyte, and only learned forty years later at a reunion that he had played soccer all his life!" (Bassett Interview.)

At graduation, Frank received his bachelors of science degree and returned to the regular Navy as an ensign in the Supply Corps. They sent him to Supply School in Bayonne, NJ, for his first six-months assignment as an officer, less than an hour's drive from home. That's where he met his future bride, Mary Ann Orecchio, who was training to be a nurse in nearby Jersey City. They were introduced through a blind date connection from a cousin's wedding. Mary Ann, who was born across from New York City in Guttenburg, NJ, was the perfect match for the young ensign. And she was four feet nine. The courtship started locally in New Jersey, but then Frank was transferred to the USS *Algol*, an attack cargo ship based in Long Beach, CA. They corresponded regularly and strengthened their relationship, and absence made two hearts grow fonder. Mary Ann completed her nurse's training, and they were married in West New York, NJ, on July 23, 1955.

While assigned as the disbursing officer on the amphibious cargo ship USS *Algol* in 1954, Frank and his crewmates were pressed into action off the coast of Vietnam. Frank was responsible for the ship's galley, and he spoke a little French. Both factors would contribute to the *Algol*'s success rescuing refugees from the fall of Dien Bien Phu. "We worked with some of the refugees in the galley to prepare foods that suited them," he recalled. "They didn't speak English and I didn't speak Vietnamese, so we worked it out in French." Somehow French and cooking always connect.

"We stripped our ship to have enough room to carry passengers," he said. In a scene that eerily previewed the fall of Saigon two decades later, the *Algol* rescued hundreds of refugees fleeing communism in North Vietnam. The Navy awarded Frank and his shipmates the Presidential Unit Citation for that service called "Passage to Freedom." The *Algol* was decommissioned and scrapped off the New Jersey Coast in 1989. Among the photographers watching his old ship sink become a fish farm was its former French chef, Frank Scolpino.

Returning to the USA, Frank next served as a supply and disbursing officer for the Brooklyn-based USS *Heyliger*, a destroyer escort and reserve training ship based in Brooklyn, NY. Later, Mary Ann and Frank moved to Naval Air Station Agana in Guam where Frank was a Material Department Head of the Airborne Early Warning Squadron 3. He also volunteered to be a nondesignated second Navigator on Navy patrol aircraft and was one of the aerial observers reporting on Chinese ship movements during the Formosa Straits crisis in 1957.

The Scolpinos' first son, Brian, was born while they were in Guam. He was later joined by brother Anthony and sister Sharon born in New Jersey years later. Brian continued in the family business as a Deputy Program Manager for Navy Air-to-Air Missiles at Patuxent River, MD. Anthony, a Commander in the U.S. Naval Reserve, is a finance executive with Hasbro, Inc. in Coventry, RI. Sharon is a sales coordinator for Structural Systems

Inc. in Thurmont, MD. The Scolpinos have three granddaughters—Gianna Marie and Stephanie Ann and stepgranddaughter Catherine—and a grandson, James Douglas.

In May 1960, the family moved back to the USA to Philadelphia where Frank put his experience in the field to work in the home office. First he was an Aviation Supply Officer then head of the Catalogs for the Navy's General Aeronautical Material and Program Branch. However, the staff desk jobs didn't help his promotion progress, so he resigned from his regular commission and moved to the inactive Naval Reserve in 1964.

He went to work for the spare parts division of military contractor Grumman Aircraft in Bethpage on Long Island, NY. During this period of the buildup of active and reserve forces for the Vietnam War, Frank worked in the Naval Air Systems Command in Washington DC. He was recalled to active duty in November 1966 and assigned to logistical fleet support for the Naval Air Systems Command HQ in Washington DC. Combining both his civilian and military experiences, Frank served as the senior supply representative on Contractor Proposals for F-14, S-3A, OV-10, and Marine Corps Harrier aircraft.

In 1969, the Scolpinos moved to the Midwest where Frank worked for the Chief of Naval Air Reserve Training at Glenview, a Chicago suburb. He was a Staff Supply Officer and later the senior supply member of the Inspector General's Team reviewing 22 different bases. He was awarded the Naval Commendation Medal for integrating reserve units into the active workforce to enhance their training and mobilization capabilities. He was promoted to Captain in 1976. Without boasting of the achievement, Frank proudly noted that promotion after so many years of challenges. "Lots of guys got promoted ahead of me and that could have been discouraging," Frank said. "But it's not the end of the world when you're passed over at first. My attitude was 'don't give up.' There were people who were my boss when I was an Ensign and (Lieutenant) JG who never made Captain. But I did," he concluded.

After ten years in the Midwest, the Scolpinos moved overseas again to the land of Frank's ancestors in Italy. Frank was named assistant chief of supply for the commander of the Naval Fleet in the Mediterranean responsible for managing NATO's (North Atlantic Treaty Organization) petroleum depots in Southern Europe. Based in Naples, he also provided support for U.S. Navy and Marine aircraft in the Mediterranean Theater. At the same time, Frank returned to sports and coached for U.S. military children whose parents were stationed in the area. Eventually, he was named chairman of the Naples Youth Council, primarily responsible for all sports programs. He also coached the American high school's football team.

Frank and Mary Ann before retirement

Returning to the USA in 1979, Frank was named director of the Defense Industrial Supply Center in Philadelphia. He held that post until 1982 when he retired from active duty in the Navy. After he left the Navy, Frank worked as a logistics engineering consultant until he retired in 1988.

Frank Scolpino's military awards and decorations list the steady achievements and modest recognition afforded to an unsung hero. He was awarded the World War II Victory Medal, the Navy Commendation Medal, the National Defense Service Medal twice, the United Nations Service Medal, the Korean Service Medal, the Armed Forces Expeditionary Service Medal twice, the U.S. Navy Expert Rifleman Medal, the Armed Forces Reserve Medal, and a Vietnam Presidential Unit citation.

In later years, Frank would fall victim to Parkinson's disease, glaucoma, heart disease, and kidney failure, leading to regular, painful dialysis treatments. During the times when we were interviewing in 2001, Frank was philosophical about his illness and didn't complain. I never learned until much later that he was on regular dialysis treatment for his kidneys. When asked about his Parkinson's, he replied with a laugh that he was in select company of Muhammad Ali, Billy Graham, and the Pope. "I'm not too steady on my feet and I can't drive now, that's all," he would say, ignoring the severity of his debilitating illnesses. "Hey! I had a great run, and now I'm slowing down. There's no use in complaining!"

"And he never did," said Mary Ann right up until he died on Halloween in 2001. He was seventy-three.

Two dozen of Frank's Annapolis classmates gathered a few weeks later in Arlington, VA. They met with Mary Ann and other members of the Scolpino family along with lifelong friends to pay tribute to the man who persevered. Mary Ann and Frank's middle son, Anthony spoke for all of them during the memorial service at the Fort Meyers Chapel on December 3, 2001.

"My father was a man of infinite patience and great compassion," Anthony told the gathering. "The three pillars of his life that clearly defined who he was were quite simply: Family, Country, and Faith." The son continued, "Frank Scolpino stood for what is right about our beloved America. He should be remembered as a role model for those who aspire to tell the truth and take responsibility for their own actions."

In the only possible reference to Frank's role as his Naval Academy class anchor, and a possible *stretch* at that, Anthony said, "He was a believer in the *underdog* and a tireless crusader for those who were unable to defend themselves or those who were down on their luck. He always saw the good things in people and never gave up on them."

After Mary Ann spoke with me about the sad news of her beloved Frank, we would connect from time to time. She always encouraged me to keep working on this book. She called it "a nice collection of memories" for her and the grandchildren.

It was my privilege to know Frank Scolpino briefly, and I am happy to share his story.

Chapter 5

Firsts, Plural

Carlisle A. H. Trost, USNA '53

The plain brown envelope arrived with a return address of Annapolis, MD. It contained a white sheet of paper engraved at the top with a small blue flag with four white stars on a small golden pole. The handwritten note apologized for the delayed response and was signed by Carl Trost. His name sounded familiar. The note was attached to the standard survey I had prepared and mailed to grads near the top and bottom of their classes with the help of the Academies' AOGs and Alumni Association. This one was completed by a member of the USNA Class of 1953. He also attached an official military biography with the heading:

> Admiral Carlisle A. H. Trost
> United States Navy
> Chief of Naval Operations

The second paragraph of the official biography told the story: "On June 5, 1953, he was commissioned an ensign, graduating first in his class from the Naval Academy. Thirty-three years later, Admiral Carlisle A. H. Trost was named the Navy's 23rd Chief of Naval Operations (CNO) on June 30, 1986. He held that post until he retired from the Navy four years later."

Carl Trost was the first Naval Academy grad and, so far, the *only* person who graduated first in the class to achieve the top post in the U.S. Navy. How he got there is a story of several other firsts. It's also remarkable that several classmates and other peers and senior officers predicted that this very bright, popular and unassumingly modest man would achieve that prominent rank.

During the 1920s depression, Luella and Elmer Trost worked the family farm an hour's ride east by horse and wagon across the Mississippi River from Saint Louis, MO. Their first-born son, Carlisle, was born at their German-American homestead in Valmeyer, IL, on April 24, 1930. Elmer continued to work the farm along with his eldest brother until depression financial pressures dictated that one of them would have to find another job. The family moved to nearby Columbia, IL, where Carl's sister, Mardelle, arrived a year later. Elmer managed a small farm near town and then went to work in a factory while Carl and Mardelle worked hard in school. Scholastics came easy to Carl. He worked on the farm, and later he clerked at Vogt's Grocery store in Columbia to pay the required tuition at the community High School in Dupo, IL, a Missouri Pacific Railroad Center. He also delivered the mail as a substitute clerk carrier, collecting a few shoulder bruises along the way.

The first military uniform worn by the future Admiral was the Army green of Army ROTC. After graduating first in his class from Dupo High, Carl went to Washington University in Saint Louis, MO. He studied mechanical engineering with a goal to become an automotive engineer. His high school success had garnered a one-year half-tuition-half-books scholarship at Washington University. But during his freshman year, young Carl applied for another scholarship and was told the odds were eight hundred to one that he wouldn't get it. So he looked around for other options.

"I heard about competitive exams for the Naval Academy being offered by our local congressman, and I took the test," Carl reported. He was soon notified that he was the only one who passed it who was already a college student, and that he would receive the congressional appointment. "I can't claim I was motivated to join the Navy," he recalled. "My Dad and Mom just couldn't *afford* college payments. *Money* is a great motivator," he added.

Carl arrived at the U.S. Naval Academy on July 19, 1949, a member of the last contingent in his class to begin plebe summer. It was the last time he would be last. Almost immediately, the maturity of a Midwestern farmer, combined with the academic preparation of a year in college, served him well. "Since I had been a Boy Scout and spent a year in Army ROTC, the military aspects of my plebe year were fairly simple," he recalled. "I was even comfortable with them. At the same time, the academics were not too tough because I had already taken some of what they were teaching. I just tried to stay out of trouble. The toughest part was just acclimating to the pressure from upperclassmen who took away time. Finally, someone reminded us that 'thirty-four thousand people have done what you guys are doing, so perhaps you could try.' That was excellent advice."

During his plebe summer, young Carl also started to sail, beginning a lifelong love affair with the sea. "We started in dingys and then advanced to 22-foot sloop-rigged knockabouts. As a class, sailing taught us more basic seamanship than anything else because we were out there on the Chesapeake interacting with the wind and the water, seeing what makes things happen."

At the end of his first year, Carl was told he ranked first in his class. "It was never a goal of mine. It just happened. I did whatever I needed to learn, what I was supposed to learn," he said. "And it was fun."

Part of the fun was intramural sports, and a teammate on the soccer team was Frank Scolpino, who was profiled in the previous chapter. "Frankie was a scrappy guy, and I remember when he turned back to our class that he was always a friendly and congenial guy," Carl recalled more than fifty years later. They renewed their friendship at class reunions throughout the years.

During his Youngster or second year, Carl met Pauline L. Haley of nearby Cottage City, MD. She was dating a classmate, and the two became friends. Friendship led to dates in Carl's senior year when romance blossomed. They were married in College Park, MD, on May 1, 1954, almost a year after Carl's graduation. The Trosts have four children and six grandchildren. Son Carl Michael is an independent sound technician in Washington DC. Daughter Laura Lee lives in Mountain Lakes, NJ, with her husband, John. They have three children: Scott, Megan, and Justin. The second son, Steve, followed Dad into the Navy. He attended the Naval Academy Prep School and graduated in 1985 and served for eight years aboard nuclear submarines. He is a commander in the U.S. Navy Reserve and lives in Potomac, MD, with his wife, Gail. They have three children: Will, Haley, and Alexa. The Trost's fourth child, Kathleen, is a special education teacher in Chesapeake, VA.

Newlyweds Pauline and Carl back at the academy

The Admiral's Official Portrait

Carl continued to enjoy his years as a midshipman and was named a six-striper and Brigade Commander in his final semester. Then, on June 5, 1953, he received a BS degree in Marine Engineering. He was also one of the few to graduate first in his class who did not go immediately to graduate school. "I was eager to go to sea, and I wasn't interested in more schooling at that time," he recalled. His first job was a gunnery and antisubmarine warfare officer and navigator on the destroyer USS *Robert A. Owens* based in Norfolk VA. The anti-sub warfare officer job served him well for later under water assignments as "you find out how hard subs can be to find."

Half a dozen of Carl's 22nd Company grads from 1953 eventually ended up in submarines thanks to the fine example and encouragement of their company officer, Lieutenant Lando Zech Jr. Zech served a distinguished career in the Navy after ranking 405th out of 914 graduates in the wartime Naval Academy Class of 1945 that graduated a year early in June 1944. His Annapolis assignment in 1952 was his first shore duty. A half century later, Lando said he remembered Carl Trost as a most unusual member of his Company. "A month or so after I arrived, I told my wife, Jo, that we had a fine company that included a pretty interesting midshipman," he recalled. "I told her that I understood that he was first in his class, but what was more important, all his classmates seemed to *like* him. He was *respected* and not just smart but a real regular guy." Lando added, "I told her that I hoped the Navy recognized him because some day he could be the CNO." Lando was the third Captain of the USS *Nautilus*, the world's first nuclear-powered submarine. He later retired as a U.S. Navy Vice Admiral and served as Chairman of the U.S. Nuclear Regulatory Commission.

Carl's career was a steady progression of challenging assignments. After a year and a half of surface duty, he moved to the Submarine

School in New London, CT. In June 1955, he was assigned to the USS *Sirago* and qualified as a submariner a year later. Two more schools—the Advanced Nuclear Power School at New London and the Naval Nuclear Power Training Unit in Idaho Falls, ID—prepared him for nuclear sub sea duty. In November 1957, Carl reported to the nuclear-powered attack submarine USS *Swordfish* in Portsmouth, NH. Two years, later he was qualified to command submarines.

One of his senior shipmates in the sub world was Jeff Metzel, who graduated "right in the middle" as he said, 430th out of the 821 members of the Class of 1947. They attended Nuclear Power School together, were stationed together in Idaho to qualify on the nuclear reactors, and then served on both the USS *Swordfish* and USS *Von Steuben* commissioning teams.[5] Metzel, who was the fourth Captain of the USS *Nautilus* and retired as a Rear Admiral in 1979, said that "Carl Trost has never stood anything but number one anywhere he's been as far as I can tell. My claim to fame is that I beat him on a quiz once. Once!" About his junior colleague, Metzel said, "Everybody knew he was gonna be CNO sooner or later."

---

[5]   Metzel recalled that his submarine class included a classmate named Howard L. "Matty" Matthews, who ranked 614th in the Class and became a submariner, retiring as a Captain. "Matty told me his father always said that if you wanted to get ahead in this world, you should always sit next to the smartest guy in the class," Metzel recalled. Matthews said, "I sat right between Bill Crowe and Jimmy Carter and that explains *their* success!" Carter and Crowe were 59th and 80th in the class respectively. James Earle Carter Jr. served as a Navy submariner until his father died in 1953. He left the Navy and returned to his native Plains, GA, where he took over the Carter farms. He was elected Georgia's seventy-sixth governor on 1971 and the thirty-ninth president of the United States five years later. William James Crowe Jr. received his PhD from Princeton and his distinguished career concluded as an Admiral who served as Chairman of the Joints Chiefs of Staff under President Ronald Reagan from 1985 to 1989. First in the Class of 1947 was Oklahoma-born James Robert Collier who became a Navy Civil Engineer and left the service after six years. The class anchor was John Frink Jones of South Carolina who retired as a Lieutenant Commander. Two other famous members of the Class of 1947 were Stansfield Turner and James Bond Stockdale. Turner was a Rhodes Scholar who ranked 26th out of the 821, and later was CIA director for his classmate, President Carter, from 1977 to 1981. Stockdale was awarded the Congressional Medal of Honor for bravery and was one of the senior Prisoners of War in the Vietnam Conflict. He ranked 129th in the Class of 1947. Chapter 21 includes names and class ranks of several other famous grads.

In his 1995 bestseller about five famous[6] Naval Academy grads, *The Nightingale's Song*, Robert Timberg called Carl Trost an ex-Whiz Kid, referring to his strong and industrious climb to the top of the Naval hierarchy (Timberg 1995, 167). Timberg, 134th out of 927 in the Annapolis Class of 1964, was a U.S. Marine Corps Vietnam veteran and Nieman Fellow at Harvard University.

Carl Trost interrupted his submarine sea duties for international schooling. First, he strengthened his German language prowess at the Army Language School in Monterey, CA. In his youth on the farm in Illinois, the Trosts had spoken enough German to give Carl the ear for it. But the intense training served to formalize and secure his fluency. In September 1960, Carl and Pauline and two children moved to Freiburg, Germany. Carl called himself a "pioneer" as the first U.S. Navy member of the first group of four Olmstead[7] Scholars in 1960. He studied

---

[6] The book's famous Annapolis grads were John M. Poindexter, Navy Vice Admiral who was President Ronald Reagan's National Security Advisor from December 1985 through November 25, 1986, and indicted in 1988 for defrauding the U.S. government and obstructing justice during the Iran-Contra scandal. He had been first among 900 in the Class of 1958. Timberg's book also included John S. McCain III, Vietnam War Prisoner of War, Arizona U.S. Senator and presidential candidate, who ranked sixth from the bottom in Poindexter's Class of 1958. Also, Robert C. "Bud" McFarlane, U.S. Marine and national security advisor to President Ronald Reagan from 1983 to 1985, was 108th out of 798 men in the Class of 1959. Virginia U.S. Senator James Webb, U.S. Marine Corps Vietnam veteran, best-selling author and former Secretary of the Navy, ranked 314th among 836 in 1968. The book also included USMC Lieutenant Colonel Oliver North, White House Contra scandal figure, who was 468th in that Class of 1968.

[7] George Hamden Olmstead had graduated second among his 102 West Point classmates in 1922 and went on to two distinguished careers in the U.S. Army and civilian financial services. As a founder of United Services Life Insurance Corporation, MGen Olmstead generously used his considerable resources to establish the foundation to educate military officers. Working with the academies to identify candidates, the Olmstead Foundation has sponsored more than 350 officers at universities overseas to help internationalize America's military leadership. Olmstead alumni include a large number of flag and general officers. Although the overseas schools' advanced degree requirements differ from those in the USA, American University in Washington DC has developed a program to recognize graduate school credits to award the officers their master's degrees in the USA.

international relations and international economics at the University of Freiberg in Germany.

After Carl completed his studies in early 1962, the Trosts returned home. Carl was named executive officer of the nuclear-powered attack submarine USS *Scorpion*. Sixteen months later, he attended the Polaris Command course at the Fleet Antiair Training Center in Dam Neck, VA. Next he became executive officer of the Blue Crew for the nuclear-powered ballistic missile submarine USS *Von Steuben* built in Newport News, VA.

In March 1965, Carl was tapped for his first Pentagon assignment as Military Assistant to Deputy Secretary of Defense Cyrus Vance and later worked for Paul Nitze. Three years later, he assumed command of the Blue Crew of the nuclear-powered ballistic missile submarine USS *Sam Rayburn* based in Charleston, SC. His next desk job was Assistant Chief of Staff for Personnel and Administration on the staff of the Commander Submarine Force, U.S. Atlantic Fleet back in Norfolk, VA. However, less than a year after moving to Norfolk, Undersecretary of the Navy John Warner called Carl back to the Pentagon where Carl became Warner's Executive Assistant and Naval Aide. Carl also later served Warner when he was Navy Secretary.

Carl was temporarily "frocked" as a Rear Admiral in June 1973, achieving star rank twenty years after his Annapolis graduation. Frocked officers were awarded and wore the designated rank although they didn't receive formal recognition and increased pay until final approval. In June 1973, Carl assumed command of Submarine Flotilla One in San Diego, CA. He also served as Commander, Submarine Force Pacific Representative on the West Coast. A year and a half later, he was back east as Assistant Chief for Officer Development and Distribution in the Bureau of Naval Personnel. One year later, he was Director of the Navy's System Analysis Division in the Office of the Chief of Naval Operations (CNO).

In August 1978, Carl was promoted to vice admiral and reported for duty as deputy commander in chief of the U.S. Pacific Fleet in Pearl Harbor, HA. Less than two years later, he assumed command of the U.S. Seventh Fleet, responsible for all U.S. Navy and United Nations fleet operations in the Western Pacific and Indian Ocean. Those duties included considerable interaction with the navies of Japan and South Korea, which recognized Carl's efforts by awarding him the Government of Japan's Order of the Rising Sun (Second Class) and the Republic of Korea's Order of National Merit.

Back at the Pentagon in September of 1981, Carl was named to a more senior post in the CNO's office as Director of Navy Program Planning. This group charted the Navy's future. "We were totally involved with strategic planning for the Navy within the specific requirements of a balanced budget," Carl explained. "We addressed questions like what ships are we going to build, how many people are we going to need and support, and how are we going to pay for it and prioritize. An interesting job, only took *seven* days per week," he laughed.

Four years later, he was promoted to admiral and became Commander in Chief of the U.S. Atlantic Fleet and Deputy Commander-in-Chief of the U.S. Atlantic Command, again, based in Norfolk. This was a joint command, and Carl said that's where he thought he would end his Naval career. However, the Navy had other plans.

Carl Trost was named the 23rd Chief of Naval Operations on June 30, 1986. He was the first and only Naval Academy grad to be first and reach the top job in the U.S. Navy. One of his predecessors was Admiral Forrest P. Sherman, who served as CNO from 1949 to 1951. Sherman had graduated second in his class of 199 in the Class of 1918. During Carl's four-year tenure as CNO, he worked for four Secretaries of the Navy: John Lehman; fellow Annapolis grads James H. Webb Jr., who was 314th out of 836 members of the Class of 1968; William R. Ball, 346th out of 743 members of the Class of 1955; and Henry "Larry" L. Garrett III. Larry Garret was Carl's last Navy boss when he retired on July 1, 1990.

Captain Henry "Hank" D. Hukill, who ranked 324th in the class, later served with Carl as a shipmate and became a close personal friend. He said, "Carl is a great guy, an outstanding leader both on active duty and after his military retirement in several senior positions in industry." Hank explained, "Although Carl is certainly proud of his achievements, he does not flaunt them."

Hank told about Carl's interview with Admiral Rickover for the nuclear submarine program a few years after graduation. The famed Admiral "didn't know everybody in the program even though people thought he did, but he knew Carl," Hank recalled. "The story goes that when Rickover had Carl in for an interview Rickover said, 'And I suppose you think you're smarter than I am.' Supposedly, Carl replied, 'Yes sir.' And he was selected.

"However," Hank continued, "one time, Admiral Rickover put Carl in his place." Hank explained that the Admiral always went on sea trials for the new subs, sending hundreds of personal letters to members of Congress and other VIPs. The letters were produced manually and individually typed long before word processors simplified the task. They described the biography of the person for whom the sub was named and were valuable keepsakes.

"Carl and I served together as opposite XOs [Executive Officers] when we built the USS *Von Steuben* at Newport News, VA. Carl was blue team, and I was gold team," he continued. "I was the Junior XO so I had to proofread these important letters word for word. The Admiral asked me if I wanted one. Obviously, I said yes. On hearing this, Carl asked me to see if the Admiral would sign one for him as well. When I approached the Admiral, he exclaimed 'Hell no!' adding 'Who's Commander Trost?'" Asked if Trost's success was bugging Rickover, Hank replied, "I don't think so. I believe the Admiral had great respect for Carl, but outwardly, he just wanted to 'keep him in his place' just as he did all those who worked for him."

Hank explained that one of their tasks during the *Von Steuben's* construction was to greet new sailors whenever they came aboard and give them a mission briefing. "One time, about two weeks later, Carl and I were walking on the dock when we spotted two of these new sailors strolling toward us. As we returned their salutes, Carl said, 'Seamen So and So, how are you?' I was flabbergasted. We met thirty guys and two weeks later, *he remembers their names?* He remembered everyone's name, and he did it on purpose because people feel a lot better when you call them by name. That's Carl." Hank added, "I'll bet he knows where every one of our classmates served and what they're doing now.

"I would introduce him to a number of people before he was an admiral, and people would ask, 'Is that the Carl Trost many think is going to be CNO?' We would go to a party, and by the end of the evening, everyone would be gathered around Carl. He just had that strength of personality."

Hank remembered his heart attack on Friday, the thirteenth of April in 1973, when he was working for Admiral Rickover at the Navy's Reactor Division. "When I woke up in the hospital, Carl was there," he recalled. Hank also noted, "Carl was one of the first to contact my wife, Ginnie, and me when our son, Maurice, a young Marine Second Lieutenant, was first declared missing, then later declared dead as a result of the terrorist attack on the Marine Barracks in Beirut, Lebanon, in October 1983. Carl kept us aware of the casualty status even though he was very busy with official duties. These actions are typical for Carl. On many occasions, when a classmate or shipmate encountered a devastating personal or family tragedy, he would be one of the first there to provide assistance."

Pressed to relay some sea stories to illustrate the more normal side of Carl Trost, Hank added, "I don't have any *bad* stories about Carl." When I pressed him for *some* balance to all this perfection, Hank finally replied, "Well, he does have *two* faults you might report. "The wives of his close friends called him 'velvet lips' because of the smooth way he would greet them whenever we gathered and first meet in a group." Then Hank added, with obvious relish, "OK, one of the *bad* things, one *terrible* thing, is that Carl and Pauline are die-hard Redskins fans!" That's from an equally ardent Dallas Cowboys fan. "I remember one time we were at the Trost's home for a Sunday dinner and a four o'clock game that ran through overtime," he recalled. "The Redskins beat Dallas on Billy Kilmer's quarterback sneak, and Carl and Pauline were celebrating so much that we didn't get down to dinner until midnight! And *my* team lost!"

Hank added that he retired from the Navy in 1975 and went to work as a Vice President for General Public Utilities in Western Pennsylvania in 1980. That was a year after the March 28, 1979, nuclear accident at GPU's Three Mile Island plant. "We needed a board member with nuclear experience and invited Carl to lend a hand. For more than a decade, he had a significant, positive impact on the safe, reliable, and cost-effective operation of GPU's nuclear and fossil fuel generating plants. All of us were amazed at how quickly he adapted to civilian life."

Carl received numerous awards and decorations during his Naval career including three Navy, two Department of Defense, one Army, and one Air Force Distinguished Service Medals and three Legions of Merit as well as more than a dozen other U.S. and international commendations.

After his military retirement, Carl formed his own business as an independent consultant in Potomac, MD. He served as a chairman of the board of trustees and the board of directors for the Bird-Johnson Company, a nautical propeller and drive train manufacturer. He also served on the boards for several other businesses with a list that reads like a corporate *Who's Who.* In addition to General Public Utilities, these include Lockheed Martin, General Dynamics, Louisiana Land and Exploration Corp., and First Energy Corporation.

Carl said he chatted with only one other Naval Academy grad who was first in his class. He was Naval Aviator RADM Malcolm Schoefell, who was first among 199 members of the Class of 1919 and later directed the Navy's ordinance bureau. Admiral Schoefell told Carl, then a junior lieutenant, "I've been told by lots of people that guys who stand first in their class aren't worth a damn for the Navy."

No one ever told Carlisle A. H. Trost that.

Chapter 6

Football to Fighter Pilot

Richard L. Olson, USNA '54

Notre Dame football played a big role in Olie Olson's life. He might not have gone to the U.S. Naval Academy if it had not been for a recruiting trip to South Bend, IN, when he was in high school and some kind words of encouragement from legendary Irish Coach Frank Leahy. There were a few other connections too, including the love of his life. All of them helped chart a remarkable course that took him from the gridiron to one of the first cockpits in a U.S. Navy jet fighter aircraft to a successful business career.

Richard L. Olson, or Olie to everyone else, was born on August 2, 1931, in Cleveland. He grew up thirty miles west in Lorain, OH, a Lake Erie steel town. He was a Depression-era baby raised as an only child by his single-mom Josephine. He never knew his father.

A strong six-foot, 180-pound All-State tackle and team captain at Lorain High, Olie was recruited by many colleges with big-time football programs including the University of Notre Dame. During the recruiting season in the fall of 1948, Olie went to South Bend and was treated like royalty, sitting on the varsity's bench for the entire home game. Afterward, he visited the locker room for a private meeting with head football coach, Frank Leahy, who wanted to talk to him about playing for his Fighting Irish.

"Leahy had been a tackle for Knute Rockne and asked me what other schools I was considering," Olie recalled. "He was trying to size up the competition, but he was also earnestly trying to understand where I was coming from. I told him I was interested in possibly going to the Naval Academy, using the prep school route through the Bullis Prep School in

Silver Spring, MD. Leahy replied, 'I'll be perfectly honest with you. I have three sons, and there would be no greater honor for me than to have one of those boys go to the Naval Academy.'"

Olie was stunned. "Man, did that ever set me off. Navy veteran Frank Leahy advised me to go to the Naval Academy, and I am forever grateful for that good advice," he said. Olie completed high school and worked again in the summer for the local U.S. Steel plant as a pipe inspector, checking pipes for cracks and pits and spot welding and sanding defects. Late in the summer of 1949, he went off to Bullis. Originally established as a preparatory school for the Naval Academy, Bullis served that function very well for the young Ohioan, providing an opportunity to enhance both his academic and athletic skills.

"The next time I saw Frank Leahy I was wearing the Navy blue-and-gold football uniform at the stadium in Baltimore in November of 1951," Olie said. In those days of the Korean War, West Point's Army teams and Annapolis's Navy elevens were football powerhouses, giving the Big Ten and major independents full schedules of national competition. The teams of pre-television days often played in neutral city stadiums to give more fans an opportunity to see their favorites in person. "I was a sophomore playing center by then," Olie explained. "The quarterback and I were warming up near the end zone with our Coach, Ed Erdelatz, watching us. It was very evident that the circus had been to town that week because the elephants and tigers had left behind a few souvenirs of their visit. Coach Leahy came over to complain to Coach Erdelatz about the field's conditions. 'Hey, Eddie,' Leahy charged, 'this field is in terrible shape!' To which Erdelatz replied, 'Hey, Frank! I'm the head football coach, not the groundskeeper!' Leahy did a 180 [degree turn] and walked off the field. They beat us 19-0."

The next year, Olie and his Navy team ventured to his hometown of Cleveland for their game against Notre Dame. This time, they played at the riverfront home of the Indians and Browns, Cleveland Municipal Stadium. They lost again, 17-6. In his senior year, when he was Captain of the Navy team, Olie returned to South Bend for his first visit since his high school days. This time, Navy was again on the losing side of a 38-7 score.

That Notre Dame visit's real significance was a blind date for Olie arranged by a family friend. He linked the Firstie Midshipman, who played center for the Navy team that day, with Doris King of Harvey, IL. She was a picture-perfect model for the Neiman Marcus Company who also worked in radio for Chicago comedian Joe E. Brown. Doris was pretty and talented enough to compete in the Miss America contest. In fact, she was Miss Illinois of 1951, and Olie was smitten. Oh, and Navy lost again, 17-6.

"In fact," Olie said, "as I recall my three Notre Dame games on the varsity, we outplayed them, but we never won. Call it the luck of the Irish."

Navy's center Olie Olson

As they say in Hollywood, he lost the game, but he got the girl. Olie and Doris, who he calls Dorie, were married a few months later. They eventually had seven children.

Despite his losses to Notre Dame, Eddie Erdelatz successfully coached Olie and other Navy footballers from 1950 to 1958 for an overall record of 50 wins, 26 losses, and eight ties. During Olie's three years on the varsity, the teams were moderately successful with records in 1951 of 2-6-1; in 1952, 6-2-1; and in 1953, 4-3-2. Those Navy teams played the best teams in America and gave as good an accounting for themselves as they got. A generation later, it may be hard to realize just how successful they were. But in the 1940s and 1950s, both Navy and Army regularly ranked in the top 20 of all college football teams. Like their counterparts in other colleges and universities at the time, football players were student athletes. The players for Navy and Army experienced the added dimension of officer leadership training in a full-time military academy environment.

Of course, a major part of Olie's military training was learning to fly while he was in Annapolis. He recalled his introduction to flying as an undergraduate at the Air Facility across the river from USNA. Olie and his flight-qualified classmates flew an open cockpit biplane with pontoon floats for wheels. Named the N3N *Yellow Pearl* and often called the *Yellow Peril*, it dated from the 1930s with quite rudimentary controls and equipment. Communications between pilots and instructors were difficult due to engine noise and the airflow past the fuselage. The rear cockpit instructor shouted instructions to the front cockpit student through a hose contraption called a "gosport." This device used a mouthpiece worn by the instructors that was connected by a hose to earphones worn by the student. Although the two could communicate in the open cockpit, the student was not able to talk back to the instructor. This device and the hardwired steering contraptions of the old plane contributed to an almost disaster in one of Olie's early flights.

"My flight instructor and I were practicing takeoffs and landings in the water up Chesapeake Bay," Olie recalled. "I had never landed before, so it was a new experience for me. A large yacht supposedly used or owned by Adolph Hitler in the 1930s was anchored as a directional guide for the planes in the landing pattern," he continued. "As we touched down on my first landing approach, I went to full throttle as instructed, causing the plane to turn to the left and head on a collision course with the yacht!

"I remember seeing people on the deck of the boat scattering to the stern of the yacht as they anticipated a collision," he added. "My instructor shouted in the *gosport*, 'right full rudder.' I panicked and applied *left* full rudder, and we were headed directly at that yacht. He somehow managed to take control of the plane, averted a collision, and flew the plane right back to the landing area in the water. We landed, and he jumped out and waded in to the shore in water up to his waist. He left me there for a half hour in the hot Virginia sun.

"When he came back, he explained, 'You're a pretty strong kid, and it was very hard to get the controls away from you. So we barely made it. *Never* grab the stick with both hands. You've got to be real gentle with it.' Then he asked me, 'Are you still planning to go into aviation?' And when I answered yes, he said, 'Rottsa ruck!'

"Then he left me there and walked away," he recalled. "To this day, I only hold the stick with one hand when I'm flying with a real soft touch."

Although football served Olie Olson very well, the many demands on his busy school schedule also hurt his academic standing and class rank. After his senior year's football season, Olie was confronted with the very real prospect of flunking out of the Naval Academy. Among the most difficult courses was "Juice," as cadets and midshipmen call Electrical Engineering. Over the years, it has contributed to many missed graduations. Midway through his Second Class or junior year, Olie realized that the difficulties he was having with his engineering courses and others were hurting his grade point average. "I knew I was near the bottom of the class, but I wasn't sure just how close I was to flunking out," he said now. Fortunately, Erdelatz was keeping track and called him in for a meeting at the beginning of his last semester in senior year.

"Olie, we've got a problem," Coach Erdelatz said. "I don't want to see you at the bottom of the class on graduation day because some folks might think we just kept you here to play football." Olie now said that he would have been *happy* to be at the bottom of the class. "I was worried I wasn't even going to make it to *graduate!*" he recalled. "Sure, some of the other guys were vying for anchor because it meant a buck from each of our classmates. That was really hard cash when you consider that we had 856 guys in the class, and nearly all of them would follow the tradition and give a dollar to the anchorman.

"Never mind the *money*, I was worried I wasn't going to make it to get my *diploma and commission*," Olie said. "And I had plans for right after graduation. Dorie and I were going to be married. Everyone was getting ready for the wedding on June 19, two weeks after graduation. I was really under a lot of pressure to pass my final exams." Olie flunked his exams the first time around, but fortunately, he was able to take advantage of the re-exam policy that let him repeat final examinations. "I can't tell you how bad I felt taking re-exams," Olie recalled. "I was studying like mad because if you failed the course, you got another shot with a makeup exam. But you had to *pass that test*. The Academy's Academic Board determined first if you get to take the makeup exam and second if you get to pass the course based upon the results of the test. Unfortunately, I was forced to take three make-ups, including Spanish, Electrical Engineering, and one other that I have conveniently forgotten. Electrical Engineering killed me at the Academy. I was so bad at Electrical Engineering that for years afterward, Dorie wouldn't even let me plug in a wall socket for fear of screwing up the lights!

"I got to be pretty good at Spanish though," he remembered. "My classmates and my teammates tried to help me out with the final exam in Espanol. Historically, the finals included a 250-word essay on a topic specified in the exam," he explained. "The essay counted double weight in the grading process, and if you did well on it, you had a good chance of passing," he continued. His friends identified an exchange cadet from Madrid and asked him to help prepare Olie for the final. The Spanish cadet wrote a 250-word essay, which was grammatically perfect. It described a clothing store that carried blue shoes, brown shoes, white shoes, etc. as well as blue pants, brown pants, and other colorful clothing articles. Olie memorized the essay.

"When finally I got to take the exam, the question on the page was a bit *different*," Olie explained with a chuckle. "It was to describe a visit to a friend. So I adjusted and responded with 'One day, I visited my friend in Madrid who owned a clothing store.' And then, I plugged in the essay that I had memorized. I passed the exam with flying colors! To this day, I can recite in Spanish the clothing store's inventory," he concluded proudly. "It's amazing what you can learn when it's *not* Electrical Engineering!"

Finally, on June 4, 1954, Olie and his 854 other classmates graduated. First across the stage at the top of the class was George Burton Parks of San Francisco, CA. Parks broke tradition as first in his Naval Academy class and joined the U.S. Air Force as a Second Lieutenant. His profile appears in the next chapter.

The Class Historian for the Naval Academy Class of 1954 is Ohioan Michael A. Nassr. He ranked 317th and also joined the Air Force where he was the first person to solo a jet without first piloting a propeller-driven aircraft. During his 27-year Air Force career, he flew eight different types of aircraft and accumulated over 10,000 flying hours, including 1,280 combat hours in Vietnam. He retired as a Colonel in 1981. Mike proudly reported that his classmates include five men who won Olympic Gold Medals at Helsinki, Finland, in 1952. They were teammates on the USA's eight-oared crew team. In 1954, Navy's team went to the Final 8 in the NCAA (National Collegiate Athletic Association) basketball tournament before losing to the eventual national champion, and their undefeated lacrosse team won the National Championship. Among his many illustrious classmates was John J. Clune, who was ranked 685th. He was Navy's first basketball All-American and later the successful Director of Athletics at the Air Force Academy. He retired as an Air Force Colonel. Another classmate was Don Walsh, who was ranked 709th. He set the world record for the deepest dive to 37,800 feet under the Pacific Ocean in the Mariana's Trench in 1960. He retired as a Navy Captain.

The Class of 1954 included 607 men or 72 percent who were commissioned and remained in the service for complete careers. Twenty-one of the 414 Naval ensigns would reach flag rank as admirals; eleven of the 221 Air Force lieutenants would become general officers, and one of the 64 Marine lieutenants would become a Lieutenant General. Among the class combat decorations were one Navy Cross, twelve Silver Stars, and fifteen Purple Hearts. Five men spent many grueling years as Prisoners of War in North Vietnam. Five members of the USNA Class of 1954 are listed on the Vietnam Wall in Washington DC killed in combat during the Vietnam War. (Nassr Interview)

After Olie finally graduated, he and Dorie were married in Harvey, IL, Dorie's hometown. Nine of Olie's classmates were there and formed the traditional sword bridge, creating "quite a show" as Olie reported in the Chicago suburb. They honeymooned at Chicago's Edgewater Beach Hotel and settled down in Annapolis with an added graduation bonus of $710 in single dollar bills from most of his classmates. Many of them had slipped the bills under his barracks room door or handed them to him during graduation festivities. "So after all that concern and anticipation,

I was finally through. And I was the anchorman," he exclaimed proudly. "Damn right I was!"

Those anchor dollars aren't the dollar bills he remembered though. The greenback he found at Notre Dame had much more significance. "I guess you could say our Saturday night first date at Notre Dame was OK," he recalled now, "but the next day was better as we got to know each other. On our way to church, I spotted a dollar bill on the ground and picked it up. Something made me stop and rip it in half for Dorie and me. We said we would always have a buck to our name if we ever wanted to put it back together," he explained. "I carried my half in my wallet for fifty years, and so did she."

One of the immediate consequences of being last in the class concerns the delicate area of first jobs or, in military parlance, the Initial Active Duty Assignment. Each military branch has a certain number of entry-level jobs to be filled by academy grads. Many of them are for training programs that begin in August after the new lieutenants and ensigns have completed their first real vacations right after graduations. However, finite numbers of openings exist for programs like flight training and other special schools, leading to a sort of limbo waiting status for grads who don't get the initial school of their choice. The waiting leads to clever temporary assignments from helping the admissions departments recruit new cadets to serving as interns in scientific labs. Athletes sometimes help with sports camps or special team practices.

As team captain for the 1953 Navy team, Olie was a natural to remain at Annapolis and help coach the football team. Eventually, it would be one of the most successful in the history of the Naval Academy. The 1954 Navy team, led again by Coach Erdelatz but now with Olie's help as an assistant line coach, would eventually record eight wins. They lost only twice, to Pittsburgh and Notre Dame. However, they ranked high enough to reach the Sugar Bowl. The team journeyed to New Orleans, LA, on New Year's Day of 1955. Navy beat a strong Southeastern Conference Champion team from the University of Mississippi, 21-0 as Olie and the others enjoyed their holidays in the Crescent City.

Back in Maryland in the new year, he and Dorie were finally alerted to attend flight school in Pensacola, FL. They arrived on the Gulf Coast in January of 1955, and he began classroom training. "I liked it, and I was good at it," Olie recalled. "I could see the immediate use of everything they were teaching us in ground school, and I felt real comfortable in the blue box Link flight simulators. I couldn't wait to get up in the air again. I just loved flying and the camaraderie of being with a group of guys who loved it too. I was like Willie Mays. I couldn't believe they were actually *paying* me to fly airplanes!"

Because his assignment had been delayed by his class rank and Annapolis duties, Olie was the only Naval Academy graduate in his flight school class. The 20 others were from college ROTC programs or the Navy's Officer Candidate School. Most of the flight instructors were experienced combat veterans who had launched off carriers during the Korean War.

Using his undergraduate *Yellow Peril* experience and taking his "soft-touch hands" with him, Olie flew the single-prop T-28 "Texan" at Pensacola. His first jet was a single engine TV-2, the Navy's version of the Lockheed F-80 Shooting Star. Next he flew the Navy's top jet trainer, the F9F-2 Panther jet that had been used during the Korean War. He also flew the swept-wing F9F-8 Cougar as an advanced jet flight instructor.

Flight training proved a boon to Olie. Thrown together with a score of other pilot candidates, he thrived on the combination of academic and physical demands. "It just excited the hell out of me," he exclaimed. "Another contributing factor was that I never met an aviator I didn't like. These were just plain good people who talked with their hands and animated voices when explaining their flying experiences."

He almost dismissed the difficulty of learning how to fly. When pressed, he admitted that learning how to drive at an early age might have helped. "I was driving my grandfather's trucks when I was eleven," he recalled. That might have had something to do with it. He remembered that transitioning from propeller to jet planes was a bit difficult. After twelve months of intense ground and flight training, he finally soloed and flew over his house. Some noisy pitch-control adjustments signaled Dorie, waving below, to pick him up at the hanger.

At the same time, Olie was playing military service football for the Pensacola Goshawks. In the days after World War II and the Korean War, the U.S. Selective Service System drafted virtually all physically fit 18-year-old young men. Exceptional high school and college football players who joined the military were given the opportunity to play service football. Military posts had their own leagues, and the teams were so talented that they also played against colleges and professionals of the still-developing National Football League. Olie's Pensacola team lost to Fort Ord, CA, for the service championships in 1956. The Fort Ord quarterback was future National Football League great Lenny Dawson, one of many professional athletes who were drafted into military service at the time.

Finally, Lieutenant Junior Grade Richard L. Olson completed Pensacola flight training, and Dorie pinned on his golden wings as a Naval Aviator. Olie was also recognized as first in his class. He had come full circle—from the top of his game in Lorain, OH, to the bottom at Annapolis and back up on top again as a Navy fighter pilot. The Navy chose him to be its first graduate student to become an advanced jet flight instructor. His work brought him in touch with the Navy's famed Blue Angels flight demonstration team. "I was assigned to the Advanced Training Unit, which shared facilities with the Blue Angels," he explained. "From time to time, I flew familiarization flights in the Cougar with new pilots assigned to the Blue Angels. Who would have thought that some day, the guy who came very close to sinking Hitler's yacht would be flying with some of the best precision pilots in the world?" he asked. "Certainly not my instructor in the *Yellow Pearl,*" he answered emphatically.

Coaching new pilots compared easily to coaching football players in the world of Olie Olson. He told of the camaraderie and teamwork involved in learning how to fly. "Going up with a guy at night and flying with all those stars was quite an experience," he recalled. "It's confusing and exhilarating and frightening and challenging, especially the first time I tell another new pilot to join up with me, and he can't distinguish between our aircraft and the millions of stars that are out there. Sure it was tense, you could hear the heavy breathing in your earphones. But those were some of the best times of my life because I was helping other young men and my peers learn something that was important and necessary in our country at the time."

After two years as an instructor, the Olsons transferred to Miramar Naval Air Station in Southern California where Olie joined the attack carrier USS *Kearsarge* (CV-33), flying FJ4B Fury jets. Years later, Miramar housed the Navy's Top Gun fighter pilot school and competition. Long before actor Tom Cruise made it famous, Miramar was training fighter pilots, and Olie was part of its roots. His duty included short patrols off the Pacific Coast as a member of the U.S. Navy's Cold War era task forces.

Although he enjoyed the flying and eventually logged more than 1,200 hours and 300 takeoffs and landings in fighter aircraft, Olie still carried the baggage of his Annapolis anchor. Despite scoring high in weapons meets as one of the top pilots in fighter competition, he was near the bottom on the promotion lists. The anchor designation didn't help at the time.

Olie is happy that the Navy has stopped tracking class rank and now focuses more on accomplishments and duty performance. He drew that conclusion from his own family. His son-in-law, Michael Duffy, retired in 2000 as a Captain after almost thirty years in the Navy after graduating from Holy Cross College in Worcester, MA. Mike recalled that he served on active duty for fifteen years before he heard the term "anchorman." Although familiar with the first in the class ranking of a few officers, Mike remembered that the modern Navy paid more attention to "how good you could drive a ship, fly a plane, or dive a submarine." "On-the-job performance is much more important," Duffy said. "Class rank is just not that important anymore." (Duffy Interview)

Another 1954 classmate, retired Navy Captain Walter "Mick" B. Hocker, who ranked 669th, agreed, saying "the biggest part of success in the Navy was where you were assigned." Then he added, "There was quite a contrast between the classroom and the reality of where you worked." Hocker, originally from Portland, ME, spent eleven years as a line officer and meteorologist on active duty until 1965. Then he served in the Naval Reserve in a number of posts, including command of several Military Sealift units in the Washington DC area. (Hocker Interview)

Still another perspective on class rank came from Admiral Gary Roughead, who ranked 267th out of 888 in his Annapolis Class of 1973 and later served as the Naval Academy's Commandant of Cadets from 1997 to 1999. "I tend to think that long ago, when the Academy provided the majority of Naval officers, perhaps class rank bias might have carried over into a career," he said. "But now that the Navy and the other services use a full range of commissioning sources, the bias has disappeared." (Roughead Interview) Admiral Roughead, who later commanded the fleets in the Pacific and Atlantic, was named 29th Chief of Naval Operations on September 29, 2007.

After completing his six-year commitment in 1960, Olie and Dorie decided to leave the Navy as Olie put in his chit and resigned. He connected with a friend of Dorie's who had quarterbacked the University of Illinois team and was serving as Head Coach for Drake University in Des Moines, IO. Tommy O'Connell needed an offensive coordinator for the Drake Bulldogs, and Olie fit the bill perfectly. His budding football coaching career was interrupted, however, by an illness in the family back home in Ohio. His mother's father, Ed Blahay, had built a successful transportation company into a freight carrier for U.S. Steel. However, Grandpa Blahay's 1961 stroke put the business on shaky grounds, and Olie was asked to help keep it running. He left football coaching, and the Olsons moved to Ohio. Olie grew the business to include more than sixty employees who used a fleet of forty trucks to deliver heavy loads for U.S. Steel. Again he thrived, more than tripling revenues during his nine-year tenure.

In 1970, he sold the business and started another. Using his extensive steel freight experience, Olie developed a port facility with eight 30,000-gallon storage tanks and large bulk warehouses to move products ranging from calcium chloride to natural rubber latex to and from Ohio and around the world. He successfully sold that company in 1972 and bought Contacts Influential, a major franchise company that provided business information services to clients like IBM Corporation and in competition with Dun & Bradstreet among others. He modestly admitted to growing the business exponentially and successfully doubling the number of franchises. That led to other business opportunities in shipping, import—export, and global asset management.

Dorie and Olie posed for the camera.

The football player turned fighter pilot turned into a captain of industry, using the same discipline and attitude that served him on the playing field and in the cockpit into success in the corporate world. At the same time that Olie and Dorie were raising their family, they devoted considerable energy to their local community. He continued to scout for the Navy football team and connected several Ohio prospects who played for the varsity. In his spare time, he was active in the local Lorain Chamber of Commerce. He was president in 1966 and was named its Man of the Year in 1968. His Alma Mater also recognized his achievements after graduation as the U.S. Naval Academy appointed Olie to its distinguished Board of Trustees.

That long-ago Notre Dame blind date led to a large family with three boys and four girls that could serve as a Navy recruiting postcard. Olie described his large family very simply if not immodestly: "Dorie was a devout Catholic, and I was irresistible."

Sons David R. Olson and Richard L. Olson Jr. graduated from the Naval Academy. Dave ranked 920th out of 934 in his Class of 1979, and Dick Junior was 967th out of 1,026 in 1986. David is a U.S. Navy Captain assigned to the U.S. Central Command. He and his wife, Teresa, have four children: Andrew, Brynn, Collin, and Evan. They live in Florida. Dick Junior (sometimes Olie is called Dick) spent seven years on active duty in the Navy. He and his wife, Lucia, daughter Remy and son David live in Chula Vista, CA. Three Olson daughters married Naval officers. Denise and her husband, Captain Mike Duffy, live in Lorton, VA, with their children: Sean, Brendan, and Morgan. Diane and her husband, Captain John Reichel, live in Vienna, VA, with their four children: Kylee, Katelyn, Casey, and Jack. Doris, who the family sometimes calls Little Dorie, married Commander Edward Schiefer. They live in Fairfax County, VA, with their children, Catherine and Aiden. The two Olson children who did not enter the Navy are Don Olson—a businessman who lives in Westlake, OH, with his wife, Elizabeth, and their three children: Michael, Meredith, and Matthew—and daughter Deneen and her husband, Jim Urhman, live near Atlanta, GA, with their three children: Tyler, Meghan, and Molly.

Dorie, the love of Olie's life, died in August of 1998, two months after their forty-fourth wedding anniversary. He told me about the two halves of that dollar bill picked up long ago on the Notre Dame campus. "When our kids were cleaning out her pocketbook after she died, they found her half in her purse, and we put them both together in her casket."

There are twenty-one Olson grandchildren, and so far, no one has attended the University of Notre Dame.

Chapter 7

First First to Switch

George B. Parks, USNA '54

J ust before the Christmas holidays in 1953, George Burton Parks stood at the top of his Naval Academy Class as he and his classmates chose the assignments that would await them upon graduation six months later. George wanted to fly like his father, an Army Air Corps aviation mechanic during World War I. He also sought a career path that would lead to command since three and a half years at Annapolis had honed his leadership skills and demonstrated his prowess at the top. He was convinced that the relatively young stand-alone Air Force would provide pilots with more opportunities for command in the same way that the older Navy favored line or surface ship officers for senior posts.

As the first in his class to choose, Parks shocked the Naval Academy by selecting the Air Force instead of the Navy for his initial assignment.

That choice would have profound consequences.

"My story is weird," George reported. "I went to the Naval Academy to become a Naval aviator with the hope that I could work through the system to eventually get to a position where I could influence the system. Unfortunately, fundamentally, as a military person, I failed."

When George selected the Air Force, the Naval Academy quickly reacted.

"They assigned a very sharp Naval aviator to me as a shadow to convince me to change my mind," he recalled. "But he couldn't and didn't."

Until the Air Force Academy graduated its first class in 1959, Naval Academy graduates chose among assignments in the Navy, Marine Corps, and Air Force. West Point graduates chose a branch in the Army including the Air Corps and then the Air Force after it was established as a separate service in September of 1947. West Point's top graduates in 1949, 1951, and 1953 chose the U.S. Air Force.[8]

For a dozen years, as many as 25 percent of the West Point and Annapolis graduates might choose to serve in the stand-alone U.S. Air Force. The Navy was not too thrilled with the practice since it had its own aviation branch. By mutual agreement, some newly commissioned officers could switch services at graduation. But that was rare and rarer still for the top graduate to switch. Later the three military academies' policies required a graduate who wanted to transfer to another service to find a corresponding graduate at that service's school who was willing to switch services.[9]

Of course, this process does not affect Annapolis graduates who choose between Navy and the Marines. About 10 to 15 percent become Marines each year.

So in 1954, George Parks's decision was so big that some Naval officers at Annapolis tried to talk him out of it. But George stuck to his decision and became the only Naval Academy graduate ranked at the top of the class to switch to the Air Force. George reported that he was influenced by his father who served in World War I as an aviation mechanic. After the World War I, George Bernard Parks came home to Okanagan in Central Washington for his high school diploma. He reenlisted in the Air Corps for flight training at March Field in Southern California. But that ended abruptly with the crash of his JN-4 Jenny training aircraft in 1920. The senior George recovered from the crash with a minor disability and then moved to Santa Monica, CA. There he went to work as an aircraft electrician for the fledgling Douglas Airplane Company. That company would eventually build the venerable DC-3 Skytrain or *Gooney Bird* that his son would fly years later. He also met up with Joy Taber, a UCLA graduate and a Santa Monica schoolteacher who would become his wife on May 29, 1930.

Their first son, George, was born on May 25, 1932; and his brother, John Walter arrived three years later. Among their souvenirs from those

---

[8]   Pennsylvanian Richard T. Carvolth III, first in 1949 and a Rhodes Scholar, died in an aircraft accident in 1954. Ohioan Gordon E. Danforth, number one in 1951, flew fighters in a 28-year career and retired as a Colonel in 1979 while the top grad in 1953, Ed D. Davis, earned his pilot's wings and served in logistics and training posts until he retired as a Colonel in 1981.

[9]   That practice, explained in 2007 by then Cadet Second Class Ben McKinney of the USAFA Class of 2009, changed to treat each request separately with decisions reached through each academy's chain of command.

days is a photo of George perched on his father's shoulders to watch the maiden flight of the first Douglas air transport, the DC-1. Both sons would follow in their father's footsteps: George as a pilot and engineer and John as a mechanical engineer for Douglas and later the merged McDonnell Douglas aircraft company.

Their father left Douglas and Santa Monica to join the U.S. Customs Service. The family moved to Los Angeles, then Nogales, AZ, and Takoma Park, MD, near Washington DC. George started high school there and also began dating a special girl named Marna Clarissa Schultz. In 1948, just before George's junior year, the Parks family moved back to the West and settled in San Francisco. George finished high school there and ranked third in his class of 325 boys and girls at Polytechnic High School. (The same school produced West Pointer Bill DeGraf, profiled in Chapter 3, in 1943.)

George was class president for the first half of the year. In his final semester, he was president of the school's chapter of the California Scholarship Federation. He also ran cross-country and track and sold ads for the school paper. And he kept his eyes on the prize: an appointment to the U.S. Naval Academy, which he had first visited as a younger man while living in the East.

George was concerned about his academic preparation at Polytechnic High School. He said it was primarily a trade school with a powerhouse football team but not too challenging academically. During his senior year, leaving nothing to chance to qualify for an appointment to Annapolis, George also joined the Naval Reserve. He drilled one evening each week at Treasure Island in San Francisco Bay. Eventually, he became an electronics technician and worked as a radar operator on a destroyer escort that occasionally ventured out of the Bay.

That preparation paid off when he received his coveted appointment in the Fall of 1949. After graduating from Poly, George reconnected with his old girlfriend, Marna. She and her parents, Leonard and Dorethea Schultz, had spent the summer in Seattle. Marna showed up in San Francisco where she and George were reunited for a few days while the new appointee was waiting for his orders to depart for Annapolis. Travel orders finally arrived July 6 with instructions to report by the 12. That administrative delay scotched George's plans to hitchhike across the country. So he spent all day flying United Airlines from San Francisco to Washington DC. He recalled it cost $170. He specifically remembered the amount because it represented about two-thirds of his total capital at the time and was a sore point because he wanted to hitchhike. However, eventually, he was reimbursed, and his bank account recovered.

Three years later, he would drive the family's thirteen-year-old 1940 Studebaker coupe back to Annapolis for his senior year. "That was a three-thousand-mile adventure," he recalled, "because the Studebaker burned enough oil to require a quart every time we filled the tank!"

During the mid-20th Century, new plebes reached Annapolis in waves, beginning with the graduates of the Naval Academy Prep School (NAPS) in Bainbridge, MD. NAPS graduates, who formed the early cadre of new plebes, were followed by regular Navy fleet appointees and students who had spent a year in college. The most recent high school grads like George arrived last.

Less than a month after hostilities began half a world away in Korea, George was sworn in as a midshipman on Bastille Day, July 14, 1950. Most of his 1,200 classmates had at least one year of college or prep school, and a fifth had prior military experience. George believed less than 30 percent of them were right out of high school like himself.

He remembered plebe summer as a blur of stencils on uniforms and blisters from rowing whaleboats. "Plebe summer was short because I only had about half of one," he recalled. "So I didn't find it all that bad." It was also helped by the presence nearby of Marna, who was driven by her parents to visit her young friend at the Naval Academy. Unbeknownst to the couple, and in an indication of the proper decorum of that era, the Schultz parents had spoken to the Parks parents and volunteered to assist the young couple "if they were so inclined."

And they were. The romance blossomed with dances called "hops," football games, and the support of family and friends throughout George's four years at the academy. Marna majored in art education at the University of Maryland at College Park, less than an hour's drive from Annapolis. She also received a diploma in Interior Design from the National Art School in Washington DC.

George pursued his studies diligently at Annapolis and thrived on it. "I liked the academy," he recalled. "The problems we faced were challenging, but I enjoyed them." He ranked among the top ten in the class throughout his four years, but it was not "cool" or "not respectable" as George put it to look like one was pursuing high grades. As a result, George recalled, most of his studying efforts were spent trying to learn his most difficult subject, the Russian language. He was not certain of finally achieving the number one rank until results of senior year's final exams were published. Number 2, by a margin of "about three-tenths of a percent" as George recalled, was a friend in his 23rd Company, James Sturgis Willis Jr. Jim Willis was the son of a Navy submariner who had died in World War II. After graduation, he became a Naval aviator and died in an aircraft accident while testing flight performance in 1961.

"I've often wondered about that," George said. "There but for the Grace of God go I. Since we were so close in school, I could have easily ended up in that cockpit instead of Jim. Who knows?"

Outside his Annapolis classrooms, George ran plebe cross-country and was a miler on the plebe track team. He also played intramural squash and singles and doubles handball well enough to be the brigade champion a few times. This prowess continued later when he was on active duty with numerous base championships. George also began running long distances again in his forties, winning the Pacific Air Forces competition at the three-mile distance. Other extracurricular activities at Annapolis included work on the radio station WRNV. He was one of the Naval Academy's broadcasters and engineers for that limited area radio station. He was also treasurer of the Trident Society, which produced a range of projects including the midshipmen guide, *Reef Points*, the quarterly *Trident* magazine, a calendar, the annual Christmas card, and art and photo club publications. George also enjoyed the Naval Academy's Foreign Relations Club and intercollegiate debate teams.

A few weeks before graduation, George was senior member of a group of USAF-bound midshipmen to meet with the Air Force Site Selection Committee. Their leader was U.S. Air Force Lt.Gen. Hubert R. Harmon, who would later serve as the Air Force Academy's first superintendent. George distinctly recalled one relatively quiet committee member, famed aviator Charles A. Lindbergh. The Lone Eagle, who was also an Air Force Reserve Brigadier General, joined the other committee members to ask the Annapolis midshipmen about life at their academy. George remembered their concerns about life at an academy remotely located away from a river and large city. At the time, he correctly concluded that the team was very close to its final decision to choose Colorado Springs as the location for the new Air Force Academy.

George also worked with his 23rd Company as part of the Sixth Battalion in its efforts to end the year on top. Each of the academies supports considerable competition among its units. Company and squadron of the year competitions provide teamwork opportunities and follow the same rigors as individual competitions: academics, intramural sports, and extracurricular activities. At the Naval Academy, the top company plays a major role in graduation celebrations. Named the Color Company because it provides the honor or color guard for the graduation parade, the top company and its commander own bragging rights at the conclusion of four-year study. One of those rights and privileges is to select an individual to affix the award banner to the Company's guidon or flag. That person was called the "Color Girl" then and is now the "Color Honoree" as the tradition continues.

As commander, when his company won top honors as Color Company for 1954, George was charged with selecting the Color Girl. Of course, he chose his fiancée, Marna Schultz. Marna, her mother, and future mother-in-law journeyed to Baltimore to pick out "*the* dress" for the occasion. In the past, the dresses had been white. But since Marna had already sewn her white wedding gown in preparation for the big event *after* graduation, she displayed her artist's flair by choosing a pastel blue. That dramatic choice became all the more evident later as the academy curator displayed her dress in the Naval Academy's museum for a few years. It later hung in a closet in the Parks' home.

On bright, sunny June 4, 1954, just before noon, George was the first of his 854 classmates to receive his diploma in Dahlgren Hall on the Naval Academy's campus. He picked up fifty-nine others and distributed them to the top academic graduates who had achieved a 3.4 GPA (Grade Point Average) or better. Then he stood with 222 other young grads, who chose to become Air Force Second Lieutenants, as General Nathaniel Twining, Deputy Chief of Staff of the U.S. Air Force, administered the oath of office. Eighty of his classmates were sworn in as Marine Corps Second Lieutenants, and the rest became Navy Ensigns. Among the latter was the anchor that day—a football player named Olie Olson. Olson was profiled in the previous chapter.

George said he didn't know Olie personally but knew who he was because "you knew who the members of the football team were. It seems to me, at the time, that there was some increased likelihood that football players would end up at the bottom of the class. This was probably because someplace in the system, on the academic board and the like, there was a bias toward not throwing them out if they got into trouble. Turnbacks [students who would repeat a year] were not unusual among athletes. We thought for a while that my roommate Carl Masters was competitive to be the anchorman." Masters ended up 39 places above Olson and eventually retired as a Navy Commander after twenty years as a surface ship's officer.

One of George's classmates who chose the Air Force took another path. Robert T. Herres of Colorado, who ranked 61st, flew fighter interceptors in air defense and worked his way through a range of Air Force assignments. Eventually, in 1987, General Herres was named vice chairman of the Joint Chiefs of Staff, the nation's second highest-ranking military officer. After he retired in 1990, he joined United Services Automobile Association, the large and well respected financial services company serving military personnel and their families. He retired as USAA CEO in 2000.

The first Marine to graduate was Clyde "Dick" Dixon Dean, of Arkansas, who ranked ninth in the class and was Brigade Captain. After graduation, Dean went to the U.S. Army Ranger School and later ran an

Underwater Demolition Team, serving two tours in Vietnam. He eventually rose to the rank of Lieutenant General and served as Marine Corps chief of staff, the third highest-ranking member of the U.S. Marine Corps. After he retired in 1987, Dean served on the board of directors for USAA. He and his wife, Helen, had five children and ten grandchildren and retired to Martinsburg, WV.

Soon after tossing his Navy dress white hat in the air, George went back to his room and switched into his new summer tan gabardine Air Force uniform. His mother and soon-to-be wife pinned on his coveted gold bars. Then George and Marna and their families and friends drove off to Takoma Park for a 3:00 PM wedding rehearsal. The high school sweethearts were married at 5:00 PM in the Takoma Park Presbyterian Church. In another sign of that bygone era, the Memorial Chapel on campus had been booked for graduation day weddings four years in advance. Marna's brother, Jim, served George as his best man. The ushers were runner-up Jim Willis and three classmates, including another Air Force lieutenant. The four new officers formed the traditional arch with their swords for the new lieutenant and his bride.

Marna and George on their wedding day

The newlyweds spent their wedding night in an Arlington, VA, motel in sight of the Pentagon. Then they chartered a sailboat and roamed over Chesapeake Bay for a week. The rest of their honeymoon was spent driving west into the sunset as they journeyed to Marana Air Base, thirty miles northwest of Tucson, AZ. There George began primary flight instruction in the T-34 and T-28 single engine propeller drive flight trainers. At Marana, George discovered that he lost vision under G (for gravity) forces experienced in acrobatic flight. "Anything over 4 Gs for 15 to 18 seconds, and I was in trouble," George reported. "To this day, I have never seen a complete loop." This was and is a significant handicap for anyone who wants to fly fighter aircraft. At six feet three, George was also too tall to fit into the T-33 jet trainer cockpit. Aviators use a maximum allowable sitting height limit to determine who can fly compact jet fighters. The sitting height limit in those days was thirty-nine inches, and George sat at forty-one. However, he still ranked first in his flying class.

Fortunately, his next stop was Goodfellow Air Force Base in Texas for the twin-engine B-25 aircraft. Those were large enough to accommodate his frame and not designed to loop. Once again, he ranked first in his class and was encouraged to remain for training as a basic multiengine instructor pilot. George eventually logged over 2,000 flying hours in the B-25, including 1,400 hours as an instructor. He moved up the ranks from instructor to the Standardization Board, conducting annual evaluations of instructors in the training wing. He was also promoted to Captain "below the zone" ahead of his contemporaries. He also became a father as Marna and George's first son, Gary, was born while they were at Goodfellow.

Flight training was not the only type of schooling George had in mind at the time. The brand-new U.S. Air Force Academy was assembling staff members, and George was eager to move to Colorado Springs to join them. But the Air Force needed pilots and would not release him from the cockpit for a desk job and academic assignment. At the same time he was teaching flying, George had been studying electrical engineering through the Air Force Institute of Technology correspondence course.

Eventually, he was chosen by the Air Force as one of the first in a group of five officers sent to Stanford University in Palo Alto, CA, to complete his graduate studies. The Air Force, at the time, released their officers to study in graduate school for a total of three years. The Stanford MSEE program was a two-year program. However, George wanted to "save" two years of time for later studies for his PhD. So he took leave (vacation time) and moved to Stanford early enough to take summer courses. Marna was pregnant with their second child, "so it was a pretty hectic time," George recalled. Lorena was born in the Stanford Hospital while George was studying. With the full support of his wife at home with two babies, George then doubled up his courses to achieve his degree in one year. He received his MS in Electrical Engineering from Stanford in June of 1959.

Next he was sent to Wright Air Development Center in Dayton, OH. There he worked as a test director for Project STEER, a part of ADVENT, the first satellite relay of ground-to-air communications for Strategic Air Command bombers. He also presented a paper on satellite communications at GLOBCOM IV, a major IEEE conference in Washington DC.

During this time, as a student and engineer, George's only flying was for proficiency and flight pay in the venerable C-47 workhorse transport. However, he qualified as an instructor for night flying to evaluate and test other pilot engineers and students. These additional duties coincided with the Air Force's roller coaster ride of not enough pilots or too many pilots soon after it didn't have enough.

Pilot shortages have plagued the military throughout history as civilian airlines put out "Help Wanted" signs for former military pilots, and the military pilots respond. Just as George was completing his research assignment, the Air Force was threatening to reduce the number of pilots retained on active duty. The combination of emerging missile technology and conversion to jets meant fewer jobs for reciprocating engine or propeller pilots like George. He was caught in the inevitable Catch-22. His Ohio engineering laboratory would not release him to train and convert to become a jet pilot, and yet the Air Force wanted him only as a jet pilot.

Researching his options, George noted seven positions for Air Force assistant air attachés in U.S. embassies based near the Soviet Union. The jobs were tailor-made for him since all seven posts required pilot engineers with graduate degrees. The officers would collect technical intelligence during the Cold War. George volunteered and was assigned to air attaché duty in the American Embassy in Ankara, the capitol of the Republic of Turkey.

In June of 1961, the Parks family departed Ohio for Washington DC where George studied the Turkish language at the State Department's Foreign Service Institute. He also took several courses in espionage and learned how to fly a new aircraft, the T-29 reciprocating twin-engine transport. After all the preparation for technical engineering and spying, flying was what kept George in the Air Force. In June of 1963, he became the chief pilot for the airplane used by the American Ambassador to Turkey Raymond A. Hare. By the time he left Turkey two years later, George had accumulated almost 3,300 hours' flying time, all of it in training or support aircraft.

The Parks moved back to the USA to Travis Air Force Base north of San Francisco. There George transitioned to another aircraft, the four-engine C-130 Hercules turboprop transport. He logged 440 hours including 60 hours combat time during the Vietnam War. He converted again in another transition, finally, to the four-engine C-141 Starlifter jet transport. Eventually, he would log 4,000 hours in the C-141 and total to 7,768 hours overall including 4,524 hours as an instructor pilot or flight examiner and 316 hours of combat time. George was awarded the Air Medal with two Oak Leaf clusters and had been promoted to Major and Lieutenant Colonel in the primary zone. He only needed command of a squadron to qualify for promotion to full Colonel. However, a conflict with a new Wing Commander during an assignment in Korea interfered. "That served to finish my Air Force career at twenty years," he said. He retired from the USAF as a Lieutenant Colonel in 1974.

While they were stationed at Travis, Marna and George bought a rundown 51-acre apricot ranch in Vacaville, CA, about ten miles northeast of the base at the edge of the Sacramento Valley. It included a 1918 raised ranch house with a walk-out basement. It was large enough to accommodate the family, and they filled it.

Their first son, Gary, who was born while they were in Texas, was an owner-operator of a truck tractor for Atlas Van Lines in Stafford, VA. He and his former wife, Karen, have two daughters: Lisa and Collette. Gary has a third daughter, Emily Grace Braun. Lisa and her husband, George Eugene Barrett, have a son named Mason Bailey Barrett. Collette married James Edmund Douglas, a University of Kentucky Air Force ROTC classmate, and they have a daughter named Cheyanne Kayleigh. The Parks' oldest daughter, Lorena, received her BS in Electrical Engineering from Syracuse University. She and her husband, Rob Bastian, have a son—Ryan—and live in Fulton, NY. The Parks' middle son, Jon, was born at the Wright-Patterson AFB Hospital and served in the Air Force as a fireman after graduating from high school in Vacaville. He's a heavy-equipment maintenance technician as a Department of the Air Force civil servant at Travis AFB. He has four children: Kiana, Shane, Kevin, and Jazmine. Kiana produced the Parks' first great-grandson, Michael, who was born in 1999. Kiana was a supply sergeant with the California National Guard and spent a year in Balad, Iraq. She was married to Shane Tyler. Shane David Parks and his wife, Jennifer, have two sons, Jacob Michael and Matthew Steven, and live in Vacaville.

The Parks' youngest son, Howard, was born at Walter Reed Army Hospital in Washington DC. He has a BS degree in Marine Engineering Technology from California Maritime Academy. Howard is a licensed Steam and Diesel Chief Engineer and worked for the Matson Navigation Company. He and his wife, Erzsebet—called Bozsi—live in Red Bluff, CA, with seven children: Casey, Christopher, Katherine, Karl, Nicholas, Sofie, and Josephine. The Parks' youngest daughter, Semra, was born in the

USAF Hospital in Ankara, Turkey. Like all her siblings, Semra graduated from Vacaville High School. Then she enlisted in the Air Force and worked as an aircraft maintenance technician. She was stationed at Mildenhall Air Base, in England, where she met her husband, David Gorst. He was an English transportation specialist as an employee of the U.S. Army. She earned her BS degree in Mechanical Engineering in Biomedical Materials Design from the University of Manchester Institute of Science and Technology and her PhD at the University of Liverpool. The English branch of family includes three children: Kayla, Katrina, and Jonathan.

During his assignments in Turkey and Korea, George had taught freshman mathematics for the University of Maryland through its overseas extension course program. Just before his official retirement in November of 1974, George began graduate studies at the University of California-Davis about 25 miles northeast of the family's apricot ranch. One day, he sat in a classroom with three other Air Force officers to take the Graduate Records Exams or GREs. He told a testing story about the verbal comprehension part of his GRE that year. "We sat there dumfounded as the test section was distributed with a major question about aviation weather," he recalled. "Each of us knew more about the subject than any test preparer certainly. But the questions were basic. Our challenge was to focus carefully on them and not go beyond the scope of what was asked and possibly make mistakes."

Obviously, George was successful once again as the University of California-Davis awarded him a Regents Fellowship based upon his high GRE scores—800 on math and 790 on verbal. UC Davis also provided a tuition waiver, and George soon found himself on the payroll as a half-time Teaching Assistant. "It had been fifteen years since I was learning in a classroom," George recalled. "Then I was a teaching assistant for an undergraduate course in FORTRAN and learning it along with my students."

He postponed and delayed taking the qualifying exam for the PhD and failed it the first time he took it. "I wasn't too pleased because I was not well prepared and did much better a year later," he said. For his research at UC Davis, George picked what he calls "an old intractable problem," the design of the very best possible electronic filter—an elliptic filter. "In earlier years," he continued, "the precise realization was of no interest because actual parts to build one were too imprecise. Fortunately, the advent of digital filtering led to precise values." George revisited the problem and developed original software programs in FORTRAN, BASIC, and one for a programmable calculator. He also used his long-ago Russian studies from Annapolis for the language requirement.

He completed his dissertation, "A Complete Process for Elliptic Filter Design," in the fall of 1982 and received his PhD in Engineering in June of 1983. At the age of fifty-one, he was the oldest student to complete a doctorate in engineering at UC Davis.

Marna and George enjoyed the California sun.

At the same time he was studying at UC Davis, George had been calling the California Maritime Academy, 25 miles Southwest in Vallejo, suggesting that an Annapolis grad with an almost PhD from the University of California system might be a good fit for their faculty. His persistence paid off, and the school appointed George an Assistant Professor in the Department of General Studies in July 1976. By the end of the next year, he had passed his PhD qualifying exam at UC Davis. He was the only member of the California Maritime Academy's faculty to complete a PhD while on the faculty. He was also fully integrated in the California Maritime environment and was elected President of the Faculty Association. He started by teaching Spherical Trigonometry and Physics and eventually taught calculus, electronics, and electricity labs in addition to computer courses such as BASIC. Among his students was his youngest son, Howard. "He managed to avoid me and vice versa during his four years at the school," George laughed. "But eventually he took my course in elementary electronics and did very well."

California Maritime Academy produces one hundred or so new merchant marine officers each year. Only a handful request Naval Science and ROTC and are commissioned in the Navy or Coast Guard. George lamented. "It's hard to put your finger on exactly who those students were and how I might have influenced them in a class or two. Yes, there are lots of people sailing ships and in other important jobs who are masters and chief engineers," he said. "But who knows what they would have done without my teaching?"

George taught at the academy for sixteen years and advanced through its ranks. After four years as an Assistant Professor, he was promoted to Associate Professor and Full Professor five years later. He explained, "I did not 'make' Department Head or Assistant Dean, so I retired in 1992. I was probably wrong to do that so early." That alluded to a restlessness that matches the cows on the ranch he chases home each day. Marna and George enjoy an active retirement, visiting family and friends around the globe.

Although he became a Life Member of the Naval Academy's Alumni Association and exchanges holiday cards with some classmates, including his former roommate, George rarely kept in touch with his former colleagues at Annapolis. He stayed away from class reunions for reasons of distance and career. "While I was on active duty in the Air Force, the Naval Academy alumni bothered me because they were a very effective lobbying group for the United States Navy. And very often at the appropriations level, their interests in calling for more ships and big aircraft carriers were inimical to mine for more and better aircraft."

After several interviews, George told me that discussions about his chapter in this book prompted him to reconnect with his Alma Mater and more of his classmates. And he was happy to reconnect.

An Ensign's First Lesson

While interviewing Olie Olson and George Parks for their chapters, I met a third classmate, retired RADM Kleber "Skid" S. Masterson Jr. who had ranked third in the class. Skid enjoyed a fascinating career in emerging technology as a computer software pioneer, but I also include him here because he told me this story about an important lesson from his first ship's commanding officer who had been anchorman in the Class of 1930.

"After graduation, I reported to the cruiser USS *Bremerton* [CA-130] based out of Long Beach, CA," Skid explained. "When I reported on board, there were very few officers qualified as Officer of the Deck. The OOD was in charge of 'conning' [driving] the ship whenever the Captain did not himself take control. It was not unusual on other ships for a dozen or so junior officers to rotate this duty since this was one of the most important qualifications for a surface line officer to attain. The small number on the *Bremerton* was the subject of considerable concern in the wardroom.

"Fortunately, soon after I joined the ship, a new commanding officer reported for duty. He was Captain R. R. Conner, known, of course, by his colorful nickname, Railroad. A West Virginian, Conner was the anchor, ranked last among 402 USNA grads in the Class of 1930.

"When Conner came aboard the *Bremerton*, he made a point of getting as many of us as possible qualified as OODs, and morale soared," Skid continued. "His leadership style in most areas of ship operations appropriately involved working through his department heads and thus indirectly to the junior officers. The results of that leadership showed up in the ship's performance as we earned many battle efficiency awards.

"The bridge, however, was where we experienced the Captain's leadership first hand. My first night watch as OOD provided one such experience.

"One clear night, we were steaming by ourselves in the Pacific. At 3:30 AM, as I was preparing to relieve the mid-watch OOD, I noted two carrier task forces on the radar that were quite close by. We were scheduled to rendezvous with them at seven AM. I asked the departing OOD, who was also the Senior Watch Officer, if he had notified the Captain about them.

"To understand his reply, I should mention one of Captain Conner's idiosyncrasies: when called during the night, the Captain would answer his phone and be perfectly alert. But he would then fall asleep and drop the phone by his side, leaving it *off the hook*. Subsequent calls would be met by a busy tone. This caused us to set a high threshold on the significance of any information we had to pass on to him at night.

"The outgoing OOD replied that he had not informed the Captain about the carriers presence because 'the rendezvous is in the night orders, and the Captain has a wake-up call for 0600 [six AM], well before the rendezvous.' I asked if I should call him and was advised that I didn't need to either.

"What happened next was, in retrospect, totally predictable," Skid continued. "The task force commander, embarked in one of the carriers, noted that all his ships were coming together much sooner than scheduled. Thus, before the time of Captain Conner's wake-up call, he put out an order on the radio. He took command of all the ships, specified a formation, and immediately executed the order. This was unusual, the normal procedure would have been to provide a preliminary order specifying the formation and to wait a few minutes before execution so that ships would have time to determine their course of action."

Skid explained that he knew where his station was relative to the senior carrier, but neither he nor the Combat Information Center had time to develop a maneuvering board solution for course and speed required to get to that station.

"Making a quick mental calculation," he recalled, "I increased our maximum speed and turned left to an estimated course to reach our station. At the same time, I told the junior officer of the deck to go to the Captain's sea cabin. I asked him to tell the Captain of the formation just ordered and our station in that formation, and that the OOD had increased to maximum speed and had come left to proceed to that station.

"The Captain replied 'very well' and asked, 'What course did he come to?' The junior officer of the deck replied correctly, 'I don't know, sir!'"

Skid added, "The next thing I heard was a seaman calling out, 'Captain on the bridge.' I looked over, and there was the Captain, in his bathrobe, heading for his chair on the starboard side of the bridge.

"I had put him in the worst possible position anybody could have put his skipper. He walked up on that bridge, and there were red lights and green lights and white lights all around him. We were cutting through the destroyer screen of the carrier group that was on our portside. Fortunately, I was going behind the stern of the carrier. That was one of the things I remembered from what Captain Conner had taught us about operating in heavy traffic: 'Even if you've got a straight shot ahead, skippers of large aircraft carriers are not always that familiar with the relative motion of ships. If you're pointing at their stern, at least they know you can't hit 'em!'

"The Captain didn't say a word. By this time, I had computed the exact course to our station, and I commenced providing a steady stream of comments to keep him informed.

"One thing you never want to hear as an OOD is the Captain saying, 'I have the con.' That phrase may seem dramatic in a Hollywood movie, but in the real-life Navy, it often meant that the OOD has lost his Captain's confidence.

"I kept up the stream of information, ensuring that everything that might be relevant was passed on. Finally, I was able to tell him, 'Captain, we are on station.'

"He replied simply 'very well' and went back to his sea cabin.

"Throughout the following days, I expected a summon for a deserved dressing-down," Skid explained. "Finally, I went to him on my own and said, 'Captain, I have been standing top watches for you for a week, and I wondered if you had anything to say about my watch standing.'

"He considered my question for a moment and then said, 'No, you are doing a very fine job.' I thanked him, and as I was about to leave, he added, 'Oh, but remember one thing. I'm paid to be Captain of this ship twenty-four hours a day. So if ever *anything* comes up that you think I should know, call me.'

"And that was it," Skid reported. "He knew that I knew what I should have done in informing him, and he also knew he didn't need to do anything more about it. Needless to say, I thought the world of him and worked hard to deserve his trust."

Anchorman R. R. Conner retired as a Rear Admiral in 1959. His former OOD Kleber S. Masterson Jr. was called Skid by his family and friends to distinguish him from his Dad. His father, retired VADM Kleber S. Masterson, had ranked 33rd in Conner's Class of 1930. Skid graduated from high school at the U.S. Navy Base at Guantanamo Bay, Cuba, before entering the Naval Academy in 1950.

After his initial gunnery job working for Captain Conner, Skid was assigned to a series of sea duty and shore assignments that combined operational savvy with emerging technology. He also acquired the first PhD in physics awarded by the University of California-San Diego. Commenting on the value of this education, Skid noted: "Most often, my jobs at sea involved nurturing new technology into the fleet and developing appropriate operational concepts. Ashore, my jobs involved analyzing future needs or developing future systems. In all of my assignments, the intellectual discipline acquired in earning the PhD played a crucial role."

He worked for the Office of Program Appraisal on the staff of the Secretary of the Navy and provided cost-effectiveness analyses demanded by Secretary of Defense Robert McNamara. It was here that he first worked for Admiral Elmo R. Zumwalt Jr. who, as the Navy's director of systems analysis, led two exceptionally successful studies in which Skid played major roles. Zumwalt, 33rd out of 615 classmates in the Annapolis Class of 1943 that graduated in 1942, was Chief of Naval Operations from 1970 to 1974.[10]

One of the studies Skid worked on led to the DD-963 class of destroyers, and the other led to McNamara's final approval of the F-14 fighter aircraft program with its exceptional Phoenix missile system. After his retirement from the Navy in 1982, Skid went to work for Booz Allen Hamilton Inc., a global consulting firm. Starting as a principal and later promoted to partner, he built six businesses: military gaming,

---

[10] During his tenure, Zumwalt issued the famed Z-grams, 119 Z-NavOp directives that addressed traditional Navy practices ranging from holidays at sea to uniform changes, including the controversial permission for sailors to wear beards.

political-military gaming, military analysis, commercial gaming, support of Navy advanced software development, and neural network technology research. After ten years with Booz Allen, Skid retired and joined Science Applications International Corporation as a senior vice president. After he retired from SAIC in 1997, he provided operations management support to a publishing company and pro-bono work mostly in education. As a member of the Society of the Cincinnati, he helped create and publish *Why America is Free: A History of the Founding of the American Republic, 1750-1800*, a supplementary text for middle and secondary school students about American history from 1750 to 1800.

Skid married Sara "Sally" Ann Cooper on December 21, 1957, at the Old Presbyterian Meeting House in Alexandria, VA. Sally is the daughter of RADM Joshua W. Cooper, who ranked 463rd out of 579 grads in the Naval Academy's Class of 1927. He was awarded the Navy Cross as Commanding Officer of the destroyer USS *Bennion* in the World War II Battle of Surigao Straits. The Masterson's first son, Thomas, arrived in 1959; and his brother, John, was born three years later. Thomas became a practicing physician and president of International Medical Publishing Company. John was an assistant counsel at the Naval Research Laboratory in Washington DC.

"If I look back on the people who had a beneficial impact on my life, I would certainly include Railroad Conner," Skid reminisced. "He was a completely self-assured person and not only taught me a lot about leadership but also about how one should measure success. I believe one should measure success using his or her own ruler, not other people's rulers," he concluded.

Skid's classmates, Olie and George, as well as the other people in the book no doubt would agree.

Chapter 8

Honest Leadership Knows No Rank

Frank C. Cosentino, USMA '66

First Lieutenant Frank C. Cosentino was not surprised to hear his name called as he walked across an airstrip in the Vietnam Highlands near Pleiku that Spring day in 1967. Bob Axley, a friend who had graduated a year ahead of him from West Point in the Class of 1965, hailed him and asked him for his DEROS—the all-important Date of Expected Return from Overseas—when he would complete his one-year tour.

"Sometime in June," Frank replied.

"Are you looking for a job yet?" Axley asked.

Frank, who was a company commander at the time and had been in combat for more than nine months, had yet to focus on his next assignment.

That was about to change.

"I'm looking for a replacement for *my job*," Axley told him.

Frank asked, "What's the job?"

"Aide-de-camp to the commanding general for strategic communications in the Pacific Theater," Axley answered. With a smile, he added that the STRATCOMPAC post was based at Schofield Barracks outside of Honolulu.

Returning the smile, Frank replied, "I believe I might be interested."

Axley, who ranked 418th out of 596 grads in his Class of 1965, quickly set up a meeting with his boss, U.S. Army BGen Robert D. Terry, who was farther south "in country" on a trip to the war zone. Terry was another West Point grad, who ranked 95th among 394 classmates in 1942.

Frank asked his friend for advice as he approached the general for his job interview. "Just be very straight forward with him. That's the kind of man he is," Axley suggested.

Frank met General Terry for the interview, which went just as his friend Bob had said: very direct and to the point.

Years later, he recalled, "In the middle of the interview, right in a series of questions about me, all of a sudden the General asked, 'And where did you graduate in the class?' I looked right at him and thought to myself, *Now, this is interesting.* And I told him I was ranked third from the bottom in the Class of 1966. Although a slow smile creased his face, the General didn't respond as he moved on to other questions."

Frank said he later learned the General already knew the answer to the class rank question and was testing his reaction. "Any man who doesn't blink when he reports he was near the bottom is OK with me" was the way the General explained it to Bob Axley, who later relayed it to his friend, Frank.

Frank's honesty came naturally, perhaps inherited, but honed throughout a lifetime of choices. When pressed to explain why, he cited his family and his upbringing. His Dad was Salvatore Cosentino, whose family came from a small mountain town in the Italian province of Calabria called Acri. Born and raised in Newark, NJ, Sal met another first generation American from Italy, Anne Casieri. Her folks were from Naples. They were married in 1940, and Sal worked in a Westinghouse factory in Newark while Anne worked in a bakery. Later, after the family moved to suburban Maplewood, she would work the counter in the famous Grunings Soda Shoppe in nearby South Orange. Frances arrived in 1942; and her brother, Frank, arrived February 6, 1944, both in Newark.

Frank worked hard in class and was a gifted three-sport athlete, so Sal and Anne sent him off to St. Benedict's Prep School in Newark. Called by many as a working guy's prep school, the school was formed by Benedictine monks. They came to New Jersey's largest city in 1857 to first serve German immigrants and then newcomers from several other countries. Despite the many changes in their home city, the prep school continues to serve today's diverse population of Newark, a few miles West of New York City. Benedict's was a sports powerhouse with top teams that attracted top college recruiters. Frank quarterbacked the football team, was a successful guard on the basketball squad, and played shortstop on the Benedict's baseball team. But football was his best and favorite.

As the successful high school signal caller, Frank won football scholarships to Holy Cross, William & Mary, and a half dozen other schools. But he was drawn to West Point. "I guess I had always watched those stories about West Point, less than two hours drive north," he explained. "I knew when the athletic recruiters approached me just how proud my parents were that I was even being considered by West Point," he continued. "I also knew several guys from the New York metropolitan area who were heading up to West Point because they wanted to play for Paul Deitzel." He was the legendary coach who had led Louisiana State University to a national championship before being lured to West Point in 1961 as the first non-West Point graduate to serve as Army's head coach.

"Of course, my decision was helped tremendously by the fact that I knew my folks could not afford to send either my sister or me to college even if I got a full scholarship," he explained. "Plus, they would be able to drive an hour and a half to attend our games. What I didn't count on was the problems I would have *academically*! I knew I was in trouble in my plebe year because I was coming from a non-technical background with not a lot of math and science courses," he continued. "My St. Benedict's classmates were going to liberal arts schools like Holy Cross or Boston College and Notre Dame, *not* to MIT or Purdue. And there I was at West Point, working on a civil *engineering* degree."

When the 850 men of West Point's Class of 1966 assembled for their plebe summer in 1962, they represented an interesting cross section of American society. In his Pulitzer Prize-winning book *The Long Gray Line*, Rick Atkinson noted, "Nearly two-thirds were the sons of military fathers, and they came as close to constituting an American warrior caste as the nation would allow." He added that two-thirds were also Protestant, and only one percent were Jewish. "Most had been varsity athletes, student government or class officers, and members of the National Honor Society" (Atkinson 1989, 14).

Frank recalled meeting his classmates for the first time: "Every time you turned around, you met achievers so and so who was 'all this' and 'all that' from their communities." He continued, "You quickly came to realize you're in pretty fast company, and so you look for the common denominators, and you begin to work together. The system fostered that teamwork," he explained.

At the time, following NCAA rules, West Point and other major schools prohibited athletes from playing varsity sports in their first year. Although he played plebe or freshman football, the academy's academic rigors prompted Frank to drop basketball. His grades were suffering, and he found himself struggling in the classroom. "Those were the days when your grades were posted each week," he recalled. "And for me, that was *not* a happy experience." However, he persevered and eventually played varsity football while keeping up with his studies.

During his sophomore and junior year, he backed up starting quarterback Rollie Stichweh, of the Class of 1965, who faced the famed

Navy quarterback Roger Staubach in the Army-Navy classic each year. Navy won in 1962 and 1963, and Army won in 1964. In Frank's senior year game in 1965, the two teams tied, 7-7. Stichweh, who ranked 516th of 596 grads in 1965 from West Point, earned the Bronze Star and Air Medal in Vietnam service. Staubach, who was 488th out of his 802 Naval Academy classmates in the same year, went on to a Hall-of-Fame career with the Dallas Cowboys of the National Football League.

Army's quarterback Frank Cosentino

The USMA Superintendent during Frank's early years at West Point was then MGen William C. Westmoreland. In his book, *A Soldier Reports*, Westmoreland described attending the 1962 Army-Navy game in Philadelphia with President John F. Kennedy, who had served in the U.S. Navy during World War II. He used the opportunity to successfully lobby to increase the size of the Corps of Cadets from 2,400 cadets to 4,400 similar to the Naval Academy's Brigade of Midshipmen.

During the game, President Kennedy asked, "General, why are there so many more midshipmen at the game than cadets?" Westmoreland explained that "the two academies operated under separate statutes which allowed the Naval Academy two thousand more men." He also pointed out that Navy had the advantage of "two thousand more men to draw from for a football team" adding, "One reason we are getting the hell kicked out of us today." After a further exchange during the game, the President said he would support an expansion bill for the Military Academy, which was accomplished in 1963 before his untimely death (Westmoreland 1976, 37).

By Frank's senior year, Stichweh and the entire defensive backfield had graduated, so the coaches asked Frank to play free safety on defense and also to return punts. He led the team in interceptions and was third in the nation with punt returns. He broke Army football single-season punt return records set two decades earlier. One was held previously by Glenn "Mr. Outside" Davis, who won the Heisman Trophy in 1946 and graduated 304th out of 310 members in the Class of 1947. Davis's classmate, Felix Anthony "Doc" Blanchard, dubbed "Mr. Inside", won the Heisman in 1945. Blanchard, who ranked 295th in the 1947 class, would go on to a 25-year military career primarily in athletics. He served as the Deputy Director of Athletics at the Air Force Academy and retired as a Brigadier General in 1971.

Frank's records, set in 1965, still stood more than forty years later.

Asked for an opinion as to why so many athletes ended up at the bottom of the class, Frank replied simply, "Maybe it's because we're constantly *running* so hard." Fred Goldsmith, who was an assistant coach at Florida A&M, Arkansas and the Air Force Academy before becoming head coach at Rice and Duke universities, provided another perspective. He explained the difference in playing football at a service academy and any other school in these terms: "At every other school in America, the *hardest* part of any football player's day is football practice. At the military academies, the *easiest* part of a football player's day is football practice" (Feinstein 1996, xii).

While Frank was pursuing his academic studies at West Point, he said, "I didn't realize my class rank was so low until they issued the graduation sheets in the spring of senior year. Evidently, the grades from my first two years dragged down my four-year average. I knew that I was graduating. There was no problem there," he reported. "It never entered my mind that I would not graduate, but I didn't realize until the end that I was that close to the bottom of the class. I never looked into it." Although he now said the importance of class rank was mind boggling at times, Frank approached it the same way he always faced adversity, with strong determination to succeed. When asked why, he responded, "I think it stems right from my grandparents who never seemed to tire at anything, whether it was working, cooking, or eating. My mother and dad worked hard, and we lived surrounded by people who *did* rather than *didn't*. They were just very hard working people, and that had a tremendous influence on me."

On a cold February night in their senior year, Frank and his classmates assembled in South Auditorium to select their branches. He remembered a Colonel asking for volunteers to go to Vietnam. And he remembered looking right and left as he and more than a 150 members of his class stood up to volunteer. He was also pleasantly surprised to find a position open in the Signal Corps. He took it, and so did the two classmates after him. Gaines S. Dyer, a Mississippian who was the football team's manager, was second from the bottom. The class goat was Robert F. Michener, author James Michener's nephew. Dyer resigned and eventually became, as Frank describes him, "an enormously successful attorney" in Mississippi. Michener completed his Army career and retired as a Lieutenant Colonel in 1989.

The top graduate among 579 members of the Class of 1966 was Wesley K. Clark. A Rhodes Scholar who attended Oxford University in England for two years, Clark would command troops in Vietnam and earn the Purple Heart and Silver Star for gallantry in action. In a distinguished career, General Clark later served as the NATO Commander during the Kosovo Conflict and retired after thirty years' service. He campaigned for the Democratic Party's nomination in the 2004 Presidential Election and is a successful businessman in his native Arkansas.

As they prepared to graduate, Frank and his roommate, Californian James McDonald "Mac" Hayes, brought some extra last minute drama to the occasion. The night before graduation, Mac received a call from his brother, Bill. He had missed his flight from the West Coast and was taking the 'red eye' due to land at JFK airport on Long Island at 5:20 AM on graduation day. Frank insisted on going with his friend to pick up Bill. "We both knew the repercussions if we missed the seven AM formation," Frank recalled, "but this was important for Mac, and I knew the roads."

"We picked up Bill and were in Mac's fire-engine red '66 Pontiac GTO, heading north on the Palisades Interstate Parkway at about ninety miles per hour. A flashing red light brought us to a halt. It was 6:15 AM when the very angry New York State trooper demanded our documents." Despite being told to remain in the car, Frank approached the trooper with his cadet ID card and a hurried explanation of the circumstances. Fortunately, the trooper had been to a number of Army football games and suddenly said, "Get back in the car and follow me!" They made it to the front gate at 6:45 AM, thanked the trooper, and ran to formation in civilian clothes. The experience cemented a great friendship of two lifelong friends. Mac, who would graduate 317th in the class, earned a Silver Star medal in Vietnam combat as a Ranger. He also served in a range of infantry assignments, completed a Master's degree from Duke University, taught at USMA, and retired from the Army as a Colonel in 1993.

Frank and Mac and their 577 classmates greeted the bright sunrise on that graduation day, June 8, 1966. After the 7:00 AM formation and a quick breakfast, Frank was rushing across campus, tidying up last minute details before reporting to his final parade formation as a cadet. Vice President

Hubert H. Humphrey and his entourage were touring the academy before speaking at graduation when Frank came upon the group and shook hands with the Vice President. Asked for his reaction, Frank said, "You couldn't miss that all-winning smile of his, and it was a neat experience."

After his parents pinned on his second lieutenant bars, Frank immediately left for Fort Benning, GA. Although many academy grads receive thirty-days' leave or vacation after graduation, in 1966, the Army was eager to get their new lieutenants in the field. Frank was in great shape as a new graduate, just six feet tall and a trim 190 pounds. He completed airborne school and switched right into Ranger School. His determination and athleticism enabled him to graduate ranked *second* among 60 classmates in his Ranger class. After nine intense weeks of Ranger School, he had dropped 24 pounds. "It was nonstop," he explained. "It was a test of your will and endurance while you were learning tactics. You would walk for thirty-six hours straight, only stopping to do map checks. We were delirious at times. It was *intense*," he said simply.

Next Frank moved to Fort Bragg, NC, for platoon leader's school. Then he was assigned to the 18th Airborne Corps in the 82nd Airborne Division. "There," he said, "you had to learn to communicate effectively at all levels—from your company commander to your worst PFC [Private First Class]. The guy who helped you with the latter, if you were smart, was your sergeant," he continued. "I loved leading enlisted troops because that was what we were trained to do. Being given a task to perform and then getting it done with others is extremely satisfying."

When pressed for a tough situation at Fort Bragg, he recalled meeting an Army Major who resented West Point grads. "He would say things like, you *goddam* ring knockers are all alike, who do you think you are?" Frank said, "I looked at the Major and just stayed away from him."

Next he attended Radio Officer's school in Fort Monmouth, NJ, and finally enjoyed the chance to be at home. On November 19, 1966, he married Marlene Franklin, from Orange, NJ. Their daughter, Jessica, was born in 1974. The couple separated a year later and was divorced in 1977. Jessica graduated from the University of Chicago and the New Jersey Medical School. She is a pediatrician, practicing and living in New York State.

A year after volunteering for Vietnam, Frank participated in a field test to check out a special radio that had been created to solve communications problems in combat. He and three other West Pointers were sent to Biloxi AFB, the Air Force Communications center in Mississippi. Although they made the special trip to check out the radio system, it just didn't work. "We spent an awful lot of time for three weeks down there trying to make this damn radio work," he recalled. "And we spent an awful lot of time eating Cajun food. But the radio simply would not function properly," he added. "In the end, they said, 'Go on home, it just doesn't *work!*"

After a brief detour to New Jersey, Frank headed off to war. Almost a year after graduating from West Point and with less than a half year of leading troops in practice, he was thrust into leading them for real in combat. When asked if he thought he was ill prepared to lead troops in actual combat, Frank replied quietly, "I *never, never* thought of that. That thought *never* entered my mind until you [the author] mentioned it." He added softly, "I knew what was expected of me." When pressed as to why he thought he was ready for the assignment, Frank replied, "If you could lead a bunch of cantankerous classmates—who haven't had enough sleep and haven't had enough food—thru Ranger School, I swear to God, you could go thru the fires of hell."

Like many combat veterans, Frank downplayed his experience in Vietnam. "We did what we were trained to do," he said simply. When he arrived in Nha Trang, he was assigned to the Second Corps Communications Center, relaying top secret and secret messages from the front lines to Saigon and the Philippines. Later he became a company commander with the 54th Signal Battalion in a combat support role. Leading teams of less than a dozen men, they drove or flew up to the tops of mountains and provided forward area communications to artillery and infantry units down below. His teams used fixed two-wing aircraft and six helicopters to move troops and equipment around the Second Corps area. "As you moved more forward, extending the reach of the troops, you had less sophisticated forms of communications," he explained. "We were there to help keep the troops in touch with headquarters."

Their mission called for quick transport of men and radios by helicopter, often several times a week. Frank described the scene on one fateful day. "We were in Pleiku and needed to transport some communications equipment back to Nha Trang. We loaded up the Huey [helicopter] with four or five guys and some radios and were trying to take off from a very small metal platform with air space restricted by some overhead wires," he explained. "That meant the pilot had to launch almost vertically. Unfortunately, that also meant he couldn't gather speed by going forward before we were airborne. As we lifted off, the chopper began the shudder, so the pilot brought it back down pretty hard. He told me we were too heavy and asked if we could unload some weight," Frank continued. "I told him we needed *all* the men and equipment, and he replied, 'OK, let's try it again.'

"So he guns it and it starts to shudder again, but instead of coming down this time, he gives it more juice, and we start to go higher. We're up about twenty or thirty feet when, all of a sudden, we start to spin. It's like a vortex spin, which is usually pretty much an indicator of a tail rotor problem," he added calmly. "So we went around about one and a half times, and he just slammed that thing down, hard," he continued.

"Later, back at the base club and after a few beers, the pilot acknowledged to me that the flight characteristics are such that if you make about two or two and a half rotations, it goes over on its side. So his quick thinking no doubt saved our lives. We came down so hard and fast that the chopper just split open, and we all tumbled out, rolling away as fast as we could to avoid what we thought would be an explosion," Frank recalled. "Fortunately, everyone was safe as the fuel cells held intact."

A couple of months later, Frank was flying in a small twin-engine aircraft, called a Caribou, which took off from Nah Trang a bit too close to another aircraft's prop wash. "We got up to four or five hundred feet, and the plane turned ninety degrees on its side and began to go down," he said quickly. "Again, I was lucky as the pilot managed to pull it up before we crashed."

Despite two close calls in the air, Frank said his worst time in Vietnam was on the ground during the Tet Offensive. The battles that some call a shocking turning point of the Vietnam War broke out in the early morning of January 30, 1968, at many cities of Central Vietnam as well as cities in the central coastal and highland areas. "We were in Pleiku City, and we didn't know who was shooting at who. Literally, the tracers were coming and going from every direction. It was an hour or an hour and a half that seemed like an eternity, and it was total insanity because we were completely surrounded," he reported. "Fortunately, our perimeter held with our fire superiority."

At one point during his Vietnam tour of duty, Frank recalled living at the end of a runway in a "hootch," a hut made from a series of pine ammunition boxes. "At Ranger School, I learned you place limits on yourself only by the number of creature comforts you can live without," he explained. "If you stacked enough of these boxes like dominoes and cut out windows, it began to look like a makeshift house. I was living in one for about a week and a half at the end of a runway when, one day, I hear banging on the outside, and this guy screaming, "Cobenzio, where are you?" It was his former roommate, Tom Carhart. "We reminisced and caught up on classmates and the war, and we both enjoyed the break from the madness," Frank said. Carhart, who ranked 384th in the class and later earned a PhD in History at Princeton University, wrote several books including an excellent series about West Point graduates (West Point Warriors: Profiles of Duty, Honor and Country in Battle).

"Looking back on Vietnam, I would say it was one of the most important years in my life and surely the best part of my time in my four years in the military," Frank said. "Everybody knew what they had to do, and we did it without the BS that I saw later in other assignments. Sure, some guys made mistakes, but when you make mistakes in combat, people get killed," he added quickly. "I was lucky because none of my guys got killed, and to my knowledge, we didn't get anyone else on our side killed."

After he completed his year's tour of duty in Vietnam, Frank moved to Hawaii for two years. First he served as General Terry's aide-de-camp at Schofield Barracks and Fort Shafter. Frank said he saw firsthand how senior military decisions are made, and he decided that he was not going to make the Army a career. "No black eye on the military," he explained quickly, "I just didn't want to be in the process as a senior officer. I wanted to go to graduate school and go back into the civilian world." After a year in the lofty world of military general officers, he was named company commander for the three hundred troops assigned to the headquarters.

He quickly dismissed the job. "From a morale standpoint, it was a cesspool. We had a bunch of smart guys poisoned to some extent by a few malcontents, and they were bored with no sense of mission. The challenge was to find a common denominator for them to rally around," he continued. "Fortunately, I found it in sports! Morale soared, and we were able to restore a sense of pride. The bonus was that it gave me a chance to compete again, albeit at a different level. But it set an example for my troops," he recalled fondly. "It was extraordinarily challenging, and I was happy to leave them after a year."

Frank's dismal class rank at West Point was another motivator. "For a long time, I had lived with that self-anointed embarrassment," he recalled. "Now I wanted to get back to New Jersey and go to graduate school and prove to myself that I was better than that," he said. When Frank notified the Army about his plans, he was told he was on the fast track for promotion to Major with a bright future ahead of him. "I knew that I had been a leader in the context of my athletic career and had been able to transfer that to my military work," he explained. "I knew that if I could do well there, I certainly knew that my discipline would serve me well," he continued. "I wanted to prove to *myself* that I could do well."

Frank was among a quarter of his classmates who decided to leave the military at the end of their four-year commitment in 1970. Less than a year later, the total reached more than two hundred, more than a third of the class. Resignations exceeded earlier classes from the 1950s and 1960s, prompting a Pentagon study of the reasons. Their analysis concluded, "Most of them disliked the Army. The major factors cited by those resigning were family separations, another imminent Vietnam tour, promotions based upon seniority, and uninspiring leaders" (Atkinson

1989, 347). Despite those resignation figures, 259 members or 44.7 percent of West Point's Class of 1966 completed more than twenty years of military service to retire in uniform.

Frank's classmate, Gerald T. Cecil—who ranked 387th in the class and later earned the Distinguished Service Cross, the nation's second highest award for valor as he led troops in the Vietnam War—served as the class scribe for many years. Jerry, who retired as a Colonel in 1984 and returned to his native Kentucky to farm and teach history at the University of Kentucky, briefly described his classmates. The clear majority, 175 men, joined the infantry, while 135 served in field artillery, 68 became civil engineers, and 66 were in armor. Eighteen joined the Air Force, and one man switched to the U.S. Navy. In addition to Wesley Clark, 15 other classmates achieved the rank of general officer. Scores were wounded in combat, and 31 were killed in action.

When he returned to civilian life, Frank pursued studies at Rutgers, the State University of New Jersey, at its downtown Newark campus. "In fact, when I applied to Rutgers, I finally looked at my West Point transcript and realized that we took a twenty-credit study load all eight semesters. I was eager to prove to myself that I could succeed in another classroom." Using the GI Bill that supports veterans' studies, Frank had also saved some of his pay from being in Vietnam and Hawaii. He obtained his Masters of Business Administration in two years while studying full time.

When asked to contrast Rutgers in 1970 with West Point in the mid-'60s, he began with the obvious difference of an urban setting with a rural campus. But he quickly switched to the class environment. "I thought my professors and courses were excellent," he explained. "And I was able to adapt quickly to the casual class atmosphere." He said the best parts of his MBA studies were the leadership opportunities. "You could sit back and go along for the ride, or you could take an active role to get your point across as you tried to shape outcomes. I liked influencing the results," he added.

"I really thrived in those periods between semesters when we would compete for assignments as interns and work in local enterprises," he continued. The first was a foray into a local retail store where he worked for the principal buyer and was introduced to the world of fashion. "It was interesting but not for me," he added. Next was a community hospital where Frank said he saw the mismatch of medical professionals trying to become administrators with little or no training or experience. "And I saw some conflicts of interest involving business investments that were questionable," he added. "The ethics of the situation disturbed me."

Frank fondly recalled his best internship assignment as the one that would set the stage for his first civilian career in the telecommunications industry. The 1968 Carterphone Decision from the Federal Communications Commission had opened up the previous monopoly enjoyed by American Telephone and Telegraph Corporation to competition for the first time. AT&T asked Frank to interview some of their former customers who had switched to competitors. "I spent four weeks visiting those customers," he explained. "Some didn't want to talk with me, so I had to be persuasive even to get an appointment. However, as a result of my interviews, I was able to produce a complete business analysis of why they had gone with the competition. Although a lower price was one factor, the overriding reason for switching away from AT&T at the time was the attitude of their sales department," he continued. "My research indicated that the sales people were simply order takers and were *not* being helpful to customers. Senior management took one look at this report and asked me to present it to their sales team."

Anyone who has worked with sales professionals knew this would be a sensitive meeting at best. "Ironically," Frank continued, "the meeting of two hundred AT&T sales pros was scheduled for the Battleground Country Club in Monmouth County, New Jersey," he laughed. "So there I was, the bearer of bad news for a roomful of sales folks who were forced to listen to my presentation." Very quickly, they evolved into a room full of *angry* sales reps who were shouting at the speaker.

When asked about the pressure at the podium, Frank laughed again. "*Pressure? That* wasn't pressure," he explained. "Pressure is when you're in the middle of a war, and guys can get killed as a result of your action."

After the New Jersey presentation, Frank said two categories of people came up to speak with him privately: those who continued to angrily deny the report and those who said, "Thanks for telling it like it is." Frank said he remembered plans for retraining, but most of all, he remembered the importance of getting facts straight and presenting them honestly and directly.

The global conglomerate International Telephone and Telegraph Corporation recruited Frank right off the Rutgers' campus. "ITT had begun a policy of bringing in new MBA graduates to gain homegrown executives," he explained. "Based at the New York headquarters, I moved through a series of interesting jobs, mostly in industrial engineering, becoming something of an expert on distribution and shipping." He recalled visiting diverse divisions that produced telephones, automotive brakes, water pumps, and electronic components as well as Wonder® bread, Hostess Twinkies® cupcakes, and Scott® grass seeds. Other parts of the company included Sheraton® hotels and Hartford® insurance products and operated the famed "Hotline" between Washington and

Moscow.[11] The company's chairman from 1979 until it was sold in 1998 was Rand V. Araskog, who had graduated 125th among 512 members of West Point's Class of 1953.

Frank recalled, "I would look at their shipping methods and suggest air freight consolidations and other improvements. They called me a 'Seagull,'" he laughed. "They said I would fly in, crap all over everything, and then fly out!" He called himself a "logistics maven," and the ITT teams sent him all over the world to assist shipping and other operational issues.

Along the way, he met Brooklyn-born Margaret "Maggie" A. Weadock, an assistant in ITT's Park Avenue offices. "The first time I met Maggie was in an argument in a business setting, and we both thought the other was pretty obnoxious," he explained with a laugh. Maggie remembered with another chuckle, "*War* at first sight! He was a new guy and very *stuffy*." Fortunately, they were reintroduced at an office Christmas party a year later and then were assigned to work together on a project. "We worked together successfully," Maggie recalled, "developing mutual respect." They began dating in 1976 and were married April 16, 1977.

Maggie brought her daughter, Casey, who had been born in 1970 in the Bronx. Casey graduated from Centenary College and lives and works on Long Island, NY. Their daughter, Jennifer, arrived in 1978 in San Clemente, CA. She graduated from Boston University and later served as an editor of *InStyle* magazine. Jenny and her husband, Christian Muirhead, live in West Los Angeles. In 1982, twin sisters Anne and Sarah were also born in San Clemente. They graduated from Bucknell University in 2004 and later shared an apartment in Hoboken, NJ, while working in New York City. Anne is in advertising for Uproar Inc., and Sarah works in public relations for Rubenstein Associates Inc.

"He still carries that military bearing, and he's still athletic," Maggie described her husband, Frank. "I love the rich tradition of West Point," she explained, remembering a reunion for a football game in 1981. "The wives were in the stands, and the men were on the field in civilian clothes, of course, when the band began to play. Immediately, the men formed up into ranks, automatically, in perfect formation, six across," she said.

---

[11]   ITT, where I worked for two decades while a member of the USAF Reserve, also fully supported its employees who were members of America's National Guard and Reserve. The company was one of thousands to officially record and be recognized for that policy by signing Statements of Support for its workers through the Pentagon's Employer Support of the Guard and Reserve (ESGR) program.

"*They* were ready to march." She also described Frank as a trim athlete who stayed engaged in sports by playing basketball and golf whenever he can. When pressed for more descriptors, she replied, "And he is a wonderful father, my girls *adore* him." She added, "He is *still* a leader able to mediate disputes and make everyone feel they are part of the solution."

When pressed to describe the links between his West Point and military endeavors and civilian business experience, Frank summed it up in one word: honesty. "We trained to be honest," he explained. "You had to be truthful. You had to know what was going on, and you had to tell the guys you were working with *exactly* what the situation was—whether it was a bucket of crap or gold—because someone could get *killed* as a result of misinformation," he said emphatically. "In business, you're certainly not dealing with the same level of intensity and consequences, but why does it [the truth] have to change?" he asked pointedly. "We're talking about *ethics*," he emphasized. "Today our society is so lacking in ethics that it's frightening. That's the most significant thing I think I brought to every position I have ever had." He continued, "Whether it's the guy who cleans up at night on the factory floor or the senior executive in a Park Avenue suite. They may not have liked what I said, but they knew that what I said was the *truth*."

At the end of 1977, Frank completed an overseas project for ITT and assessed his future. "I wanted to move from headquarters to a field unit because I had had enough of headquarters," he recalled. "Fortunately, I connected with the group executive of ITT's Cannon Electric connector business on the West Coast. The boss there told me, 'Look, you've already been an aide to one general, you might as well be an aide to another civilian general.'" Finally, back in a line job, he progressed well up the corporate ladder. He worked for the ITT Components Division, a $25 million company taking electronic components made in the Far East and Europe and putting them to work in a range of industries. He shed the division's red ink and turned a profit. He was named its president in 1986. However, two years later, excessive travel for a company some people called "I Talk and Travel," plus a change in reporting relationship, prompted Frank to explore other opportunities. He became a Vice President of Avnet Inc., a major components distributor, also in Southern California. However, he said he still spent too much time traveling as a road warrior.

"One night, I found myself sitting in a hotel room in Salt Lake City on another trip away from home," Frank recalled. "I called my sister in New Jersey to find out about our Dad, who had been ill. "When I complained about my job, Fran suggested that I speak to her husband, Sal Davino, the entrepreneur whose business developing New Jersey shopping centers was exploding. The next day, I called Sal, and we both realized quickly that it was a good match. I moved the family back east to New Jersey and took all of my experience in a large corporation to work in a smaller one. In 1988, Frank became the seventh employee as Vice President of Development for Fidelity Land Development Corporation. In the ensuing eighteen years, the company expanded to forty employees and amassed a portfolio of almost four million square feet of prime New Jersey commercial real estate. "We were able to grow a nice business very successfully." Maggie and Frank lived and worked in Readington, a suburb in the country not far from his Newark roots. "We developed shopping centers and other commercial properties, primarily in New Jersey," he explained. "And when I hopped on an airplane, it was for pleasure!" he reported happily.

The United States Congress BRAC (Base Closure and Realignment Commission) included historic Fort Monmouth in New Jersey in 2005. The redevelopment of this 1126-acre site and its economic revitalization required an experienced leader. As a result, that public service gene nurtured at West Point many years ago was reactivated in 2006 by a recruiting call from New Jersey Governor Jon S. Corzine. Frank left the Fidelity Land Company to accept an appointment as the Executive Director of the State's Fort Monmouth Economic Revitalization Planning Authority.

Executive Director Frank Cosentino

"We're working to come up with a plan to replace the twelve to twenty thousand jobs directly and indirectly affected by the post's closing as well as redeveloping the real estate in ways that are consistent with the needs of the affected communities and the region in general," Frank explained.

"If ever there was an effort that required the highest ethical standards and absolute public transparency, this is it," he said. "It's a unique opportunity for me to give back to my home state a legacy of which to be proud," he continued. "I love my job," he added simply. The Authority's plan was scheduled to be submitted in 2008.

"Other than that and moving to West Long Branch to be closer to work and the Jersey Shore," he remarked dryly at the time, "things are quite dull."

Chapter 9

Seeking Opportunity

James E. Love, USAFA '69

Like many black men born in the south at the beginning of the 20th Century, Leon Love moved north for opportunity during World War II. He found it in Milwaukee, WI, with two full-time jobs in that lakeside city's famed meat packing business. By their example, Leon and his wife, Thelma Adams, instilled in their six children the importance of hard work and education. Their oldest son, Jimmy, worked hard enough at his studies to graduate as valedictorian, first in his winter Class of 1964 at North Division High School. North Division was one of two city schools with predominantly black populations. At six feet two, Jimmy also played forward for the school's varsity basketball team. But he found himself unsure of the future. He just knew that the part-time job arranged by Leon for him and his younger brother, Leon Babe, cleaning up in the slaughterhouse, was not going to lead him to where he wanted to be.

"I was a jock and an artist in high school," Jimmy recalled. "I had no idea what I wanted to do except that it was not to work in that packing plant. I was leaning toward being a commercial artist though I wasn't sure I could make a living at it."

Fortunately, the North Division Blue Devils' basketball coach was a former U.S. Marine who talked to Jimmy about attending a military academy. Coach Vic Anderson called it a good opportunity. So did Conradeen Young, the mother of Jimmy's teammate and friend, Clarence. Mrs. Young was raising her family as a single Mom after her husband had died while serving in the U.S. Navy. Talking about the military, she urged Jimmy to "take that opportunity if it comes to you." She stressed the quality of the education, opportunity to serve and travel, and all the positives that military service included.

A different Blue Devil connection, at the college level, was Michael "Mike" W. Krzyzewski, who graduated 568th out of 800 in West Point's Class of 1969 and served as an artillery officer in the USA and Korea before returning to his Alma Mater as a basketball coach in 1975. Krzyzewski often spoke fondly of his days at West Point both as a cadet and coach. In 1980, he moved to Duke University where he successfully coached those Blue Devils to championships year after year. Coach K believed that the service academies need to be more daring in their recruiting. He suggested, "Why not go to the 25 biggest cities in the country and find inner-city kids who are valedictorians and salutatorians in their class? Or class presidents. Regardless of their SAT numbers, they're clearly leaders. Army is about finding and teaching leaders. Accept 25 a year. Some may be athletes, others won't be. Some may flunk out; others will be great officers. Take some chances, but take chances on kids who have proven they have some guts and desire already. Don't just look at numbers. My last captain, Matt Brown, from the Class of 1979, finished in the bottom ten in his class and now he's a battalion commander. There's more to this than numbers." (Feinstein 2000, 267).

Jimmy Love accepted the encouragement of family and friends and agreed to attend the U.S. Air Force Academy Preparatory School in Colorado Springs, CO, after he graduated from high school. The Prep School is located on the grounds of the Air Force Academy complex but separated from the main campus cadet area by a few miles of winding roads.[12]

Those winding roads weave through the Air Force Academy's 18,500 acres, which are located in an hour's drive south of Denver on Interstate 25. The grounds are split into five large areas: the academic campus, the

---

[12]   Each of the service academies has a preparatory school offering students extra academic help to enable them to succeed with college level courses. The USMA's prep school is located at Fort Monmouth, NJ, about 50 miles south of New York City, or about 100 miles from West Point. The Naval Academy's prep school is in Newport, RI, about 400 miles North of Annapolis. The schools' one-year programs teach basic studying skills and offer special post-graduate high school programs. Each year, nearly all the one hundred or so graduates of each academy preparatory school are able to enroll in *their* academy after they successfully complete studies. Many of the students are inner city kids or recruited athletes who might not have received the same level of undergraduate preparation experienced by their peers.

service and support areas, the staff family housing, an airfield, and the wilderness. The campus houses approximately four thousand Air Force Academy cadets and also includes the Air Force Academy Preparatory School, which has two hundred students. They are located at an altitude of 6,380 to 8,040 feet above sea level. The place seems and is huge almost like a national park. And in fact, it is a major tourist attraction in the State of Colorado. Just about every day, small prop-driven airplanes and gliders whir and soar overhead. Occasionally, billowing parachutes dot the sky. All cadets can learn to fly the gliders, and many also learn the important skill of jumping out of perfectly good aircraft. Parachutist's wings above a left breast uniform pocket often indicate Air Force Academy grads. Those cadets who are physically fit for pilot training also receive their initial flight training at this Academy.

Smiling sentries greet visitors at the two main gates, the ends of west turn exits from I-25. The Northern post leads past the BUFF, a B-52 bomber used in the Vietnam War. It's one of nine vintage USAF aircraft strategically placed throughout the Academy's grounds. Signs warn of deer and elk crossings, adding caution to drives on twisting roads that wind their way up to the campus. The main campus area lies out in a large gray granite rectangle with the Chapel wall at the West. Dormitories, classrooms, the library, dining hall, and administrative offices surround thousands of terrazzo tile squares in the two-tiered courtyard. The buildings carry names of Air Force heroes, ranging from the dining hall named for aerial bombing pioneer General Billy Mitchell to a dormitory named for Captain Lance P. Sijan, a graduate of the Air Force Academy's Class of 1965. His F-4C Phantom jet fighter exploded and crashed into the Laotian jungle on his sixty-seventh combat mission during the Vietnam War. Despite a compound broken leg and several other severe injuries, Sijan eluded capture for more than six weeks and then died as a Prisoner of War. To date, he is the only Air Force Academy graduate to receive the Medal of Honor. Sijan ranked 413th among his 517 classmates.

Jimmy Love and all other new student cadets arrived at the service academies with the wonder of new beginnings. Leaving the comforts of home where they were often significant and successful individual achievers, they are thrown together anonymously with others just like themselves. Upperclassmen and women rudely introduce the new recruits to the rigors of military life. "In one word, it's a shock," recalled Jimmy.

Military life is a shock in any circumstance, but to an 18-year-old black man from Milwaukee in 1964, it was even more so. "I had grown up almost isolated in a black community," Jimmy recalled. "Now, for the first time, I was thrust into an environment that I had never before experienced. It was a big change for me. The prep school eased the transition somewhat, but it was still a big change. Actually, I looked at the academic and military parts of my transition as an adventure."

When Jimmy completed his prep school year successfully and joined his basic cadet classmates in 1965, the U.S. Air Force Academy included nearly four thousand cadets—all male. There were a handful from foreign countries, and few were native Americans or of Hispanic origin. Five other black men were members of Jimmy's "doolie" or freshman class.

Jimmy reported that his biggest adjustment was to decide how to approach being black in an almost all-white society. "The rest of it was exciting," he said. "But how I conducted myself as a black man was to be an important issue." In many ways, his demeanor set the stage for his life's work that was to follow years later. Jimmy's college days were the era of American history with civil rights awakenings. Race riots in Watts, Newark, and Detroit punctuated the unsettling times. Jimmy adjusted to his first year in Colorado Springs in a manner that appeared to be successful. He worked at his academics and sports and found he liked the rigors and discipline of military life. He also decided to blend in with his classmates as best he could to be one of the guys. He avoided confronting prejudice and went along with all the racial jokes and other slanders. When he completed the prep school, he continued with this attitude as a Basic Cadet at the Academy. Peer ratings and evaluations by his classmates midway through his freshman year at the Air Force Academy confirmed he was "getting along," ranking him 99th out of 1,000 cadets in terms of military bearing and congeniality.

However, near the end of his first Academy year as he matured, he began to question his own attitude toward his identity. "I almost reversed what had worked for me," he explained. "I became the opposite of what I had been. I confronted who I was and how people interacted with me. Although I didn't pick fights, I did pick opportunities to challenge and speak about racial issues. And when I had the opportunity for assignments, I tried to work into the assignment some kind of racial aspect to tell my story," he recalled. In his sophomore year, *Ebony* magazine published an article that questioned Abraham Lincoln's status as a great emancipator or white supremacist. "I took it to my History class so we could talk about it," Jimmy recalled. The instructor appointed another classmate with an opposing *New York Times* review, and we debated it. It was very helpful to me and to the others to understand different points of view."

After the class debate, the instructor, an Air Force full Colonel, called Jimmy aside and asked, "What is it that black people really want?" Jimmy reported, "I thought his question was really interesting because I hadn't been to any race consciousness classes yet. It seemed clear to me that black people wanted just what everyone else wanted, and I told the

Colonel that. I thought we just wanted the opportunity to be able to live our lives like all Americans, to move freely, and to enjoy the freedoms and responsibilities that everyone else had in our country." Years later, Jimmy is still not sure if his white teacher asked the question because he didn't know or if he was somehow testing this young black future officer to see what *he* wanted.

As they moved through the upper classes, some of Jimmy's classmates reacted adversely to his newfound militancy. Evaluations by his peer group plummeted. A few weeks before graduation, his AOC (Air Officer Commander) called him into his office to tell him he was near the bottom of the class, both in terms of peer ranking and the overall Military Order of Merit. "I guess I wasn't too surprised about the academic side because I had not worked that hard in the classroom," Jimmy recalled. "But the peer-group ratings surprised me. So I asked why, and he shared some reports that contained language like 'he spends too much time with his soul brothers.'"

Jimmy was surprised at the intensity of their criticism. "At first, I was hurt because no one had ever put that into perspective for me," he said. "I think we were all unsure of what to do at this stage in our history. But I also knew that, someday, I wanted to be able to help others to avoid the pain that I felt then."

Those times included a very public display by two young African-Americans at the 1968 Olympics in Mexico City—John Carlos and Tommy Smith. Jimmy recalled, "I felt pride at what Carlos and Smith had done, and I understood their actions to be a statement and form of peaceful demonstration—a way to bring public attention to a situation of unfair treatment and racism. I thought then and still think today that we need to be more candid in discussions about race, human relations, and tolerance in order to move toward a better place or existence. It felt good to see persons in the spotlight speak out and reinforce some of what I felt inside."

During Jimmy's junior year, Columbia University sent a package to the Air Force Academy's Psychology Department, urging them to establish an Afro-American Society at the Academy. The Chairman of the Psychology Department gave the letter to John Hopper, one of Jimmy's five classmates who were black. Hopper, who would go on to a distinguished career as a general officer in the Air Force, called a meeting of his classmates who were black. "We discussed the proposal and saw real conflict in creating a separate group within the larger brotherhood of the Cadet Wing," Jimmy recalled. "Finally, we decided we would ask the Air Force Academy to respond positively. No one wanted to sign the letter and make waves, so I did it. They didn't know what to make of it then. But a few years later,

I was back at the Academy, and I learned that they had created a Black Studies group. The programs that had been suggested and that we had struggled with earlier had been adopted. I considered that progress."

In addition to Love and Hopper, the Class of 1969's other cadets who were African-Americans were Rich Spooner, Walt Howland, Ken Little, and Ken Stevenson.[13]

During his academy years, Jimmy Love continued to play sports and practice his art. "I sure did like to play basketball," he recalled. "Although I was a starter on the freshman team, the rest of my career was spent as a benchwarmer. I was a scrub. My 'showtime' was at practice." During Jimmy's playing days, the team never won too many more than they lost, suffering—like many academy sports teams—from lack of players with big-time ambitions and big-time physical stature.

"Sure, basketball took its toll," Jimmy recalled. "I wasn't much of a student." His modesty got in the way of the reality. As an artist, Jimmy continued to practice his craft at the Academy, where he was art editor and cartoonist for the underground cadet newspaper, the *Dodo*. He also

---

[13] John D. Hopper Jr., ranked 477th, was a command pilot who worked in a range of distinguished assignments ranging from flying C-130s in the Vietnam War, where he earned the Distinguished Flying Cross and three Air Medals, to Commander of the Operations Group responsible for Air Force One. He logged more than 3,900 flying hours in twelve different aircrafts. Hopper also taught at the Air Force Academy and, in 1994, served as the Academy's first Commandant of Cadets who was black. Lt.Gen. Hopper was Commander of 21st Air Force and later was Vice Commander of the Air Education and Training Command responsible for recruiting and training for the entire Air Force.

Richard E. Spooner, 628th, was a master navigator with 2,900 flying hours who flew F4s Phantom fighters during the Vietnam War where he earned the Meritorious Service Medal and Air Medal. He spent ten years on active duty before transferring to the Air National Guard. He rose to the rank of Major General and became the Air National Guard assistant for technology integration, intelligence oversight, and information operations. He was responsible for assisting and advising the chief of the National Guard Bureau on technology, intelligence, and information operations issues impacting the Army and Air National Guard. He also served as a Director of Intelligence Programs for defense contractor Lockheed Martin Corporation.

helped design one of the most lasting mementos of his Class of 1969, the Class Crest for the class ring.[14]

Jimmy's head basketball coach was Bob Spear, whose tenure at the Academy ran from 1957 to 1971. One of Spear's key assistants was Hank Egan, who graduated 648th among 797 classmates in 1960 at the Naval Academy. After he completed his Navy obligation, Egan got his coaching start in 1966 at the Air Force Academy. He was to have an important role in the development of Jimmy Love three years later. One of Jimmy's teammates was Gregg Popovich, later head coach of the NBA's San Antonio Spurs. Popovich and Love played together for two years. The future NBA coach was team captain as a senior and Air Force's leading scorer for a team that was 12 and 12 in the won-loss columns. He graduated in the middle of the class in 1970, with a degree in Soviet Studies, followed by five years' active duty. He returned to Colorado Springs to coach for six years as an assistant to Egan and then later hired Egan as an assistant for the Spurs. That Spurs team included perennial All-Star and original U.S. Olympics Dream Teamer David "the Admiral" Robinson, who graduated from the Naval Academy in 1987. Jimmy kept in touch with his former teammate and coach, who sometimes treated him to a pair of tickets when the Spurs visited Washington to play the Wizards.

Walter T. Howland, 530th, was another Air Force navigator whose distinguished career included combat crew duty in Vietnam, where he earned the Silver Star and four Distinguished Flying Crosses, two Meritorious Service Medals, and twenty-six Air Medals. He earned an MBA and taught at the Air Force Academy and Fayetteville, AR, State University.

Kenneth H. Little, 604th, was a combat photographer who commanded the Photo Squadron at Tan Son Nhut Air Base in Vietnam during the Vietnam War and later worked as a film editor for Universal Studios in Hollywood.

Kenneth E. Stevenson Jr., 634th, became a clergyman in New York.

[14] Each class at all of the academies designs a special crest as a lasting memento. The crest usually includes scenes of the academy and significance of the four years that class spent there. It appears on class rings, graduation invitations, shirts and beverage glasses, alumni magazines, and virtually everywhere the class trumpets its year. A large relief of each class crest graces a wall near the chapel at the Air Force Academy. Virtually all the crests include the class mottoes. The Class of 1969's was developed and produced in Latin and reads, *Esse Non Dideri* (To be not to seem).

"When I was at the Academy, I was not the model cadet, and through the years, that took its toll," Jimmy said. "So at the time of graduation, my GPA was 1.99. Several of us were in trouble of not graduating, and I was at the bottom of the heap. The Academy was not going to graduate or commission me, and that was a real wakeup call," Jimmy recalled more than three decades later. Six senior cadets were told to meet a board of officers who would determine if they would graduate.

Jimmy met with his basketball coach and asked for his advice. "Coach Egan really influenced me." He said, "Jimmy, you've got yourself in a *real* mess. What are you gonna tell this Board?" I told him I was going to tell them the truth: that I came to the Air Force Academy to play basketball." Egan advised, "Yes, that's right, and the best thing you can tell them *now* is that you want to be a model officer."

Fortunately, the Air Force gave Jimmy and the others one more shot at the free-throw line. He was offered a special creative writing course to make up his for his academic deficiency. That worked, but not before another strong influence became involved in Jimmy Love's difficult progress through his final days of cadet life. "Through all this time, I had pretty much kept my folks out of the picture concerning my academic situation," Jimmy admitted. "Oh, I kept in touch with them regularly, but I hadn't told them I was in danger of not graduating. When I finally admitted that, my Dad was so upset that he called the Commandant of Cadets to find out what happened."

Each academy has a superintendent or president and academic deans like most postsecondary schools. They also have Commandants of Cadets who are responsible for the academies' military training. There is no way to overemphasize how much these people epitomize the military presence on each academy's campus.

The Air Force Academy Commandant who Leon Love called about his son was BGen Robin Olds. Robin Olds would have been a poster boy for commandants. He had graduated 193rd out of 513 members of the USMA Class of 1943, where he was an All-American tackle on the West Point wartime football team. Olds was a no-nonsense fighter pilot—the only USAF ace who shot down enemy aircraft during both World War II and the Vietnam War. His chest full of ribbons included the Air Force Cross, the nation's second highest recognition for bravery. Another legendary Air Force General, cigar-chomping Strategic Air Command leader Curtis E. LeMay, called Olds his mentor, saying, "If I had to single out anyone, I would say Robin Olds made the greatest impact on me" (Puryear 2000, 201). Just before coming to the Air Force Academy as commandant of cadets in December 1967, Olds had completed 152 combat missions and served as commander of the Eighth Tactical Fighter Wing in Thailand during the Vietnam War.

Olds was matched against Jimmy's father, Leon, a hardworking native of Wynne, AR, who had lived through many difficulties and was still then working two jobs to keep his family intact in Milwaukee. Jimmy was his first son to attend college. Leon knew Jimmy had attended his classes. He had done *all* that the Air Force Academy had asked. Or so he thought. Since Jimmy had not involved his parents as he worked to resolve graduation issues in Colorado Springs, his father didn't know anything about this process.

All Leon Love knew was that his oldest son was being denied his diploma and second lieutenant bars, and he wanted to know why. So when Leon called General Olds, he asked the general if Jimmy was being discriminated against because he was a young black man.

One can only imagine the test of wills between these two men in June of 1969. One was an experienced military veteran accustomed to the spit and polish of orders given and received without question. The other was a soft-spoken, concerned civilian father, who was unfamiliar with the rigors of military schooling but *convinced* that his son was being denied his reward for five years' effort.

Jimmy said, "I don't think there was discrimination or any institutional problems at the time, but my father didn't accept that. He had just seen too many instances of unequal treatment in Arkansas and Wisconsin. I'm certain he was respectful, but I'm also certain he was blunt. I was *so proud* of my Dad in his talk with General Olds," Jimmy reported.

After the conversation between the General and his father, the possibility of a misunderstanding prompted Olds to summon Cadet First Class Love to his office in Harmon Hall. The building was named for U.S. Air Force Lt.Gen. Hubert R. Harmon, USAFA's first Superintendent. Harmon ranked 112th out of 164 in the Class of 1915 at West Point. As another famous member of the "Class the Stars Fell On," he was a successful aviator who took many West Point traditions with him to Colorado during his pioneering 1954 to 1956 tenure. He was officially recognized as the Father of the Academy as part of the Air Force Academy's 50th anniversary celebrations in 2004. The Academy was also designated a National Historical Site that year.

Harmon Hall is a large imposing building not far west of the famed Air Force Academy Chapel, that school's most distinguished edifice. Its three stories loom large over the campus terrazzo tiles, where—in his first year—Jimmy and the other doolies squared corners as they rushed to class. Harmon's cold glass-and-steel exterior houses the beginning and the end of Air Force Academy life. It holds offices for the Superintendent and Admissions Department as well as the Legal Staff and Public Affairs Director. The building seems to rest firmly on two large lobbies with the backdrop of the majestic rampart range of the Rocky Mountains. Although the north entrance is empty, the south's is stuffed with memorabilia.

The western wall includes General Harmon's plaque while a bookcase contains his three-star flag and desk plate. He gazes solemnly across the lobby at another, much larger silver-and-gray plaque that's topped with a giant set of command pilot's wings. Unlike the more well-known and visible "Bring Me Men" sign that graced the entrance ramp for more than forty years and was removed in 2003, the Harmon plaque had not yet been gender-neutralized as of 2005. Four columns of dates, from 1959 to 2059, are listed below the heading. Next to each date is a smaller plaque, engraved with the names of each class's top graduate from 1959 to the present, including several in this book.

Their names share the lobby space with figures and mementos from other aviation and Air Force heroes. Bronze busts of Orville and Wilbur Wright face these top graduates. So does the bust of Dr. Theodore von Karman, the scientific architect of the modern United States Air Force. Glass bookcases hold models and commemorative plaques and framed certificates from overseas visitors from Argentina to Egypt. One diorama contains the figure of the early aviator Octave Chanute in his two surface-flying machine seven years before Kitty Hawk. In the lobby's northeast corner, the bust of General Curtis E. LeMay seems almost mellow without his ever-present cigar. However, a visitor senses the former Eighth Air Force leader of the Air War against Nazi Germany and founder of the Cold War's Strategic Air Command would be pleased with his neighbors, the men and women who were top in their classes.

Back in 1969, Jimmy remembered General Olds as a straight shooter who was down to earth. He easily related to cadets both as a group and individually. He met Jimmy Love, discussed his situation, and promptly concluded, "We are going to graduate and commission you and get you to work out in the Air Force."

The Class of 1969 received their diplomas and commissions from President Richard M. Nixon on June 4, 1969. In those days, only the 25 Distinguished Graduates were given their diplomas by the distinguished keynote guest. First of the 683 to walk across the stage in Falcon Stadium was Steven Ross Sturm, who then went to Oxford University as a Rhodes Scholar. He served a distinguished 25-year career largely in political-military affairs positions. He retired as a Colonel in 1994 and remained in Brussels where he continued his political-military affairs career as a civilian in NATO.

Fourth in the class was Howard Lindsey Parris Jr., a service brat who lived in Atlanta, GA, during his Academy years. He was a math major, the captain of the cross-country and track teams, and later the Class President. A few years after graduation, he became the '69's scribe, preparing a Class update every quarter for publication in *Checkpoints*, the USAFA alumni magazine. Lindsey served 22 years on active duty in the

Air Force in a variety of disciplines, retiring a colonel in 1991 when he became a management consultant. Three decades after graduating, when asked to characterize his class in one word, Lindsey said "cohesive." He said he knew Jimmy well, perhaps a bit better than his other classmates who were black, because both had been varsity athletes throughout their Academy years.

Lindsey and Jimmy described the environment at the academy in the late 1960s in similar words of equality, opportunity, and teamwork. Neither mentioned discrimination, or anything close to it, as a defining characteristic of his Academy experience. The N-word was seldom heard. Jimmy remembered hearing it only once—in his basketball team's locker room freshman year. "I came into the room and heard one of my teammates saying it," Jimmy said. "I confronted the guy who used the word, and he reacted by saying, 'Come on, Love, you're different. You're not like those other guys.' I didn't like that at all and told him so. I never fell out of friendship with the guys, but it hurt. You know that people you love sometimes disappoint you. This was one of those times."

Lindsey also recalled hearing it only once. "I was a first classman, leaving the mess hall, and overheard a handful of young black cadets, either doolies or third classmen, chatting together when one of them remarked something to the effect, 'One of these days, you'll look out at this whole terrazzo, and there'll be nothing but niggers from end to end.' That's close to what the cadet said. I immediately stopped them all as a group, put 'em up against the wall [in a brace], and gave them a short talk along the same lines that Jimmy Love would have delivered had he been there. We just didn't tolerate that there."

Lindsey reported the class included 468 men who went to flight training—430 as pilots and 38 as navigators. Another twelve went to medical school and served as flight surgeons. Nearly half would serve more than twenty years on active duty.

After graduation, Jimmy Love first worked as a space system surveillance officer at the Space Defense Center in Colorado and later at Shemya, AK. He worked on a global sensor network to monitor United States and international missile launches and orbits. His initial assignment in Colorado conveniently kept him close to his Alma Mater. He was also able to rekindle a relationship with a young lady who was eventually to become his wife. During junior year, they had attended a dance with other partners but were introduced and knew each other casually. Beryl Elizabeth Cook was the daughter of Ann and Edsel Cook, a senior U.S. Army NCO who was assigned to nearby Fort Carson. Becky and Jimmy began dating right after graduation, and the relationship flourished. They were married in the Air Force Academy Chapel on February 1, 1970.

During his second assignment in Alaska, Jimmy recalled reading Air Force newsletters that referred to newly emerging personnel policies, which the military called "Social Actions." It occurred to the young First Lieutenant that this might be a field worth pursuing, so he volunteered for additional duty. Social Actions included human relations training and counseling for drug and alcohol abuse. It was also the department that reviewed and worked on complaints about discrimination.

"I had originally thought I would only stay in the Air Force for my five years' commitment," Jimmy reported. "But I kept getting these great assignments that were challenging and interesting. I loved the work that I was doing."

After Alaska, he and Becky moved to Cleveland, OH, where Jimmy was chief of the recruiting support branch. He directed administration, personnel, supply, real estate, transportation, and communication services for 57 recruiters in northern Ohio. Next they moved to his father's home state and Jimmy's first assignment in the burgeoning field of Equal Employment Opportunity. Called EEO in the civilian world, it was Military Employment Opportunity or MEO within the military. The U.S. military made the simple distinction that Equal Employment Opportunity applied to civil servant employees and Military Equal Opportunity (MEO) applied to military personnel in uniform.

In 1974, just five years out of the Air Force Academy, Captain Love was named MEO officer for Little Rock AFB in Jacksonville, AR. He resolved race, ethnic, gender, and sexual harassment complaints through formal investigation. He was also chosen by the Air Staff at Air Force headquarters to develop and conduct problem-solving workshops and seminars. As a Human Relations Group Facilitator for two years, he developed and taught a range of programs in human relations while advising senior officials on their status.

He was a front-line pioneer in the relatively new world of MEO, which was receiving support at the time all the way from the top. General David C. Jones, who was Air Force chief of staff from 1974 to 1978, was a major proponent. His chief of chaplains, Father Henry J. Meade, reported later that Jones "was particularly interested in minorities." "He introduced human relations programs in the Pentagon to address racial issues and demanded that all attend . . . Jones wanted impediments to minorities halted" (Puryear 2000, 251).

The Air Force recognized Jimmy's unique abilities in the new MEO field and sent him to the Air Force Military Personnel Center in Universal City, TX, in 1978. As the Center's Chief of Human Relations and Equal Opportunity, he analyzed affirmative action plans and results, chaired committees that updated the Air Force Affirmative Action Plan, developed a complaint-processing manual, and continued to consult for higher headquarters.

That assignment brought Jimmy Love almost full cycle back to his days at the Air Force Academy when he was named an Academy faculty recruiter in 1981. He screened all applicants to help determine Air Force staffing at all three military academies. The three schools support an officer exchange program to give cadets a broad range of exposures to the other military services. For example, the Air Force Academy staff includes several from the Army, Navy, and Marine Corps, including faculty members and a USMC Major who serves as an Air Office Commanding (AOC) for one of the Air Force Academy's forty cadet squadrons. Each of the officers is a very visible representative of his or her service during this special duty assignment. Unlike the exchange of cadets among students who study for one brief semester at another academy, officer staff assignments include a limited number of positions for a year or more. They are controlled by the individual services and their personnel departments who are controlled by people like Jimmy Love.

When Jimmy concluded his faculty recruiting assignment, the man who had graduated last in his Class of 1969 was chosen to attend the prestigious Air Command and Staff School (AC&S) of Air University at Montgomery AFB, AL. Without the distractions of basketball and youth, he graduated from AC&S with academic distinction in 1984. Then Major Love was assigned to Europe as Director of Personnel (Human Resources) for the Headquarters of Allied Forces Central Europe in the Netherlands. He was responsible for the personnel administration and information management programs, supply services, training, and financial services needed to support one thousand Air Force employees in the Netherlands.

Major James Love, USAF

Jimmy, Becky, and Gregg at a basketball game

That assignment was followed by a move to the Royal Air Force Base at Mildenhall, in England, where Jimmy became deputy group or base Commander. As the Assistant City Manager and later as Mission Support Commander for a community of eleven thousand people, he directed human resources, civil engineering, law enforcement, security, disaster preparedness, education and training, information management, family support, and morale and welfare services. Mildenhall was a major staging and gateway base for KC-135 tankers and C-130 transports and other aircraft and crews stationed temporarily in Europe. Finally, in 1990, the family returned to the USA and an assignment at the Pentagon. Then Lt.Col. Love was named Acting Director, Military Equal Opportunity at Air Force headquarters. He monitored and developed equal opportunity policy for three million employees in the Department of Defense. He analyzed trends and formed corrective actions. And he exercised oversight of all the Air Force's equal opportunity programs.

Although some observers might indicate that he was ideally suited for the job, Jimmy was quick to point out that MEO is a career area peopled with all types of individuals. One of his first bosses at the Pentagon was an Air Force Colonel named Robert Brady who was a pioneer in the field of MEO. He is white. "No one questioned Brady's sincere interest or his qualifications, and I think that's important," Jimmy said. "Sometimes we have a tendency to look for very specific credentials when we staff certain jobs. We can carry that a little bit overboard, especially when we're dealing with minorities or women. We think we need to have a woman or a minority in the job. I don't think that's necessarily the case. I believe you must look at the quality of the individual." That's an experienced human resources executive speaking, practicing what he preaches. He was also the product of a family and school environment that recognized opportunity and took advantage of it. "My father always said, 'Nobody can ride your back if you're standing up,'" Jimmy recalled. "Those kinds of teachings for me came through a prism of skin color. I learned to take what you have and try to work with it."

Like all other matters of public policy, MEO and EEO in the U.S. government reflect the will and wishes of the president and his political appointees who assume senior positions in his administration. The Department of Defense is no exception. Jimmy's first assignment in the Pentagon introduced him to the subtle emphasis that can make the difference between robust, active MEO and EEO programs and passive ones that merely meet minimum requirements. For example, the latter would assess results of military promotion boards and analyze data to indicate if minorities were being promoted at the same pace as the majority. Fortunately, Jimmy worked for an experienced MEO executive who was legendary, Claiborne D. Haughton Jr. Successfully overcoming numerous physical and family handicaps, Haughton achieved a senior executive position to direct proactive policies and practices, which fully endorsed MEO principles.

Jimmy and his colleagues were able to produce significant programs that promoted minorities and women. These included a series of recruiting brochures: *African-Americans for America's Defense, Hispanics for American's Defense*, and *Women for America's Defense*.

"We were able to publish these booklets, which included a chronology of contributions by different groups, as recruiting tools," Jimmy said. "We distributed them to schools, libraries, and military recruiters. The Government Printing Office even sold them. These publications had a significant impact on the street to support recruiting."

After nearly thirty years in uniform, Jimmy retired from active duty in the Air Force on September 30, 1993, as part of a selective early-retirement program. He linked up with an entrepreneur friend in a startup consulting business. He led a team of investigators, trainers, and mediators to assist discrimination complaints stemming from government regulations concerning disabilities, equal pay, and age discrimination. Meanwhile, his old job in the Pentagon was converted from a military position to a civilian as the Defense Department tried to provide some continuity to the function. So after a year in the private sector, government service beckoned once again.

Jimmy returned to the Pentagon in 1994 as the Defense Department's Deputy Director, Military Equal Opportunity. He served on Defense Department staffs of Richard B. Cheney, Les Aspin, William J. Perry, William S. Cohen, and Donald H. Rumsfeld during the administrations of Presidents George H. Bush, William J. Clinton, and George W. Bush. He developed and monitored Equal Employment Opportunity policy for

3.2 million DOD employees. These responsibilities included analyzing affirmative action trends and recommendations for the Defense Equal Opportunity Council, the senior advisors to the Secretary of Defense on training matters, complaint processing, women and minority representation issues, and sexual harassment. He has planned and organized annual Department of Defense participation in conferences, special observances, and national forums from groups ranging from the National Association for the Advancement of Colored People to the famed U.S. Army Air Corps group, the Tuskegee Airmen.

Equal Opportunity is a topic that often leads to conflicting points of view with many opinions concerning issues of quotas and fairness. Jimmy reported that he and his Defense Department colleagues use more facts and figures and hard data to understand what has happened and to predict where the military and civilian sectors are heading. "We've got a lot of perceptions and anecdotes regarding progress and lack of progress, but the facts help us separate fiction from reality," he said. He and his team conducted the landmark 1995 Sexual Harassment Survey of 76,000 men and women in uniform. A year later, they conducted a similar study concerning MEO relationships, attitudes, and experience. "These surveys told us quite a bit about the perceptions of the military forces," he said. "Today, if folks want to understand what's happening on these issues, we can produce trend lines to analyze so that actions can be taken as appropriate. These are very powerful tools at work in our ability to effectively manage the human resources available to us."

As they celebrate more than thirty-eight years together, Jimmy and Becky Love combine professional careers with raising a family successfully. Becky runs the training program for the National Protection and Programs Department for Homeland Security in Washington DC. The Loves produced three daughters, and Jimmy said their success is his proudest achievement. Their oldest, Jhvoir, is married to Army Sergeant Terrence Hollis and assists a veterinarian in Newport News, VA. They have two sons, Dajhi and Terrence. Second daughter, Niambi, works as a government background investigator in Orlando, FL, with her husband, Oscar Blodgett, a former *Washington Post* accountant who owns and manages a youth football league in Brevard County. They also have two sons, Marcus Trevian and Kobi Arend. The youngest daughter, Brioni, works in Quality Assurance for Wells Fargo in Phoenix, AZ, and married Michael Mudler there in 2007. Becky also has five siblings; and the families keep in touch frequently via trips, telephone, and e-mail.

In the early part of the 21st Century, Jimmy continued to work hard for the rights of others. And in 2004, his efforts received special recognition from one of the premier Civil Rights organizations, the NAACP. The

National Association for the Advancement of Colored People presented Jimmy the Benjamin L. Hooks Distinguished Service Award to recognize his efforts on behalf of members of the military in his role as acting director for military equal opportunity, Office of the Deputy Undersecretary of Defense for Equal Opportunity.

Jimmy said that he was surprised to receive the award, saying, "I've only done what I think we all do, and that's my job! And I love doing it. I'm humbled because of the company of people who have received this award before me." When he accepted the Award, he modestly added, "I have heard many acceptance speeches, but what I remember most are two words—'thank you.'"

Looking back at his Air Force Academy experience, Jimmy said he learned a lot about himself. "I learned the value of perseverance and the value of working with a team," he reported. "You learn you can do things either as you push yourself or others push and pull you up. I wouldn't trade that experience for anything. And the relationships that developed are lifelong connections to a super group of people," he concluded.

Chapter 10

The Historic Sailor

Charles Todd Creekman Jr. USNA '69

Todd Creekman's love of history, combined with strong Navy family roots, led him to Annapolis and a thirty-year career in the U.S. Navy. When he was a young boy, he heard lots of military and sea stories from many members of his family. As a result, he was always interested in details of the past. Then he lived through modern history during his Naval career. So after he retired from the Navy, he became Executive Director of the Naval Historical Foundation. However, although his heritage and Naval history were important parts of his life, Todd Creekman never took a single academic history course while at the Naval Academy where he graduated first in his Class of 1969.

Many of Todd's ancestors wore military uniforms. His grandfather, James Lemuel, enlisted in the U.S. Navy in 1913. He worked his way up through the ranks as a Chief Petty Officer and was commissioned from the ranks as a "mustang." That's the term used to describe officers commissioned after prior enlisted service. James served on the battleship USS *Nebraska* before World War I and spent his 34-year career in the supply field. He retired as a Lieutenant Commander after World War II. Along the way, he met Mildred Todd ashore in Norfolk, VA. They married and had three sons. The oldest was James, who spent 28 years in the U.S. Army and retired as a Colonel in 1970. The youngest, David, retired as a U.S. Air Force Colonel in 1978 after a 27-year career. The second son, Charles Todd Sr., known as Chuck, enlisted in the U.S. Navy just before World War II. He rose to storekeeper first class and qualified for the Navy's V-12 commissioning program. He went to the University of

Minnesota and became an Ensign in October of 1945. He met Virginia "Ginny" Chapman from Minneapolis, and they were married on February 22, 1946.

Their son, the historian Todd Junior, was born on October 23, 1947, in the Naval Hospital in Portsmouth, VA. His sister, Laura Lee Creekman, who arrived three years later, eventually became a teacher in Lynden, WA. Todd and Laura's father was a naval aviation supply officer who served on aircraft carriers USS *Coral Sea* and USS *Enterprise*. Chuck Creekman retired from the U.S. Navy as a Captain in 1970, a year after watching his son become the newest military officer in the clan.

Like most military families, the Creekmans moved around with assignments ranging from Virginia to Hawaii to Tennessee. They were also assigned to Canada where Todd's Dad was an exchange officer with the Canadian Navy in Montreal. Eventually, the Creekmans settled back in the Tidewater section of Virginia when Todd Junior was a sophomore in high school. After a couple of years in the Quebec Province, the new tenth grader's French language skills were *tres excellent*. That helped him fit right in for his three years at the then-new Frank W. Cox High School in Virginia Beach. He was part of its first graduating class where his strong academics led Todd to graduate near the top of that class of 500 students in June 1965. He was accepted by two top schools, the University of Virginia and Duke University.

But the subconscious influence of his father, uncles, and grandfather attracted him to the military. Those attractions, combined with some pleasant experiences during excursions on his father's ships at sea, lured him to the Naval Academy. He recalled having visited the school when he was younger but doesn't remember too much about it. But he does remember that he always loved the sea and history, especially military history.

"I went to the Naval Academy pretty much idealistic and blind to all of its nuances," Todd recalled. "On the night before I was due to report, my folks and I stayed with some of their Navy friends in Annapolis. I remember being dropped off at the main gate to begin my adventure. Almost immediately, the upperclassmen kept us so busy so quickly that I didn't have a chance to react. I just recall the stress and tension right from the beginning, and that it lasted for all four years. I remember we were continually under observation and required to try to be perfect in respect of bearing, deportment, uniform, and performance in every way: academic, military, and athletic. I guess I reacted OK because we quickly became part of a team with the plebes rallying around each other," he continued. "Everybody got into trouble since, by definition, you screwed up regularly. But you did the best you could while trying to help others. I remember pride in being there and a determination to do well. There's something to be said about *stick-to-it-ive-ness*. It was not a laid-back, joyous experience, that's for sure." Unlike many other graduates, Todd said he doesn't recall a time when he wanted to leave.

A dark-haired, long-legged, skinny guy who had less than 150 pounds on a six-foot frame, Todd said he was not particularly athletic; and that posed some challenges for him as a plebe. "Running was not a problem," he said, "but other athletics like swimming gave me fits." Midshipmen and other Navy folks spend considerable amounts of time swimming, preparing for emergencies in the water. Todd spent a lot of time learning how to swim throughout his plebe summer. His friends recalled teasing him about the Naval Academy's tests in the 1960s that included practice jumps off a 20-foot tower into a pool, fully clothed, to simulate abandoning ship. Midshipmen learned how to convert their clothing into floating life preservers and were required to swim a mile. His friends recalled that Todd was a regular member of the "swimming subsquad," a form of detention for swimmers who couldn't quite keep up with the others. "Yes, I spent hours and hours in daily practice," Todd admitted, "but by the time I was a Firstie, I think I was getting a B in swimming because they made you swim a lot."

On dry land, he found out that he was coordinated enough to shoot straight. He scored expert on the firing range. That led him to try out for the Academy's pistol team, where he was very successful in competitive matches and earned Second Team All-American status. Later he recorded expert with both the M-1 rifle and the .45 pistol.

Academically, he started out majoring in French, building on his *Quebecois* experience and high school prowess. However, he switched to engineering when he realized that he was good at it. "I thought it might have more utility for a naval career!" he exclaimed later. He kept up his French and was able to use the language to good advantage throughout his career. He also remembered that he never had a course grade of less than the coveted A, but high class rank was not his goal. "My goal was to get on the Dean's List," he recalled. "With a star on your collar and extra visibility, that might lead to some extra privileges. I wanted to excel," he continued, "because it was something I could do well."

He was a member of the First Company with several upperclassmen who were doing very well academically, and he remembered that they set a good example for high standards. "People were helping me with my athletics, and I was helping others with their academics," he recalled. However, he said he had "no idea" of that help's significance until a class reunion more than thirty years later when a classmate reminded him that he would have flunked out without Todd's help. "Evidently, I tutored him in math, and that helped him. I just don't remember it! Funny how teamwork works," he mused. He was also part of a group of classmates who ranked near the top in their class. "I don't remember competition among us, and eventually our military rank would figure in the mix, so I really didn't know I was going to end up in the top spot until my senior year," he explained.

Todd roomed with two classmates for most of his time at the Naval Academy and remained in frequent contact with both of them nearly four decades later. Each one added his own perspective on their friend, the historic sailor. Tennessean Pem Cooley said Todd was "the one who comes to mind who said he was going to make a career of the Navy." New Yorker Brad Beall called Todd "one of the smartest guys I ever met." He added, "Many of the smart people you meet have egos to match. That amazing thing about Todd is that there is no arrogance or superiority." Pem served in submarines and went to divinity school after postgraduate studies at Georgia Tech. A Presbyterian minister in Atlanta, GA, Pem remarked, "Todd looked at things the way they were supposed to happen at the Academy. He would say, 'Let's do it together, and let's have fun doing it.'" Pem, who ranked 55th in the class, was also a mechanical engineer; so he shared many classes with his roommate.

Brad was an economics major who said he struggled with engineering courses. He graduated 331st in the class and went to law school after serving on destroyers, including Vietnam combat duty. He eventually became a lawyer and later worked in the general counsel's office of the Defense Department's Medical School in Bethesda, MD. Brad recalled having to leave their room to study since so many classmates would visit Todd for advice, which he freely dispensed. "I used to study in the library because there were so many guys coming to our room for extra help," he added with a chuckle.

"One evening," Brad remembered, "I asked Todd for the formula for a specific math problem. He replied that I should not try to *memorize* it but rather to *learn* it." Brad said his response of "memorization was how I pass" led Todd to a three-page explanation that *derived* the formula in question. "Todd didn't memorize, he *derived* it," Brad said with a bit of awe.

Both roommates remembered that Todd's best times at the academy were during exams. "He loved final exams," Brad recalled. Pem added, "He didn't have much to do except help us." Brad added, "Todd *remembered* what he read the *first* time. Getting ready for exams was truly review for him. At ten PM, he would turn out the lights, saying, 'I've got to get a good night's sleep!'" Brad said he and Pem used penlights to read after lights-out.

Brad said that Todd's only problem at the Naval Academy was that he *always* followed the rules, sometimes to the extreme. "I was not exactly a full-time rule follower," Brad admitted. That led to a classic roommate conflict. Dormitory rooms at all of the academies are neat and tidy, in inspection order, virtually all the time. In the late 1960s at the Naval Academy, roommates would determine each day who was the ICOR (pronounced "eye-core"), the person In Charge of the Room. That designation enabled inspectors to determine who was responsible for tidiness when roommates were absent.

Brad explained that, by their final year, most Firsties were "cut some slack" in the room inspection world. "However," he explained, "Todd wasn't buying into the upper-class privilege. We knew that our rooms were only going to be inspected every two or three weeks." He explained, "So there was no reason to go that extra mile each day in making beds properly and all the other finer points for a room inspection when you could estimate the time for the next inspection. But Todd wasn't buying it.

"Finally, it reached the stage where he wanted to fix up the room, and I wanted to let it go with the minimum, and we had a pretty fair argument," Brad recalled. "Brad," Todd said, "*I'm* ICOR, and *you've* got to make up your bed better than just covering up the top of it." Brad said he finally went to the sign on the door and flipped over the ICOR. "'There!' I said firmly. 'Now I'm in charge of the room!' He said then, 'But you can't do that! It's *my* turn!' So I gave him two choices. One, I'm in charge of the room. Or two, you're in charge, and I'm not making the bed. Either way, I'm not making the bed. Clearly, this was almost a dilemma for him." Brad laughed more than thirty years later. "Todd is absolutely unflappable. By the way," Brad concluded, "we were never put on report."

Both Pem and Brad recalled that Todd never mentioned history during his academy years, but neither of them was surprised at his second career. "I believe his family's heritage had a lot to do with his love of Naval History," Brad concluded.

While Todd was moving smoothly through his four years of mechanical engineering studies at the Naval Academy, he discovered, during his summer cruises, that he also loved going to sea. Although many of the Naval Academy's top students were encouraged to pick nuclear-powered submarines or aviation, Todd wanted to serve on board surface ships. So he chose destroyer duty on service selection day. He remembered that choosing a "surface line" job also came with sixty days' leave as an added incentive. He was selected as a Trident Scholar, and his independent study project reflected the complexity of his studies. Titled *Morphology and Kinetics of Precipitation in Ternary Cobalt-Base Alloys*, Todd's material science project explored the effects of adding cobalt to steel alloys. At the top of his class, he was offered a Churchill Scholarship for graduate school in the United Kingdom. But the lure of sea convinced him to postpone his studies.

Todd was the first of his 865 classmates to walk across the graduation stage that sunny June 4, 1969, on what he called an absolutely glorious day. Graduation speaker Secretary of the Navy John Chafee urged the graduates to help win the war in Vietnam. Up in the stands at Memorial Stadium, Todd's parents, Chuck and Ginny Creekman, found themselves sitting next to O'Dell and Virginia Red of Lafayette, LA. Their son was Richard Preston Red, a former Marine enlisted infantryman who had entered the Naval Academy as one of eighty-five former Navy seamen and Marines through an appointment from the Secretary of the Navy Paul Nitze. He had graduated from the Naval Academy Preparatory School at Bainbridge, MD, in 1964, and was the last man in that class to be accepted by the Naval Academy for its Class of 1968. Academic issues at Annapolis led him to repeat a year to become the last member of the class to turn back to the Class of 1969. Richard had combined his studies with varsity sports, playing tackle on a successful Naval Academy football team with a record of five wins, four losses, and a tie during the 1968 season. "When I came back from final leave ten days before graduation, I found out that I was going to be the anchorman," Richard recalled. "It was nothing I aspired to," he added simply.

On graduation day, the crowd roared in special recognition of the man who was last in the class. More than thirty-five years later, Richard would relate the story of how his father told him that Chuck Creekman turned to the Reds on graduation day and said, "Twenty years from now, *everybody* will remember your son, and no one will remember *my* son."

His classmates certainly appreciated Richard's position, dutifully contributing 864 one-dollar bills that a friend, who was roommate, collected in a pillowcase for the Class of '69's anchorman. "What did you do with the money?" I asked. "I had one *great* party that evening," he laughed in reply. "And thankfully, my parents helped me hang on to most of it." Then he added very thoughtfully, "It was a terrible thing that the guy ahead of me got nothing, and the guy behind me didn't get to graduate."

Richard returned to the Marine Corps and learned how to fly Boeing CH-46 Sea Knight helicopters. He proved the adage that "timing is everything in life" when asked about duty in the Vietnam War. "Just missed it," he said quietly. He completed his military service in 1981 and moved to southern Louisiana. There he worked in the oil-and-gas business in mineral leasing, pipeline right-of-ways, and seismic testing. When I caught up with him in 2004, Richard said he was "mostly retired but battling cancer with surgery for a carcinoma and the beginnings of intensive radiation treatment." Then he said directly, "I've got a real good oncologist and a lot of confidence in him with a real positive outlook on my future." He concluded our first conversation by saying, "I can't tell you how much support I've gotten in calls and e-mails from my classmates. That means so much to me. It really helps." A few months later, he reported in an e-mail, "Thanks be to the Lord, plus the prayers and support from so many of you and the expert care of a professional medical team. I am cancer free!" Then he added comments about his plans to connect with classmates at reunions and the Army-Navy game that illustrate the special bonds that many of these grads have with each other. Sadly, Richard's cancer returned and he passed away in 2008.

Todd Creekman's Mother and sister pinned on his Ensign bars as his justifiably proud Father beamed on that 1969 graduation day. He received a Bachelor of Science degree in Mechanical Engineering and accepted the prestigious Burke Scholarship that offered two years of sea duty followed by two years of graduate school. Since most new Ensigns assigned to the fleet spent their first three years at sea, Todd rushed to learn as much as he could in the shorter time period. "I was very fortunate," he explained, "because my first assignment provided the full spectrum of experiences from standing watches to many that involved other sea-going tasks."

He also tasted an immediate abundance of genuine Naval history firsthand. Todd's initial sea duty was first lieutenant for a relatively new destroyer, USS *Hoel* (DDG-13), a 437-foot guided-missile destroyer based in San Diego. It was headed for the war in Southeast Asia with a crew of 24 officers and 331 enlisted men. "Hole" or "Hoe-Well," as some people pronounced it, was the second U.S. Navy vessel by that name. The first one had been sunk by Japanese naval action during World War II. On Todd's first cruise in 1969, he and his crew left the West Coast and passed over the spot where the first ship had been sunk in combat 25 years earlier. "We were en route to another war in the Pacific but took time out to lay a wreath on the sea to mark the memory of those sailors lost in the first *Hoel*," he recalled. *Hoel* also crossed the equator, a special event always full of pomp and tradition. Next they sailed to New Zealand to help celebrate the two hundredth anniversary of the discovery of that country by Captain Cook. "It was almost a paradise, very friendly and intriguing," he recalled. "We enjoyed a series of visits to a couple of ports and then stopped in Australia before heading off to war," he reported. The first tastes of New Zealand whet his appetite for a return visit later in his career.

Todd enjoyed the Z-Gram regulations.

Lt. Creekman radioed his position.

Soon after the pleasantries of history and diplomatic protocol, the new ensign was part of *Hoel's* crew that began fire missions supporting U.S. Marines and U.S. Army soldiers fighting ashore as part of the Vietnam War. "We were in the war, but we were fortunate since we didn't take any incoming fire," he explained. *Hoel* provided gunfire support with five-inch guns and also plane guarding as they escorted the carriers that were launching the aircraft that were flying in their task force. "Plane guarding was a fairly boring operation until an emergency developed," Todd recalled. The war came home to the young Lieutenant JG and his crewmates when a Navy A-6 fighter-bomber returned from a mission over Vietnam and crashed, killing both crew members. *Hoel's* rescue boat crew, including Todd, watched helplessly as two empty helmets floated to the surface.

Todd wanted to learn more about the gunfire support mission, which he thought was an unworldly experience. "You're sitting there on the ship, a couple of miles offshore, listening to calls for fire support from the troops on the ground," he explained. "You're firing this way and that at their command far away." Many of the rounds fired by the *Hoel* went four or five miles to their targets, and the distance and terrain obscured their destruction from Todd and his shipmates. To learn more about the mission, Todd went down below decks to the magazines and loaded five-inch rounds in the drums. Then he moved up to the gun mount and watched while it was automatically shooting. Next he went to the gun plot where they were taking the commands and pulling the trigger. Finally, he revisited the Combat Information Center where he and the others would plot targets. "I went through the whole process to get the full picture because here, we were fighting a war and engaging in combat, but it was kind of one-sided combat, and I wanted to experience it as much as I could."

He remembered one call for a fire mission in the middle of the night that almost proved disastrous. The ship was supporting a combat harassment-and-interdiction mission when a faulty projectile "blew off the end of our gun barrel," he said calmly. "One of the gun crew guys fired off a round and said it didn't feel quite right to him, so he opened the door to the gun mount, and he could see light coming through the deck below. The shell had exploded in the gun barrel. Fortunately, the blast pattern was out and down. Some of the shrapnel penetrated down two decks, through the berthing compartment right below, where some of my sailors were sleeping. The errant shell actually sliced right between racks and through the shower in the head," he continued. "Luckily, the only injury was a slight nick on the leg of one of our sailors. But it reminded us how dangerous firing was."

Todd remembered his first two Pacific Cruises as great training grounds as a chief bosun's mate and others took over his education. "We learned how to steam independently and form up with other ships," he said. He also served as a Combat Information Center Watch Officer, Junior Officer of the Deck, and then Officer of the Deck. Like all apprentices, he learned from his mistakes. "One day, we arrived in American Samoa to refuel, and I really screwed up," he remembered. "I was aft [in the back] and we were trying to handle the mooring lines, but we didn't do it quickly enough so we managed to wrap a mooring line around our propeller. This was not good," he recalled sheepishly. "We sent divers down to clear the line, and then I was reprimanded by Captain Paul Asmus. He chewed me out better than anyone ever did in my life. Then he put me in hack, and it was not a pleasant time. That meant you could not go ashore, and you were basically confined to the ship."

After cramming three years of sea-duty learning into two years, Todd returned to the classroom on land. He took his scholarship to Atlanta to the Georgia Institute of Technology and discovered that his Naval Academy math and engineering skills had not rusted from two years at sea. He found Georgia Tech to be "comfortable and conservative" despite antiestablishment turmoil that was complicating matters for the military on many campuses at the time. "The Georgia Tech students were so conservative that, when a Hare Krishna group would show up with their tambourines and hands out for contributions, the *students* would run 'em off campus," Todd laughed. He also found the academic load of 12 to 15 semester hours per week a respite from the 18 to 21 hours he had experienced in Annapolis. "It was a pretty good setup, and I even managed some good grades," he recalled fondly. "And for a complete change of pace, I even met the girl of my dreams!" he exclaimed.

She was a Delta Air Lines stewardess (flight attendant) whom Todd described as blonde, petite and soft-spoken, lovely and charming. Deborah Carole Adams had come to the big city of Atlanta from a small town in Western Georgia called, ironically, West Point. After a traditional courtship and proper family introductions, the couple was married on September 9, 1972. Todd may be the only Annapolis graduate to have married in a West Point Church. It was the Presbyterian Church of West Point, GA. After a week's honeymoon in Jamaica, helped by Debbie's Delta connections, the newlyweds settled back in Atlanta as Todd completed his master's degree. Their early married life followed the familiar pattern of travels to exotic ports as Debbie joined the legions of Navy wives reuniting with husbands in far-off lands. They remembered two special trips to the Mediterranean Sea with vacations in Palma, Majorca, and Naples, Italy. "These were major excursions in those days as the wives and families organized charter flights to meet up with the ship's crews overseas," Todd reported. "Of course, sometimes they went to all that trouble and expense, and the ship would be diverted while the families waited in ports like Hong Kong, so the reunions were extra-special when they actually happened."

The Creekmans would eventually have three daughters. Amanda Elizabeth was born in 1978 and followed her father's love of history to the College of William & Mary, where she graduated and later married a fellow historian, Justin Isaac. In 2005, they produced the Creekman's first grandchild, Thomas Aubrey. Jennifer Carole, who was born in 1981, also attended William & Mary. She married Salvador Bezos in 2004. Their third daughter, Caroline Louise, who was born in 1988, went to the Culinary Institute of America in Hyde Park, NY, to pursue a degree in baking and pastry arts.

Todd remembered that Caroline's birth coincided with his command of the frigate USS *W. S. Sims* (FF-1059) in Mayport, FL, when Dad was forty. "It was interesting being the old man [Captain] and coming aboard the ship with a new baby. It gave the sailors a different perspective of the boss."

Although his academic prowess led to the offer of PhD studies, Todd was eager to get back to sea. So he took his 1973 master's degree in Mechanical Engineering from Georgia Tech and returned to active duty. He was named the first Weapons Officer for the new USS *Moinester* (FF-1097) in Norfolk, VA. *Moinester* was a destroyer escort, later called a frigate, under construction in Norfolk, VA. "We were with the ship as it was being built and became "plank owners,"[15] the Navy's label for the original crew on a brand-new ship." Todd said the commissioning crew formed special bonds because each member was a new crew member charged with learning and performing his job on board but also setting the standard of operation for the new ship.

In 1976, *Moinester* deployed the new U.S. Navy antisubmarine warfare system tactical towed-array sonar to the Mediterranean for the first time. The ship's towed-array sonar included a series of complex underwater microphones that could detect and track submarines of the Soviet Union during the frequent "cat and mouse" games of the Cold War in the Mediterranean Sea. He saw face-to-face confrontations between the USSR (Union of Soviet Socialists Republics) submarines and the U.S. frigates, including one collision that resulted from a Soviet sub's attempts to figure out how the U.S. ships were always nearby when it surfaced.

As Weapons Officer, Todd was responsible for the ship's firepower, including the five-inch .54-caliber gun, the torpedoes, and an antisubmarine rocket launcher (ASROC). Sheepishly, he remembered a training exercise in Cuba at the Guantanamo Naval Base where he was *almost* involved in an international incident of historical proportions. "We were shooting seaward [*away* from Cuba] at an aerial target that was being towed," he explained softly. "We had ceased firing when the target continued moving inbound toward the island. All of a sudden, the gun started up again and continued to track the target, firing at it

---

[15]   The term refers to the practice, on older ships with wooden decks, to cut up excess pieces of boards from the decks and present them to the original crew as souvenirs. The Naval Historical Center is one of the organizations that maintains wood from old ships, labeled and stored for "plank owners" who surface from time to time looking for mementos, usually four-by-four-inch boards suitable for mounting on a plaque.

automatically! By now, Castro's Cuba was providing the backdrop for our target practice. Fortunately, our errant five-inch shell landed in the water although it might have been within the three-mile limit of Cuba." That shell landing in the warm sea put the young weapons officer in hot water for another chewing out by another Captain. Happily, no one on the Cuban side seemed to notice. After two years on the *Moinester*, Todd transferred to the staff of Destroyer Squadron 10 and served as a Staff Operations Officer for a second antisubmarine warfare deployment.

In the winter of 1978, the Creekmans moved to Newport, RI, for a year's study, at the Naval War College, focused on sea power strategies. He remembered sharing ideas with other U.S. Navy Lieutenant Commanders but again took no history courses per se.

A year later, Todd and Debbie and baby Amanda moved overseas to Auckland, New Zealand. Todd was the U.S. Navy's exchange officer with the Royal New Zealand Navy for two years, and he loved it. He worked as the Staff Antisubmarine Warfare Officer, serving alongside many New Zealanders who had been trained by the British Navy. And he viewed firsthand their respect for English traditions. One dramatically contrasted the New Zealanders' past with the Americans. Todd explained that, in 1979, sailors in the Royal New Zealand Navy still lined up each day at noon for rum rations. "As duty officer, several times I had to supervise as the sailors 'fronted up' to be served their 'tot' of rum," he recalled. "Also, during this time, the Prince of Wales, a Royal Navy Officer, married Diana at Buckingham Palace," he continued. "So we all took a break from our duties half a world away to gather around a silver punch bowl and toast the Prince and his new bride." That sense of history continued to influence Todd Creekman.

Returning to the USA in 1982, Todd was named Executive Officer of USS *Richard L. Page* (FFG-5), a frigate based in Norfolk, VA. He completed a deployment to the Persian Gulf during the Iran-Iraq War. "Our biggest enemy was the sand and the heat," he reported. "Sometimes the visibility from sand in the air was worse than fog," he explained. "The environment was very challenging there." He also wangled a side trip to Saudi Arabia as an exchange officer with the U.S. Air Force to observe airborne warning and control system (AWACS) operations. He managed to connect with Debbie's brother, then U.S. Air Force Sergeant Norman Adams.

More than a dozen years after graduation, Todd was finally posted to the Pentagon as a junior Commander. He was a Fleet Modernization Program Coordinator on the staff of the Deputy Chief of Naval Operations for Surface Warfare. Todd worked on the reactivation of battleships in the 1980s as once again history inserted itself in his career. Battleships, huge gun-firing platforms of an earlier Navy, were being transformed into modern fighting machines. "The blend of modern missile technology with almost-archaic ships was fascinating," he recalled. On the famed USS *Missouri* one day, he was crawling through the uptakes or smokestacks that served to exhaust burnt oil from its powerful boilers. "I discovered the *Missouri*'s honeycombed bomb deflectors left over from World War II attacks, and that gave me a better appreciation of what they faced during those days," he said.

Finally, in 1986, he received his first command, USS *W. S. Sims* (FF-1059)—a 438-foot, 3215-ton fast frigate based in Mayport, FL. For two and a half years, Todd took his 300-man ship literally around the world during a wide range of Cold War assignments. He remembered balancing the challenges of training exercises and engineering inspections with real-world surveillance of the Soviet Navy. The Navy's regular requirements for Basic Engineering Casualty Control Exercises were sometimes challenging. BECCE (pronounced "Becky") provided some white-knuckle times for Captain Creekman and his crew. "Once we were on station in the Aegean, among some nice Greek islands, watching an anchored Russian task group of a couple of cruisers and destroyers," he recalled. "We steamed past them, doing our regular monitoring, and then would begin our practice drill by shutting down our boilers and drift for a while before we relit the fires and steamed up again. None of this is automatic," he explained quickly, "it takes a while. We would be drifting for about an hour before we completed our exercises and got back into action," he continued. "Fortunately, my crew was good enough that we could do everything required for BECCE while still doing our monitoring." He proudly recalled another tour in the Caribbean Sea where the *Sims* successfully stopped drug runners. A nice liberty stop at the island of Saint Lucia also brought a smile. "Prince Charles was there for a celebration, and we were part of a Navy contingent that saluted them," he recalled.

Next he broadened his fleet experience with a formal introduction to aircraft carrier operations. He joined the staff of the Commander, Carrier Group Four in Norfolk, VA. Todd served as Surface Operations and NATO Exercises Officer from 1989 to 1991 and saw firsthand the workings of the brown-shoe Navy as Naval aviators are called. "Until then, my only experience with carriers had been plane guard duty and following carriers, dodging their garbage," he reported. "This assignment was very broadening, learning the language and culture of aviators."

Throughout his career, Todd had never had an assignment that directly applied his engineering education. That was to change when he joined a repair ship, the destroyer tender USS *Samuel Gompers* (AD-37), at the end of the Gulf War in July 1991. In retrospect, that could not have been better timing. He caught up with the *Gompers* in the Persian

Gulf, once again in the summer, as it was beginning to repair overworked ships that had been on duty throughout that conflict. Although based in Alameda, CA, the ship spent considerable time in the Middle East where its 1,200 crew members fixed ships that were tired and in need of repair. "One interesting part of this assignment was the male-female mix of the crew," Todd recalled. "We had about eight hundred men and four hundred women working on that ship, perhaps the most of any in the fleet," he said proudly. "Our ship's motto was "Service Supreme," but we had a slogan—"We fix 'em to fight!" And *that* was a strong indication of a customer service ethic that we all cherished."

Todd returned to the East Coast in 1993 for a three-year tour as Operations Officer and Chief of Staff for the Commandant, Naval District Washington. That assignment offered him more opportunities to witness history in the making since his organization provided administrative support for the Navy throughout metropolitan Washington DC. They provided considerable ceremonial, security, and legal support for the Navy in the nation's capital. In 1996, Todd was able to get a final assignment that brought him directly into the world of Naval history. He was named Deputy Director of the Naval Historical Center based in the Washington Navy Yard. It was frontline history, and he loved it. "History and heritage always intrigued me, and now I was working *on* it and *in* it every day," he reported. His office was upstairs from the Naval Historical Foundation whose Executive Director, retired Navy Captain Kenneth Coskey, was ready to step down from his second career. In July 1999, Todd retired from active military service and moved downstairs, eventually to succeed Coskey. Since 1926, the Foundation has supported naval heritage to preserve and promote naval history across a wide range of outreach programs. It could not have been a better match for the man and the job.

Both of his Naval Academy roommates were able to attend Todd's retirement ceremonies in Washington. The minister, Pem Cooley, recalled that big event included a significant spiritual dimension shared by the 150 guests. "Todd is a good guy, but never what we might call flashy about his faith," Pem reported. "However, at his retirement, he spoke about his family and shipmates and the other folks who were significant in his life," Pem continued. "He concluded by saying that his key shipmate was Jesus Christ." Pem explained that Todd had participated in a Bible study program called Disciple. "With Todd's encouragement, we were able to introduce that program successfully in our own church," he concluded.

The Annapolis Class of 1969, with a motto "'69 Is Mighty Fine," included 764 men who entered the Navy as Ensigns and 105 new Second Lieutenants in the U.S. Marine Corps. Five grads returned to their overseas countries, and five men were not commissioned due to medical restrictions.

Of the new Ensigns, the surface Navy claimed 31 percent while 18 percent went to nuclear power training (most then serve in submarines), and naval aviators comprised about 49 percent. The remaining two percent were commissioned in the restricted line communities such as Supply, Public Affairs, Civil and other Engineers, Intelligence, and Cryptology duty. Many classmates served in Southeast Asia during the Vietnam War. Eight were wounded and received the Purple Heart while one—Steve Hanvey of South Carolina, who ranked 159th—also received the Silver Star in Vietnam. Two men—Scott D. Ketchie from Alabama, who ranked 260th, and Californian Arnold Winfield Barden, who ranked 678th—were lost in combat in Vietnam.

Coloradoan John "Mike" M. Lounge, who was ranked ninth, received his astronaut wings in 1981 and flew three NASA missions, logging 482 hours in space. Several members served in command positions during the First Gulf War in 1990. James F. McGovern, who ranked 625th, was Acting Secretary of the Air Force briefly in 1998 and 1999. Venezuelan Tito M. Rincon, who was ranked 342nd, was Minister of Defense in his country from July 1997 to February 1999. The class included nine men who reached flag rank and three general officers.

When speaking about his second career, Todd said simply, "I love my job. We are five people full-time who are helped by a range of part-time volunteers, and each day, we connect interested citizens to yesterday's Navy." He described the joy of connecting individuals, often Navy veterans and their families, with the past. "We put on programs, we publish books, we support a lot of research," he explained. "These are all important functions. But it's the *personal* matters of history and heritage that mean a lot to the people who reach us, and," he added. "Many of those people and their ancestors made a difference in our history."

He told the story of a California woman who lost a very dear friend in World War II on a ship off the Normandy beaches. "She had always wondered about her friend. 'What had happened to him? Had his body been recovered?' With fragmentary information, we were able to reconstruct that, in fact, her friend had died and was buried in France. But his family moved his remains back to a cemetery in California. She was able to visit her long-lost friend's grave not far from where she lives."

Another call from the New Zealand embassy in Washington triggered a happier result. They had been contacted by a couple from New Zealand who had discovered a long-lost leather wallet when they opened up an old couch to refurbish it. The wallet contained an American Marine's identification card and photos of his family and friends. Todd and his colleagues were able to locate a U.S. Marine Corps veteran in the

Midwestern USA and return his long-lost wallet filled with memories more than fifty years later.

Not long ago, a World War II Japanese naval pilot in his eighties contacted the Foundation with a most unusual request. He wanted to connect with the surviving family of a U.S. Naval aviator who may have been the first man he shot down in combat over Iwo Jima in 1944. Again, with some fragmentary information, Todd was able to locate the man's brother and his nephew, who was also the dead pilot's namesake. "We would never know completely," Todd explained, "but the timing matched, and we could be sure at least that this man was killed that day."

Todd described a poignant meeting near the historic USS *Constitution* in Boston Harbor in the Summer of 2003. "Here we had a Japanese family, led by the pilot, and eight Americans, coming together to connect in peacetime almost sixty years after war." Todd said the Japanese pilot felt it was important to honor the memory of this fallen American. "To their credit, the American family took this tribute graciously in the manner it was extended, from one warrior to another." Todd concluded, "It's the safeguarding and the respect for the history and heritage and, if possible, that personal connection to the individuals who made up that history that we work on every day here."

The historic sailor had found his place.

Chapter 11

Public Service Continues

Charles R. Reed, USAFA '70

When I first caught up with Chuck Reed, he was the City Councilman representing 96,000 people in the Fourth District of San Jose, a booming metropolis of nearly one million Northern Californians. As one of ten members of the City Council, Chuck and his five-person staff dealt with budgets, goals, priorities, and strategic plans for San Jose. In November 2006, he was elected Mayor of San Jose, the tenth largest city in the USA.

These full-time duties cap a career of volunteer public service that began when he reported to the U.S. Air Force Academy in 1966. He later rose to command the 4,400-man Cadet Wing as the senior cadet officer in his USAFA Class of 1970 and graduated first in its Military Order of Merit. Twenty-seven years later, his daughter, Kim, achieved the same prominence in her USAFA Class of 1997. Her story appears in Chapter 19. Service academy historians believe their achievements are unique.

Charles Rufus Reed was the only son of Ambers Reed Jr. and Estelle Robinson of small towns outside Hattiesburg, MS. They moved to Southwestern Kansas during World War II and married in 1947. Chuck was the firstborn, arriving on August 6, 1948. His sister, Sandy, followed in 1950. She's a retired journalist nearby in Saratoga, CA. His other sister, Junette, was born in 1952 and died in a motorcycle accident while Chuck was at the academy. Chuck grew up knowing the value of hard work in the rural and flat Midwest, recalling his first job sweeping floors at the age of eight. Garden City High School served the local communities, and Chuck thrived there, earning mostly As and Bs in his class of 250 kids.

Introduced to public service and politics at an early age, he was a member of the Student Council in Kindergarten. A dozen years later, he was elected president of his high school class of 1966. He captained the Buffaloes football team where he punted and played defensive safety. In the winter, he was a six-foot, 160-pound forward on the state championship basketball team. Then he ran the mile on the Spring track team to stay in shape. Summers included American Legion baseball and odd jobs in construction in the town along the banks of the Arkansas River.

"I decided I wanted to go to the most challenging school that I could find and that we could afford to attend," Chuck recalled. "I was looking for a challenge, and the Air Force Academy offered all those opportunities." Although it was only a six-hour drive west from home, he actually saw it for the first time when he went there for his physical exam during his senior year. Then Congressman Bob Dole nominated him based upon the usual process of a local nominating committee's interviews. (Chapter 21 describes the academies' admissions processes.)

As a result of his sports conditioning, Chuck was in great shape when he arrived at the Air Force Academy on June 27, 1966, with 1,034 other men in the Class of 1970. "I won't say that I enjoyed BCT [Basic Cadet Training]," he reported later. "But I thrived. Physically, I was in great shape, so while it was challenging, it wasn't too bad for me. I was in good condition and highly motivated to succeed." When asked why, he responded, "I had decided I wanted to go to the Air Force Academy. It was my decision, and I had decided I was only going to do it once, and that I was only going to do it very well. I was in the process of proving to myself and finding out how far I could push myself, how far could I go, and how high could I jump. It was, for me, part of growing up. One of the reasons I chose the academy was that it looked like the toughest place in the country that I could afford to go to."

He did find the military confining however. "I didn't much like being a 'prisoner,' and the loss of freedom and liberty was tough to deal with at first. I remember I ran the assault and obstacle courses very comfortably. Mostly, I remember it was about running all the time." He was also thriving academically. He took "double overloads," or extra classes, and regularly stayed up until 2:00 AM studying. That was despite the fact that *Reveille* was always at 6:00 AM each day. "This was a process of learning and growing," he recalled. "I wouldn't want to do it again, but at the time, that was important to me."

Chuck's academic class rankings at the end of his first semester were near the top. He began classes as an Electrical Engineering major and then switched to Soviet studies. However, he took as an omen a lowly grade of C in Russian language studies and switched to International Affairs.

All the academies provide cadets and midshipmen with formal leadership training both inside and outside the classroom. West Point's Brigade of Cadets, the Naval Academy's Brigade of Midshipmen, and the Air Force Cadet Wing assign literally hundreds of positions to students to run their own organizations at all levels. Although the public might view these positions in special parades and formations, the student officers also manage specific duties designed to teach them about leadership and organizational behavior. Their duty assignments are 24/7, and they often lead to conflicts as the supervising cadets ask their peers to conform to their authority. Leadership assignments begin during the early days of Basic Cadet Training or Plebe Summer when new cadets and midshipmen become element or squad leaders, directly supervising a handful of peers. Responsibilities increase at every level up the organization. The top cadet or midshipman officer commands the entire student body with extra duties, responsibilities, and challenges.

When Chuck was a Two Degree Junior, the Commandant of Cadets named him the Wing Sergeant Major, the highest-ranking post for his class. A year later, he was named Wing Commander. Chuck said the best part of being Wing Commander was "the chance to lead and learn." The worst part, he explained, was "having a few thousand people upset with you every once in a while when you had to order them to do something they didn't want to."

In a story reminiscent of every school superintendent who makes the calls to close schools for a snow day off, the USAFA Wing Commander decides each weekday if the four-thousand-person Cadet Wing would form up and march to breakfast. "One day, I made the wrong choice at 0600 [6:00 AM] to march in formation to breakfast. Fifteen minutes later, we had bitter cold and snow, but it was too late to rescind the order. We were all freezing, so I just stood outside and watched everyone enter the dining hall. It was pretty obvious that I stood there to say, 'Here I am guys, I screwed up!'"

Finally, on graduation day, June 3, 1970, then Secretary of Defense Melvin R. Laird presented Chuck his diploma as the 16th man of 744 to cross the stage in Falcon Stadium. Eventually, he would record a GPA of 3.86 to achieve that class rank academically when his class graduated. His Military Point Average (MPA) and his high peer review led to his rank at the top in the Military Order of Merit, which combined the MPA and peer review.

Cadet Wing Commander
Charles R. Reed

San Jose Mayor Chuck Reed

    The first graduate to receive his diploma was Stephen J. Berta of Du Quoin, IL. Berta was one of 428 grads to enter pilot training and flew C-130s after he completed his MS in Aeronautical Engineering at Purdue University. He was killed in an aircraft accident near Nuremberg, Germany, in 1974. Last in the class was William R. Alexander of Trenton, OH. He flew C-130s at Dyess AFB, TX, and left the service in 1976. Later he flew a wide range of aircraft as a Captain for American Airlines.

    Class Scribe Richard S. Rauschkolb, who was ranked 228th in the class, called himself "a military brat who attended four different high schools and later had an unusual career." Dick, who was a tremendous help to me in the book's development, served in Thailand during the Vietnam War. He earned an MA degree in Middle East Studies at the Naval Postgraduate School and Defense Language Institute in Monterey, CA, and later taught at USAFA. He was Executive Officer to the Commander in Chief of the Pacific and Deputy Military Assistant to the Chairman of the Joint Chiefs of Staff, Admiral William J. Crowe Jr. He graduated from National War College in 1988 and became the Deputy Director of Admissions at the Academy. He served in Riyadh, Saudi Arabia, during the First Gulf War and retired as a Colonel in 1997 as Commander of the Air Force Historical Research Agency at Maxwell AFB, AL. During his 28-year career, Dick served on the Academy's Association of Graduates (AOG) Board of Directors. In 1999, he was named the AOG's Vice President of Communications.

The Class of 1970 motto is *Ense Petit Placidam* (By the Sword We Seek Peace). The class produced fourteen general officers led by USAF General Gregory S. Martin, who ranked 214th, who rose to be Commander of U.S. Air Forces Europe and Air Force Material Command. Lt.Gen. Timothy A. Kinnan, who ranked 97th, won the Risner Trophy as the Outstanding Fighter Pilot in the Air Force. George R. Keys Jr., ranked 56th, was one of the first African-Americans and one of three members of the class named Rhodes Scholars. He is a lawyer.

Dick proudly reported that the Class of 1970 has a reputation of supporting the Academy and cadets and had the highest number (66) of Sabre Society donors of any USAFA class. The Sabre Society includes donors who annually make unrestricted gifts of $1,000 or more to the Air Force Academy Fund.[16]

Dick recounted that their 1970 class also included 78 navigators, and that 317 members of the class stayed on active duty until retirement. More than 80 served in Reserve Components. Classmates received virtually every major military decoration, including the Air Force Cross awarded to Tilford Warren Harp, who ranked 151th, who retired as a Colonel in 1994. Others received five Defense Distinguished Service Medals, four Silver Stars, 193 Distinguished Flying Crosses, and 1,242 Air Medals. Thirteen Purple Hearts were awarded, and the class has nine members on the Academy's War Memorial that honors graduates who were killed in combat.

When Chuck Reed was in his third year at the academy, a mutual friend arranged a blind date for him with Paula Weeg of Rockford, IL. Paula was a sophomore at Loretto Heights College in Denver, studying to become a nurse. They dated for the next two years and were married in

---

[16]   Although they are tax-supported institutions, all three academies rely on contributions from alumni and other private funding sources. Private philanthropy provides major parts of new facilities and programs beyond government funding.

Rockford on June 6, 1970—the Saturday after Chuck's graduation. They honeymooned in a cabin on Lake Michigan.

Paula remembered when she first met Chuck that he was "tall, thin, and solid." When pressed for more details, she added with a chuckle, "With more hair than he has now." She described him as "serious and driven with an intensity about what he believed in." Then she suggested that he also had "a funny side and a very soft, sensitive side" as she recalled some poetry and paintings that Chuck produced in his youthful days. Today, she said, "He is very much the same. He's committed to what he is doing with a strong intensity and is very honest. He also still has that very funny side, especially when he's with our son."

After their honeymoon, the newlyweds moved farther east to New Jersey. Chuck switched out of uniform into civilian clothes to attend the School of Public and International Affairs at Princeton University on a Woodrow Wilson Fellowship. In what he laughingly called "a real hardship tour," Chuck studied public affairs and community programs. However, the tour would eventually redirect his life.

One of his projects was an internship at the United Community Center in Brooklyn, where he learned how to work in community organizations at the local level. The Center's director, Morris Eisenstein, profoundly affected the young graduate student. Chuck remembered vividly that Morris asked, "What kind of world do you want to live in?" And he answered with the statement, "*You* get to *chose* by what you do to affect what *kind* of community you live in." Chuck recalled thirty years later, "There's so much truth in that question and answer, and so much of it depends upon public service." Chuck received his Masters of Public Affairs from Princeton in 1972.

Paula and Chuck returned to military life when he became an official Air Force spokesman. He was named Information Officer for the 306th Bomb Wing at McCoy AFB in Orlando, FL.[17]

However, turmoil around racial issues in the early 1970s attracted him to the field of Social Actions as an Equal Opportunity Officer. He explained the move, "I thought I might be able to do some good in that field." And so he went back to school, albeit briefly. The Air Force sent him to social actions training at Lackland AFB, TX. There he learned about how society's race relations and drug abuse problems had moved into the military. He learned how to help military people and their bosses to deal with them. Unfortunately, when he returned to Orlando, one boss

---

[17]   The name of the since-deactivated Florida air force base survives in the three-letter symbol familiar to all who fly to the Magic Kingdom as MCO.

didn't want to hear the bad news. That led to some anxious moments for then-young Lieutenant Reed.

Chuck's headquarters had established a special communications loop, a chain of command authority that enabled Social Actions officers to report local problems to higher headquarters outside of the normal channels. Chuck had done an administrative investigation of a unit and concluded there was considerable discrimination by the commander. His message fell on deaf ears with that commander's local supervisor, so Chuck took his assessment to higher headquarters. When this information exchange was made known, the base commander "went ballistic," Chuck recalled. "He called me into his office and threatened to court martial me." Lieutenant Reed then went to the JAG's (Judge Advocate General) office for legal counsel and discovered that the JAG also *worked for* and *sided with* the commander. The commander was even more upset when he learned of that visit. In the final analysis, however, the chain of command worked successfully to solve the problem without repercussions for the messenger. It also gave Chuck considerable insight into the possibilities of his future profession as a lawyer.

Next Chuck moved overseas to Thailand during the Vietnam War as an Equal Opportunity Officer for the 17th Air Division at U-Tapao Air Base. "My job was to hang out with the troops to find out what was happening before it blew up into real trouble," he explained. "I had a pass to the NCO Club and regularly visited all the 'gin joints' off base at all hours, just trying to figure out how everyone was getting along. My boss was a one-star general who wanted to hear about problems before his colonels did. So I was out gathering intelligence from all the guys. If there were bad things happening, I thought I could find out about them in bars before they hit the base." Dressed in civvies, he would look into a bar and literally see racial polarization and anger right in front of him. It was visible in segregated establishments and Afro haircuts and special-brotherhood secret handshakes called the "dap." "We had big issues to keep people focused on loading bombs and making sure the aircraft were maintained," Chuck recalled. "So we worked on all the distractions during off-duty time to make sure they didn't interfere with getting the job done."

After six months in Thailand, Chuck was reunited with Paula and moved to Hawaii to work in Equal Opportunity at Hickam Air Force Base. Their daughter, Kim, was born there, arriving on their fifth wedding anniversary in 1975. However, despite the idyllic setting and second honeymoon with Paula, Chuck still chafed at the restrictions and uncertainty of future assignments that are part of being on active duty in the military. So, with the end of hostilities in Vietnam and subsequent staff reductions in the military, he took advantage of an early-out release program and left active duty.

By now, Chuck had decided to become a lawyer, so the Reeds moved to Menlo Park, CA, where Chuck entered law school at Stanford University. In 1978, he received his Juris Doctorate degree and took an internship in San Francisco in employment-related fields. He focused on sex and race discrimination cases, building upon his experience in the military. Meanwhile, Paula, who had completed her nursing studies, began working with cancer patients as the Reeds were growing accustomed to living in Northern California. She eventually became an oncology nurse and directs a clinic for a medical practice in Sunnyvale. Chuck described Paula's work. "It's a tough job. She works much harder and much longer than I do." Paula added, "I love working with people, and I am very happy to be able to do what I do."

As Chuck began practicing law, he quickly recognized the significant business benefits of networking through organizations like the local Chamber of Commerce. In the early 1980s, San Jose and Santa Clara County were continuing to boom as companies like Apple Computer and Cisco added new luster to the traditional technology successes of older firms like Hewlett-Packard. Business and government partnerships prospered, unhindered by past traditions and cronyism. However, much of the boom had passed by downtown San Jose in favor of the newer suburbs. The San Jose Silicon Valley Chamber of Commerce decided to expand to revitalize the downtown region. And Chuck helped, too, as a Chamber Director, Board Chair, and President of the San Jose Downtown Association among other volunteer duties.

He and Paula had always been interested in the arts, so they naturally gravitated to the theater and concerts available in town. He remembered seeing Noel Coward's *Private Lives* and deciding to volunteer to help with fundraising to bring more live theater to San Jose. The San Jose Repertory Company's board chairman at the time was Phil Hammer, whose wife, Susan, would eventually serve as San Jose's Mayor. He welcomed Chuck's efforts to help, first, as board counsel and then a board member. Chuck also served on the San Jose Symphony's Chairman's Council. Proving he is not afraid to look silly in public, Chuck is a regular performer in the annual satirical review of local politics, which raises funds for the San Jose Stage Company.

Paula and Chuck's son, Alex, was born in 1983 in Mountain View, CA. Unlike his father and older sister, he showed absolutely no interest in the military and attending a service academy. He studied political science and economics and received his BA degree in 2005 at Santa Clara University near San Jose. That eventually led to work for a Washington DC think tank, an NGO or Nongovernmental Organization working to prevent the spread of weapons of mass destruction.

Chuck threw his full energies in to his legal career and said, "One good thing about the legal business is that you can change directions easily." He started in commercial litigation doing trial work and then became a solo practitioner, emphasizing land use, real estate, and environmental law. He joined a small firm in 1981, which grew to include eighteen lawyers with Chuck as Managing Partner.

Chuck's successful professional career has enabled him to satisfy his drive to support his local community. When asked why he has recorded such an impressive roster of local public service, Chuck replied simply, "Duty, Honor, Country." Repeating the motto West Point adopted in 1898, he continued, "That stuff doesn't change. I think public service is something that you should do. One of the reasons I went into the legal profession is that I wanted something where I could earn enough money in my day job that I could do public service on the side. And that's what I've done."

Following the earlier lead from Morris Eisenstein in Brooklyn, Chuck first began to get involved in volunteer public service at the local level. He joined a committee for daughter Kim's school in Berryessa in the northwest area of San Jose. "I wanted to have an effect on how my kid's learning progressed," he explained. He began by working on the school district's human resources task force and progressed to fundraising. That eventually led to his efforts to create the Berryessa Education Foundation, which he served as president from 1992 to 1997. Next he began working on city-governing activities in his local district. "My problem is that I can't just sit there if there's a problem and no one is addressing it," he explained. "I'm happy to let someone else take it, but if no one will, I'll usually step in."

Chuck's activities support the Modern Proverb, "If you want something done, you should ask a busy person." He attracted enough attention as a willing and capable volunteer to be chosen for more duties at the city and county levels. These ranged from a neighborhood association and shelter foundation to a wide range of voluntary advisory boards and committees. He also helped create the Santa Clara County Land Trust and worked on the Greenbelt Alliance campaign as he expanded his open-space and environment commitments. After eight years on the City of San Jose's planning commission, the Sierra Club and other environmental groups recruited him to join the County's Planning Commission. He called that group "civilized" because it met only once a month to protect open spaces like ranches, parks, and golf courses.

In the early 1980s, San Jose transitioned from citywide or "at large" City Council representation to elect representatives by district. Businesswoman

Shirley Lewis was the first to run from the Berryessa district, and Chuck decided to support her as a volunteer campaigner. He walked the district, handing out fliers and speaking with voters. He discovered that he liked the experience. So he combined his volunteer committee work with some politics, primarily through "get out the vote" efforts for his favorite candidates and office holders.

Eventually, Margie Matthews succeeded Shirley; and six years later, she asked Chuck to help pick her successor. At lunch, one early-December day in 1998, Margie asked Chuck to run to succeed her. At first, he declined, but then they reviewed the list of possible successors and did not see any viable candidates. During this time, Chuck and Paula had been considering semiretirement. The law practice had just produced its best year ever, and both of them were ready for a possible move to the Sierra foothills that frame the Eastern side of California's Central Valley. After meeting with Margie, Chuck concluded that no one else was going to run. So he asked himself, "Who's going to do that job?" He decided that he could be semi-retired in the mountains or semi-retired in San Jose, so he chose the latter course.

He called Margie, who had two more years left in her term, and accepted her offer of help. So in February 1999, he began to reduce his work at his law practice to prepare for his next career as an elected official. At first, he continued a part-time law practice working with Steve Roth, a U.S. Army Vietnam veteran in the firm of Reed & Roth, which provides a range of legal counsel, including real estate and business transactions, and tax advice. However, with his election as Mayor, he put his law practice on hold and officially switched to inactive status with the California Bar.

Chuck said he enjoyed campaigning, which he called "just being out, talking with people. San Jose and my home district really reflect the American dream for new citizens," he explained. "As a result, I have learned so much about so many other cultures. People who have come from so many other countries where the political system is 'crud' appreciate that we will pay attention to them even if they're not rich and powerful. There's tremendous psychic reward in associating with people like Vietnamese immigrants, for example, who paid a terrific price to come to this country. I really enjoy that. I like to say that we are carrying a message that all citizens are entitled to respect as full participants in our democracy," he continued.

He was elected in November of 2000, gaining 60 percent of the votes cast, and was reelected in 2004 with 86 percent of the votes. As an elected official, Chuck constantly attends community events so he can meet his constituents outside the sometimes-forbidding confines of an office. "I like to go to events so I can meet up with friends and also so that strangers can feel free to approach me, and they do." He helps people with issues with government, and he helps candidates run for other elections. He also helped to promote private and public partnerships such as the effort to create a new multimillion-dollar Vietnamese Cultural Heritage Garden among other projects. About a quarter of San Jose's eighty thousand Vietnamese immigrants live in Chuck's home district. Although he quickly said he represents all of his constituents, he described a special relationship with the people from the war-torn country of his younger days in the U.S. Air Force. "We share that tie to their country," he explained. "And they appreciate the link, even forgiving my terrible attempts at the Vietnamese language because I try." The local Vietnamese Council of Elders named him Council Guardian and presented him with a native *Ao Dai* ceremonial dress and hat that he wears proudly on special occasions.

Although Latinos represent the largest ethnic group in San Jose, about a quarter of the city's citizens originated in Asia. In addition to the Vietnamese, a large number of Chinese, Filipinos, and Koreans live there. More than half of the people in Chuck's district have Asian or East Asian origins, including a large number of Sikhs and Hindus from India. He recalled carrying literature in eight different languages when he was campaigning through the precinct. "Those new Americans are wonderfully enthusiastic about their adopted country, and they come here with impressive backgrounds."

Asked what it's like to be the wife of a politician, Paula first replied, "I'm very proud of him," adding, "those values that I first saw in him haven't changed any. His honesty, commitment, critical thinking skills and ways to deal with people fit nicely with his work." Then she added, "I haven't had to do a whole lot other than to support him in what he does, and I'm glad he does it."

Chuck found the bane of most politicians—fundraising—less of a burden in San Jose, which enforces strict $250 limits on campaign contributions. When pressed about the downside of being a politician, he replied, "I try to follow the rule from General Carl Spaatz, which was 'Never tell a lie but don't blab the truth.' That not blabbing the truth part can be hard sometimes as I bite my tongue, but I like to be a part of making sure that my city is going in the right direction."

Working on the City Council for his district led Chuck to respond favorably to many colleagues who urged him to run for Mayor in 2006. He successfully campaigned City-wide and came out on top in the June primary. Then he won the runoff in the November election. Asked later about his new post, he replied, "It's a lot more fun than I thought, and I am enjoying it."

Although he has received several awards for his work, he tended to downplay the recognition in the spirit of "doing this because it needs to be done." Conversations with Chuck Reed soon led to an understanding of this basic belief that he stated very simply, "Whether it's military service or community service, I don't care where you are. Everybody should do service." This is a man who practices what he preaches.

Chapter 12

Negotiating Nukes and Nerds

Paul H. Nelson, USMA '71

Paul Nelson's pioneering work made Saddam Hussein nervous long before the despotic Iraqi leader expelled United Nations weapons inspectors, and the search for weapons of mass destruction was well-known. As a West Point graduate and U.S. Army officer based in West Germany during the Cold War, Paul led an inspection team that methodically assured compliance with arms reduction treaties. That experience taught Paul and other inspectors how to do their jobs effectively and contributed to huge reductions in arms among dozens of countries. It also set the stage for other later inspections in Iraq and North Korea. Still later, it prepared Paul for his second career, leading technically savvy nerds who taught ordinary people how to best use their computers.

In December of 1987, U.S. President Ronald Reagan and Soviet General Secretary Mikhail Gorbachev reached agreement to eliminate all nuclear-armed ground-launched ballistic and cruise missiles with ranges between 500 and 5,500 kilometers. One major significance of their historic INF (Intermediate-Range Nuclear Forces) Treaty was that it was the first one to include provisions for people to witness compliance with the dismantling effort. American and Russian teams familiar with the nuts and bolts of weaponry were charged with assuring that the treaty's provisions were put into effect. Then National Security Advisor U.S. Army General and later Secretary of State Colin Powell asked the U.S. Defense Department to come up with inspection teams to monitor its execution.

From January to June 1988, the military services assembled twenty teams of experts to inspect the Soviet's compliance with the Treaty. A senior Lieutenant Colonel or Colonel from a U.S. Military Liaison Mission headed each ten-member team. Lt.Col. Paul H. Nelson, USMA Class of 1971, was named one of the U.S. Army Team Chiefs based upon his considerable experience with the Russian military. Each inspection team included three types of experts. Army and Air Force weapons technicians versed in the USA's Pershing and Ground-Launched Cruise Missiles could look at the Soviet weapons and understand their complex operations. Experienced military and civilian analysts brought their expertise in intelligence, geography, and new weapons systems to the disarmament process. And finally, linguists from all the services could translate and remove language barriers.

When Paul described the team's composition, he also relayed a story about an added benefit that resulted from the translators' participation. "We put linguists on each team to ensure we could communicate and preclude misunderstandings," he said. "Most of these folks were sergeants or chief petty officers, NCOs [Noncommissioned Officers]. The unintended consequence of using them was a degree of discipline and structure in each team that otherwise would not have been injected into the inspection process. Because we worked in two-person elements, these folks were often subgroup leaders. The Russians wouldn't or perhaps couldn't believe that these people were really NCOs because we all wore civilian clothes. The American NCOs operated on a level commensurate with company grade officers in the Soviet military. We were two very different military systems, but ours demonstrated a rather profound lesson of democratic professionalism for the officer corps on both sides, especially for the Soviets. They really only believed us when they saw these same American NCOs later as escorts wearing their full uniforms."

He concluded with a statement echoed by virtually all of the subjects in this book time and time again, "We really do have the best armed forces in the world." Historian Stephen E. Ambrose wrote about one of the main reasons: "No other army emphasizes democracy the way we do, because we have learned and know that democracies produce great armies" (Ambrose 2002, 94).

The Cold War NATO teams were facing adversarial counterparts equally adept in their fields. "No one could know what the environment would be when we visited these sites," Paul explained. "We were literally writing the book on weapons inspections and disarmament, and there was a lot of uncertainty as to the process and the eventual outcome." He remembered it as a cooperative environment because it was clear to him that the Soviet leadership had said, "Make this work." Occasionally, they would find a reluctant commander who was being asked to dismantle his life's work; but generally, military order on both sides prevailed. The teams visited 124 sites in the former Soviet Union during an almost nonstop inspection tour. They were the most sensitive military posts in the one-time enemy's arsenal. And they were opened wide for the inspection teams who were matched by similar Soviet teams who visited 50 sites in the United States. The teams visited four kinds of facilities: training, production, storage, and missile operating bases. The latter were staffed by the elite Soviet Strategic Rocket Forces. They were the best of the Soviet military forces, and the tip of the Soviet spear pointed at NATO.

Along with his peers, Paul and his team planned, trained for, and conducted the first inspections of Soviet strategic weapons bases. "We worked with many Soviets who had never met Americans and had never planned to," he reported. "And we set precedents for treaty-compliance regimes that continue to serve us well today, for both conventional and weapons of mass destruction sites. In fact, we were able to set up a template for inspections that was used for other treaties, including work in Iraq after the Gulf War." He said the UN inspectors used their techniques for discovery successfully for several years in the 1990s. "We knew we were successful all along," he explained, "but it was confirmed even more when Saddam Hussein pulled the plug and wouldn't let the UN inspectors inside Iraq any more to do their jobs."

He described his first trip to Sverdlovsk in the Ural Mountains, in August 1988, to inspect a production plant for the Soviet equivalent of GLCMs or Ground-Launched Cruise Missiles. "Sverdlovsk had been a 'closed city' in Soviet terms," he explained. "The last American to drop in was Francis Gary Powers when his U-2 was shot out from underneath him during the Eisenhower administration. Our movements as a team were tightly constrained within the provisions of the Treaty and subjected to lots of Soviet press attention. It was a far cry from my next trip, which took place six years later."

The American inspection teams entered the Soviet Union through Moscow for everything west of the Ural Mountains and the small town of Ulan-Ude for everything east of the Urals in Siberia. All-day trips by aircraft, bus, train, and truck were not uncommon. The Americans, who were the first westerners to ever visit the site, tried to lessen tension by telling personal stories and even brought family photos to share with their hosts.

But Paul remembered one uncomfortable episode where that attempt at friendliness backfired. They were about halfway through the inspection at the base when they took a break for lunch. "For the sake of conversation, I was just asking our host about his family," Paul recalled. "In a very defensive reaction, he said my question was a *provocation*. I turned to the Russian escort from Moscow and explained that I was not trying to pry but was just trying to be polite. The escort, who I had known from an earlier assignment in Potsdam responded, 'Look, Colonel, *you* are the *first* Westerner ever to come to this site. Not only is this officer required to let you in to see some of the most secret weapons of Soviet history, but he's required to welcome you and host you and feed you and let you see anything you want. It's a *total* contradiction of everything he has ever been trained to do. Keep in mind the folks who are being inspected are not the same folks who are visiting the U.S. And then you bring these guys from Moscow with you telling us how to do our jobs.'"

The end result of these inspections was either agreement on what was there or not. In fact, Paul recalled, "We almost always agreed on what was there. The technical violations of the treaty that occurred were solely attributable to the people who wrote the treaty and not to the people being inspected because some of the weapons had different characteristics than someone at the treaty table had anticipated. It was never an attempt to hide something. The treaty itself was only a 39-page document compared to others that could run hundreds of pages. That left a lot of room for interpretation, but we learned a great deal as we progressed."

As a result of the treaties and the inspections, both the Americans and the Soviets actually destroyed the weapons they maintained. Paul reported that the method used to destroy weapons was very telling. The U.S. dismantled its weapons; the Soviets chose to launch and destroy theirs. They fired off 42-ton solid-fuel rockets that were not equipped with warheads. "This was a testament to the reliability of the Soviet's weapons," he recalled. "Over several months, they launched 72 SS-20s [missiles] without a single misfire. *That* was impressive!" he exclaimed.

Paul was also impressed with the fact that the inspectors had progressed to the point that proper on-site weapons inspections had become routinely accepted. "It is low cost and convincing," he explained. "It doesn't take an understanding of technical things. It takes the understanding of trained and disciplined eye witnesses. And I knew it was effective when we were talking to others who might not understand all the parameters, including our elected officials, and all of us liked the accountability of the process. We also liked the fact that we were sparing lives by disarming belligerent powers—by destroying their weapons systems peacefully. It's a much more civilized approach to warfare than Clausewitz's definition of war as a continuation of politics by other means. This was a peaceful kind of warfare that was practiced. You go in unarmed, fully declaring your intent with the other side that you're going to inspect and destroy their weapons, and they are doing the same thing on your side."

Paul's life story includes a 26-year career in the U.S. Army before he moved to the front lines of global society's Information Technology. His grandparents Olaf and Christine Nelson came to the United States from the island of Fyn in Denmark and settled in Racine, WI, a beautiful city on the shores of Lake Michigan. Their clan numbered nine boys and six girls, including Viggo, Paul's father. Viggo's sister, Effie, was a high school classmate and friend of a neighbor named Mildred Hansen who lived a couple of blocks away. Mildred's parents had emigrated from the outskirts of Copenhagen. Eventually, Viggo and Mildred met and fell in love. They were married on December 16, 1938. During World War II, Viggo served in the U.S. Navy Seabees while five of his brothers served in other branches of the military. All of them returned home safely. A carpenter who never attended high school, Viggo urged his kids to pursue higher education.

Mildred and Viggo Nelson would eventually have a daughter and four sons who would also prosper in Racine. They all studied hard and did well to graduate successfully from Horlick High School. First-born Evelyn graduated from Dominican College and became a teacher and social worker. Marv graduated from the Milwaukee School of Engineering and worked at Caterpillar Tractor. Bob was another teacher who graduated from the University of Wisconsin-Milwaukee and served as that city's assistant superintendent of schools for technology. The youngest son, Frank, studied nursing at the same school, earning his RN degree and later assisted an orthopedic surgeon.

The Nelson's fourth child was Paul, who was born in Racine on January 7, 1949. A strong, silent type, and serious even as a youngster, he would be big enough to play football and wrestle for the Horlick High School Rebels. He was intrigued at the prospect of flying and possibly attending a military academy after graduation. When he was a junior in high school in 1965, Paul visited the Eastern United States with Jack Ahlgrimm, a bachelor friend of the family who was a juvenile judge. Jack spent enough time with the Nelson boys as a mentor that "some folks thought he was keeping us juvenile delinquents out of trouble," Paul said dryly. They went to the Nation's capitol "to meet our Congressman and see how government was put together" and then up to New York for the World's Fair. Another important stop was West Point. "Although I was not able to meet up with any cadets or staff when we visited the first time, it was certainly an impressive place," Paul reported. "I remember being struck by the strength of the granite cliffs along the Hudson. At the time, I was more interested in flying and going to the Air Force Academy. But my eyesight wasn't good enough to pass their physical. And the Naval Academy wanted me to go into the Marines," he continued. "So I decided to try for West Point."

Paul reported to the Military Academy on July 3, 1967, and remembered his plebe summer as physically challenging. However, the former high school athlete didn't have too much trouble with his stamina. His wrestling training provided great preparation. "The military stuff was tough, but one of my roommates, Charles M. Heinbach Jr., had gone to the prep school [USMA prep school at Fort Monmouth, NJ], and he showed me the ropes," he recalled.

Their other roommate was Paul B. Watkins, a big football offensive guard on the Army football team. He had been recruited from Spring Branch, TX, to play Army football. Paul Watkins remembered meeting Nelse, as he calls Paul Nelson, when they were both plebes. They roomed together in Company A-1 for four years, which was an unusual situation since most cadets switch companies and roommates after one or two years. He graduated 279th in the class. Watkins spent five years in field artillery and airborne duty, including overseas tours in Germany and Italy, before he eventually returned to Texas. He owns three businesses—a title company, a land-surveying company, and an electrical contractor—and is based in Dripping Springs. It is what he calls "a little bitty town" west of Austin.

More than forty years later, Paul Watkins recalled, "When we arrived at West Point, Nelse and I were both athletes, and we were both pretty big guys, and maybe people kept us together and out of the way. I was from Texas, and I had never seen a winter as cold as it gets at West Point. I was surprised the first time it snowed. It was bizarre to me as somebody who barely owned a coat. For fresh air, Nelse opened the window and kept it open," Paul remembered with a shiver. "I was freezing, but we ended up having to compromise. The compromise was that the window would only be *half*-opened!" he laughed. "That meant we would only have *half* as much snow on the floor. I think because we could compromise is why we stayed such good friends," he added.

Paul Nelson's strong Horlick High preparation made him an above-average student at West Point. He enjoyed successful math and science programs and validated the foreign language requirement with his German prowess, so he had a bit more flexibility in taking elective courses. As a six-feet-three wrestler, Paul weighed in at 195 pounds to fight in the heavyweight class. He described his intercollegiate wrestling team as "so-so," and he wasn't able to help it too much when he broke his neck in practice during his senior year. Given a fifty-fifty chance of paralysis with surgery, Paul decided to "live with it," but the injury did keep him from serving in Combat Arms branches after gradation.

He was a general engineering major whose best class was German. Paul Watkins remembered struggling to study the Russian language at West Point while his roommate breezed through German. "Years later, I laughed at him trying to learn Russian," Paul Watkins remembered. Paul Nelson's worst classes were Military Science, which Paul and his classmates called "military art."

One day, in the first semester of his senior year, Paul got into an argument—what he called a "stupid, teenager beef with an instructor" that kids do sometimes. "I didn't know my place there and was disrespectful. I chose to challenge a Captain who was one of my instructors," Paul reported simply. He described the verbal confrontation's outcome in two words: "He won."

As a result of the conflict, Paul was promptly and severely punished. A discipline board dropped him from the middle of the class in ranking to the bottom. He was told he would not graduate on time with his 728 classmates and would have to repeat the Military Science course after the rest of his classmates had graduated in June.

While his 728 classmates spent June 9, 1971, listening to Defense Secretary Melvin R. Laird and becoming new Second Lieutenants, Paul and five others at the bottom of the class were in temporary limbo. For the next month, they went to special repeat classes each morning, six days per week. In the afternoons and on Sundays, they studied and also worked on their suntans. Eventually, they all graduated at the bottom of the class and were commissioned on July 2, 1971, as a select group with a later date of rank than their classmates.

The Class of 1971 graduated commissioned officers in all four branches of the United States military as well as new officers from several allied nations ranging from Korea to Thailand. Among the more prominent members of the class are Rhode Island U.S. Senator John F. Reed, who ranked 16th; Ambassador-at-Large Lt.Gen. Dell L. Dailey, USA Ret., who ranked 249th; and two USMA superintendents who are both also retired U.S. Army Lieutenant Generals—Franklin L. Hagenback, who ranked 385th; and William J. Lennox Jr., who ranked 58th. BGen Patrick Finnegan, USA Ret., who ranked 23rd, also served as USMA's Dean of the Academic Board. In addition to twelve other general officers, the class included numerous leaders of civilian enterprises and government agencies who followed the class motto Professionally Done.

After his own commissioning in July, Paul drove back to Wisconsin. He flew to Europe with his brother, Frank, and Judge Ahlgrimm for a month's holiday in England and Ireland before reporting to active duty.

During Paul's senior year, his brother, Bob had introduced him to a teacher colleague, Mary Farrell, of Cincinnati, OH. Mary had spent eight years teaching in Catholic schools there as a Sister of Mercy of the Holy Cross. After she left the convent, she pursued her official Wisconsin teaching credentials to teach in public schools. Paul and Mary became friends, kept in touch through a long-distance romance, and were married on January 29, 1972, at St. Vincent's Church in Cincinnati.

Their relationship also strengthened what Paul calls a spiritual dimension in his life. "That's just one other part of our lives, but it's a very important one," he said firmly. The newlyweds packed everything they owned into Mary's 1969 Volkswagen Beetle and drove from Ohio to Fort Benning, GA. There they dropped off some of their wedding gifts and continued on their journey south to Coral Gables, FL, for a honeymoon. They also visited Mary's Grandfather, Pop Farrell, then ninety-three, who had been unable to attend the wedding.

With his proficiency in German, the new Second Lieutenant was sent to Darmstadt in West Germany in 1972. His old roomie, Paul Watkins, teased, "His first job was a real *toughie*—managing ski slopes!" First as a platoon leader and later as a company commander, Paul worked in personnel and administration for the Army's Fifth Corps. "I learned what the real Army was all about," he reported years later. "Everything from race relations and drug abuse and counseling, we were basically taking care of soldiers." Next he moved from the Frankfurt area to southern Bavaria and the U.S. Armed Forces Recreation Center at Garmisch at the foot of the Zugspitze—Germany's highest Alpine peak. Garmisch hosted the 1936 Winter Olympic Games. After World War II, the U.S. established a recreation area there and operated three hotels, a campground, and a recreation lodge for U.S. military personnel and their families. Captain Nelson first served as the Center's adjutant and then was the headquarters detachment commander responsible for 200 soldiers.

Mary and Paul liked living overseas. Mary met Franz Paul Eder, a renowned German master wood-carver, and apprenticed to him for two years of study. That led to a hobby she continues today. Among her many projects was a wooden shoe carved to mark the birth of Heather Watkins, the firstborn daughter of Paul and Judy Watkins. The Watkins family treasures it to this day. Paul Nelson was able to extend his assignments in Germany, which he recalled as "a time when we met a lot of lifelong friends and enjoyed a great quality of life there."

They also registered with the local West German authorities and were able to adopt their first daughter, Sabine, in 1977, just before they were due to return to the USA. Their second daughter, Sara, was born a year later at Fort Bragg, NC, while Paul was attending the Army's six-month Foreign Area Officer Course. Next the family reported to the Defense Language Institute in Monterey, CA. "At that time, the Army needed officers who were proficient in Arabic and or Russian," he reported. "I chose the latter because I was very interested in returning to Eastern Europe." Language training was followed by studies for a Masters of Arts degree in National Security Affairs from the Naval Postgraduate School at Monterey. Less than a decade after graduating near last in his West Point class, Paul Nelson had collected a Master's degree and was pointing his Army career in a new direction.

They returned to West Germany in 1980 for a two-year postgraduate program at the U.S. Army Russian Institute back, again, in Garmisch. The Institute provided basic understanding of the Soviet culture, people, and military. It also helped Paul to refine his Russian language skills and led to a three-year assignment as an American Liaison Officer to the GSFG, the Group of Soviet Forces in Germany. Major Nelson was stationed in Potsdam in the German Democratic Republic, the official title of the former East Germany. He and his team observed the maneuvers of 450,000 Soviets troops in the buffer zone between NATO and the Warsaw Pact forces. "I gained an extensive understanding of the Soviet military, their hardware, the military culture, and the Russian people," Paul recalled.

He vividly remembered the death of a good friend and coworker, U.S. Army Major Nick Nicholson, who was shot by a Soviet soldier on March 24, 1985. In his chilling report, "*The Last Casualty of the Cold War*," Paul's former boss, retired U.S. Army MGen Roland Lajoie, wrote about the cold-blooded murder that took the life of his friend. Mary and Paul often timed return visits to Washington DC each year to enable them to attend an annual memorial service for Nicholson at Arlington National Cemetery. His widow, Karen, who never remarried, worked for the U.S. Army's survivor benefit programs. Paul said she and her daughter remain forever part of the extended U.S. clan of former Russian Foreign Area Officers and their families.

Paul and Mary and their daughters returned to the USA in the summer of 1986. Major Nelson reported to work as an Intelligence Analyst for the Defense Intelligence Agency at the Pentagon. He brought his firsthand observations and experiences from the field to headquarters, which welcomed his insights. The planners were especially interested in the assessments of Paul and others who had watched contingents of the Soviet's 40th Army Division in Afghanistan at that time.

Mary and Paul at a Founder's Day Dance

Another classmate, James H. Cox Jr., who ranked 301th and said "anonymity was my middle name," also served as a Russian Foreign Area Officer in a 31-year military career that was followed by arms-control duty with the U.S. State Department. Although classmates who knew each other by name, Paul and Jim actually became friends when their career paths crossed years later.

Jim relished the story when, one time, the two West Pointers were together as eyewitnesses to history in Germany. On November 9, 1989, Paul flew to Berlin on a TDY (temporary duty) assignment. Jim was assigned to the U.S. Military Liaison Mission in Berlin when they caught up with each other. As friends were taking Paul around his former home, they couldn't help but notice that crowds were gathering near the Berlin Wall. Jim called the scenes "joyous chaos" and remarked directly, "Nelson arrived one *afternoon*, and *that night*, the Wall came down!" Jim said he saw his friend a few days later, and Paul laughed, "Well, I guess I've done enough here. Time for me to go home."

Jim Cox called the fall of the Berlin Wall "the most exciting day of my life," as he reminded us that most military people, who train for war, are joyful with peace.

After nearly twenty years of observing Russia from afar, the Nelsons finally moved to Moscow in 1992 when Paul was named Assistant U.S. Army Attaché for American Ambassador Robert Strauss. He was named

Army Attaché a year later when he was promoted to full Colonel. His boss was the Defense Attaché, U.S. Army BGen Gregory Govan. Govan eventually became an Ambassador for the U.S. State Department and later served as Chief Delegate to the Joint Consultative Group of the Treaty on Conventional Armed Forces.

One of his colleagues there was classmate Jim Cox. They served overlapping tours of duty in the Russian capital. They also shared a promotion party when they were notified that they were promoted to full Colonel at the same time. Jim recalled travels to a military industrial complex in the Ural Mountains and a visit to the Continental Divide. "We were the first Americans there since Francis Gary Powers dropped in and were enjoying a much friendlier reception," he explained. "Our escorts drove us to this tourist spot with colored bricks so you can stand for a photo with one foot in Europe and the other in Asia. As we're snapping pictures, one of the Russians turns to us and says, 'I'm kinda confused now. What are you guys? Are you *Friend* number one or *Enemy* number one?'" Cox said he replied, "It really doesn't matter, so long as we're *number one!*" The Russian answered back, "The world is too confused. I can't figure this out."

The 1993 change in U.S. government administrations brought in Ambassador Thomas Pickering, who provided "superb leadership" according to Paul, during the October crisis that year when President Boris Yeltsin evicted the Russian Parliament by force. Paul recalled that Yeltsin used the Kantimirov Tank Division to shell the Parliament, which was located right next to the U.S. Embassy compound. "We were under siege for two days and were very fortunate that only one of our people was wounded," Paul reported. "After the hostilities ended, I went out to the railhead where the Kantimirov tracked vehicles were loading out and gave a thank-you gift to the division commander for his troops' accurate shooting."

Three decades after graduating at the bottom of his class, this career soldier witnessed firsthand the two defining moments signaling the end of the Cold War: the fall of the Berlin Wall and the breakup of the Soviet Union.

In addition to his diplomatic duties, Paul's two-year tour focused primarily on peacekeeping and arms control. "We knew, at some point, that the U.S. Army or possibly other NATO forces might be going into the Balkans with elements of the Third Infantry Division," he explained. "So we affiliated that division with elements of the Russian's 27th Guard Motorized Rifle Division. Our staff made numerous visits to come up with the rules of engagement in both languages so that Russian and American soldiers could operate together." He believed that training paid off handsomely as the two armies began to operate successfully in Bosnia and Kosovo.

With two attractive teenaged daughters, the Nelsons were quite visible, especially among the small American community in the Russian capital. Dad took action that *some* fathers and mothers might appreciate more than *most* daughters and sons. "I knew Sabine and Sara were going to get some attention from the two dozen United States Marines who kept us safe at the Embassy," he reported. "Fortunately, the Army had produced a rather stern-looking photo of me for visas and other official needs, and there were quite a few of these 'sour-faced tough guy' photos left over in the wrong size. I took the stack of the extra ones and went around, visiting these outstanding Marines. I introduced myself to each of them, shook their hands, and presented them with a picture labeled: *Sabine & Sara's Dad.* As a result, all the Marine security posts had the photo mounted on their walls, and the Nelsons went home to the USA with two single daughters."

Colonel Paul Nelson, Army Attaché

In 1994, they completed their duties in Moscow, and Paul returned to the Pentagon as Chief of Staff for the On-Site Inspection Agency. That was the same group he had worked for as a team chief for the INF Treaty compliance six years earlier. He told a story about a later trip back to Russia to contrast the changing times. "I made several visits back to Sverdlovsk in the Ural Mountains, which was still the center of Russia's defense industry. Lots of changes had taken place: the country had changed its name to Russia, and the city had reverted back to Yekaterinburg from Sverdlovsk. My status changed from being the team chief of a ten-person inspection team on my first two visits to being the U.S. Army Attaché. The reception of the city went from reluctant to enthusiastic," he continued. "On my last visit in 1994, I went to an arms bazaar as an invited guest. Others included representatives of the production facility selling computers and shovels and a reception at the newly opened U.S. Consulate."

Throughout this time, Mary had kept studying and working outside the home while she and Paul raised their daughters. Mary received her BS in Mathematics from Marquette University in Milwaukee, MI; her masters at George Mason University in Fairfax, VA; and her PhD in Math Education from the University of Colorado at Boulder. While they were stationed in Moscow, she worked for the U.S. Department of Commerce, searching for scientists who were interested in internships to the United States. She accompanied Paul on two visits to the former Soviet heartland. He said she was "considerably more welcome than I since she offered visas, plane tickets, and an opportunity to get infected with capitalism." He said all of the relationships were very different as the highly talented folks in this formerly closed city anxiously sought to open the proverbial window to the west. "The whole nature of the adversarial relationship we had grown up with turned around and forced the leadership of the countries as well as the military to fundamentally change how we dealt with each other," he reported.

Unlike some other academy graduates from the bottom of their classes who were regularly reminded of their positions by other graduates, Paul was not. "Jim Cox was one of the few graduates who I served with," he explained. "However, neither my class rank nor where I went to school were ever an issue with me or the people I worked with." He seemed to have followed the advice of a Regular Army Captain who addressed the issue when Paul was a senior at West Point. "He told me class rank would make a difference in two ways: one was where I sat when I graduated and, two, where I sat when I came back to watch football games. And he was right."

Paul said, "I was taught very early in my military career that the job isn't nearly as important as who you're doing it with. I was lucky in my military work that there were relatively few of us in the [Russian area] career field, and we had repeat contact with the same people. We were either working in Russia or back in the Washington DC area. Those interests and our friendships kept us together." His old boss from Moscow, BGen Greg Govan, called these special Foreign Area Officers the Band of Brothers.

After nearly three decades in uniform, Paul Nelson said, "I'd done all the fun jobs, so I decided it was time to retire." He left the service in Washington DC in June of 1997. His first civilian resume described a rather unique range of capabilities, including "an arms control operator with extensive experience in implementing strategic and conventional treaties." Fortunately, he reconnected with Bill Richardson, also from the Class of 1971 but from the Air Force Academy. They had met on a flight to Greece in 1974. William E. Richardson was ranked 34th among the 694 members of his class, worked in computer science for the Air Force, earned a PhD from Oxford University in England, and later taught at the Air Force Academy. He retired as an Air Force Colonel in 1994. They had stayed in touch, and Bill convinced Paul to join him in Colorado at the Educational Services Division of Sun Microsystems Inc., the scientific computer company.

Paul became Operations Manager and Chief of Staff for Sun Educational Services and held that post until he retired again in June 2005. He explained at the time that Sun employed some 1,300 people at 250 locations in 63 countries around the world. "We taught people how to use Sun computer systems so they could get the most out of them." Paul modestly reported that he ran the headquarters, maintained worldwide quality, and led a team of talented, self-proclaimed geeks who maximized the utility of Sun systems. Mary said he moved to the civilian world "just like it was another Army assignment." Paul would not disagree. He maintained that the Sun employees, who some might call nerds, were not all that different from soldiers. "We worked together to get the job done," he said. "I mostly gave direction to some very talented, highly energetic young people who were responsible for producing our hardware and software courses in quality formats—on time and on budget."

Mary managed to keep up her math studies and teaching credentials during a series of eighteen global moves. In 2005, she completed her PhD and continued teaching, working in the University of Colorado's Department of Applied Mathematics in Boulder. Sabine earned her BA degree in English from George Mason University in Virginia in 1997 and worked at Sun as a contract administrator. She and her husband—sales executive Michael Scanlon—live with their sons, Ben and Alex, and daughter, Isabel, in Thornton, CO. It was a nice and close twenty-minute drive from grandparents Paul and Mary. Daughter Sara earned her BA degree in Education from Trinity College in Washington DC and her MA and teaching certification from Loyola University in Baltimore. She teaches special-needs students at a Maryland high school.

Like most fathers, Paul is very proud of his children. He chose to emphasize their spiritual sides when he described them. "We were fortunate that religion and the spiritual dimension lent some more discipline to our lives," he explained. "Parish life helped determine how we raised our children and, to a large extent, determined with whom we interacted. It was certainly a focal point in our lives," he continued.

"For example, many of the same people that we met early in our lives in Germany eventually moved and retired to Washington DC. We stayed in touch and were together there at Our Lady Queen of Peace Church in Arlington, VA. Our Pastor, Father James Healy, often called it 'Our Lady Queen of the Perpetual Revolution'. We continued to attend Church together, and that meant that we maintained relationships across continents and generations with people with whom we shared values. It was very comforting to keep the church family together. And those connections provided many of the mechanisms by which our daughters learned the values that guide them today."

After his second retirement and during our last conversation, Paul described his hobbies as skiing, biking, and hiking when not playing *opa* (grandfather) to the children. In fact, until he retired, he biked the ten-mile roundtrip to and from his office each day.

Unfortunately, this wonderful life would end much too soon. On March 1, 2006, Paul and Bill Richardson and two other friends were enjoying one last run down the mountain at Breckenridge Ski Resort when a skiing accident killed Paul instantly.

More than three hundred family and friends gathered three days later for a funeral mass at their parish, St. Louis Church, in Lafayette, CO. That was followed a few weeks later by a memorial service attended by hundreds more back East in the Army Chapel at Fort Myer, VA. Paul was cremated and buried at Arlington National Cemetery.

This very strong, faith-filled family supported each other despite their terrible loss. Although she continued to teach at the University in Colorado, Mary considered the possibility of teaching math at West Point.

Chapter 13

Preacher's Kid Walks in Heavens

David C. Leestma, USNA '71

Dave Leestma is a preacher's kid whose father interested him in the Navy while his uncle attracted him to flying. His success at the Naval Academy almost led to submarine duty; but eventually, he graduated first in his class, flew Navy jets, and then walked in space as a NASA astronaut. Later he worked in the space program as an administrator.

Born on May 6, 1949, David C. Leestma was the third child of Reverend Dr. Harold and Lois Leestma, who spent their early years of marriage in a series of assignments for the Reformed Church of America. Originally from Michigan, the Leestmas had four children. Mary, Peter, and then David were born in Muskegon, MI. When Dave was a toddler, the family moved to Grand Rapids where his brother, Mark, was born. Then the family moved to Munster, a small town on the Illinois border between Gary and Hammond, IN. Famed *Hour of Power* radio minister Robert A. Schuller invited Harold to join him in Orange County, CA, as he began his Crystal Cathedral Ministries; so the Leestmas eventually moved to the West Coast.

Although no one in the immediate family had served in the military, Dave's Dad had piqued his interest in the Navy by regularly sharing books of Navy adventures with his son. Dave's Aunt Suzanne, his father's sister, was married to Frank Pettinga, a physician and private pilot in Michigan. Uncle Frank took Dave up in his single-engine Cessna when he was eight, and the young nephew was hooked on flying. "After we took off and I looked down, to me it was just thrilling to fly," he recalled excitedly. "I used to dream about it all the time." Dave took that interest in flying and the Navy and applied to the Naval Academy. He was also motivated to go "away" to college and knew that his family's limited financial resources made college costs daunting.

Dave was a small dynamo with reddish brown hair just five and a half feet tall and weighing in at 125 pounds. He played water polo and golf instead of the traditional high school team sports of the 1960s. Fortunately, academics at Tustin High School came fairly easy for him. During his high school senior year, Dave went to the Marine Corps Air Station, at nearby El Toro, for his Naval Academy Admissions physical. He was examined by a U.S. Navy physician who told him he would need a waiver for his eyesight, which then measured 20-25. "Your height is OK at five feet six," the doctor said. "But at 125 pounds, you don't have a snowball's chance in hell of getting into the Naval Academy," the doctor advised directly, adding, "Sorry, son." Dave said he walked out of that medical examination thoroughly discouraged but extremely motivated. He said his motivation to excel comes from his mother, who constantly challenged her children to be more competitive. "We used to play a lot of games when I was growing up, and it was always cutthroat," he recalled with a smile. "Board and card games like Monopoly®, Clue®, Rook® and bridge challenged all of us kids to win."

Dave successfully gained some weight and juggled school and sports to graduate as salutatorian among his 450 classmates at Tustin High in 1967. With his nomination from Congressman James B. Utt of Orange County and appointment from USNA, he went off to see Annapolis for the first time.

After his cross-country flight, the first sign of the Naval Academy that Dave saw was the football stadium. Less than an hour's drive east of Washington DC, on U.S. Route 50 or southeast of Baltimore on Interstate 97, the Navy-Marine Corps Memorial Stadium appears on the horizon. It is the 30,000-seat field for all Navy home games except the last of each season against Army. Built in 1959, the stadium is located a mile from the campus, which compactly combines old and new facilities in a beautiful 338-acre site. Separate locations of the Yard and the football stadium sometimes prompt the brigade of midshipmen to march to their home games through city streets. Despite numerous distractions akin to World War II newsreels of the allied forces' triumphant march through liberated Paris, the brigade manages to keep its ranks reasonably disciplined and aligned right. That is, until they reached sight of the stadium where eager friends and family members literally pelted the ranks with candy. When my wife and I attended a game in the 1990s, midshipmen scrambled to catch the trick-or-treat goodies, assuring sugar highs for the games.

When Dave first walked through the Academy's gate, he thought, *This place is kind of neat.* "But," he quickly added thirty years later, "you just don't get much time to enjoy it! I had just turned eighteen, and the place hit me like a ton of bricks because I had absolutely no prior experience with the military." He remembered that the initial shock "took me totally by surprise." Fortunately, his strong academic preparation served him well as he buried himself in his classes. Told to avoid aeronautical engineering because it was too difficult, the competitive juices nurtured by his mother kicked in. "Of course, I signed up for it. I like challenges," he said. He recorded a 4.0 grade point average by the end of his first semester.

Unfortunately, that high academic mark was posted on his company's bulletin board, and the upperclassmen in his company began to notice the short, redheaded kid from California. That was not the kind of attention the young plebe needed. Dave said what happened next illustrated why the academies' adult company and squadron officers serve their schools very, very well. "As part of leadership training, the upperclassmen train the underclassmen, and that's all well and good," he explained. "But you're still seeing kids runnin' kids. At some very important times, it's *critical* that adult supervision kick in." As soon as Dave's high grades were posted on the bulletin board after Christmas vacation, a couple of upperclassmen confronted him and charged, "Mr. Leestma, we *obviously* have not been paying *enough* attention to *you*." From then on, they paid him too much attention, almost harassing him with extra military training. And his grades plummeted. A few weeks later, his semester GPA had slipped below 2.0.

Told one day to report to his company officer's office, "I thought I was in danger of being thrown out," he recalled. The young U.S. Navy Lieutenant in charge of his company asked the plebe, "What's going on?" And the plebe nervously replied, "Nothing, sir!" The company officer repeated the question, which resulted in the same reply from the shaking plebe. "Well," the wise Lieutenant replied, "I can *guess* what's going on, and I'm going to have to do something about it." Harassment by upperclassmen lessened, and Dave was able to better balance his military life with his academic life. He jumped back into the scholar groove, recording another 4.0 at the end of his first year. His classmates called him the Wiz or Wizard long before Harry Potter tales, and he used that moniker later as his call sign when he flew Navy jets.

North Carolinian William Trigg Long, who roomed with Dave for three years, remembered him as a brilliant guy who seemed to do everything effortlessly. "He didn't even seem to study *that* much," Bill recalled. "I asked him how he did it, and he explained, 'I just pay attention to what's going on in class.'" Bill claimed Dave had "a photographic memory and an amazing ability to put things together." He also marveled at Dave's nightly bridge playing and a sports schedule that made him a "big" golfer, sometimes playing four times per week with the varsity team. "Golf was a great way to get away from the Yard," Dave recalled, and he still plays today.

Bill also remembered "legions" of girls from his high school who provided a steady stream of letters to cram Dave's mailbox full of admiring letters. "And he wasn't even *that* good looking a guy!" the old roomie added with a laugh. Bill,who would rank 217th in the class, majored in ocean engineering and then served five years on submarines. He spent a year as a systems analyst before going to medical school at Georgetown University in Washington DC. He's a Manhattan dermatologist who also teaches clinical dermatology in the medical school residency program at New York University. "Dave Leestma was one of those guys who had it *all,* including a strong spiritual sense," Bill added. "But never in a *showy* way," he concluded.

Dave Leestma relished the memories of his time at the academy. "I love mathematics, and I loved airplanes, so I was doing something I liked to do," he explained. Throughout his four years at the Naval Academy, Dave thought he was going to end up in submarines because, as he said, "Some of the 'smart' guys were steered in that direction. Or maybe to fly. You had to go study nuclear power, and you had to go get interviewed by Admiral Rickover," he said. "That was a big deal that I thought would be a great experience." Luckily, Professor David Rogers, one of Dave's aeronautical engineering teachers, knew he was more interested in flying blue-sky aircraft than driving underwater ships. He told Dave that a visit to Admiral Hyman Rickover, the legendary father of the nuclear submarine, implied a commitment to work in submarines. Dave had naively misunderstood the notoriety his number one class standing entailed.

"I went up to the office that was arranging interviews in the next few days for the admiral and told them that I wanted to cancel mine," he recalled. "They were surprised at my request and told me that I had to call Admiral Rickover's office directly. So I did. The admiral's aide told me the wheels were already in motion for my interview, and if I was going to cancel, I had to talk directly with Admiral Rickover. I was more than a little surprised at that but figured, 'OK, here we go.' The aide got Admiral Rickover on the phone for a brief conversation. He promptly asked, 'Mr. Leestma, I understand you don't want to come for an interview. Why's that?' I replied, 'Sir, because I want to go naval aviation.' The phone just went dead. That was it, he had hung up.

"Although I was shook at the time, I was glad I didn't go see him," Dave recalled three decades later. "My whole life would have been different. Sometimes doors open and doors close not because of your own doing. I only realized that later. It still scares me that I was so close to taking a wrong path, and I didn't even know it. At the time, I might not have felt

I had a choice, but I did. To me that proves that people should follow their dreams."

Another grad, who completed studies at Annapolis a year earlier, told the story of *his* interview with Admiral Rickover. Kevin W. Sharer, who majored in aeronautical engineering and ranked 58th among 838 classmates in 1970, started out wanting to be a pilot but failed his flight physical. He decided to switch to nuclear subs and went to see Admiral Rickover. "I told the Admiral that nuclear subs were my second choice, and that was *not* the message the admiral wanted to hear," Kevin recalled in a *New York Times* interview published June 20, 2004. "However, after about forty-five seconds, Admiral Rickover said, 'Get out.' That was high praise because it meant you had been accepted." Sharer served on two attack submarines and then worked for General Electric and MCI before joining Amgen Inc. in 1992. Eight years later, he was named CEO of Amgen, the world's largest biotechnology company, which *Forbes* magazine named its Company of the Year in 2004.

Updating the interview process, I asked a more recent Naval Academy grad in the surface nuclear branch about *his* selection experience. New Yorker Daniel I. Doyle, who ranked 467th among 942 members of the Class of 2001, said he had heard about the "infamous" Rickover interview stories. "I didn't experience any 'steering' in my community selection," Dan explained. "Information was available about the nuclear program, but it wasn't pushed. Halfway through our senior year, we entered our preferences online through a web-based program indicating our top three community choices and found out on Service Assignment night by opening a small envelope that had the final results in it." He added that "everyone who selected conventional surface got it, so there were no surprises there, but some people, who had dreamed their whole lives of being SEALs or pilots, were devastated when they weren't selected." He concluded, "However, we all supported each other and made the best of our assignments." Dan started out as a surface warfare officer (SWO) on a guided-missile frigate, USS *De Wert* (FFG 45) and then studied to become a nuclear SWO. He joined with other SWOs and future submarine officers for a year of intense training at the Naval Nuclear Power Training Command and Nuclear Power Training Unit in Charleston, SC, before his first nuclear tour of duty. In 2005, he became a reactor department division officer on the nuclear-powered aircraft carrier USS *Theodore Roosevelt* (CVN 71).

Dave Leestma was subject to some additional pressures, both seen and unseen, at the Naval Academy. He was urged to remain in the front lines as a "ship driver, pilot or submarine driver" in the surface Navy. Although he picked Naval Aviation, his marginal eyesight disqualified him for pilot training. So he was assigned to become a Naval Flight Officer, the second-seat weapons systems officer in Navy aircraft. At the time, many NFOs were former pilot trainees, and the Naval Academy's senior officers were not necessarily pleased that their top student was taking that path. Dave believed he was part of the change to upgrade the status of that career field.

June 9, 1971, was a sunny beautiful day as Dave led his 874 classmates across the stage at Memorial Stadium to receive diplomas from Chief of Naval Operations Admiral Elmo Zumwalt.

The Naval Academy's Superintendent then was RADM James F. Calvert, an experienced surface ship officer who wanted more graduating midshipmen at sea. He had graduated 113th out of 615 men in the Naval Academy's Class of 1943. Calvert was widely quoted as saying "since N-A-V-Y spells O-C-E-A-N" and had ordered all aviators to serve on a ship for a year before going to flight school. Although Dave had asked to go to graduate school immediately, the Navy assigned him first to sea duty in Southern California. He was assigned to USS *Hepburn* (DE-1055) based in Long Beach. This 438-foot, 3238-ton destroyer escort, staffed by 20 officers and 300 enlisted men, was preparing to deploy to Vietnam War duty in the South China Sea. Fresh from Annapolis, Dave was named First Lieutenant Afloat, handed a stack of training manuals, and told to go to work.

Among his first on-the-job trainers were bosuns—a contraction of boatswains mates—the backbone of the Navy. Bosuns work as the important and very necessary general-purpose deckhands on a ship. They sometimes stand watches on the bridge and are responsible for the ship's general cleanliness. They run all the ships' boats as well. One assignment opportunity intrigued the new ensign. Dave decided to learn how to be the Officer of the Deck (OOD), directing the helmsman to steer the ship when the Captain is absent from the bridge. In less than six months, the ensign was a fully-qualified OOD, helping to drive the $100-million ship with senior lieutenant junior grade officers reporting to him.

As he was preparing to depart this temporary assignment for graduate school, Dave was called into the office of the ship's Captain who told him, "Hey! We don't want you to leave! We want you to stay! If you stay here in the surface line, you'll be an admiral before you know it!" Once again, the young officer was forced to choose. He rejected more pleas of senior officers who were trying to chart another course for his future. Dave politely declined and reported up the California coast to Monterey for the Navy's postgraduate school. Wartime urgencies gave him one year to complete his master's degree including his thesis. And complete it he did, earning a MS degree in aeronautical engineering from the U.S. Naval Postgraduate School in January 1972. Highlighting that graduation was dinner with his parents and the commencement speaker, former Naval Academy Superintendent Admiral Calvert. This time Dave recalled an enjoyable social evening when "I found out that the admiral was a real person." He also remembered that this time, the admiral didn't try to talk him out of his chosen path to naval aviation.

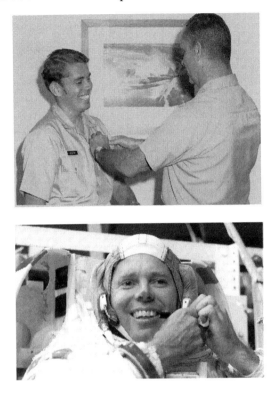

Ensign Leestma received his flight wings.

Astronaut Leestma checked his equipment.

Dave switched back to the East Coast for Naval Flight Officer training at Naval Air Station Pensacola in Florida. He graduated first in his class in early June and was preparing to move up to Glynco, GA, for advanced training. In the meantime, his Father had just completed the work for his PhD, and the family was organizing a party in Tustin to celebrate this important achievement. Dave decided to fly out west to attend. Planning ahead, he wondered if his Mother might be able to scout up some dates for the celebration, so he asked her for some matchmaking help. Lois called some of her friends and arranged dates for her 24-year-old bachelor son on Thursday, Friday, Saturday, and Sunday.

On Thursday, Dave escorted his first date to the big party for his Dad. Unbeknownst to him, one of the guests was Patti Opp, the Friday night's date, who attended Thursday's party and watched him from afar. The next night, Dave drove over to pick up Patti. She was a perky college coed who had been called to be Dave's date by his 85-year-old Great Aunt Betty Albers. He took her to watch his old softball team play a pickup game. He told her he would hit a homerun for her, and he did. They had a great time and followed the game with an ice-cream treat. "I was just smitten by this girl," he reminisced simply, but he was faced with a social dilemma: two more dates had been arranged for the rest of the weekend. He called Saturday's and smoothly explained the situation, leading to a cancellation. Then he called Patti, and they enjoyed another date Saturday night. He was starry-eyed and in love. However, for Sunday morning, his Mother had arranged for still *another* young lady to drive him to the airport after they attended church together.

As they walked into church, who would be in the pew watching his every move? Patti—who glared at him with "glacial stares" that demanded explanation. However, Dave was unable to tell her what transpired until much later that night after he had returned to Florida. Dave called Patti from Pensacola at 1:00 AM for some late-night explaining. First he reached her Mother who told him that Patti didn't want to talk with him. Dave persevered and convinced his new friend that he was only interested in *her*. He flew back and forth a few times as cross-country hops helped the long-distance romance blossom.

At the same time, Dave was training in Georgia to be a tactical fighter Radar Intercept Officer or RIO. RIOs were responsible for the offensive and defensive systems in high-speed fighter aircrafts like the F-4 Phantom, the Navy's workhorse in the Vietnam War. Based upon his superior performance in training, Dave was selected to work in fighters. He had earned his wings and was chosen for readiness training. He wanted to fly on the West Coast because that's where all the fighter squadrons were gearing up to go to Vietnam. "I got my orders, and they said VF-124 Gunfighters, and I thought that was a mistake," he recalled. So he went to his Captain, who just smiled and said, "Son, the F-14s are just starting to train and get ready to go as a brand-new airplane in the fleet. The Navy has been assigning lots of folks, many of them senior flying officers, to the new bird." He explained, "But they realized they don't have any SLJOs.[18]

"Guess what?" he continued. "You're going to be a SLJO, but you get to fly the F-14!" With that bluntness, Dave became the very first nugget (a rookie straight out of Navy flight school) RIO for the Navy's then

---

[18]   S——Little Jobs Officer, then U.S. Navy slang for 'go-fer,' the person who goes for this and goes for that, getting the tasks, large and small, that no one wants, but must be done.

brand-new F-14 tactical fighter. He was to be based in Miramar Naval Air Station in San Diego, and he was one happy camper.

Dave managed to get back to see Patti a few weeks after their first dates, and this time, he wasn't burdened by schedule conflicts. The relationship strengthened, and eventually, they set a date to be married—Independence Day of 1974. But first, he had to unload his bachelor car. It was a 1971 Pontiac Firebird Formula 400 that he said, "Passed everything but the gas station." He also added that he knew Patti was "the right one because I was willing to sell the car" at her request. They bought a *family* car, an Opel sedan. They drove back east on their honeymoon as Dave was assigned to Virginia Beach. He was moving east ahead of his squadron, and the newlyweds were on their own. "Being by ourselves, without family or friends, kind of glued us together," he reported. He also introduced Patti to the austere life of a military officer in transition at a new base. After a quick three-day trip across country, he remembered the honeymoon coming to a quick halt when they checked into the cement-block BOQ (Bachelor Officers' Quarters). The newlyweds remembered a Spartan room with two twin beds and a quarter refrigerator plus a steel desk and a single chair.

After two nights in the BOQ, Dave reported on Monday morning to the squadron where he was told to fly back to California immediately to pick up the new aircraft. He recalled, "Here I've been married for a week. We don't have a place to live, and I'm leaving my new wife to go back to where we used to be. Plus when I get back to California to pick up the airplane to fly back east, we take it on a test flight, and it breaks!" He didn't return for a week. However, Patti adjusted, found a suitable apartment, and settled in. It was the beginning of a vagabond life so familiar to military couples.

Dave was flying off the USS *John F. Kennedy* (CV 67), an 80,000-ton attack aircraft carrier with a crew of 4,500 men. Launched in 1967, the "Big John" was a multi-mission carrier that spent considerable time in the Mediterranean as part of the United States' presence in the Middle East. Dave was the first F-14 RIO to land on the *Kennedy*'s huge flight deck. He also tested the ship's inertial navigation system and was involved in several other firsts, which set the stage for other technical experiments later with NASA. He remembered flying in the Mediterranean and intercepting Russian Bear bombers that flew too close during Cold War "cat-and-mouse games." He also proudly recounted getting his "one-hundred traps patch," signaling one hundred safe landings aboard the carrier. Although he flew several times per week, Dave reported that flying was a collateral job. His primary job was to learn and perform in a series of assignments ranging from maintenance to operations to administration.

After Patti completed her studies and received her degree from Old Dominion University in Virginia, she was able to join other Navy wives who visited their husbands during their deployments in Europe. The couple recalled some nice holidays in Rota, Spain. They also met up in Naples, Rome, Florence, Barcelona, and Majorca with a special Christmas leave (vacation) in Munich, Germany. Dave reported that he spent two and a half years of their first four years of married life at sea.

In early 1977, during the last of his three *Kennedy* cruises, his operations officer, then Commander David Sjuggerud, saw an announcement that NASA was again recruiting astronauts.[19]

He urged Dave Leestma to apply. Leestma said Sjuggerud was an imposing figure and quite convincing—"a big guy in heart and stature." He had ranked 581th out of 927 graduates in the USNA Class of 1964 after playing football with Roger Staubach of the Class of 1965. "He came to me with this little article in the paper that explained they were selecting a new group of astronauts," Dave recalled. "Eventually, a hefty applicant package caught up with me in the ship's mail. However, by the time I got it, there wasn't enough time to complete it. I figured, 'Here I am, a guy stuck out on a ship in the middle of the Mediterranean, and there's no way I can get this done on time.'" In the spirit of anyone who has ever justified procrastination, Dave told himself, "I'll never get in, and besides, they'll never pick me because I'm a RIO, not a test pilot."

So he passed up that opportunity and eventually received orders to transfer to Air Test and Evaluation Squadron Four(VX-4) at Naval Air Station Point Mugu, on the Pacific Coast, fifty miles northwest of Los Angeles. Picking up on his earlier flight test experience in the F-14, he conducted the first operational testing of new tactical software for the aircraft and its avionics, including a programmable signal processor. He also helped write the F-14A's tactical manual that described how to use it in combat. Although happy to return to Southern California, he and Patti were taken aback when two other members of the squadron were selected by NASA. "I finally figured out that the *worst* thing that

---

[19] NASA selected its first astronauts in 1959 from among 500 candidates. The seven original Mercury astronauts were all military pilots. Later, NASA sought civilians with extensive flying experience, and then the requirements changed to emphasize academics. In 1965, six scientist astronauts were selected from a group of 400 applicants who had PhDs or equivalent experience in the natural sciences, medicine, or engineering. NASA accepts astronaut applications on a continuing basis and selects candidates as needed.

could happen to me would be *not* to apply, so I got back on track," he explained.

Dave wrote to NASA and received another hefty applicant package. But this time, he completed it and mailed it in. He also applied officially through the Navy's chain of command for approval to switch to the space agency. He was called for an interview in January 1980 and spent a week in Houston at the Johnson Space Center.

"I remember we were pretty excited to be in the running," he recalled, "but it was kind of strange because all twenty of us were competing against each other. The final interview was amazing, spending an hour talking to people who had walked on the moon, flown Apollo, and done all the things I had dreamed of. However, I didn't hold much hope because all the other mission specialist candidates had PhDs." He also noted that his group of twenty was one of four or five to be considered. "I figured that they were gonna pick maybe twenty from a qualified pool of more than one hundred, so I was not very optimistic," Dave explained. That attitude was strengthened when he completed the process and was told, "Don't call us, we'll call you"—a familiar refrain for so many job applicants.

Dave went back to Point Mugu where he and Patti were expecting their first child in May. And NASA never called. He figured, "It's like *any* job interview. If you're really gonna get hired, they follow up with other interviews, right?" Wrong.

More than five months later, on May 27, the phone rang at 6:00 AM, waking up Dave and Patti and their new three-week old son, Ben. On the phone was George W. S. Abbey, then Director of Flight Operations for the Johnson Space Center. He was calling from his office in Houston where it was 8:00 AM. He introduced himself and asked Dave if he still wanted to be an astronaut.

Dave replied, "Sure! Yeah, I'm still interested."

And George said, "Well, we'd like you to move to Houston and become an astronaut."

Dave recalled he replied, "Oh, yeah. Great! Yes!"

And George said, "OK, you'll be hearing from someone with the details, but we'd like you to report July first. See ya then."

And then George hung up. Dave said he got off the phone and exclaimed, "Wow! July first. That's in a few weeks!"

And then he turned to Patti, who asked, "*What's* in a few weeks?"

Dave said, "I told her they wanted me to be an astronaut. And she asked, 'Does that mean we have to move to Houston?'"

Any partner who's ever taken a new job and then spoken with a "trailing spouse," can appreciate that situation. This new opportunity was further complicated by a three-week-old infant and grandparents living nearby within easy driving distance for ready babysitting duty. That contrasted to a pending transfer many miles away to Houston. Plus a newly occupied house to sell.

Dave replied to his wife's question softly, "I said, 'yes.'"

Patti answered, "You didn't say yes, did you?"

Dave remembered later, "I wanted to say, 'Whaddya mean, did I say yes? Of course, I said yes!'"

Then she asked again, "You didn't say yes, did you?"

Dave said, "I was so excited that I didn't sit still for several days. Wow! Being an astronaut! I can't even imagine that!"

Like all the partners of the grads of this book, Patti was asked to comment on and describe her husband, specifically in this important, life-changing exchange. However, in the fine tradition of Annie Glenn, the wife of famed astronaut and later Ohio U.S. Senator John Glenn, Patti declined to be interviewed. One can only imagine . . .

Eventually, the couple worked out the details of the move and their new lives. Dave reported in July, and Patti avoided the Texas heat and stayed in California for the summer. She sold the house, and she and Ben joined Dave in Houston after Labor Day.

They've been there ever since and have added five more children to the clan. Patti home-schooled all of them. Ben grew up to be an Air Force pilot after graduating 124th among 929 grads from the USAFA Class of 2002. Later he flew F-15Cs out of Mountain Home AFB, ID. Dave explained that Ben chose the Air Force Academy rather than Annapolis despite appointments to both schools. "He came to me and told me, 'Dad, I'm going to go Air Force, and I hope that doesn't offend you.' He said he knew all the stories about the Naval Academy and my time there and added, 'I don't want to spend the next four years trying to follow your footsteps and filling your shoes. I want to do this on my own.'" Dave added proudly, "I thought that was a very mature statement for an 18-year-old."

The other Leestma children are all Texans. Katie was born in Webster in 1981. She graduated from Texas A & M College of Veterinary Medicine in 2007 and works in California. Emily, who also was born in Webster in 1983, graduated from Texas A & M in 2005 and married Joe Dalton. Three more children were born in Nassau Bay, TX. Peter, who was born in 1986, joined the Class of 2009 at USAFA in July 2005. Mary, who was born in 1988, majored in education at Texas A & M while Caleb, who arrived in 1989, hopes to attend a service academy.

When Dave reported to the Johnson Space Center on the first Monday morning in July of 1980, he met his eighteen other colleagues in the NASA Astronaut Class of 1980. They were immediately dubbed the 'Needless Nineteen' by the *other* astronauts who were waiting for *their own* flights and missions. The veterans saw the rookies as more competitors for coveted spaceflights. NASA saw them as a steady stream of talent for the many space shuttle flights planned for the next decade. At the time, the space agency's plans for the shuttle program anticipated more than 40 flights per year. Including Dave, the 1980 class had eight pilots and eleven mission specialists. NASA had picked 35 others two years earlier, but they were yet to make their first flights. As a result, the 54 newbies were contending for flights with the two dozen earlier Apollo astronauts who were ready to return to space again. Eventually, all nineteen flew, including Jerry L. Ross, who would make seven spaceflights.

Dave's preparation for spaceflight began immediately. He detailed it in his preface to *Before Lift-off*, a book written by veteran space writer Henry S. F. Cooper to describe the mission of the *Challenger* STS 41-G space shuttle.

> Learning about the NASA organization and operations, becoming conversant in the endless stream of NASA's technical acronyms, assisting in the design and development of future space systems, participating in the testing of current or proposed space hardware, learning *how* to read abbreviated flight checklists and discovering *why* each step is done in a particular order, involving oneself in hundreds of other scientific issues and engineering tasks—these are all parts of an astronaut's introduction to space-flight training. (Cooper 1987, ix)

When the *Challenger* launched with Dave aboard from Kennedy Space Center, FL, on October 5, 1984, it was its sixth flight and the thirteenth space shuttle flight. The seven-person crew was the largest to fly on a single spacecraft until then. Like all NASA crews, they had bonded together as a family during their year's intensive training. Veteran commander, then U.S. Navy Captain Robert L. Crippen was making his fourth Shuttle flight. The pilot was U.S. Navy Commander Jon A. McBride, Dave's former squadron mate at Point Mugu, with two payload specialists—oceanographer and Australia-born Paul Scully-Power and Marc Garneau, the first Canadian citizen to serve as a shuttle crew member. Dave was one of three mission specialists. The other two were veteran Dr. Sally K. Ride, the first American woman in space, and U.S. Navy Reserve Commander Kathryn D. Sullivan. Dave's mission was the first time two female astronauts flew together in space.

Kathy became the first American woman to walk in space when she and Dave performed a three-hour Extravehicular Activity or EVA to demonstrate the feasibility of actual satellite refueling. "It was pretty exciting to do an EVA on your first flight," Dave recalled. "When you're inside the shuttle, the biggest thing is the visual scene as you look outside, but when you're inside, there's always something else in your vision," he explained. "When I stepped outside the hatch, I got this *enormous* sensation of *falling* because there was nothing in my vision except the earth many, many miles away." It was so exciting that he reported that, after landing, the medical team reported that his EKG heart rate, which measures his pulse rate, peaked when he stepped outside the hatch.

After Dave and the rest of the *Challenger* crew landed safely on October 13, 1984, he was reassigned as a CAPCON or capsule communicator for the next nine space shuttle missions. These included three space lab flights, two for the Defense Department, and four other communications satellite flights.

However, while Dave and his crew were preparing for his next flight, NASA launched the 25th shuttle mission, STS-51L, for the Teacher in Space Project. Dave and his colleagues were training in their Texas simulator when they took a break to watch the Florida launch at 11:38 AM on January 28, 1986. They were as shocked as any other observers to see the ill-fated *Challenger* explode seventy-three seconds later, taking the lives of seven crew members, including New Hampshire school teacher Christa McAuliffe. These were their friends and fellow astronauts, and Dave remembered a very real sense of purpose to find out what happened and to make sure it didn't happen again.

"We know the risk of spaceflight," Dave explained. "And we know how important it is for the space program to continue, but safely." He contrasted the loss of the *Challenger* with the loss of the *Columbia* and its crew while reentering earth's atmosphere on February 1, 2003. "Both of these losses were terrible, but two issues contribute to different reactions to the *Columbia*. First, he explained the shuttles are a lot older, so there are technology-aging questions. Second, the cause of the first accident was relatively quickly understood, and the lengthy analysis of the second accident has led to more questions about flying shuttles," Dave said.

Dave's second spaceflight launched August 8, 1989. He was again a mission specialist and was one of five military crew members on board the STS-28 *Columbia*. The others were Commander USAF Colonel Brewster H. Shaw Jr., Pilot Navy Commander Richard N. Richards, mission specialists USAF Major Mark N. Brown, and Army Lt.Col. James C. Adamson. Adamson was 162nd among 800 grads in West Point's Class of 1969. That mission carried a number of classified military payloads. It was the 30th space shuttle flight, and the first flight of the refurbished *Columbia* since difficulties experienced on the 61-C mission that launched on January 12, 1986. During the flight, the crew experienced a few minor problems but completed 98 orbits and returned safely to Cape Kennedy after six days in space.

After his *Columbia* mission, Dave was named NASA's Deputy Director of Flight Operations. Based at the Johnson Space Center, Flight Operations' two divisions managed staffing and budgets for both the 100 astronauts and their 40 aircraft. Dave was introduced to the complex world of major departmental budgeting, and he remembered considerable pressure to reduce the number of T-38 aircraft used by the astronauts for training. "Every year, we had to listen to charges that the T-38s were 'just for you guys to go joy riding around to maintain the astronaut's flyboy image,'" he explained. "And every year, we faced budget cuts within NASA." He said he always answered with one simple fact: "There is no other place where you can train an astronaut where his real-time decisions have real-time consequences. You cannot do that in a simulator. You can *only* do that in flight," he added emphatically.

Eight years after their initial flight together, Dave was reunited with Kathy Sullivan for his third shuttle flight when the STS-45 *Atlantis* launched from Kennedy on March 24, 1992. For this nine-day mission, the crew conducted a dozen experiments ranging from studying atmospheres and climate to weightlessness and vision. They also conducted a Shuttle Amateur Radio Experiment for crew members in space to converse with amateur or ham-radio operators worldwide, including students at several selected schools. Ham radio operators use two-way radio stations from their home base to communicate with each other using voice, computers, and Morse code. Dave applied for and received his ham radio license, N5WQC, from the American Radio Relay League or ARRL. NASA engineers built a two-meter antenna that could only be used in line of sight from *Atlantis*. Dave placed the antenna in the shuttle's window whenever he was able to communicate with other ham operators on the ground. "Line of sight is pretty good when you're in space," Dave explained offhandedly.

The project was a huge hit. "Sometimes we might get a bit jaded about spaceflight," Dave reported, "especially here at NASA where the space program is all around us 24/7. But many people in the world take an *enormous* interest in spaceflight. The ham radio community would have considerable interest because they often help in global communications. And of course, we flew over them regularly, so that added to the excitement." Dave obviously enjoyed the experience. One of the only times during our interviews that he actually *bragged* about his many accomplishments was when he reported that he actually *conversed* with ham radio operators on all seven continents. "I got a small band of guys at a research station on Antarctica too," he said proudly. Using his spare time in space, Dave connected with literally thousands of ham radio operators. They followed up conversations with registers or QSL[20] cards that certified the conversations took place by specific call signs. Dave reported that he signed several thousand cards that were verified by replaying recorded tapes of the mission. He also said that he was the first person to talk on two-meter waveband to all seven continents including a research station on Antarctica.

Ham radio publications and other media thoroughly reported the plans for the *Atlantis* mission and its radio experiment. Dave recalled flying over New Zealand and connecting with an operator in that country. Since it was nighttime in the South Pacific, Dave suggested that the operator look up to the sky to see if he could see the *Atlantis's* flight. "We're coming directly overhead," he told the operator. "Why don't you run outside and see if you can spot us?" The man did and came back in to report he had seen the *Atlantis*. Dave recalled the experience like it was yesterday with the boyhood enthusiasm that drives so many people into space. "It was really neat!" he said enthusiastically. "It wasn't anything technologically sophisticated. It was a nice connection between space and the ground."

When he spoke of this time in space, Dave said, "I was chided for spending too much time on the radio. But it was fun, and I enjoyed using my spare time to connect with other hams on the ground." The problem was simply the distinctive chatter between the tight confines of *Atlantis* and the myriad of operators on the ground. "This program only worked when you talked, so our conversations distracted some of the crew," he explained.

Commanding *Atlantis* was then U. S. Marine Colonel Charles F. Bolden Jr., who graduated 359th among 836 in the USNA Class of 1968. Bolden, who was making his third spaceflight, later retired as a Major General. The pilot, who was on his first spaceflight, was then USAF Major Brian Duffy, who graduated 469th among 756 in the USAFA Class of 1975. In addition to Dave and Kathy, the third mission specialist was Mike Foale, also making his first spaceflight. Payload specialists were Byron Lichtenberg, making his second flight, and scientist Dirk Frimout, the first Belgian to fly in space.

Following this flight, Dave worked briefly as Deputy Chief and acting Chief of the Astronaut Office. In November 1992, he was named the Director, Flight Crew Operations Directorate. During his tenure, NASA

---

[20]   The abbreviation QSL has been used for more than a century by telegraphers, Morse code operators, and other electronic communicators. In any language, QSL means "I can acknowledge receiving this" while QSL? means, "Can you acknowledge receiving this?"

and the Russian Space Agency successfully flew 41 Shuttle flights and seven Mir missions. Dave was responsible for the selection of Astronaut Groups 15, 16, and 17, which totaled several dozen new astronauts. Now Dave Leestma was making those exciting 8:00 AM calls!

He remembered one particular call that instantly took him right back to a U.S. Navy aircraft carrier at sea. "I called an F-14 pilot named Susan Still, and I reached her ready room, but I didn't give them my name when I asked for her," he recalled. "In the background, I heard them tell her someone was on the line, and she said she was running out the door for another flight. I said that I would call her back in about two hours. When we were finally connected, Susan asked, 'Why didn't you say *who* you were, and I would have come right back in?' And I told her, 'No, I thought *you* needed to make that one last F-14 flight without *my* distraction!'"

Two other memorable calls went to Scott and Mark Kelly, twin brothers who were U.S. Navy pilots but stationed separately. "I reached one right away but not the other. After I told the first one that he was selected and we went through all the excitement that entails, he asked, 'I promise I won't tell him, but did my brother make it?'" Dave said he let him know but asked him not to tell his brother. "It took me another hour and a half to reach the other brother," Dave continued. "When I finally did, he said his brother had received *his* call, but he had *not* and was really anxious to say the least." Dave concluded, "It was pretty neat to get *both* of them."

He also remembered reaching Dr. Don Pettit on a cellular phone when he was hiking in the mountains of New Zealand. "Those new astronaut calls were the great calls you like to make," Dave said. "You reach them and say, 'This is Dave Leestma,' and the excitement grows with every word. Then I ask, 'Do you still want to come to Houston?' And you know something? I've never had a *no!*"

Dave continued to progress through NASA's operational and engineering hierarchy, supervising upgrade modifications of the avionics for the agency's T-38 aircraft. In 1998, he was named Deputy Director of Engineering, in charge of the management of Johnson Space Center Government Furnished Equipment (GFE) Projects. This was NASA's "in-house" contracting department, building projects like the treadmill for the space station. In August of 2001, he was assigned as the Johnson Space Center's Project Manager for the Space Launch Initiative, responsible for all JSC work related to the development of the new launch system. That program evolved into the Orbital Space Plane Program. Dave was later named Assistant Program Manager for NASA's Orbital Space Plane and worked for more than two years, planning the design of the new craft that was to serve as the transfer vehicle for space-flight crews to and from the International Space Station. However, that program was cancelled in early

2004, and Dave was transferred to work as the Manager of the Johnson Space Center Space Exploration office. That office managed the Space Exploration program as described by President George W. Bush in early 2004. It included a long-term human and robotic program to explore the solar system, starting with a return to the Moon that would ultimately enable future exploration of Mars and other destinations.

When asked to describe what it was like to fly in space, Dave first reported in the preface of Cooper's book, "You can't describe it, and it's best to talk with other people who have been there. We just look at each other and nod." A few years later, he said, "The memories tend to dull with age just a little bit." But then he waxed eloquent as he described what happened whenever he visited a public forum. "As an institution, NASA wants to talk about the technical accomplishments and our achievements in space," he explained. "And that's important. But invariably, the audience wants to hear the experience itself. They ask about what it *feels* like when the rockets go off. They ask about what it *feels* to look down at the earth. I like to talk about that *more* than seven million pounds of thrust and four and a half million pounds of fuel."

Dave then warmed to the task of telling, rushing to repeat what he has, no doubt, explained hundreds of times with the same enthusiasm that a new father uses to describe his newborn or a grandmother tells about a grandchild. "When you talk about watching a sunrise or sunset, it's really difficult to put that in words," said Dave. "It happens very rapidly, almost instantaneously bright in thirty seconds from dark to sunrise. Just before the sun comes up on the horizon, it begins to brighten in the atmosphere. You start seeing the weather bands that are very close to the earth. First they're oranges and yellows with a black area above. Then there's a band of blue that comes out. It's just a spectacular color, and it changes in brightness and intensity as the sun comes up. You can see the bands of color. Cameras can't even begin to give you that. One time, we started to count, and we saw between eighteen and twenty-four shades of blue. Some are more spectacular than others, but you get one every forty-five minutes, either a sunrise or sunset. It's spectacular."

Trying to explain in more detail, Dave reminded the listener that NASA's computer constantly tracks the shuttle's flight. "Most of the time, you're over water, of course, so you don't have a clue where you are," Dave recalled. "But after a while, we can figure it out, and you can know where you are by the colors below. Certain shades of greens and browns tell you we're over the Midwestern United States. Or if it's got this reddish-colored dirt, it's Australia or maybe the Namibia Desert. Other colors tell you it's a brownish color of China or the white of Siberia."

In the epilogue to his book, Henry Cooper described the impact on the NASA crews of the *Challenger* accident: "They will no longer have the same infectious confidence. An innocence has been lost" (Cooper 1987, 257). Dave Leestma talked about the 1986 *Challenger* accident and the 2003 *Columbia* tragedy very philosophically, almost religiously, perhaps reflecting his upbringing as a preacher's kid. "You never even think about what could happen again," he said. "Well, maybe you do, but you really don't," he concluded.

The official web site maintained by NASA displays many of the photos from space at http://eol.jsc.nasa.gov/. Photos are displayed with three locations listed below in a multiple-choice, interactive geography game online. Dave Leestma occasionally takes a break from his day-to-day work and plays the game by covering up the offered choices. He's pleased that he, more often than not, guesses the location in space correctly, peering at his desktop screen instead of out the shuttle window.

The wonder of it all still shines through in his voice.

Chapter 14

Growing Up To Be an Astronaut

Richard A. Searfoss, USAFA '78

Some seven-year-old boys want to be firefighters or police officers when they grow up. If you live on an Air Force Base and your Dad's a pilot, you might think about flying. And if you're seven years old in the early 1960s, you might even aspire to go to the U.S. Air Force Academy, graduate first in your class, and become an astronaut. That's what Rick Searfoss did.

Richard Alan Searfoss was born on June 5, 1956, in the base hospital at Selfridge Air Force Base near Mount Clemens in Michigan. His Mom was Mary Catherine Spencer, and his Dad was Stanley "Jerry" G. Searfoss. Jerry was first a U.S. Air Force navigator for HU-16 amphibious aircraft and then went to pilot training. He flew huge C-124 Globemaster cargo transport aircraft and later switched to fly the C-135 Looking Glass airborne command post for the Strategic Air Command. He transferred again to become an aerial refueling pilot, flying KC-135 tankers. Rick and his younger sister, Debbie, who arrived in 1958, lived in Nebraska, Mississippi, and South Carolina before they moved to New Hampshire in 1966. Jerry was assigned to Pease AFB near the coastal city of Portsmouth and retired from the Air Force in 1973. Mary died in 1978, and Jerry later met and married Barbara Taylor in 1981. Rick's sister, Debbie, majored in International Business at Auburn University in Alabama and became a banker.

Rick always wanted to fly and remembered many hours spent building aircraft models of the planes of his dreams. He was surrounded by pilots and living on air force bases, so flying was a natural part of his life. He studied hard in school and also joined the Boy Scouts, working regularly on his merit badges to achieve the coveted Eagle Scout rank in 1970. A year later, he visited the Air Force Academy for the first time. It was during a trip to the Philmont Scout Ranch in Cimarron, NM, about 200 miles south of the Academy. He thought it was pretty neat and knew he wanted to go to USAFA. Rick was a top student at Portsmouth High School and also played soccer and ran track as a hurdler and jumper. Eventually, he ranked second in his class academically. He also placed second in the triple jump in the New Hampshire State meet in 1974. That impressive combination of academics and athletics served him well when he applied to the Air Force Academy.

He believed growing up in a military family helped prepare him for the rigors of military life at the academy, but it was his academic preparation that was to have a more lasting effect on his life as a cadet. Soon after his arrival in Colorado Springs on the first of July in 1974, Rick and his classmates took batteries of tests to determine their academic levels for first semester classes. His first perfect score in his first major exam, a chemistry test, gave him the confidence to think he could continue his success. "In many ways, I was lucky because the academics came relatively easy for me," he explained.

Several of Rick's classmates at the academy were Mormons, members of the Church of Jesus Christ of Latter-day Saints. "I had been raised Base Chapel Protestant," Rick explained. "My Mother was Methodist, and my Father was a Baptist. However, at the end of my sophomore year, a friend introduced me to some of the concepts of the Mormon Church, and I decided to learn more. My French literature professor that semester was also a Latter-day Saint," he continued. "And that helped me to a better understanding of the faith."

That professor was retired Air Force Colonel Robert M. Atkinson, who teaches Air Force Junior ROTC at Patchogue-Medford High School in Medford on Long Island, New York. Then Captain Atkinson taught French during two different tours at the Academy. He also encouraged Rick to strengthen his French language skills with studies overseas. To illustrate the strength of those skills, Atkinson recalled a Survey of the French Literature class with a dozen students, including two native speakers. "Rick was number one in that class too," he reported. Rick stayed in touch with his former teacher and took a letter from his AFJROTC program into space on his second shuttle mission. The Long Island school proudly displays the memento in its trophy case.

In the fall semester of his senior year, Rick moved to Salon de Provence in the south of France where he attended L'Ecole de l'Air, the French Air Force Academy. All three academies support exchange programs with counterparts in several overseas countries. Rick and Californian

Scott Richardson, who was majoring in engineering sciences and ranked second in the class, enjoyed their time in France. "It was wonderful," Rick recalled. "There we were in the hometown of Nostradamus and learning more about the language and culture of France."

Back in Colorado Springs, Scott's roommate was Michael J. Mitchell, an International Affairs major from Garden Grove, CA. Mike, who volunteered that he was in the middle of the class, said, "Rick and Scott were great friends of mine at school, and still are. Although I have always been in a little bit of awe at their abilities and drive, to their credit, they were never in awe of themselves," he continued. "I always felt their equal even though it would have been nice if a *tiny bit* of their smarts had rubbed off on me. Mike was also an Eagle Scout,[21] and he and Rick served the Boy Scouts in a summer leadership program as rangers at the Philmont Scout Ranch. I never saw him have so much fun as when he was working with younger scouts and getting them ready to go out on the trail," Mike reported.

Rick agreed with that assessment, adding, "I love the outdoors, and I loved the opportunity to work with the Scouts." He continued, "This was supposed to be *work*, but it was also a very effective real-world leadership experience. We were dealing with kids and didn't have the hammers [threats] of consequences that we had with basic cadets back at the academy." He concluded, "This was one of our very effective leadership programs, and your motivation skills were very much in evidence."

Mike told one story of the differences between Rick and Scott and some of his other classmates. "In our senior year, during Easter vacation, five of us rented a house in Newport Beach, CA. We all drove down to relax on the beach a few weeks before graduation. Rick and Scott spent what seemed like half of the time studying for academic scholarship tests they were preparing to take. The rest of us were at the end of our four academy years and enjoying ourselves. The contrast was striking and a reminder that they didn't attain their status as first and second in our class without hard work and constant dedication," he added.

Mike flew transport aircraft, augmented C-130s in Special Operations and C-12s in Latin America, as well as F-18 fighters with the Spanish Air Force in a 20-year career that included State Department duty as an

---

[21] The three academies' admissions departments report that 10 to 15 percent of the members of each entering class are Eagle Scouts. Discussions among fellow Admissions Liaison Oficers concluded the Scouts help themselves by learning early as teenagers about how to set goals and achieve them, setting the stage for more achievements later in life.

Assistant Air Attache in Argentina and an assignment to the Spanish Air Ministry in Spain. He also logged two Master's degrees: Systems Management from the University of Southern California and National Security Affairs from the Naval Postgraduate School in Monterey,CA. He retired as a Lieutenant Colonel and was later Chief Operating Officer of the software development company, SabiOso Inc., in Clearfield, UT.

After graduation, Scott went to the California Institute of Technology in Pasadena for his MS degree in Aeronautics and later earned a Masters in Business Administration from the University of Southern California. He worked at several Air Force research labs and was a future threats analyst and, later, a Colonel and program manager in the USAF Reserve. Scott worked as a project manager and systems engineer for Northrop Grumman Corp. and as a general manager and program manager in high-tech ceramics firms. He has authored numerous publications and is an inventor on a patent for a clutch system using a ceramic-matrix composite.

Another one of Rick's classmates, Floridian Michael A. Valdivia Jr., recalled that Rick's class rank once prompted the future astronaut to take extra action academically. "I remember that we were in Ninth Squadron together in our two degree [junior] year," he explained. "And Rick's academic advisor told him he might have a chance at being 'number one,' so he double loaded some courses one semester. At the time, most of us took 22 credit hours per semester. Double loading meant 28 to 30 hours of class per week.

"I would call that stubborn determination and an indication of how hard Rick and others worked to succeed," said Mike, who was ranked 535th in the class. A rare medical condition forced Mike *out* of the military at graduation, but he still managed to stay connected to the space program, working at the Kennedy Space Center as a shuttle payload engineer first for Rockwell International and later Lockheed Martin Corporation. He and Rick remain lifelong friends, sharing a love of flying and space.

When asked what was the toughest part of his four years at the Air Force Academy, Rick replied in two words: "Mickey Mouse." That's the timeless vernacular for the nitpicking overzealousness that sometimes permeates bureaucratic organizations like the military. He said he appreciated the importance of the military discipline and leadership development programs at USAFA and went along with them enough to make the Commandant's List. "But," he clarified, "I had some problems with folks who were hyper-military and neglected their academic responsibilities. Taxpayers were spending a lot of money to send us to the academy," he said bluntly. "And I felt it was an important part of your duty as a cadet to maximize the learning while not letting anything else, including military duties, interfere with that learning process." He cited the time-honored time punishment of "tours" as the absolute worst part of the academy experience because it just wastes time. He marched a dozen tours during his four years.

During his senior year, Rick realized he was going to graduate first in his class, and he was awarded a National Science Foundation Fellowship. "I knew that eventually I would fly, but I was focused on going to graduate school *first*," he recalled. Rick said he had not seriously considered becoming an astronaut right away because the National Aeronautical and Space Administration (NASA) had not been calling for very many astronauts at the time. However, in his senior year, NASA began picking the shuttle astronauts. And he knew he was on track with those childhood dreams.

Secretary of the Air Force John Stetson presented diplomas to Rick and 980 other grads on May 31, 1978. Rick received his BS degree in aeronautical engineering and earned the Harmon, Fairchild, Price, and Tober Awards for top overall academic, engineering, and aeronautical engineering achievement. He also received the Air Force Aero Propulsion laboratory Excellence in Turbine Engine Design Award. As a result, he picked up a three-year National Science Foundation Fellowship that he used successfully to study for his MS degree in Aeronautics at the California Institute of Technology in Pasadena.

While he was attending graduate school at Cal Tech, Rick went to a single adult retreat sponsored by the Mormon Church. There he met Julie McGuire of Glendale, who was home for the summer from Brigham Young University and working temporarily at the Jet Propulsion Labs in Pasadena. Julie remembered being impressed that Rick was getting his master's degree at Cal Tech because "that was a tough school," and she also remembered his super-strong level of intensity that remains to this day, adding, "He is one of those people who drinks water from a fire hose!"

After he completed his MS at Cal Tech a year after graduation, Rick fulfilled his lifelong dream when he entered pilot training at Williams AFB near Phoenix, AZ. And he loved it. Despite the rigors of learning to fly, Rick was able to continue seeing Julie in both Los Angeles and Utah where she was completing her degree in elementary education. After long-distance dating for nearly a year, the couple married on January 4, 1980, in the Los Angeles Temple of the Church of Jesus Christ of the Latter-day Saints. They briefly honeymooned in coastal Santa Barbara and Solvang, the old-style, Danish-theme town. Rick quickly returned to pilot training, and Julie settled temporarily in Arizona as an Air Force wife in their first of nine homes. Julie liked to cook and considered herself a good one, so she said she was chagrined that her new husband lost weight when they were newlyweds. "Here I was cooking away, and he was running so much and losing weight that my in-laws thought I was *starving* him!" she laughed. Julie said, "My husband definitely has his head in the clouds sometimes. He just thinks at a different level than a lot of people." She added, "I like to call myself his grounding wire. He's an outside-the-box thinker, and I'm an inside-the-box thinker," she continued. "We're a good pair." Rick and Julie have three daughters. Megan was born in England in 1983, Elizabeth in Idaho in 1985, and Camille in Houston in 1994.

When he was at Williams learning to fly, Rick thrived, but the second stage of his training brought a mysterious stomach ailment that first baffled doctors. Exploratory surgery diagnosed the condition as chronic appendicitis, and he missed eleven days of training. Julie said she knew her husband was a hard worker, "but that illness really told me more about his intensity," she explained. "He worked even harder to get back on track because there was no way he was going to slip back to the next class in his training." Later she explained that Rick's intensity doesn't compete with others. "He competes with the standards that he sets for himself."

During flight school, Rick discovered that he especially liked low-level flying at 420 speedy knots (483 mph) just 500 feet above the desert floor. "This was great flying, and I just loved it," he recalled enthusiastically. He decided he wanted to fly the two-seat, swing-wing F-111 jets. The F-111s were specially equipped with low-level flying terrain-following radar systems to avoid radar detection. Graduating from pilot training in 1980, he and Julie moved overseas to England. There Rick joined the 48th Tactical Fighter Wing, known as the Statue of Liberty Wing, in Great Britain. They flew F-111F fighter-bombers from the Royal Air Force Station at Lakenheath, seventy miles northeast of London.

In the early 1980s, NATO pilots like Rick were very busy responding to concerns about the "Evil Empire" of the Soviet Union. As a young lieutenant right out of pilot training, Rick was fortunate to move quickly into the left seat as an aircraft commander. "There was no question that we were on the front lines," Rick explained. "We were involved in numerous NATO exercises to hone skills with the Royal Air Force and other allied air forces." The 48th also "sat alert" on call for immediate launch for three- or four-day periods per month. His first mission as a young flying Lieutenant in Europe was an exercise to simulate attacks on ships in the Irish Sea. An experienced WSO (pronounced "whizzo") or Weapons Systems Officer in the right seat called the altitude over the intercom and brought them down below the 500-foot minimum. "It was just great flying," Rick recalled again. "The F-111F was a very demanding system, and we operated it at very low levels to avoid radar."

He also liked the flying environment overseas where, sometimes, NATO pilots would telephone call each other, take off, and engage in some friendly but intense dogfights over European skies. Rick said he loved the ability to arrange and fly into a *furball*. That's an aerial engagement where both airplanes are scooting around in every which direction, and their contrail paths look like pieces of hair in a fur ball. In the 1980s, these engagements took place when pilots flew into predetermined airspace to tangle without face-to-face preparation briefings. The various NATO air forces maintained areas where anyone was fair game and could be "jumped" at any time by any other aircraft if they were flying in that airspace. The surprise nature of the "jump" helped to make the training more realistic. As another pilot put it, "You never know in combat when and where the bad guy is going to show up."

Among Rick's 48th wing mates at Lakenheath were two other pilots who later became shuttle astronauts.[22] His USAFA classmate Kevin R. Kregel eventually flew four spaceflights. Kregel piloted the shuttle *Endeavor* (STS-70) in 1995 and *Columbia* (STS-78) in 1996. Then he was

---

[22]   At the beginning of 2004, NASA reported that the astronaut corps included 34 from the Air Force Academy, 17 from West Point, and 51 from Annapolis. Some suggested the disproportionate number of USNA grads resulted from a U.S. Navy bias in the early astronaut selection system that has since been corrected. It may have been perpetuated by George W. Samuel Abbey who graduated 128th out of 855 in the Naval Academy's Class of 1954 and then became a USAF pilot. Abbey joined NASA in 1964 and worked in senior flight crew operational posts until he retired in November 2002.

NASA Astronauts from the Service Academies listed alphabetically:

Air Force Academy: Blaha, Bloomfield, Bobko, Boe, Bridges, Brown, Casper, Chilton, Covey, Drew, Duffy, Dutton, Gardner, Grabe, F. Gregory, W. Gregory, Gutierrez, Halsell, Hammond, Helms, Henricks, Johnson, Jones, Kelly, Kregel, Lee, Lindsey, McMonagle, Precourt, Searfoss, Sega, Shriver, Stott, Veach, and Virts.

Military Academy: Adamson, Aldrin, Borman, Clifford, Collins, Forrester, Gemar, Kopra, McArthur, Mullane, Peterson, Scott, Spring, Wheelock, White, Williams, and Worden.

Naval Academy: Anders, Bolden, Bowen, Bowersox, Buchli, Bursch, Cabana, Cassidy, Coats, Creighton, Culbertson, Curbeam, Duke, Edwards, Eisele, Foreman, Freeman, Frick, Givens, Gorie, Griggs, Ham, Hire, Hobaugh, Irwin, Jett, Lawrence, Leestma, Linenger, Lopez-Alegria, Loria, Lounge, Lovell, McCandless, McCool, Nowak, O'Connor, Oswald, Phillips, Readdy, Reightler, Schirra, Shepard, Shepherd, Smith, Springer, Stafford, Thorne, Thuot, Walker, Williams, and Zamka.

the spacecraft commander on the *Columbia* (STS-87) in 1997 and the *Endeavor* (STS-99) in 2000. Another member of the 48th, William G. Gregory, who ranked 15th among 900 members of the USAFA Class of 1979, later piloted the *Endeavor* (STS-67) in 1995. Bill recalled running on Lakenheath's track-and-field team with Rick, and later the two of them were together as astronaut classmates in 1991.

The Searfoss family enjoyed their European assignment and then headed back to the USA, where Rick was stationed at Mountain Home AFB in Idaho, until 1987. He continued to rack up awards. First he was a distinguished graduate of the USAF Fighter Weapons School, and then he was named the Tactical Air Command F-111 Instructor Pilot of the Year for 1985. He also graduated at the top of his class from Squadron Officers School and was selected one of the Outstanding Young Men of America in 1987. A year later, he was sent back east as the U.S. Air Force exchange officer at the U.S. Naval Test Pilot School in Patuxent River, MD. He remembered flying U.S. Navy A-4s, T-2s, and T-38s and even logged about fifteen hours flying helicopters. They practiced short-field takeoffs and landings but never had the opportunity to land and takeoff from carriers.

Rick called that assignment his "Air Force Appreciation Tour" because he and Julie learned more about life in the Cold War Navy with its many separations and overseas deployments. They contrasted it to the lives they had known in the Cold War Air Force, where most couples were stationed together, with only occasional separations. Rick also noted a considerable difference, at the time, in how the Navy pilots approached their flying regulations. "The Air Force operational philosophy was 'If the regs [regulations] don't say you can do it, you can't do it,'" he explained. On the other hand, he saw Navy pilots subscribe to the philosophy, "If the regs don't say you *cannot* do it, you *can* do it!"

Rick went from being a student on the East Coast back to teaching in California. He was named a flight instructor at the U.S. Air Force Test Pilot School at Edwards AFB. At that point, fulfilling his lifelong dream, he finally applied to NASA to become an astronaut. He was selected for the astronaut program by NASA in January 1990 and became an astronaut in July of 1991.

Rick sounded like baseball great Willie Mays when he talked about his reaction as a 35-year-old to finally reaching NASA at the Johnson Space Center in Houston. "Somebody pinch me, I can't believe I'm here." Right after arriving in Texas, he flew T-38s jets, usually used for high-speed flight training, in what he called "serious grown-up flying." This reaction came from a pilot who had accumulated more than two thousand flying hours at the time. He said the instrument check ride on the T-38s was "probably the toughest instrument check ride anywhere."

After Rick finished his initial training, his first job was the one he called the *best* job in the astronaut's office *other* than flying. Affectionately labeled "Cape Crusader" and officially part of Astronaut Support Personnel team, he helped strap the astronaut flight crews into their shuttles just prior to launch. Rick's voice lowered an octave when he described how he was the last person on the launch pad, closing the door prior to launch of the Shuttle *Discovery* (STS-48) on May 6, 1991. "It really got to me," he recalled. "I will never forget that feeling. I knew then that I was really part of America's space program."

That wonder would continue throughout his tour of duty with NASA. Although based in Texas, the astronauts would fly to Cape Kennedy in Florida for more training and the launches into space orbit. As fellow astronaut Dr. David A. Wolf would exclaim when they took off in their T-38s from Texas for Florida, "*We're going where the rockets are!*" Rick remembered, "We worked really hard, long hours, but we were just like kids. It was like not having a job because it was so much fun. Plus the entire team was simply outstanding."

Rick prepared to fly his T-38.

Astronaut Rick Searfoss

The Astronaut Mission Support office provided considerable training for new astronauts like Rick. Attention to detail took on new meaning since every step they took directly affected the lives, safety, and mission success of their fellow astronauts. This assignment also enabled Rick's supervisors to watch him in action as he performed the necessary tasks on ground and the launch pad to help the flying mission succeed. He worked directly on a half-dozen missions from June of 1991 to August of 1992. Rick reported that the Astronaut Mission Support provided high visibility and realistic practice too. "If you do a good job, you're gonna get some good feedback from the commander of the mission," he recalled. "And if you screw up, the whole world's gonna know it." He said U.S. Navy Captain John O. Creighton, who commanded the Space Shuttle *Discovery*'s mission on September 12-18, 1991, was one mentor who provided good feedback. "Creighton was very helpful in telling it like it was, and that helped all of us." Creighton ranked 68th among 868 graduates in his Annapolis Class of 1966.

All of his continued success on the ground paved the way for Rick's selection to fly in space. In August of 1992, he was selected for his first mission. He was named pilot for the Space Shuttle *Columbia* (STS-58) on a seven-person life science research mission. It was scheduled for launch from the Kennedy Space Center a year later. "I was pretty ecstatic," he recalled enthusiastically. "It was finally happening after all those years of anticipation! At first, you're still doing your old job and beginning to get ready for the flight mission," he explained. "However, even when all you're doing is training for the mission, it's still hard work. My first commander provided a good analogy using school grades. He said training is pretty good. 'It's a solid "B" I guess. But I tell you what, when we're on orbit, it's an "A plus" and then, between missions, sometimes it's a "D"!' I would second that assessment," Rick reported.

He remembered his first mission for the anticipation and the excitement, but those memories were tempered by his waiting for his two later flights as well. "The rookies [first-time astronauts] are real anxious and want to get going, so the inevitable delays seem that much longer," he recalled. "The veterans don't complain as much. In fact, one advantage of the delays is that you get a chance to decompress your days, and it's a great way to taper into a mission."

His recalled his first liftoff from Cape Canaveral as "sitting on top of a train wreck that pushes you up into the atmosphere." He said, "You're clobbered from behind by this irresistible force that's pushing you along with lots and lots of vibrations. As the pilot, you pare down your whole world to the workings of the main engines. There are countless systems that the pilot, flight crew, and support teams are responsible for, but the pilot's job is to concentrate on those main engines and react to their power. They are your first priority. In the final analysis, the pilot is the first person who can sense a problem with the main engines and do something about it."

Rick's first mission launched October 18, 1993, and the crew performed a wide range of medical experiments on themselves and forty-eight rats. They explored scientific knowledge of human and animal physiology in the weightlessness of space. He recalled that his first commander had encouraged him to blur the distinction between the orbiter crew and the payload crew. "We are one crew on this mission despite our different roles," he said, "and I followed that good advice to the letter."

After 225 Earth orbits, Rick brought the *Columbia* home safely at Edwards AFB in California on November 1, 1993. It was NASA's last planned landing at Edwards before switching landings to Cape Canaveral. After that, the agency moved landings to Florida so the shuttles would not have to fly piggyback on the Boeing Shuttle Carrier Aircraft. After a few weeks' debriefing, public affairs work, and decompression, Rick began his second desk job in software verification for NASA's Shuttle Avionics Integration Laboratory or SAIL. He and his team tested all the new software changes and the integration of new hardware and software on NASA's systems. He was the Astronaut Office representative for both flight crew procedures and shuttle computer software that was being developed by IBM Corporation. The team looked at systems in all phases of spaceflight: launch, orbit, rendezvous, and reentry. The cockpit was set up to have as much fidelity as possible to the real shuttle with respect to avionics issues. "For example," Rick explained, "they have identical wire lengths because signal transit times had to be precisely the same to duplicate the shuttle avionics functions. Realism was key in all the work that we did."

He also served as the Chief of the Astronaut Office Vehicle System and Operations Branch, later called Spacecraft Systems. He led a team of consultants made up of several operational astronauts and support engineers. They worked on Shuttle and International Space Station systems development, rendezvous and landing or rollout operations, and advanced projects initiatives. One of their projects was the technical development of the actual rendezvous techniques, enabling U.S. astronauts and Russian Space Agency cosmonauts to dock successfully during Mir missions. They developed and used special software that could be used on portable IBM ThinkPad® computers on board the spacecraft. Evolutions of that work led later to more realistic applications software used on the international space stations.

It also prepared him for his second mission, which was to include the third docking of an American spacecraft with the Russian space station, Mir. Its international component also included a ten-day orientation trip to Russia and a veteran crew. On March 22, 1996, Rick piloted the Space Shuttle *Atlantis* (STS-76) on a nine-day mission. STS-76 was a night launch, so the rumbling train wreck had its lights on. He said he enjoyed working with the Russian cosmonauts who he described as "very talented and dedicated." Although American astronaut Shannon Lucid spent a year in Russia and spoke enough of the language to get by, she was helped by one of the Russian crew members who spoke some English. "We got by with that old standby language, 'pointy-talkie' as well," Rick recalled. The *Atlantis* crew brought the Mir almost two tons of water, food, supplies, and scientific equipment. They also transported Shannon for her six-month stay in space. That mission also included the first-ever space walk on a combined Space Shuttle-Space Station complex. The flight crew conducted scientific investigations, including biology experiments sponsored by the European Space Agency, plus several engineering flight tests. After completing 145 orbits, Rick once again landed the *Atlantis* at Edwards AFB on March 31, 1996. Originally scheduled for Florida, this California landing was unexpected due to overcast weather problems on the East Coast.

By now a two-flight veteran, Rick was ready for a break after his two-weeks' debriefing, but NASA had other plans. "Usually you have a month off to reconnect, but in week three after the mission, the deputy chief tapped me on the shoulder with a special request, 'We want you to be a branch chief,' he asked. 'When do I start?' I answered. 'The staff meeting's in less than an hour,' he replied." It appears the "just in time" nature of personnel moves affected NASA just like any other large organization. He was able to compromise his schedule slightly with three weeks' vacation that included a family reunion in Montana.

Rick worked more on software for another year until he was picked to command his third mission. That was a seven-person crew on the Space Shuttle *Columbia* (STS-90) in a Spacelab/Neurolab mission. It launched from the Kennedy Space Center on April 17, 1998. The crew both operated the spacecraft and served as subjects for 26 individual life-science experiments focusing on the effects of microgravity on the brain and nervous system. Rick said STS-90 was unusual because it was a joint venture of six space agencies and seven U.S. research agencies and nine countries. After successfully completing 256 orbits, Rick finally brought the shuttle down in Florida though again weather was a factor when he landed hard in high winds. This mission, the last of NASA's 25 Spacelab projects, was also to be Rick's final spaceflight.

During his Air Force career, Rick had logged over 5,000 hours' flying time in 61 different types of aircraft. "I was blessed," he said, "with being able to achieve my three primary personal objectives: *never* have an assignment out of the cockpit, *never* set foot in the Pentagon, and finally, *command* a space mission."

Twenty years after his graduation from USAFA, Colonel Richard A. Searfoss retired from the U.S. Air Force and the NASA Astronaut Corps on December 31, 1998. He was awarded the Legion of Merit to mark the close of his distinguished career. His other decorations include the Air Force Distinguished Flying Cross, usually awarded to the Commander of any Space Mission, the Air Force Commendation Medal, the Air Force Meritorious Service Medal, the Defense Meritorious Service Medal, and the Defense Superior Service Medal. He also received three NASA Space Flight Medals, the NASA Exceptional Service Medal, and the NASA Outstanding Leadership Medal.

His academy friend, Mike Valdiva, noted, "Rick has a very deep and true love of flying that he has obviously had since he was a kid." When he described Rick and the other astronauts he has met, Mike called them "your classic overachiever types, so focused on their love of the space program and our country." Mike also added that he saw Rick work with his "nose to the grindstone" both at the academy and after he graduated. "He *earned everything* he got by working *hard*," he said emphatically. His other friend, Mike Mitchell, added, "Rick has been blessed with some capabilities and experiences that most of us don't have." And then he concluded, "So he wants to really make a difference in whatever he does."

Julie describes Rick as "thin and tall, almost six feet with long legs." She added, "Our oldest daughter was glad to inherit his long legs because she's a ballet dancer, but fortunately, he didn't give her his flat feet," she laughed. Julie said her husband has maintained his fitness and mentioned his running regimen in a steady routine of six days per week. "He ran a lot more miles last year than during the past twenty and keeps track of all his running in a logbook."

In 1999, the family moved to Florida where Rick began to work for the company that supported the Space Shuttle, United Space Alliance. At first, he was local consultant for the Houston-based company. However, he would often stop by the Cape Canaveral Visitor's Center and joined their Astronaut Encounter program. Next he started his own company dedicated to sharing with the public much of what he had learned from space. As an accomplished professional speaker, Rick was able to share his messages of leadership and teambuilding to many thousands of people each year.

Eventually, however, the cockpit lured him back to flying. So in 2001, the family transferred to California where Rick went back to work for NASA as a research test pilot. He flew out of the Dryden Flight Research Center at Edwards AFB, NASA's primary installation for flight research.

When asked how often he was able to fly in his new job, Rick replied with the typical pilot's response, "Not often enough!" But he did admit to three or four days per week in F-15s, F-18s, T-38s, and other project aircraft.

I was in the midst of interviewing Rick for this chapter when seven NASA crew members perished as the Space Shuttle *Columbia* was lost during reentry on February 1, 2003. The next day, I wrote to Rick and Julie expressing sorrow on behalf of my wife, Barbara, and me and so many others. He replied with thanks, writing simply, "Yesterday was numbness, shock, and disbelief. Today it's really sinking in, and messages from people who care really help." Painful reactions led to changes in plans and procedures, but the experience reminds all of us of the perils of space exploration. A few weeks after the *Columbia* tragedy, Rick submitted his resignation from Dryden, saying, "It was time for me to move on."

Since then, Rick has been constantly seeking opportunities to promote space exploration and travel. In 2004, he was selected to assemble a team of pilots and former astronauts and serve as the Chief Judge for the highly successful and innovative Ansari X Prize competition. Several organizations competed for a $10 million prize as the first privately financed team to develop and fly a reusable human-carrying spacecraft. Dr. Peter Diamandis, founder and chairman of the X Prize Foundation, said, "Rick's extensive career in aviation and space . . . made him the perfect candidate to be our Chief Judge." The Ansari X Prize was designed to promote the private, commercial space industry. Organizers hoped the incentive would mirror the $25,000 offered in 1919 by hotel owner Raymond Orteig to the first person to fly nonstop from New York to Paris. That prize, of course, went to Charles Lindbergh and his *Spirit of St. Louis* in 1927.

Rick and the Ansari X Prize team worked to bring the entrepreneurial spirit to space with hopes to travel into space the way we now travel on commercial airliners. He reported enthusiastically, "It's a joy to have this ringside seat on history. I'm deeply honored to witness and verify the efforts of bold, creative, and courageous private teams to reach space, make history, and pave the way for many thousands more in the future." On October 4, 2004, Judge Searfoss declared that the Mojave Aerospace Ventures team completed two qualifying flights of their SpaceShipOne vehicle to win the X Prize. He certified the results with the announcement, "After careful review of all requirements and technical data, I declare that Mojave Aerospace Ventures has indeed earned the Ansari X Prize by flying a reusable three-person suborbital spacecraft to one hundred kilometers altitude twice in two weeks."

Also in 2004, Rick connected with another Air Force Academy graduate, Rob "Waldo" Waldman, who was ranked 290th in the Class of

1990 and later flew F-16 aircraft in 65 combat missions over the former Yugoslavia during Operation Allied Force. The two men work together, sharing leadership and teamwork training for a wide range of business and government clients. Rick's web site, www.astronautspeaker.com, provides information about his development programs.

Like many successful people, Rick attributed his success to setting goals and lots of hard work. But he tended to dismiss its importance with an almost "Aw, shucks, no big deal" attitude frequently voiced by many other successful people. While I was interviewing Rick in 2003, *Sports Illustrated* magazine named champion cyclist Lance Armstrong its Sportsman of the Year for 2002. In the cover story, noted *SI* columnist and author Rick Reilly reported that Armstrong, with an almost superhuman practice of mind over matter as a cancer survivor and then four-time Tour de France winner, was interested in going into space someday. When told about that interest, Rick responded the way he always does when someone asked about the future of space travel. "He certainly has the physical fitness part down," Rick said. "Hopefully, within a few years, he can buy a ticket on a suborbital ride for a reasonable price."

That boy who dreamed of flying long ago now helps others achieve their dreams, both on earth and in outer space.

Chapter 15

From GI to Guru

David A. Anstey, USMA '82

Online enterprises of the 21st Century economy have created
considerable demand for people with new skills. Traditional preparation
paths—such as undergraduate and postgraduate college, university, or
technical school training, apprentices, and internships—often fail to
meet the needs for qualified technologists. This seems to be particularly
onerous in the world of software. The word "guru" labels people as hard
to find as their mythical mountaintops. Software techies come in all sizes
and shapes. American and global dot-com companies are filled with
very young former nerds who are now creating complex systems. At the
beginning of Y2K, a forty-something ex-Army Ranger might seem out of
place in that world. But being out of step never stopped Dave Anstey in
the past, and he's not about to let it stop him in the future.

Dave was born on Christmas Eve of 1960 in Santa Fe, NM, but raised
in Estes Park, CO. It is "a stunning place" where, he said, "You're ruined
for life. It's absolutely gorgeous, an incredible place." The soaring Rocky
Mountains provided a spectacular backdrop for young Dave, his mother,
Elsie, and his stepfather, Ron Cotten. Ron was a civil engineer for the U.S.
National Park Service and nurtured Dave's exploration of the picture-
postcard outdoors as he developed an interest in the Army. His biological
father, Arthur Anstey, had been a U.S. Navy machinist mate in World
War II. He and Elsie had split when Dave was three years old, and Elsie
raised Dave as a single Mom with help from her mother, Inez Brown. Inez
spoke to her grandson entirely in Spanish so the youngster was bilingual
when he started school. Dave thought using both languages surely helped

him, albeit subconsciously, in later life as he wrote in multilayer software languages. Elsie worked outside the home as a secretary for the National Park Service. That's where she met and later married Ron. All four adults strongly influenced Dave, who was an only child. He was a scrawny little kid who enjoyed the outdoors and thrived on camping in the woods. Boy Scouts served his needs, and Colorado's Rocky Mountains captivated him. Elsie succumbed to brain cancer when her son was twenty and a junior at West Point. Inez died seven years later.

At Estes Park High School, Dave was the smallest freshman boy. He was one of the original nerds, working on his Data General computer in the mid-1970s long before most kids had Apple computers or PCs. Thanks to the relative wealth of the Estes Park community, the school system was well equipped. Its computer labs were state-of-the-art, and Dave loved working on their computers. He also studied reasonably well enough to graduate in the top third among his ninety-two classmates in 1978. Extra-curriculars ranged from Scouts to leadership on the Student Council where he served as president in his senior year. He also played coronet in the school band and was a photographer on the *Whispering Pine* yearbook staff. By senior year, he was a five-eight, long-distance runner who racked up two-mile races for the Bobcats track team and generally presented himself as an ideal candidate for admissions to USMA.

"My family didn't have a lot of money," Dave explained. "So I knew that funding my education was going to be an issue. West Point was the best of all possible combinations for me and my education." His stepfather's younger brother, John, was an influence too. "My Uncle John graduated from the Air Force Academy in 1973 when I was in junior high school, and I was impressed with all the ceremony and the mystique of the military," he recalled. John P. Cotten, who ranked 276th among 844 grads, was an Air Force Civil Engineer for six years.

So with the full support of his parents, Dave left the Rocky Mountain high and flew east for the first time to join 1,395 other classmates on July 6, 1978, in the Long Gray Line. His eventual low class ranking at West Point would contrast sharply with his steady rise to the top of the software-consulting world less than two decades later.

"I look back on my years at West Point very fondly," Dave recalled. "I actually had a lot of good experiences, and I felt like the Academy was the place where I finally grew up. I was definitely a kid when I arrived. I didn't really know much of anything about teamwork; and, as an only child, I had never experienced the necessity of sharing. So for me, it was a good exposure to a lot of things that every one needs in their lives. Plus, I had never been east of the Mississippi, so the introduction to another part of the world was very helpful.

"I loved the military side but not the academic side of life at West Point," Dave explained. "I wasn't very fond of studying, but 'playing Army' was fun. It was something that I enjoyed. I enjoyed the challenge and the outdoors. The interesting camaraderie in life in the military in that we're all in it together was a real benefit for me. However, I certainly didn't study properly and didn't take academics seriously. I mostly enjoyed the military part of West Point. The annual Sandhurst[23] competition with four-member teams, for example, was a lot of fun for me, and I was good at it."

Perhaps one of the keys to understanding Dave's future success lies in exploring this competition, especially the final initiative obstacle. He explained that software development consists of seeking patterns and eliminating the wrong ones while focusing on the right paths to complete tasks. He compared software development to strikingly similar military leadership challenges of getting a dozen people to move from Point A to Point B. "That's the hardest thing to do because you've got to get inside someone else's head to get them to do what you want," he explained. "Writing software code is much, much simpler compared to that.

"A lot of people take leadership for granted," Dave continued. "If you have an analytical pattern, you solve it by eliminating the approaches that don't work. That may be OK for software, but it won't do when you're dealing with people. People bring their emotions, knowledge, and prejudice and even fear to the situation. It's much more complicated. As a leader, you've got to build consensus, or you're not going to get anything done, much less get a dozen folks to follow you through unknown

---

[23] Sandhurst is a yearly timed competition that tests military skills over a 6.5-kilometer course. Based upon military exercises at the Royal Military Academy at Sandhurst, England, West Point's competition originally matched cadet company representatives against each other. Eventually, it pitted thirty-two West Point company teams against others from U.S. Army ROTC units, Sandhurst, and Canada's Royal Military College. Each nine-member team includes at least one female member and a member from each of the four academic years. Opening with the firing range, cadets next don protective equipment for nuclear, biological, and chemical site exercises. Team members dismantle and assemble an M-60 machine gun and an M-249 squad automatic weapon. They navigate a field itinerary with eight grid coordinates and cross a river with a one-rope bridge. After the entire team crosses the bridge, they crawl through a tunnel and run uphill to a wall obstacle and then rappel down a cliff. They also face an unknown obstacle that tests initiative. David Lipsky's excellent description of the modern West Point, *Absolutely American*, included a thorough review of the Sandhurst competition in 2002.

wilderness. As I've gotten older, I realize that what I learned about leadership at West Point serves me almost every day. I have also concluded that leadership is less about committee thinking and more about achieving the objective through common understanding and motivation."

Jeff Poulin, who ranked 10th in the class, remembered Dave as a friend who was right at the top militarily but not a strong student. He quickly said, "Even folks at the bottom of the West Point class are like the top of any other school." Sounding like a recruiting poster, he added, "I believe West Point preparation is second to none." He reported that confidence building is just one part of the difference and focuses on planning when he connects the success enjoyed by Dave and others after graduating from West Point. "They taught us there to plan and plan again," he recalled. "And Dave was a master at it. 'Does it take five minutes to move forty troops from here to there?' he would ask and then add, 'Did you try it?'" He said the practical use of case studies made it realistic, and "I believe that surely helped Dave and the rest of us." Jeff spent ten years in the U.S. Army as a Ranger. He earned a PhD in Computer Science from Rensselaer Polytechnic Institute in four years and later worked as a Computer Systems Architect for IBM and Lockheed Martin Corporation.

Another classmate and company mate in D-4, Paula Hartman Koehler, remembered Dave as a hardworking military guy with a great sense of humor. She said she was "as shocked as anyone" with his success in the computer field. "But that just shows you how hard it was at West Point, and how well prepared we were," she added. Paula majored in mathematics and ranked 174th in the class. Right after graduation, she married another classmate, Perry L. Koehler, an engineering officer. She served in the Army's Quartermaster Corps for five years before resigning to work in industry. Paula described Dave as "sort of a string bean, fairly thin, maybe six feet two" and sandy hair. Paula and Perry saw Dave in 2002 at their class reunion and said he had not changed too much. "He is still one of the funniest people I know," Paula said directly. "Any time you spend with Dave *always* makes your day better. We had a great time at West Point and didn't concentrate too much on academics." She remembered the 'pet rock' craze during their junior year. "We decided to get Dave a pet *lawn*. We pulled up some sod from the Supe's [Superintendent's] lawn, put it in a box, watered it, and took care of it for a while as a diversion. That was one of the ways we just tried to get through and enjoy ourselves."

At graduation on May 26, 1982, Dave's inattention to academics took their toll. He ranked fifth from the bottom of his class. Later he would joke about it, saying he would tell people who asked that he graduated in the top 100 percent of his class at West Point. He's unsure about who was actually last in his class, naming two classmates who might have been '82's goat. Dave laughed, "The big joke used to be that the *dumbest* guy in the class was *next* to last because he didn't get the money!"

First to receive his diploma in 1982 from Texas U.S. Senator John G. Tower was Peter R. Mansoor of Sacramento, CA. Mansoor chose the Armor branch and was assigned to the 3rd Armored Cavalry Regiment with duty at Fort Bliss, TX, where he met his wife Jana. The Mansoors have a daughter, Kyle, and a son, J.T. (John Thomas).

He spent much of the next two decades in cavalry regiments in Germany and at the U.S. Army National Training Center in Fort Irwin, CA. Like many top graduates, Mansoor eventually earned a Master's degree (1992) and PhD (1995). After completing his studies in military history at the Ohio State University in Columbus, he returned to West Point to teach it there for two years. His dissertation on the development of combat effective infantry divisions in the U.S. Army during World War II formed the basis for his first book, *The GI Offensive in Europe: The Triumph of American Infantry Divisions, 1941-1945.*

After a Pentagon assignment as the Special Assistant to the Director of Strategic Plans and Policy from 1997 to 1999, Mansoor moved to Fort Hood, TX, to command the 1st Squadron, 10th Cavalry, the "Buffalo Soldiers" of frontier history fame. While at Fort Hood he also served as the Operations, Plans, and Training Officer (G-3) for the 4th Infantry Division (Mechanized), and was selected for early promotion to colonel and command of the 1st Brigade, 1st Armored Division in Germany. After attending the Army War College, Mansoor deployed to Iraq, where he commanded the Ready First Combat Team in Baghdad. After finishing his first 13-month combat tour plus another year in Germany with his brigade, Mansoor was appointed a senior military fellow at the Council on Foreign Relations in New York. Later he was founding director of the U.S. Army/Marine Corps Counterinsurgency Center in Fort Leavenworth, KS.

He returned to Iraq from February 2007 to May 2008 as executive officer to General David Petraeus, the commander of Multi-National Force-Iraq, who was ranked 39th among 833 graduates in his West Point Class of 1974. Mansoor retired after his Iraq duty and was named to the General Raymond E. Mason, Jr. Chair of Military History at Ohio State University. He published *"Baghdad at Sunrise: A Brigade Commander's War in Iraq,"* in September 2008.

Academy grads say that their schools never look as good as they do in their car's rearview mirrors as they finally drive away after graduation. Following a popular tradition at all of the academies, Dave's cadet car was a hot one. He bought a black 1981 V-8 Chevy Camaro with a T top and "four on the floor" stick shift.

Graduates also bore their younger compatriots with endless tales of WHIT. That double entendre was not necessarily humor; it represented claims by the older grads that "We Had It Tougher." Dave recalled a different twist from an old grad who visited West Point while he was a cadet. "He was walking across the apron in front of Washington Hall where we had just come out from noon meal formation. He was an elderly gent with a topcoat and alumni armband, slowly making his way across the field with the help of a cane. He spotted the three of us from my company, and we saluted automatically. The old man pointed at the plebe who was with us and called him over with an inquiring wave. We didn't know if he was going to jack him up or ask a question. Then he privately said something to him. The plebe answered, drawing a laugh from the old man who ambled on his way. The plebe came back to us, and we asked, 'What was that all about? Was he looking for the new gym or something?' 'No,' said the plebe, 'he wanted to know if this place still *sucks* as badly as it did when he was here.' The plebe answered, 'Yes, sir, it does.' And the old grad laughed and said, 'Yeah, I thought so.'"

For Dave's graduation, both his Dad and Stepdad flew east to commend their son. In a moving commissioning ceremony that sunny May day, each of the men pinned on one of Dave's shiny, new gold second lieutenant bars. Following the rounds of graduation parties and weddings, Dave headed back out to Estes Park for a well deserved, month-long graduation leave. One night, he and Ron went out to dinner at a local restaurant called the Other Side. Dave noticed the young woman who was the assistant manager, a former fellow student at Estes Park High named Cindy Acton. They began dating, and then he left for Officer Basic Training at Fort Bliss near El Paso, TX. He proposed over Labor Day weekend, less than three months after they first met; and they were married November 20, 1982. A week later, Dave started Ranger School at Fort Benning, GA.

Without the tedious academic loads that had dogged him at West Point, Dave thrived at soldiering full-time. He downplayed his experiences at winter Ranger School. Most observers described Ranger School as one or two steps from pure hell. However, Dave explained, "During my Cow summer [just before junior year] at West Point, I had gone to Airborne School at Fort Benning, so I had a leg up on some of the guys who hadn't jumped yet. But Ranger School cured my itch for all things challenging. I was content to take people's words for it that things were difficult after that experience."

After Ranger School, the Ansteys moved to Europe. Dave was sent to the Fifth U.S. Air Defense Artillery Group at Holzwickede in Northern West Germany in the waning years of the Cold War. They were first lines of air defense against the possibility of an attack by the Soviet Union. With the passage of time, his five-and-one-half years in the Army now seemed to have flown by quickly. But it was tedious work on the front lines of NATO's borderline front against the USSR. And Dave's West Point class rank still dogged him. "I wanted to be in the infantry, but I was ordered to Air Defense, one of the worst assignments you could get at the time," he recalled. When he noted that this was an important but undesirable assignment, he also reported that many of the people who staffed it were West Point graduates who had been at the bottoms of their classes.

"We were entrusted with what was probably the nation's most sensitive weapons material," he recalled. "For example, in my last year in Germany, I was an emergency actions officer who certified people for important tasks. We went to the special NATO weapons procedures course, and we knew the ropes. Many of the folks who literally had their fingers on the triggers had not graduated anywhere near the top of their classes. But we were properly prepared and supervised, and we did our jobs correctly at the height of the Cold War."

During the Ansteys' three-year assignment in Germany, Dave became embroiled in an incident that resulted in a written reprimand, effectively ending his military career. He and Cindy returned to Fort Bliss to finish out his military service commitment, bringing home their sons, David and Zachary, who were born in Germany. Fort Bliss and El Paso are 330 miles from Dave's Santa Fe birthplace. The post and city have evolved from a small sleepy 19th Century infantry outpost to a town that was an ideal place to seek a civilian job. But Dave's West Point experience interfered. "I think I ended up near the bottom of my class at West Point because I never cared much for academics and never thought that I would work in academics," Dave explained. "In fact, I had every intention of becoming a lifer in the military, and so I thought my military work would count more than my academics. Ironically, when I was in El Paso getting ready to exit the military, I tried some of those career outplacement services. I joined other grads trying for interviews with high-end *Fortune 500* companies. However, my GPA at the Academy followed me and prevented me from joining a big business like many of my classmates. It's too bad that so many initial hiring decisions are based upon a person's GPA.

"In a way, though, it helped motivate me because I wanted to show everybody that being at the bottom of the class doesn't prove anything," he continued. "So, I was faced with very few options when I got out of the Army in the summer of 1987. Fortunately, I had taken computer science in high school, and my major concentration at West Point was Systems Analysis, which was basically computers. Although I've always enjoyed the world of computers, when I worked in the Army's Air Defense, I didn't see a computer for five years!

"When I got out, I needed a transition mechanism to get me into civilian life," Dave explained. "So, I hooked up with a defense contractor, doing research analysis and maintenance for a small company by that name. They needed some help in software, and I needed a job.

"I took a 30 percent pay cut and started at the bottom, programming IBM AT/286 personal computers and Digital Equipment VAX 11/780 computers. Luckily, the cost of living in El Paso was reasonable. His first company was Research Analysis and Maintenance Inc., which provided systems and software engineering and technical support services to the U.S. government and private industry. It was a leading business owned by a woman. With typical bluntness, Dave said the contrast from working with combat Army men on the front lines to a business owned by a woman presented no problem. "I learned a lot and contributed to our success," he recalled. "They gave me a great opportunity to develop software for surface-to-air combat systems. It was a great entry-level job as a software engineer.

"Then I parlayed that experience into an Operations Analyst job at CASE [Combined Arms Systems Engineering] for the Battlefield Integration Center in General Dynamics' Fort Worth Division," Dave reported. CASE was like one of those *Fortune 500* companies that had ignored Dave in his job search less than two years earlier. Now he was experienced in the burgeoning world of software development, and suddenly his West Point class rank didn't matter. His resume at CASE lists an impressive array of ever-increasing responsibilities. To the layperson, it's gibberish; to the computer cognoscenti, it's a veritable All-Star scorecard.

Dave was a Project Leader who helped design a real-time simulation system for Air-Land combat used in the Army's Battlefield Integration Center. He worked with a large computer system that modeled theater-level combat operations and provided analysis tools down to the battalion level. All the transactions and events that took place were reflected in real time in the computer. Combat commanders in the midst of fighting saw the results of enemy conflicts as they occurred. Real-time feedback added realism to the conflict. Dave didn't mention the irony of creating the necessary technical tools used by his higher-ranked classmates still in uniform. He specialized in linking high-powered, 32-bit VAX computer systems and sophisticated SUN intelligent terminal systems with programs written in scientific FORTRAN and connected via ETHERNET. He studied and learned how to use Relational Database Management Systems produced by Oracle Corporation, the world's leading supplier of software for information management and the world's second largest independent software company.

Every day, he was using the discipline of the military in the world of computing. And he thrived on it.

His work at General Dynamics attracted the attention of several outside consultants who waved new opportunities at him. So he commuted to Dallas to work for Database Consultants Inc. They provided systems to clients as diverse as ARCO, MCI, and the Fort Worth Police Department. Years later, he would serve as an outside consultant project manager for General Electric's electronic commerce efforts.

"Part of that consulting life is the need to share information and publish," Dave explained. "Fortunately, I enjoy writing. To me, it's a logical extension of what I like to do, which is to help people as a consultant. In the field of IT [Information Technology], publishing gives you exposure, and exposure generates demand, which feeds on itself. If you're good, publications help you to network. It's the way we market ourselves and our capabilities to prospective clients."

Clients called the shots, and the consulting programmers responded. In fact, that response led to the acronym for Dave's company, POCSOL Inc. "We would be working on a project with a certain set of specifications, wants, and needs," Dave explained. "And inevitably, the client would ask for more. 'Can you just add this or that?' was the question." And Dave and his team would respond easily, "Sure, Piece Of Cake, Speed Of Light!" It led to the acronym POCSOL, which forms the name of his company today.

Dave's resume described his climb up the corporate ladder, from software engineer to operations analyst, programmer, and project manager. His acquisition of vast information technology experience is a tribute to the discipline he learned from his parents, schools, and military service. Like many of his West Point classmates, Dave is an accomplished author and public speaker. He has written more than a dozen papers with titles like "Object Mapping in the Relational Database" and "Designing Class Hierarchies in Oracle 8.1." He is the author of *High Performance Oracle8 Object-Oriented Design* and a contributing author for *Advanced Database Technology and Design*. He has also addressed numerous international computer conferences as an expert in Oracle database development. Like most other successful computer companies, Oracle encourages its customers and clients to operate users' groups. These groups provide important feedback to the company as it designs its products to serve users' future needs.

Dave has designed and developed many Oracle-based applications and client and server systems. He has also managed numerous large-systems development projects, mentored junior developers, and helped to develop corporate application development methodology standards. He was chairman of the Oracle Development Tools Users Group's Web Committee from 1999 to 2001. He served as Editor-in-Chief of the Group's *Technical Journal* for four years. He is a past president of the Fort Worth Oracles Users Group. He served as a member of the Board of Directors of the Oracle Development Tools Users Group (ODTUG) since 1998 and was elected its president in 2002. He retired from the group at the end of 2005.

The early part of the 21st Century saw Dave adjust to two major transitions. He and Cindy divorced in October 2001. As his marriage came to an end, Dave took on a long-term software project in Louisville, KY, flying back and forth to his house in Texas each week as he pursued new work in a difficult economy. Ultimately, Dave would relocate to Kentucky in mid-2003. Not to be deterred by a diminishing demand for IT services and a slow economy, Dave met the challenge by co-founding an Academy graduate business networking group to help promote business relationships among service academy alumni in the Louisville area.

While working on the long-term project in Kentucky, Dave met up with Jennifer Staunton, a New Jersey native who had settled in Memphis with her parents and four siblings. Jennifer received her bachelor's degree in Education from the University of Tennessee and her Master's degree in Education from the University of Louisville. She specialized in instructional design and distance learning systems. After a fourteen-month courtship, Dave and Jennifer were married in Memphis on May 24, 2003.

Dave continued to consult with a wide range of clients as their Oracle expert. He also continued his love of adventure and the outdoors through activities as diverse as long-distance running, handgun shooting, and orienteering. But he balanced them with more-relaxed pursuits like cooking, wine tasting, and guitar playing. Jennifer commented just before their marriage that "Dave is different. He has such a diversity of interests and skills. He's my renaissance man."

Dave completed the Bataan Memorial March.

*Dave and his son,
the Army medic*

On March 21, 2004, Dave successfully completed the Bataan Memorial Death March at White Sands Missile Range, NM. Entered in the "Male Over Forty" group, Dave and his longtime friend and former Marine, Mike McDonough, completed the 26.2-mile march through high desert terrain in six hours and 23 minutes. Michael M. McDonough graduated 184th out of 888 in the Naval Academy's Class of 1973 and served as a field artillery officer. In civilian life, he worked in information technology. Dave and Mike entered as individuals and ran together throughout the gruesome trek. The March, which included more than 3,000 starters and 1,800 finishers in 2004, honored the survivors who defended the Philippines during Word War II. Of the experience, Dave said, "This was a significant event for two reasons. First, it was a tremendous physical challenge and gave me a sense of focus for months beforehand. Second, Mike and I both felt honored to participate in an event that respects this great group of veterans. It was humbling to meet several of those gentlemen before the race."

The two friends returned in 2005 to participate in the March once again and shaved more than thirty minutes off of their time from the previous year, completing the race in five hours and fifty minutes. Although the event became more taxing as the participants get older, neither has ruled out another trip to do it again.

Dave and Jennifer enjoyed some other, more relaxing travels with a 2006 trip to Napa, CA, to attend a Mastering Wine course sponsored by the Culinary Institute of America. At the same time, he proudly reported that his son David had enlisted in the U.S. Army. After completing Basic Training at Ft. Benning, GA, David completed medical training at Ft.

Sam Houston, TX. He also married longtime sweetheart, Rachel Olsen on May 26, 2006. Then he was assigned as a combat medic with the 101st Airborne Division (Air Assault) and served a combat tour in northern Iraq from September, 2007, through November, 2008.

Dave Senior officially moved back into another classroom in 2006 when he joined a few younger students at the College of Business of the University of Louisville. He pursued a Masters of Business Administration (MBA) degree with a focus on entrepreneurial thinking. This time around, Dave reported much better scholastic performance and graduated from the program in May of 2008.

James "Jay" F. Jennings—the Class of '82's alumni note keeper or scribe, who was ranked 379th—said that Dave is a fairly typical classmate. In 2002, Jay reported, "My classmates' current professions include priests, ministers, and missionaries, warehouse shipping managers, corporate pilots, Wall Street bankers, college professors, policemen, homemakers, physicians, lawyers, engineers, delivery truck drivers, pharmaceutical sales reps, corporate recruiters, telephone company executives, cyber-business owners, doctoral candidates, and a park ranger. Sixteen are deceased. The most common occupation is still the profession of arms."

Chapter 16

A Grad Who Defied Labels

Karolen Kay Fahrni, USAFA '85

When I first connected with Karolen Fahrni, she was running the assignments division in human resources at her Alma Mater, the U.S. Air Force Academy. I reached her in the Department of Personnel while trying to learn more about the academies' staff recruiting activities. When I described this book, she promptly volunteered that she was "probably last" among the ninety women in her class of 945 who graduated there in 1985. An award-winning gymnast and captain of the academy gymnastics team, she later coached the sport for the Academy. Then she commanded squadrons and worked in protocol and personnel departments around the world.

Karolen was very up front about her class ranking as she described working each day in an environment that charted success by using the alphabetic GPA and numeric MPA (Grade and Military Point Averages) to determine rankings. When she worked at the Air Force Academy, U.S. Air Force Lt.Col. Karolen Kay Fahrni regularly reminded her coworkers that the academy may rank and label students using those letters and numbers, but the regular Air Force and the rest of society use job and life performance as better measures. They also provide recognition through challenging new jobs, promotions, and awards.

Karolen's class was the sixth to include women, and she was one of its pioneering students. She was also a varsity gymnast from a military family, who worked diligently at her sport four hours each day. Much of that determination came from her father and mother, who she called "dirt poor" South Dakotans born in the Depression and accustomed to hard work. Dad was Leonard W. Fahrni, a small-town athlete good enough to earn a work-study athletic scholarship at Black Hills State University in Spearfish, SD. He was also recruited into baseball's minor leagues and, in 1994, would be inducted and recognized in Black Hills's Hall of Fame. While in college after the Korean War, Len joined the U.S. Marine Corps and was commissioned as a USMC Second Lieutenant when he graduated in 1955. He attributed much of his later success in life to his early military training. Len married his high school sweetheart, Helen Waterland, from Central City, SD, on June 5, 1955. Then the two of them left home and raised three kids at various military assignments around the world. Len spent two combat tours in Vietnam and ended up at Camp H. M. Smith in Hawaii where he retired in 1976 as a USMC Lieutenant Colonel. He developed a rare blood clot and lost his left leg to surgery in 1994.

Like many military families, the Fahrnis moved often, transferring to fourteen duty stations in twenty years. They enjoyed their last tour in the Aloha State so much that they retired there and started second careers in real estate. Both of Karolen's brothers worked in the family business. Older brother Len worked in property management while younger brother Allen became a realtor.

Karolen was born May 11, 1962, in Oceanside, CA; and her family moved to Northern California then to North Carolina, New Jersey, Rhode Island, Hawaii, Japan, and finally, back to Hawaii. Although she never spent more than two years in the same school, she was a top student at suburban Mililani High School, less than an hour's drive from Honolulu. She was also a successful and good-looking blonde gymnast, attracting more than her share of admirers. She remembered, during her junior year in high school, that a teammate's brother graduated from the Air Force Academy and returned home to sing its praises. As Karolen planned for college a year later, she was ranked academically among the top 10 of her graduating class of 200. An Air Force lieutenant, who was a recruiter and a recent USAFA grad, spoke glowingly of comfortable camping in the beautiful Rocky Mountains. He mentioned a cadet car and enough other faux attractions to entice Karolen to apply to the Air Force Academy. She remembered going home that night to tell her folks that she wanted to go for an appointment. "Of course, I was a bit late in a few minor details like writing for a traditional nomination," she laughed, "but we didn't let *that* little detail stand in our way. My Mom helped me work the system through the gymnastics coach. I ended up getting into the Academy Prep School, which really helped me."

Shortly after Karolen's high school graduation, the Fahrnis flew to Montana for a family reunion and then sent their only daughter off to Denver. Relatives met Karolen there and drove her to the Academy Prep School on the USAFA campus grounds. It was July 22, 1980; and, like virtually all the people I have interviewed about their academy experiences, she called it "a date I will always remember." Karolen recalled, "The next thing I know, I'm looking at a chalkboard with those statements that tell you about the proper responses,[24] and it's a real shock. Fortunately, I wasn't totally unfamiliar with the military like some of my classmates. Eventually, we got through it, helped by people I remember like USAF Technical Sergeant Johnnie B. Graton who asked, 'Where is it written in stone that life is fair?'"

Academically, Karolen was also in for a few surprises. "You go from being an overachiever in high school, and then you reach the academy, and you get your first D or F because everybody there is a 'brain,'" she complained. "At first, it was a setback, but what do you do?" she asked. "If you want to succeed, you must work hard at it." And work hard she did. "Except for the first holiday after prep school, I spent *every* summer at the Academy in Summer School, making up for courses that I failed," she recalled. "I only went home for the Christmas breaks."

She pursued a "Basic Academics" major, which she called her "BA." Although that allowed her to take a range of electives, the core curriculum of engineering-oriented courses, like thermodynamics, still dragged her down. "I liked the law classes and took every one I could, but classes like 'aero' and 'astro' still hurt my GPA," she said in a determined voice. "However, there was just no way I was not going to graduate on time."

At the same time she was working hard academically, Karolen was one of only eight to ten female cadets who competed on the Academy's varsity gymnastics team. That year-round sport included NCAA Division I meets that began in November and concluded with league, regional, and national championships in April. "I can remember one year, when one of my teammates was injured, that the cadet who was our manager actually competed on balance beam because we needed a minimum of five gymnasts to compete," she recalled. During her senior year, Karolen was elected Captain of the gymnastics team. She enjoyed that leadership position because she liked the interaction among hardworking people who were more or less capable athletes. She called herself the "glue" who helped keep her team together as they handled the stress of competition in an environment made more difficult by the demands of a military

---

[24]   "Yes, Sir"; "No, Sir"; "No excuse, Sir"; and "Sir, may I ask a question?"

I mentioned this exchange in 2005 to then Cadet Fourth Class Laura Kate Martineau of the Class of 2009 who updated me with three more in use:

"Sir, may I make a statement?"; "Sir, I do not understand"; and "Sir, I do not know."

academy. "We used to laugh when we would compete against athletes from civilian schools, and they would complain about their so-called 'busy' schedules with nine hours of class per week," she explained with a hint of irony.

"I think you have to be very disciplined to be an athlete at any college but especially at an academy since you must balance your classroom, military, and athletic responsibilities," Karolen remarked. "You go to school, you go down to the gym then to the library and come back to your room and go to bed. Time is critical, and so is your physical well-being. For example, I don't know too many athletes who would pull an all-nighter to study or write a paper. *Not* because they wouldn't want to, mind you, but because the lack of sleep would affect performance in other areas."

At the beginning of her two degree or junior year, Karolen was assigned to Squadron 22, which included only one other female cadet from her Class of 1985—an English major named Lynn Steer. Lynn was also outspoken and a basketball player from Colorado Springs. As the only two female two degrees in the Squadron, they were assigned to be roommates. "We didn't see eye-to-eye at first," Karolen recalled. "At taps, the lights were out in our room because I was too tired to keep reading by flashlight. And of course, Lynn had lots of extra reading for her major. Fortunately, she ended up graduating as a successful English major. Later she was nice enough to give me some of the credit because I forced her to manage her time better, to go to sleep at night, and to be alert and ready for class in the morning. She said she was awake for classes, and that really helped."

As an undergrad, Karolen said she was not too aware of class rank. "My focus was on survival, not class rank," she explained. "I think my first F was in computer science where we were working on programming. Ironically, years later, although I'm not an expert, I'm comfortable with computers." Cadets' Military Performance Averages include reviews by peers. "We really didn't like peer rankings, and I can remember a comment that went, 'She doesn't smile enough in the halls.' My reaction was 'OK, you don't say that about the *guys!*" Both Karolen and Lynn didn't remember much discrimination as female cadets, but they did recall being singled out as athletes. Karolen said, "We sat together as a team for lunch, and that was always a sore spot because non-athletes thought you were getting away with something that *they* had to do."

The Class of 1985 had assembled on June 22, 1981, with 1,466 basic cadets. Four years later, 945 graduates listened to U.S. Air Force Secretary Verne Orr urged them to lead the Air Force into the 21st Century. Karolen was among the 644 members of her class to enter Undergraduate Pilot Training, and another 46 classmates reported for navigator training. That total of 690 out of 946, or 73 percent, responded to the "needs of the Air Force" during that period, reflecting an admissions process that favored candidates who were flight qualified. Three-quarters of the 945 grads remained in uniform after seven years, and nearly 40 percent reached the twenty-year retirement milestone in 2005.

Karolen's parents pinned on those bars.

The class scribe, Tennessean Lt.Col. Frank Quintel "Q" Williams, who was ranked 876th in the class, earned a Master's Degree in Physical Sciences from the University of Houston, TX, and was a space operations officer. He said the class included two members of the Thunderbirds Aerial Demonstration Team and more than ten successful CEOs. Twenty years after graduation, the roll call had been depleted by the deaths of twenty-two members, including eleven from aircraft accidents.

After graduation and a brief stop at Disneyland with her folks, Karolen flew back east where she and Lynn took a Caribbean cruise with a ship full of what they called "newlyweds or nearly deads." Then she reported to Vance AFB in Enid, OK, for Undergraduate Pilot Training. UPT is the Air Force's intense one-year school and flying program to produce pilots.

She successfully completed all the rigorous classroom requirements and began to enjoy flying. First she flew the sit-side-by-side T-37 Tweet jet trainer and then upgraded to the sleek T-38 White Rocket supersonic jet trainer. She had logged over 130 flying hours and soloed, well on her way to becoming a pilot, when she hit a roadblock. She was about three-quarters of the way through her training in March of 1986 when she failed her contact check ride. Pilot training includes a series of difficult exercises and tests designed to check the pilot trainee's progress. Despite a dozen successful flights in the T-38, including a couple of solo flights, she was unable to complete the necessary contact check ride.[25] Like all T-38 students, she was given two more chances to pass but was unable to complete that phase of her training. "I washed out, plain and simple," she lamented. "It was a shock, and I was disappointed, but I knew I had given it my best shot and was determined to get on with my life in the Air Force."

After leaving Vance, Karolen set out to find another job in the Air Force. "When you wash out, you have no clue as to what's available since all the emphasis until then has been on flying," she said. "I called up other people that I knew to explore other career paths." One suggestion was to join the missile career field. Karolen had visited Minot, ND, during a program called "Operation Third Lieutenant" between her third and fourth class years to introduce cadets to active-duty Air Force jobs. "I had no desire to be a 'pioneering woman' in that field, sitting underground with a gun strapped on my waist, 24 hours a day, ready to launch a nuclear weapon," she said very directly. "I wasn't ready to do that."

After considering several job fields, she became an assistant acquisitions officer for Satellite Support Systems at Sunnyvale Air Force Station in California's Silicon Valley. For nearly two years, she worked at Sunnyvale, later named Onizuka AFS to honor astronaut Ellison Onizuka, the USAF Colonel who perished on the *Challenger* Space Shuttle. She managed a

---

[25]   Another USAFA and Vance UPT graduate (our oldest son, USAF Major Kevin A. Hoppin, ranked 477th in his Class of 1990) described the contact check ride as "the one where you must demonstrate an ability to fly the aircraft under a range of exercises before you move on to the next phase of training. You perform all sorts of High-G aerobatic maneuvers including loops, barrel rolls, cloverleaves, split Ss, and Immelmans. You also perform stalls and the ability to land the aircraft safely and consistently. One of the main challenges is keeping the aircraft in your airspace. At Vance, they took western Oklahoma and cut it into a dozen or so pie wedges using a compass-like device. You had to use the navigational instrument as well as ground reference to stay inside your piece of the pie. But the biggest challenge was performing loops requiring 10,000 feet of altitude in a 12,000-foot block. Most people busted by going out the top or bottom. People used to graduate from pilot training with 190 hours. The contact ride is around Hour 130, and you could still wash out in Hour 189." (K. Hoppin Interviews)

$287 million annual budget in a program control environment. They tracked satellites and space shuttles and other classified projects using many new one-of-a-kind computer systems.

The "World Series" earthquake that hit Northern California on October 17, 1989, threatened to wreak havoc on the base and its operations. Karolen's quick action helped protect Air Force computer resources and valuable data during the aftermath. She later received the Air Force Achievement Medal, which cited her for "leadership, supervision, and decision-making capability instrumental in the successful mission restoral efforts after this catastrophic event."

Later organizational changes led to another assignment as the executive officer to the station or base commander at Onizuka. In December of 1987, First Lieutenant Fahrni was named headquarters section commander for the 1004th Space Support Group. Once again learning a new career field, she was the direct administrative boss for 300 officers and airmen and concerned about their military responsibilities away from their jobs. The 300 included approximately 45 WAF or Women of the Air Force. Her primary duties included all discipline matters, courts martial, and discharges. At the same time, her additional duties ranged from public affairs and protocol to career counseling. She performed these duties so well that she was recognized with several awards in 1989. She was named the base and U.S. Space Command Company Grade Officer of the Year. She also received the Meritorious Service Medal at the end of her tour of duty in May of 1990. The MSM, rarely awarded to junior company grade officers at the time, noted her "professional skill, innovative approach, and exceptional dedication to duty." Karolen's California experiences laid the foundation for her future dealings with complex staffing issues, developing her skills as "a people person."

After she left California, Karolen was assigned to two consecutive overseas assignments, once again, in a new career field. She became Chief of Protocol first for Osan Air Base in Korea and then for Tempelhof AB in Berlin, Germany. Both high-visibility jobs demanded considerable tact and organizational skills as she entertained high-level visitors and interacted with host-nation dignitaries as well as senior U.S. military and diplomatic officials. Her Berlin work coincided with German reunification and the closure of the U.S. air base, resulting in even more intense protocol challenges. Once again, her success and outstanding efforts were noted with the first Oak Leaf Cluster awards to both the Meritorious Service and Achievement Medals.

Captain Karolen Fahrni returned to the USA in 1993 to take up several new posts at her Alma Mater. She remembered, "At first, when I drove back on the academy grounds, I still got that sick feeling in my stomach that I was a lowly cadet all over again. When I finished at work and drove off base to my home, I thanked God that I didn't have to face all that cadet BS." At first, she was the gymnastics coach, but she also taught four physical education courses with a total of 200 male and female cadets. The courses ranged from water survival and unarmed combat to self-defense and volleyball. She experienced time demands and schedules similar to the ones she had experienced as an undergraduate. But now, she was also spending weekends scouting and recruiting new cadet athletes. "It was one of the most intense times in my working life," she recalled. After a year, she was assigned the additional duty of Executive Officer or deputy to the assistant athletic director in charge of all twenty sports except football, volleyball, and basketball. Her teams racked up impressive records with three national championship appearances, ten team records, six All-Americans, and two Academic All-Americans.

One day in May of 1995, Karolen went to the academy's dental clinic for her annual checkup and cleaning. The dentist, Lt.Col. Robert C. Wahl, was very helpful. She remembered returning to her office and telling a friend, "The dentist that checked on me today was a really neat guy, but I'm sure I'll never see him again." That night, the cleaning caused her some tooth pain, so she called up the dental clinic for some relief. "The clinic staff people were very concerned," she recalled, "and with hindsight, they might have even been playing matchmakers. They arranged for me to meet that same dentist who everyone calls Dr. Bob. Later *he* ended up calling *me* to check on the tooth, and we chatted for a while. I remember thinking, *Is this guy really calling up to check on my tooth or is he gonna ask me out?* After about an hour's conversation, he asked me out to the movies. He assured me that he did not get my phone number from the records, which would have been inappropriate." She described Dr. Bob as "a really straight-laced Iowa boy."

Not too long after they started dating, Bob received orders to transfer to Offutt AFB near Omaha, NE, about 600 miles east of the Academy. The prospect of a long-distance relationship didn't appeal to either of them. Neither did the difficulty of obtaining concurrent Air Force assignments, which are reserved for married couples. So they decided to follow their hearts and were married. Their wedding took place on New Year's Day of 1996 in Moanalua Gardens, a private park in Honolulu. Several years later, Karolen said, "Dentists are very precise and careful people. Why he married me, I don't know because all I've done is brought total random chaos to his life! But it works, and we work really well together." Eventually, Dr. Bob would become a stay-at-home Dad or, as he called it, "A Family Dynamics Engineer and Consultant." Karolen and Bob had two children:

Mikaila Kalani, who was born in 1999, and Justus Rider, who arrived in 2001. Of motherhood, Karolen said, "It's just so scary being a parent, but you make choices."

*Bob and Karolen
and Mikaila and Justus*

When I first spoke with Dr. Bob, he said his wife was very fun-loving and very driven, a "can-do type person who gets things done." He said her independence was nurtured by her parents and believed the Air Force Academy fostered that independence. He also said Karolen was a very good worker who thrived in the military. He described his wife as "very attractive with long blonde hair" and a trim figure of 128 pounds on a five-feet-six gymnast's frame.

In 1996, Karolen concluded her first assignment at the Air Force Academy with the second oak leaf cluster to the Meritorious Service Medal. She then moved to rejoin Bob in Nebraska where she was assigned to the Civil Engineering Squadron as squadron section commander at Offutt. Although similar to her first California job after pilot training, now she was responsible for hundreds of airmen and officers charged with building, maintaining, and protecting the huge Nebraska base. However, after a year, the Air Force restructured her job and assigned her to the human resources or personnel field. With no formal training, the new Major Fahrni was assigned to work with what she affectionately called "the hogs."

She remembered fondly, "They were a great group of folks who took great care of me. And we got the job done." She plied her trade in the personnel arena, transferring skills learned in other areas of interactions with people of all ranks. She worked successfully for four years as the chief of senior officer matters in the Assignment Division for the U.S. Strategic Command at Offutt. After only two years in the career field, she was named the Command's Personnel Manager of the Year 1999. A year later, Dr.

Bob completed his twenty years and retired from the Air Force, and they decided to try to move back to Colorado Springs. At the conclusion of her tour in Omaha, Karolen received the Joint Service Achievement Medal for leading the hogs to successfully support this Unified Command.

In May of 2001, sixteen years after graduating from the Air Force Academy, Karolyn returned for the second time to become Chief of the Assignment Division and Senior Officer Matters for the academy's personnel department. She and her four-person team of NCOs specified, recruited, and assigned jobs for virtually all of the academy's 1,000-person military staff, excluding cadet assignments. She also handled the delicate assignments of placing senior officers, colonels, and general officers in their new assignments once they concluded their tours of duty at USAFA.

Karolen thought she might have been the first graduate to come back to have the key job of recruiting new staff members in personnel. "It's funny," she said. "When I first met the Dean, he said, '*Ah ha*! It's great we've finally got a grad back here in the personnel shop who can understand our problems.'

"Then the Dean asked me, 'So, what did you major in?'

"I looked right at him and replied, 'Graduation.'

"And he paused, slightly confused, and said, 'No, really, really, what did you major in?'

"And again, I answered directly 'Basic academics' and his jaw dropped as he recognized that he was talking to 'one of *those*' who were *not* in the top half of the class."

Despite that initial surprise, Karolen believed the Dean was happy with the job that she did. "Those were very difficult times for a combination of factors. The increased operational tempo in the regular Air Force was taking more people away from the Academy. It was part of my job to make sure that we kept staffing at the proper level." Later the job would become even more complex when several senior officers at the Air Force Academy would be reassigned in the midst of the 2003 disclosures about sexual harassment of female cadets.

"It is always very interesting at USAFA because everything is measured in the institution. It was kind of a joke between my boss and me as we heard all the time that I would be considered a 'bottom of the barrel, dregs of society' graduate. So I would sit in these meetings when they have these kinds of conversations about our cadets, and I would try to bring a certain dose of reality to the discussions. Sometimes they would start talking about jocks and bottom feeders, and I would say, 'Now, wait just a minute, that would be me! *That* usually got their attention!'"

From the time when an Air Academy was a gleam in the eyes of early aviation pioneers, it has always been an important objective of USAFA to produce pilots. And throughout its history, the U.S. Air Force Academy has struggled with the proper mix of graduates who are qualified to become pilots and those who are not. During most of its 50-year history, the Air Force Academy's admissions criteria favored applicants who were physically fit to fly. In fact, in many classes that entered in the 1980s, only 25 percent of the new freshmen were not qualified to fly. Less than perfect eyesight and vision less than 20-20 were the primary disqualification. We Admissions Liaison Officers used to say, "You *can* get into the Air Force Academy if you wear glasses and can't pass the flight physical. It's just *twice* as difficult." To my knowledge, no one in the Admissions Office ever disputed that assessment.

Karolen recalled vividly a meeting where she was not only one of the few women in the room but also one of the few officers of either gender who was not wearing the flight wings of a pilot or navigator above their uniform pocket. The discussion was focused on encouraging more graduates to fly, addressing a pilot shortage at the time. Karolen thought it was ignoring those who would not fly. "Finally, I'd had enough," she remarked. "I spoke up and asked, 'Why are you slamming support officers? How has this institution swung so far off its main mission of producing Air Force officers, *some* of whom will fly?

"All of a sudden, it got to be real quiet in the meeting room, so I concluded with a simple statement, 'I might not be a pilot, but I'm still a warrior.' At the end of the meeting, the Commandant of Cadets—BGen S. Taco Gilbert—said to me, 'Thanks for bringing us back to reality.'" She added later, "I appreciated his support." Gilbert graduated 23rd among 981 in the Class of 1978.

Karolen was one of the few female officers in the Academy's senior staff, but she never considered herself a pioneer. "All of the female officers provided role models for cadets who number 4,000, including less than 600 women," Karolen said. She added, "As a woman in the military, we're always scrutinized. You have to be better at what you do. That's just the reality of the situation in society. I was not a ring knocker [bragging about being a grad], so many folks didn't even know I was an academy grad. And there were still some who questioned women in uniform. Even in the 1990s, I was there with a group of male cadets who were still saying that women should not be at the academies. I just said 'get over it' and went about doing my job."

Her former academy roommate, Lynn Steer, took a different approach. After graduation, where she ranked 470th, she completed pilot training at Reese AFB, TX. Next Lynn flew KC-135 refueling tankers for five years in the Air Force. Faced with a non-flying desk job, she chose to resign and become a civilian pilot. Lynn flew Airbus A320 aircraft for United Airlines, based in Denver. She and her husband, Eric Lewis—a commercial software database administrator—have a son, Duncan, and a daughter, Rebecca. Lynn said, "I loved every minute I spent in an Air Force uniform, and I am never going to malign my school or the military. It just appeared to be easier for men to gain rank because they're encouraged to have wives and children. *I believe* women in the military have the spouse or child option, *but* at the expense of rank."

Lynn recalled going back to the twentieth-year anniversary celebration of the pioneering women at their Alma Mater in 2000. "I saw a panel of high-achieving women from the Air Force Academy," she explained. "They were diverse in many respects, and most of their jobs were related to aviation and aerospace of course. But there was one very obvious thing they had in common: no husbands and no children. Males don't *have* to have a wife to be successful, but you're *supposed* to. As a woman, you cannot have a husband and children and be successful. At least, that's the message I got. It's just too bad because it really limits the opportunities," she said. Lynn and Karolen remained good friends and were able to visit each other often. Of her former roommate, Lynn said in 2003, "Karolen is very honest and does not suffer fools easily. But the problem is she's a woman. If you're strong and opinionated as a woman, you're labeled as a bitch right off. Fortunately, she has the ability to be tactful." (Steer Interviews)

One fall day, late in 2002, Karolen discovered a bump in her scalp and decided to go see her doctor, who quickly recognized symptoms of a melanoma cancer. He sent her to the University of Colorado Hospital in Denver for immediate treatment and surgery just before the Thanksgiving Holiday. Karolen bluntly described the procedure, "They took a baseball-sized chunk of skin out of my scalp behind my right ear and reconstructed it. Then they took out forty lymph nodes down my neck." Classified as a Stage III Melanoma, her cancer required extensive chemotherapy—five days of treatment followed by a few weeks off. The cycle was repeated four times that winter and spring; at the same time, Karolen and Bob were completing construction of their new house.

"When I first got the news, I called it the pits," she recalled. "But I was determined not to let it take me." Her father had lost a leg to a blood clot ten years earlier. "He's the real hero," she reported. "He's been through a lot. I'm the daughter of a one-legged Marine," she said firmly. "Need I say more? I'm not giving up any time soon. I'm thankful every day that I wake up, and I'm still with us."

During our interview process, I would contact Karolen and Bob for updates and to ask about her progress. My wife, Barbara, is also a cancer survivor and a strong supporter of anyone who endures those challenges. With the typical layman's uncertainty, at one point, I finally asked Karolen, "Was it serious surgery?" "Yes," she replied, "and I've got the scars to prove it." Then she provided the details that appear above. Later she concluded, "But I'm happy to be alive and looking forward to spending a lifetime with Bob and our children. Nothing else bothers me too much now."

While Karolen was fighting her cancer, she was on medical leave from her job in the Air Force Academy's human resources department. She returned to work in August, right after the school's very public scandal involving sexual harassment and rape of female cadets. Of her own cadet days, she recalled, "I think I felt 99 percent safe, but I was always aware that there were some bad eggs there," she explained. "However, when you read a girl's comment that she had twenty lemon vodka drinks before this happened, I say, '*Hello*, what were you thinking or *not* thinking at all?' However, rape *is* rape, and that *does not* excuse the behavior," she added quickly. "I *do know* that they have a lot more educational programs now about date rape, but the institution itself sounds like they didn't necessarily handle these things correctly in the past."

Upon returning to work, Karolen saw that the academy had beefed up the cadet counseling center and put in place a wide range of other improvements. "People are coming forward a little bit more," she remarked. "However, a briefing on the results of a cadet wing survey in late 2003 reported cadets who are minorities feel integrated; but the problems still persist. They've got a long way to go, and it will not be solved simply," she concluded.

Early in 2004, Karolen saw an opportunity to take another assignment back home in Hawaii at Hickam Air Force Base. Hickam was the headquarters for the Pacific Air Forces or PACAF, the command team for the 45,000 military and civilian USAF employees in the Asia-Pacific region. The headquarters included 500 officers and 400 enlisted employees, and Karolen was named their administrative commander with responsibilities ranging from facility management to discipline. Although it had many similar duties to her work in California and Nebraska, the new job brought more challenges because her squadron had so many senior officers and NCOs.

"In many ways, the base is like the Pentagon without the building," she laughed. "I have never seen so many Colonels and Chiefs in my life!" She quietly added, "I'm pretty insignificant here in the big picture, just trying to help these folks do their jobs and getting ready to retire from active duty."

Each of the book's grads helped me tremendously as we explored their own lives and the influence of their families, friends, and academy experiences. During the interview process, we would often talk regularly and then move on to our other projects for a while. When Karolen started up her new job in 2004, I was working on other chapters and scribe notes and didn't call her for several months.

On April 1, 2005, I called her for an update. Someone in her office told me she was at home, and that her illness had returned. So I sent her this e-mail:

> Dear Karolen, I called your office and they told me you were having some more health problems. Be assured Barbara and I are praying for your speedy recovery from this latest setback. Here, hopefully to cheer you up a bit, is my first Draft of your Chapter. I look forward to discussing it with you soon. Meanwhile, be well and know the snow is almost gone on Peaks Island—no foolin'! Chris

She quickly replied,

> Chris, Great to hear from you—yes the cancer is back and it's not good. They will medically retire me and I will keep enjoying the time I have with my family. Everything happens for a reason—it is a funny twist that we came out to take care of my Dad and now my family will take care of Bob and the kids. My e-mail automatically erases any attachments—can you send the text to me in the e-mail? Thanks again and God Bless :) Karolen.

That was the last I heard from her. In a few weeks, she passed away.

I called Bob and Lynn in May, and they told me the details of her passing. In February 2005, Karolen and Bob took the kids and returned to Colorado for snow and skiing. During their holidays, Karolen began to notice some health problems and checked herself back into the hospital for tests when they returned home. Tripler Army Hospital doctors discovered the relapse of malignant melanoma. "We didn't realize the cancer would progress as fast as it did," Bob explained. "And we were never able to get ahead of the disease." He added that the oncologist was "really super and did everything he could for her, but the disease moved too quickly." After ten days in the hospital, Karolen asked to return home for hospice care so she could be with her family and friends.

Shortly before she passed away, USAF General Paul V. Hester, PACAF commander, presented Karolen with a medal. She asked him, "Sir, can I ask you one thing?" And the general replied, "Of course." Karolen urged, "Well I wish that you get somebody to replace me for my troops right away." Bob said that the general recalled that this was a typical concern of Karolen, looking out for her troops. No one who knew her well was surprised.

Among those who visited was her old USAFA roommate, Lynn Steer, who marveled at her resolve. Another grad, Kimberly Ann Green Davis, also visited and later wrote the tribute "Gone but Not Forgotten" for the AOG's *Checkpoints* magazine. Kim was an instructor pilot and USAFA Women's Tennis Coach who graduated 898th among 1,074 in the Class of 1988. She is a tennis professional and Co-chair of the U.S. Professional Tennis Association's National Women's Committee in Colorado Springs.

Kim's alumni magazine tribute included reminisces about a happy day skiing in Breckinridge, CO, before Karolen's final illness. She wrote,

> Karolen told me that she wanted me to remember her most in this way—on the slopes, deep in the powder, sun shining, and blazing a trail on a double black diamond. I remember that day how Karolen yelled for me to come her way through the trees—once again challenging me to better myself and have fun at it! I followed her and watched as her beautiful spirit shined through layers of ski clothes as we were alone together experiencing the beauty of the Colorado Mountains.

Kim concluded, "Our last conversation together before she died was especially meaningful. Karolen held my hand and told me that she was at peace with God, and that she had put her trust in Him and His plan for her. She was grateful for the time that He had given her and thankful for all of the blessings that He had bestowed on her." (Davis Interview.)

Bob said simply, "I was so impressed with Karolen and the way she carried herself in those last months. One thing that really amazed me in the last couple of weeks before she passed away was that she sat down and wrote letters to the kids for each one of their birthdays right up until they're eighteen. And letters for when they get married and have their first child." He continued, "I thought that was pretty neat." Then he added, "I would try to comfort her and tell her we're gonna be OK, and I found that she was the one who ended up comforting me." He concluded, "She was one strong lady."

Karolen helped the family plan her funeral arrangements, which included services led by their former pastor and longtime family friend Reverend Richard Matsushito. She was cremated, and some of her ashes were distributed to the sea in a small family ceremony at Ko Olina Beach on Oahu's western shore. "That's a place where the family had enjoyed many happy outings," Bob reported.

Lt.Gen. Victor E. Renuart Jr., Vice Commander of Pacific Air Forces, visited Bob and asked to arrange a memorial service on base at Hickam. "At first, we were reluctant," Bob explained, "because Karolen had said she didn't want a big formal memorial. But we agreed to General Renuart's suggestion and were glad we did, because many people were able to pay their respects to Karolen and acknowledge the impact she had during her career. The service was held at Hickam in the Nelles Chapel, which was filled with family and friends. General Hester presented Bob and Karolen's mother with American flags in shadow boxes. "It was a beautiful ceremony and proved helpful during that difficult time," Bob recalled.

This remarkable woman received two other tributes: Each year, the Air Force Academy's top female gymnast receives an award in her honor, and PACAF designated a section of its historic headquarters building with a plaque on the wall in the area where she last served. It's now the Fahrni Commander's Support Suite.

Bob explained, "Our children are very young now, and I don't know how much they will remember about their mom. Hopefully, these honors and family and friends will help keep her memory alive. I want the kids to know what a special person their mother was and how much she loved them."

Hopefully, this chapter will help that understanding too.

Chapter 17

Life's Zigs and Zags

Terrie McLaughlin-Galanti, USAFA '86

Sometimes the paths of life twist more like a Monte-Carlo Grand Prix than the straight U.S. Interstate Highway System. Terrie McLaughlin-Galanti has zigged and zagged ever since her birth on January 11, 1965, in San Bernardino, CA. She was the first child of Thomas and Jackie McLaughlin, who moved the family to Naperville, IL, when Terrie was nine years old. Tom was a sales manager for Pfizer, using his BS in chemistry from Marquette University in Milwaukee to work in pigments and minerals. Jackie was a homemaker, raising Terrie and her brothers, Michael and Steve, who were born in 1966 and 1969. Terrie reported a normal childhood filled with schoolwork and play that led to Naperville Central High School, a strong Northern Illinois suburban institution where nearly all graduates went to college.

Before she completed high school in 1982, Terrie had played center for her high school basketball team for two years and had earned another varsity letter on the track team as a four-hundred-meter sprinter. She was also president of the Math Club, an organization she described, two decades later, as one of the most "un-cool" organizations in her school. "But I really liked the challenges of math competition," she reported.

Most high school guidance departments arrange College Fairs each fall that enable students and parents to learn about opportunities available to them after high school. Naperville Central is a top high school, so its fair regularly attracts a good crowd of college representatives. Depending upon the location and interests of the school, most college fairs include a wide range of exhibitors who set up modest tabletop displays. Traditional colleges and universities as well as trade schools and the military services send their recruiters and volunteer representatives to display information about their institutions. The service academies' liaison officers put on their uniforms and distribute materials and describe their programs to parents and students who visit their tables. Often the fairs are the first time a prospective cadet or midshipman meets a military officer. The programs also provide good opportunities to dispel confusion about the academies' admission processes. That confusion stems from common misunderstandings about congressional nominations. The demeanor and body language of parents and students speak volumes to observers about genuine curiosity, interest and/or reluctance to consider military service.

Terrie recalled her College Fair as a very positive and helpful experience, where USAFA liaison officer Air Force Reserve Major George Gulick told her about the Air Force Academy. "I liked the challenges and opportunities at the Air Force Academy and also at the Naval Academy, especially for electrical engineers," she recalled. "And I wanted to serve my country. I thought the military offered a great opportunity for me as an individual and as an engineer."

She was well prepared to apply to USAFA and USNA. She also sent in her applications to Notre Dame and the University of Illinois, where she could have used an Air Force ROTC scholarship for part-time military studies. However, the prospect of a complete, well-rounded education—combining academics, leadership, and athletics—convinced her to go to Colorado Springs and the Air Force Academy. Eventually, both her younger brothers would follow their big sister into uniform through the University of Illinois' Air Force ROTC program. Mike became an Air Force pilot, achieving the rank of Colonel below the zone, and Steve completed his military service and became a partner at the management-consulting firm of Bain and Company in Chicago.

On June 28, 1982, when new appointee Terrie McLaughlin arrived at the Air Force Academy with her 1,482 other classmates, she was well prepared *and* ready. At the end of her junior year in high school, she had attended the Summer Scientific Seminar Program at the Naval Academy. Those one-week sessions are used by the academies to recruit and acquaint top candidates with a sampling of life as a cadet or midshipman. Programs range from dormitory living and meals in the dining hall to sample classes and activities intended to introduce candidates to the academy. During her senior year, Terrie had also attended the Air Force Academy's special appointee orientation weekend. So, unlike nearly half her classmates, Terrie had actually spent some time at the academy before that first day, which all cadets and midshipmen call the longest day of their lives.

However, Basic Cadet Training still loomed as a large shock. Starting with the first day's harsh transition, Basic McLaughlin, as she was called then, was thrown into an intense six-week period called "beast." The "basic" label instantly describes the contrast in lifestyles new cadets and midshipmen experience. To reach the Air Force Academy, Terrie and her classmates had achieved considerable success if not fame and notoriety. A typical entering class at any of the three academies includes scores of high school class academic valedictorians and student council or class presidents, hundreds of Eagle Scouts, and varsity team captains. Eighty percent of them have just completed the last semester of their senior year where they have been at the head of their schools, literally and figuratively. Many have just finished rounds of awards celebrations, team banquets, and graduation parties. Their appointing Congressional representatives or Senators have greeted them warmly while proud parents have placed photos and news items in local newspapers. These folks have been riding on the tops of their local worlds, flying high.

Then they arrive at their academy where one—to three-year-older upperclassmen and women—called the cadre—burst their balloons.

"Basic!" the upperclassmen and women shout, "get in line and wipe that smile off your face! There are just three things I want to hear from you: 'Yes, sir; no, sir; and no excuse, sir!'"

Terrie recalled, "For someone accustomed to doing a good job and succeeding at almost anything I had tried, this was an emotional adjustment to say the least. My classmates and I were now the lowest of the low. I had been prepared and told that the best thing I could do was to try to have a sense of humor and keep my focus. But it was shocking and not at all easy. Almost immediately, they tore you down and took away your identity. Then they began the process of building you up as a member of a team, earning respect and the right to be recognized."

Team building during "beast" takes many forms. Plebe summer or Basic Cadet Training, with the inevitable acronym of BCT as it's officially called, throws basics together in organizations called companies or flights or platoons made up of 100 strangers seventeen to twenty-one years old. Their senior cadet and regular military instructors overload them with too many conflicting orders, too many tasks, and not-enough time to complete them. Although more recent "kindler and gentler" changes have certainly improved the tone and the respect of "training" new cadets, the pressure to succeed is real and ever present.

Time pressure is an enormous motivator. One of the cadets who I served as a Liaison Officer was David Suzuki, who graduated seventh in his Class of 1991 at the Air Force Academy. He said, during his cadet days, "If you wait until the last minute to do something, it only takes a minute to do." That seems to be a survival strategy for many cadets and midshipmen. David's twin sister, Karen, who ranked 20th in their class as the Suzuki twins achieved prominence as the first brother-sister twins to graduate from a U.S. service academy, recalled her basic training years later when she gave birth to her first child. "I remember the first thing I learned in basic training has actually been a most important lesson when my baby was born: 'Never pass up a chance to eat, sleep, or go to the bathroom.' This lesson started the first day at the Academy," she recalled. "We were in a small group for in-processing and passed from one upper-class cadre member to another. Around six PM, our cadre asked if we had had dinner yet, and we said no—we hadn't even had *lunch* yet!" (Suzuki Interviews)

Beast summer or plebe summer experiences were a series of many, many last-minute experiences for overstressed cadets and midshipmen. Far from frivolous, however, these pressures are designed to practice quick decision making at the very beginning of officer development. Eventually, of course, these basics would progress through their leadership development to the point where their quick decisions would affect the lives of the soldiers, sailors, marines, and airmen assigned to them.

Terrie said she learned one of her young life's best lessons during her fourth-class (first) year. As part of their training, cadets and midshipmen receive regular feedback from their instructors. They also review their fellow cadets to provide them with additional assessments by members of the team. These frank exchanges tell cadets and midshipmen how their peers think they are performing. The reviews provide real and helpful insights. The top and bottom two assessments are offered verbatim and are often even more enlightening. "I thought I was doing just fine," Terrie recalled. "I was working with my teammates, and I thought we were right on track. But the peer ratings told me I was not as effective as I could be. To put it bluntly, my peer ratings said I had a lot of talent and ability but was not helping the *team*. I think that was the greatest thing that could have happened to me at the Air Force Academy. Right at the beginning, it caused me to step back and say, 'OK, I need to do well here, but there are other things that are also very important.' It really helped me to work better with others," she explained. "It was a part of officer development that I was definitely lacking, and I learned from it. I learned the importance of working with others rather than just striving for success myself."

With Terrie's strong academic preparation and love of learning, she thrived in the charged academic environment of the Air Force Academy. Unlike virtually all other top-tier universities, service academy instructors and professors are teachers first and researchers or authors second. Her electrical engineering studies included courses taught by teachers with proper academic credentials and practical experience as working engineers. Each of the academies offers dozens of academic majors that reflect both traditional higher-education scholarship and military officer development for the specific needs of the individual services they represent.

At the beginning of her 1984 junior or second class year, Terrie's AOC (Air Officer Commanding) told her she was ranked first in her class. "It wasn't something we kept score of," she recalled, "so it was a bit of a surprise. I had continued to progress in teamwork, so I really wasn't paying all that much attention to my individual records. In fact, teamwork at the Air Force Academy involved lots of help checking laboratory results at eleven o'clock at night. It was a real contrast for me later when I got to graduate school where the learning process was more individual. I learned that the team building at USAFA was not always a priority for individuals at other institutions. That was another shock at another stage of my life."

During her senior year at the Air Force Academy, Terrie was interviewed for the prestigious Rhodes Scholar Program. Throughout the years, all of the military academies have recorded an impressive number of graduates who have been awarded special graduate scholarships. Rhodes Scholars numbered 86 at USMA, 44 at USNA, and 33 at USAFA.

Terrie remembered the Rhodes Scholar qualifying questions from an Air Force Captain, a woman who was a history instructor at the Air Force Academy at the time. She posed several queries to the top graduating senior in 1986 that might have been inappropriate for a male questioner. The Captain asked, "Suppose you earn this scholarship and then you decide to stay at home as a parent after these wonderful educational opportunities, how can you justify using these opportunities and staying at home?"

Terrie recalled that she felt very strongly as she replied as a 20-year-old graduating senior when she said, "There is no more important job than the formation of the souls and the minds of children and what they can provide to our world in the next generation. I thought if that's the path my life takes, then I will use the opportunity that I've had and the things that I've learned to really help my children.

"In the 1980s, people truly believed that, as a woman, you could do it all," she remembered. "*Now* people realize that you cannot do it all, or certainly that you do not *have* to do it all. I don't know if the pressures to nurture are societal or biological. I believe it's a very personal decision that each parent must make as they feel it's appropriate."

Then Vice President George H. W. Bush presented Terrie and her 960 classmates their diplomas on May 28, 1986. As the top graduate, Terrie enjoyed her short-lived fame including a public affairs-sponsored visit to New York City and an appearance on ABC television's *Good Morning America* program. After a brief vacation leave at home in Illinois, she flew back to Colorado Springs, picked up her trusty 1984 Toyota Corolla, and drove to Los Angeles for temporary work as an Air Force intern. Graduate school beckoned at Stanford University in Palo Alto, CA.

Each year, the service academies send the overwhelming majority of their graduates to the military workforce or basic officer training schools. One or two top graduates in each academic major are released temporarily from military duties to attend graduate school. This practice dates back to the early days of West Point. A review of the initial assignments of graduates who were first in their classes, reveals that most of them went to graduate school right after graduation. The time spent in school is simply added to the active-duty commitment required of all graduates.

Terrie spent a year at Stanford where the contrast between her undergraduate and graduate studies was striking. "It should not have been a surprise to me because the Air Force Academy was producing well-rounded officers and Stanford's Graduate Engineering School was producing graduate engineers, but it was still quite remarkable," she explained. "I had never met so many people who were just pure engineers who lived *for* and *loved* the subject." She also contrasted the striking difference in levels of cooperation among students that she had been accustomed to at the Air Force Academy.

As Terrie was completing her MSEE at Stanford University, the Air Force was keeping track of her and ready for her to start her work outside the classroom. Four hundred miles south of Palo Alto, the Air Force Systems Command operated a major satellite and communications systems acquisition organization at Los Angeles Air Force Station. Among the Center's units was the Defense Dissemination Program, which collected, analyzed, and presented overhead satellite information for U.S. military forces. The DDP's Program Manager was equipped with state-of-the-art technology and charged with finding the "best and the brightest" technologists to use it effectively.

In 1988, BGen Jean E. Klick was vice commander for the Air Force Space Systems Division. She also ran the DDP and MILSTAR programs. She charged her deputy, Colonel Don Fisher, to scour the Air Force for the best people he could find. "I was able to recruit and hire at the top of the list," Fisher recalled. "Terrie McLaughlin was certainly one of the many great hires that I made with that authority. It was clear she had a great resume and was bright and extremely articulate. After I brought her in to the program, all the other qualities that made her a great young leader became immediately obvious."

Initially, First Lieutenant McLaughlin was Deputy Program Software Manager for DDP. After a few months, her boss was reassigned, and Terrie replaced him. Fisher reported, "She worked for three years in the program and received a succession of very responsible jobs. We gave her as much as she could handle, and she could handle an awful lot. As a junior Captain, she was put in charge of a group of senior Majors and Lieutenant Colonels and got them to work for her successfully.

"As a very young officer, she basically had the future of our program in her hands. She handled that marvelously," Fisher continued. "She's extraordinarily bright with communications skills that are very highly developed. She makes everybody feel comfortable around her. She's a consummate team player. When she's working on somebody's team, she's giving them 100 percent, and when she's the leader, she's able to get 110 percent out of her team."

Fisher said that after working with Terrie for a couple of years and giving her really significant responsibilities—from software engineer to being in charge of all future development in the program—he was about to send then Captain McLaughlin onto even bigger and better assignments. "I made it very clear that I thought she was going to be the first lady three-star or four-star general," Fisher recalled.

Meanwhile, Terrie had begun a friendship with one of her fellow program managers, Captain John Galanti. John, of Buffalo suburb Lackawanna, NY, had completed his electrical engineering studies at Syracuse University in 1983 and was commissioned through the Air Force ROTC program there. Terrie and John started dating in 1988. A year later, John resigned from the Air Force to go to work for Hughes Aircraft in Los Angeles. The couple was married April 21, 1990, in Naperville, IL. Two years later, they thought seriously about moving back east and starting a family.

Terrie remembered lengthy discussions with her new husband and her boss about their future plans. "I was concerned about balancing work and home life," she recalled. Fisher had the same memories. "Our talks about *where* she would go in the Air Force were balanced about her discussion about *what* was going to be important to her in the long run," Fisher said. "Terrie was not necessarily concerned with being the greatest officer that the Air Force ever had but with being the greatest Mom that ever was. This was certainly something that I subscribed to," Fisher continued. "I told Terrie that if *anybody* could balance the responsibilities that would

278 Same Date of Rank

come with being a great officer and a great mother, you would be the one person in the world that I thought could do that. I tried to make her understand that 80 percent of Terrie was way beyond what some people can do at 100 percent."

Terrie replied, "That may be true, but that was not the route I was prepared to take. I didn't want to work at the 80 percent level in a career and 80 percent for family and see where that would lead. I *knew* I wouldn't be satisfied with that."

Fisher recalled that he and Terrie talked about her career many times over several months. "She told me she was thinking about motherhood and getting out of the Air Force." He remembered that it was a very emotional experience for both of them. "We both knew what she was going to be giving up with that decision," he said. "Today I would probably support that decision even more than I did years ago," he said. "I'm sure she's making an extraordinary contribution to the country as a wife and parent and member of their community." Fisher later retired as a full Colonel and moved to Bend, OR, where he worked in technology for the public school system there.

The Class scribe for 1986, U.S. Air Force Lt.Col. Robert A. Colella, who ranked 196th academically, reported nearly two decades later that more than half the class remained in uniform. Bob has flown both B-52 and B-2 bombers and was Commander of the 96th Bomb Squadron at Barksdale AFB, LA. In 2004, active-duty classmates numbered 409 while 108 were in the Guard or Reserve. Others worked in the U.S. government including the Federal Bureau of Investigation. Several flew for United Parcel Service, United Airlines, and Southwest Airlines while other classmates worked in technology firms like Gateway, Microsoft, and Inflow. Others worked at home.

Members of the Class of '86 saw combat in all U.S. operations during their careers, including the Kuwait and Iraq Desert Shield and Desert Storm, Northern and Southern Watch, Kosovo during Operation Allied Force, Enduring Freedom, and Iraqi Freedom. One classmate, then Captain Scott "Spike" Thomas, safely ejected from his damaged F-16C fighter over Iraq during Desert Storm and was rescued after two hours on the ground. Another, then Captain T. O. Hanford, was the F-16 pilot who located Air Force Captain Scott O'Grady when he was shot down over Bosnia during Operation Deny Flight. Graduates were working in the Pentagon when it was attacked on September 11, 2001. Several classmates flew the Air Force One aircraft for the 89th Airlift Wing at Andrews AFB, MD, ferrying the President and other dignitaries around the globe. Many maintain their ties to their Alma Mater by serving as Academy Liaison Officers, helping to interview new candidates for admissions or Air Force

ROTC scholarships. When this book was written, twelve members had retired; and eleven had died, including several in aircraft crashes.

Terrie resigned from active duty in the Air Force in 1992 and joined Aerospace Corporation in Virginia as a project engineer. Meanwhile, John switched from Hughes to Aerospace, and they both worked on satellite communications. While John severed all his official links with the Air Force and switched to the civilian side of the business, Terrie became an Air Force Academy Admissions Liaison Officer. She remained in the Air Force Reserve from 1992 to 1996. In 1992, they moved from Los Angeles to suburban Virginia to start their family. The birth of their first child, Laura, in July 1993, prompted major changes in their lives. "We decided that one of us should stay home with Laura, and I volunteered because both of us believed in the importance of full-time parenting at home," Terrie reported.

She told the story of a dear friend from the Air Force Academy's Class of 1984, Marybeth Peterson Ulrich. She was Terrie's mentor as an upperclassman at the Academy. "She was a terrific help, and we remain very good friends to this day," Terrie reported. "She seems to have balanced work inside and outside the home very well. Sometimes I find myself wishing I could be more like Marybeth, but that's just not me."

Marybeth Peterson graduated 53rd in her 1984 Class of 1,027 as a political science major and then went to Air Force Navigator School. She eventually logged almost 2000 hours as a navigator on KC-135Q air refueling tankers and other aircraft. Later she earned her PhD in Political Science at the University of Illinois through the Air Force Institute of Technology graduate school program. She returned to the Air Force Academy to teach political science from 1993 until she resigned her regular commission and transferred to the Air Force Reserve in 1999. She is also an Admissions Liaison Officer for the Air Force Academy. Her full-time job is teaching international relations and national security strategies as a Civilian Title 10 professor at the Army War College in Carlisle Barracks, PA. Along the way, she married Mark Ulrich—a fellow graduate student from Illinois—who's a mechanical engineer for Ingersoll Rand. Marybeth and Mark have had four children but suffered the loss of one in 2000.

Marybeth said, "*Any* working mother is very conflicted." She looked at Terrie and said, "Here's someone who could have done any number of things both at work and in the home, in or out of the Air Force. But I think it comes down to your identity." Marybeth said, "For me, I just know I wouldn't be happy staying home. Somehow for me, my work brings something to what I do and who I am at home. My identity is wrapped up in the balance of work and home."

Terrie concurred, "One could ask if Marybeth is *less* of a parent because of what she does outside the home. I'm sure the *opposite* is true! I believe Marybeth is *more* of a parent because she balances. Everybody makes his or her choices. And everyone does what's best for their family. When I see Marybeth and look at all that she has done, I ask how could she have done it? But I always come back to the answer. I may have been able to do this, but it was not the best choice for me and my family."

Marybeth believed that Terrie was influenced by her own Mother who raised her family without the distractions of a job outside the home. Jackie McLaughlin died from a sudden brain aneurysm in 1991 at the age of forty-nine. Terrie reported that her mother was initially opposed to her going to the Air Force Academy because she was concerned about Terrie's ability to handle it emotionally. Terrie said now, "My Mom was probably almost right. From her perspective as a parent, she may have given me good advice, and I chose to follow a different path. Even though I was successful there, it was a real challenge for me." Although her mother was a traditional stay-at-home mom, Terrie said Jackie encouraged her daughter to combine her work with her family and her work outside the home. Terrie said that one must look at what is done by today's stay-at-home parents as she and others volunteer to make communities effective. "Schools, churches, and other organizations rely on so many volunteers to serve their communities," she reported. "Everyone needs to make the best of the intellectual challenges that come with various degrees of involvement and make them work to build strong families and communities."

Men and women at the service academies number approximately 85 percent male and 15 percent female. Many of the male cadets come from traditional homes with two parents and a nuclear family. As a result, they might be considered more traditional in their attitudes toward women. On the other hand, many of the female cadets are more likely to be risk takers, athletes, and leaders who have chosen nontraditional roles for themselves. The 85-percent-male-and-15-percent-female ratio reflects similar numbers in the military services. Unfortunately, the smaller numbers of female officers leads to an even smaller number of senior officers through resignations and attrition. Marybeth Ulrich noted that the Air Force provided virtually no role models for its young female officers. "After I graduated, all the senior officers I saw who were women were either single, divorced, or married to pilots," she recalled. "I could not identify one who was raising a family and enjoying success as a senior officer."

Terrie Galanti's marriage and family are the key factors in her life. She and John are as intense and as relaxed as necessary as they enjoy their relationship. Their family expanded quickly when little Laura was two years old, and John and Terrie learned they were to be parents of triplets. Doctors ordered Terrie to restrict her activities for four months; and then Elizabeth, Stephen, and Matthew arrived on May 24, 1996.

In her initial response to my survey for this book in 2000, she replied, "The paths of my life since graduation from USAFA have taken some interesting turns—not what I would have predicted as a newly commissioned USAF lieutenant!" That phrase prompted the title of her chapter.

"The triplets' arrival solidified our decision for me to stay at home," Terrie reported when we first began to chat. "In a way, it's really ironic how it worked out. Describing the parenting of four kids under four is difficult to explain. You just have to *experience* it. There are so many aspects to it, and certainly, teamwork is important. As a parent, you want to devote true attention to each child. We constantly juggle time for each child, and I would like to say that our kids are well behaved because they are accustomed to patiently waiting their turn."

When asked how her prior academic and project management success helped her as a mother of four small children, Terrie replied, "It's very humbling to be a parent. You think you have a big influence, but each child has his or her own style. We never put them in the same clothes. One likes to play soccer, and another would rather coach. In our family, we have tended to downplay the triplet designation and treat each child as an individual. In fact, when the three youngest started kindergarten, we had to explain to them what it [being triplets] meant because classmates had mentioned it. 'Oh, we have the same birthday,' they replied with no reaction."

Terrie's graduation photo

The four Galanti children at Mom's twenty-year reunion: Mathew in front, Stephen and Elizabeth side by side, and Laura in the back

When all four kids began spending time in school each day, Terrie was asked about her spare time and replied, "We live in chaos at times, but I try to add organization and discipline whenever possible!" She continued her lifelong interest in choral singing, including the Air Force Academy's Catholic Choir. Terrie sings alto in the choir at St. John Neumann Catholic Church in the Northern Virginia community of Reston. She also taught in the Church's religious education program. She has pursued her interest in working with young people as a Girl Scout camp volunteer, an after-school science program teacher, and as a Fairfax County Public School substitute teacher. "I was interested in becoming a teacher when I was in high school, but I was strongly advised to consider engineering because of my math and science abilities."

She also keeps her hand in higher education as a volunteer member of the military academies' Congressional selection panel. She assists Representative Thomas Davis of the Eleventh District in Northern Virginia. Nearly twenty years after her own college application process, Terrie observed a much more diverse group of candidates at the beginning of the 21st Century. "Today, these kids bring a lot more to the table, and I think that's healthy for the academies, the military, and our country," she said. "They are still very high-quality applicants with strong academics and leadership and a mature desire to serve their country."

Terrie told the story of a reception for candidates that Tom Davis hosted so his appointees and their families could get to know one another. The speakers were a 1950s-era West Point grad and two young men who were then at the Air Force Academy. "All three described the same important values of teamwork, dedication, and sacrifice even though they were generations apart," Terrie recalled. "All of us, including the newest high school graduates, were very impressed with the sentiments of that continuity."

Since Terrie was the first woman to be first in her class at the Air Force Academy, her portrait hangs in the ninth corridor of the fourth floor at the Pentagon along with other Air Force pioneers. A smaller version hangs in the chapel at the Air Force Academy. Both her friend Marybeth and her old boss Don Fisher mentioned the portraits; Terrie did not. When I asked her about it, she simply said that one of these days, she will take her own children to see it but not just yet. "Like any parent, I'm trying to balance what I did as a student with what I encourage my kids to do now, without too much pressure on them. I just want them to do their best," she concluded.

Astronaut Rick Searfoss, who ranked first in the USAFA Class of 1978 and is profiled in chapter 14, said he knew about Terrie's achievements. When told about her current status as a stay-at-home mom raising four children, he said promptly, "You know what? She's doing the toughest job *anyone* could ever have." This comment came from someone who flew three times in space.

Terrie added, "As our children are growing older and more independent, I look forward to a time in the future when I may pursue a degree in education. Our kids have received tremendous support from our public school system—ranging from special education to gifted and talented services. And I see a unique need for enthusiastic and dedicated individuals in public education. I also plan to consider working in a low-income or disadvantaged community." She concluded, "I suppose the desire to serve and give something back to the nation that gives us so much never really disappears—we simply 'zig' and 'zag' along the way."

Chapter 18

One of the Few and the Proud

Eric L. Kapitulik, USNA '95

Ask anyone who's ever met a member of the United States Marine Corps to react to the encounter, and they will undoubtedly mention *pride*. Many people think the Madison Avenue advertising campaign that recruited Marines as the "*Few and the Proud*" was a natural fit. When I began to look for Marines at the top and bottom of their Annapolis classes to include in this book, I called the Naval Academy's Alumni Association and the Naval Historical Foundation. I reached Colonel John W. Ripley, USMC Ret., who ranked 11th from the bottom of his 788 classmates in the Class of 1962. After I described my research, John told me about a grad from the Class of 1995, Eric Kapitulik, whose efforts had been described in *Shipmate*—the Naval Academy's alumni magazine—and a few other media outlets. So I called this one of the few and the proud and introduced this project. At first, he didn't want to participate, saying there were others more worthy with better tales to tell. With the help of Colonel Ripley and others, we were able to convince him to be part of this book.

It's an understatement to write that the very modest Eric Kapitulik inspires.

When speaking about his success in life so far, Eric said simply, "I attribute *everything* that I have been able to do to my parents, the Naval Academy, and the Marine Corps." Eric said he just *knows* he was in the bottom 10 percent of his class at Annapolis. "I don't know too many Marines from the top of my class, sir, but I know plenty from the bottom," adding, "none closer to the bottom than myself." His successes since then make him a prime example of how the service academies produce leaders who use their mental toughness and physical strengths and courage to care for others.

Eric was born on September 17, 1972, the third child of hardworking parents in a small town in rural Connecticut called North Grosvenor Dale. It's about twenty minutes south of Worcester, MA. His father, Louis "Lou" Peter Kapitulik, was a Connecticut State policeman who spent most of his career as a detective before he retired in 1990. Asked for the ethnic origins of his family, Eric proudly replied, "The Master Race. Polish"—then he added quickly—"and Czechoslovakian." When asked about any prejudice he might have experienced, he responded simply, "No, no, sir." He proudly reported longtime roots in the community, citing a Kapitulik Road named for his great-grandfather that runs west of Quinebaug Road north of town. His mother, Louise Claire Bouthillier, was originally from another small Connecticut village with the big-city name of Brooklyn. She taught French in the Edwin O. Smith High School in Storrs, home of the University of Connecticut.

Louise and Lou were married September 10, 1966, in Wauregan, CT, and have two other children. All three were born in Putnam, CT, not far from the one-hundred-acre Kapitulik farm, and all attended the private Pomfret School nearby. Monique was born in 1969 and graduated from Brown University in Providence, RI. Later she returned to Pomfret as dean of admissions and later worked as director of development at Quinebaug Valley Community College in Danielson, CT. She and her husband, Bruce Wolanin, Pomfret's head hockey coach, have three sons: Blake Eric, Ian Bruce, and Calvin Louis. Maria was born in 1971, graduated from the University of Vermont, and lives nearby with her husband, Robert Viens, the mayor of Putnam, CT. Maria teaches English as a Second Language at Marianapolis Preparatory School in Thompson, CT.

When he described his rural background in the Nutmeg State, Eric explained, "We originally had animals on the farm, but by the time I was growing up, we were pretty much down to chickens and Christmas trees. And my Dad was pretty casual about the trees." He recalled the year his Dad donated *all* the trees to the Boy Scouts for them to sell as fund-raisers for their programs. Louise and Lou scrimped on their modest incomes to send their three children to Pomfret. The small private boarding-and-day school for 350 students, tucked away in northeastern Connecticut, would have a huge influence on all the Kapitulik children. Pomfret is less than fifteen miles south of their farm, a tiny rural community an hour from Hartford or Boston in an idyllic country setting.

In numerous conversations, Eric deflected his achievements and gave credit to his parents. "*They* are the ones who sacrificed so my sisters and

I would have the opportunities that we did," he said directly. "I have got a *terrific* family."

At Pomfret, Eric was a three-sport varsity athlete: he ran on the cross-country team, played point guard on the basketball team, and midfielder on the lacrosse team. Academics took a backseat to sports, as Eric was comfortable with a B—average that placed him in the bottom half of his class of 90 students.

As he recounted his high school days, it sounded like Eric was enjoying the role of big man on campus. He ran cross-country well enough to attract attention as he won the New England Prep School Cross County Championships. That led to this featured item in the coveted *Sports Illustrated* magazine "Faces in the Crowd" section on February 20, 1990:

> ERIC KAPITULIK N. GROSVENORDALE, CONN. Eric, a senior at the Pomfret School in Pomfret, Conn., ran a 3.1-mile course in 17:13 to win the New England prep school Class B cross-country championship. He has also finished first in 29 consecutive dual meets.

Eric is a big blond handsome athlete, a strapping six-footer who tips the scales at a muscular 205 pounds now. That's twenty pounds over his high school weight, but he reported his Mom's home cooking back then was balanced by his constant running. "I always shed a lot of weight when I run regularly," he explained. "Plus, my Mom's cooking sometimes totaled five thousand calories for one meal!" When asked about his favorite meals from that home cooking, he replied, "I don't think we have enough time to tell you about *all* my favorites growing up. My Mom is the world's *greatest* cook!" he added enthusiastically. When pressed for a specialty, he cited her roasted venison with onions and mushrooms and garlic. The deer were locally procured as the Kapitulik farm was a favored hunting spot for Eric, Lou, and other family members and their friends. "We picked up a lot of venison and turkey on our farm," he recalled. Although other sports interrupted his hunting, those forays gave him an appreciation of and skill with firearms that would serve him well later in the Marine Corps.

"Visiting my house in the hunting season is hilarious," he laughed. "My Dad is like the 'Don' of North Grosvenordale when all his friends come over to hunt."

He remembered, as a youngster, listening to stories about military service from his father's relatives. "When you see people you know who have been in the military and you listen to their stories, you just *know* that the military is a way of life that is important and necessary," he explained. "It's sort of what we *should do*," he said simply. He used the same phrase later when he saw a Naval Academy coach explain to befuddled and nervous plebes, "That's all right, we will all make it. It's *what we do!*"

Eric enjoyed every bit of his high school days, especially sports, and thought they would just continue in college. When asked a decade later about what he was planning to do after high school graduation, Eric recalled, "I was just thinking about playing sports in college, *somewhere.*" College recruiters fueled those dreams as he heard from Syracuse University and Penn State, among others, including West Point. Eric's Dad, Lou, had been an Army enlisted infantryman; and his great uncles had all served in the military.

Eric and his Dad visited USMA, and Eric remembered spending a weekend there and deciding that was *not* where he wanted to be at the time. A bit later, a Naval Academy coach approached him with an offer to attend their one-year Prep School, called NAPS for Naval Academy Prep School, in nearby Newport, RI. "Going the prep-school route was attractive for three reasons," he reported. "First, it gave me another year of getting bigger, faster, and stronger. Next, it would help me academically. And third, I could put off for a year where I was going to go to college."

During his NAPS orientation on his first day in uniform, Eric remembered sitting on a bus with his lacrosse stick in hand and a name tape on his shirt. "This older guy in uniform comes up to me and says, 'Eric, I just want to tell you that you should thank your high school counselor because the reason you got into school here is that his recommendation was the *best* teacher recommendation I've read in twenty-two years in education.'" Eric recounted later, "I thought quickly of Mr. Hagop Merjian, the wrestling coach in my high school. Although I didn't wrestle on his team, I worked with him in the summertime, building stone walls. So we had a good relationship. I am always grateful to Mr. Merjian for that good start. And he surely influenced me tremendously in what I did later in life."

Eric jumped at the chance to continue his education and physical development less than an hour's drive from Mom's home cooking. But he was shocked when he got to NAPS. "At first, it was *horrible*," he recalled. "Not to sound arrogant," he apologized, "but I went from being a big fish in a small pond, with people telling me I was *the man*, to just being *another guy*. I didn't mind the yelling and screaming part," he explained quickly. "My Dad was a loving but strict father and I've got two *older sisters*, so I was used to hearing directions and criticism. But overall, NAPS was a *huge* and painful maturation process for me."

He struggled academically. His class at NAPS started with 320 students, and more than 100 dropped out before the year was completed. Eric had a 1.99 grade point average and almost didn't graduate. At the end of the year, another one of his lacrosse teammates, Matt Foxman, from Silver Spring, MD, also had a 1.99 GPA.

"On the day that final grades were posted, Matt and I went to see our lacrosse Coach, Dave Disciorio," Eric explained. "We knew we're both in trouble because you needed a 2.0 to progress to the Naval Academy. Coach Disciorio took one look at us and said sternly, 'You two *dummies* stay right here while I go talk with your teachers.' Matt and I just sat in the coach's office, wondering what was next," Eric recalled. "We fooled around, tossed a ball back and forth, and killed time with no idea about what was going to happen to us," he continued. "Finally, when the coach came back after an hour, he told us the *good* news and the *bad* news. Fortunately, my trigonometry professor had recomputed my grade, from 74 to 75, because my Coach reminded him that I had gone to every single extra session for his class. That one point for extra effort made the difference, and I was finally able to graduate with a GPA of 2.002. Matt spent another year at a civilian community college before we were both teammates again at the Naval Academy." Matt eventually graduated with the Class of 1996, also ranked near the bottom of his class, and served in the Navy as a Surface Warfare Officer.

Eric said he enrolled at the Naval Academy because he was influenced by the men and women in uniform that he met at the Prep School. "I may not have been the *smartest* student at the prep school, but I was *smart enough* to realize that I had the best friends in the world in my classmates," he reported simply.

Eric recalled his first visit to the Annapolis campus as a NAPS student. "It was *beautiful*," he exclaimed emphatically. "Oh my god, this place is *so* pretty, I thought. It was also a little bit daunting because I had come from a small town and was moving a long way from home. The challenge of it, and my parents' guidance, kept me going," he recalled. He was also well prepared for the military side of Annapolis life. "From the very first day at the Academy, we knew what was expected of us," he reported. "Of course, I was nervous, but those of us who had already been through the NAPS indoctrination were better prepared."

The Naval Academy coaches had been recruiting him for the cross-country team, but Eric had been telling *them* that *he* wanted to play lacrosse. He made the varsity lacrosse team as a plebe and enjoyed tremendous success with his team, which was ranked in the top 10 in the country during his playing days. The Navy team's record was good enough to gain NCAA Tourney berths in three out of Eric's four years as a varsity midfielder and defenseman. Eric was the Naval Academy's Defenseman of the Year in his senior year and was chosen to play in the NCAA's Lacrosse North-South

All-Star Game in Baltimore that spring. When asked about the All-Star game experience, he said, "It was a nice honor but sort of anti-climatic because, for me, the biggest thing about playing lacrosse was the chance to be with my teammates."

Asked about his academics at the Naval Academy, Eric stumbled and replied, "They were a challenge from the word *go*." And then, he added, "I was focused on lacrosse and doing the things I needed to do to become an officer." His grades suffered, and he recalled that the technical courses were the toughest. He thrived in the leadership courses both because he was enjoying them and because he could see its direct application to his future plans as an officer. Although Eric was never in danger of flunking out, he said he was never that confident as a student midshipman. Difficulties in engineering courses and failures in courses like calculus kept him in summer school each year, depriving him of the sea cruises and other special summer programs that midshipmen say balance the rigors of the school year.

Living in Bancroft Hall as a plebe, Eric was part of 20th Company for two years. His Company Officer, Marine Captain G. E. Warren, provided Eric with his first daily contact with a U.S. Marine Corps officer. "He was a great guy, and he made a tremendous impression on me," Eric explained directly. "I guess, at that point, I thought maybe the Marine Corps would be a good place for *me*." During his second two years, Eric was assigned to the Fourth Company. That Company Officer, Marine Captain T. J. Chamberlain, was another strong influence. Eric said he also thought that the midshipmen headed into the Marine Corps seemed to be in a lot better shape than the Navy folks. "I just thought the Marines at the Academy were guys who were more like me," he recalled.

One of those classmates was Douglas A. Zembiec, a wrestler from Albuquerque, NM, who remembered meeting Eric during Midshipmen Leadership Training at Quantico, VA, after their plebe year at the Academy. "We were in pugil stick competitions, and I made it to the finals," Doug recalled. Pugil sticks combine four-foot poles with boxing glove-like padded devices at each end and have been used for years to simulate hand-to-hand combat. "I ran out to the middle of a circle, and another guy ran out and stood next to me. The ref blew his whistle, and I was clocked [hit] immediately! I was hit by a 'killing blow to the head' as they say, and I was upset because I didn't even get a chance to fight! I never saw it coming," Doug exclaimed. "I ran back to my team and asked, 'What in the hell happened?' They told me, 'Don't worry, that was Kap, and he's a lacrosse guy. Just chalk it up to experience!' After that Kap [Eric responds quickly to both names] and I became best friends."

When asked to confirm that Eric was in the bottom ten percent of their class, Doug responded quickly, "Without a doubt, on a good day, downwind with a tailwind." That translated to a statement that he might have been even lower, perhaps in the bottom five percent, without his drive and energy. Doug said he remembered the announcements for Class Selection night in the spring of their Firstie year. "Around 1800 [six PM], the loudspeakers in Bancroft Hall boomed, 'Senior Midshipmen ranked one to 100, report to the Second Wing for service selection.' Those announcements ran all night," Doug continued. "Finally, around one or two o'clock in the morning, they called for Midshipmen ranking 700 and below. We all lined up in the wing, one of several large hallways. *That's* where I saw myself and Eric and all our buddies!"

When asked to summarize his four years at Annapolis, Eric quickly responded, "My friends and lacrosse." A lacrosse injury to his ankle in his sophomore year led to surgery that kept him from summer training at the halfway mark. After playing in the NCAA Tournament in his Junior Year, Eric had a second surgery on his ankle and again had to attend summer school to catch up on his academic requirements.

After completing his Senior Year, graduation day loomed bright and sunny and full of promise. Eric said he approached his graduation from USNA much like his graduation from Pomfret and NAPS. "I was proud and pleased that I was completing that stage, but I was also a bit sad that our great times were drawing to an end. It was very bittersweet," he said quietly. "I was almost happiest for my parents."

On June 3, 1995, Secretary of the Navy John Dalton urged 778 new Naval Ensigns, 119 new Marine Corps, six Air Force, and two Army lieutenants to succeed. Eric received his BS degree in Economics and officially ranked 772th out of the 916 members of his class, which included 810 men and 106 women. His father, Louis, and his grandfather, Louis Kapitulik Sr., proudly pinned on his Second Lieutenant bars.

I asked Doug Zembiec to describe his friend Eric, and he said, "We always called him pretty boy." Then he quickly added, "But he's the *toughest* pretty boy I know." Eric "would give you the shirt off his back," Doug emphasized. And more than once, he did even better. Doug remembered sweating and freezing through the Infantry Officers Course in Quantico, VA, after graduation. "We were in one of the final events in a twelve-day mock war," he explained, "with very little sleep, maybe two to three hours a day. You're starving because they limited food to only one packaged MRE [Meal, Ready-to-Eat] a day, and you're probably burning over 5000 calories each day," Doug continued. "I'll never forget because the blizzard of '96 hit that year, and we had a pause in our training. Eric offered me his precious MRE. I said no, I wouldn't take it. Finally, Kap stubbornly said 'Fine, I'll leave it here, so you better eat it' and off he ran. After a slight hesitation, I ate it quickly."

While virtually all of his graduating classmates took off for a month's leave or vacation, Eric's low class rank led to orders requiring that he immediately report to Quantico, VA, for the Basic School of the U.S. Marine Corps. Simply quoted, the School's mission is "to educate newly commissioned or appointed officers in the high standards of professional knowledge, esprit-de-corps, and leadership required to prepare them for duty as a company grade officer in the operating forces, with particular emphasis on the duties, responsibilities and war-fighting skills required of a rifle platoon commander. The Infantry Officer Course will further enhance the war-fighting skills of the newly designated infantry officers."

However, nothing is simple about the Basic School. All combat-ready Marine officers matriculate through the school's six-month program. They study leadership, communications, decision-making, and other military skills against a background of military history and theories of war. With his athletic prowess and five years' preparation at NAPS and USNA, Eric arrived at the Basic School well prepared. He found it long but not that challenging physically. As famed Major League Baseball pitcher Dizzy Dean said, "It ain't bragging if you can do it." Each week, Eric and his fellow Marines logged around 35 miles of running, hiking, and crawling. Eric and Doug added lifting weights for four or five days and added numerous pushups, pull-ups, and parallel dips in what Eric called, with a laugh, "*manly* exercises" until they burned out and rested for the day.

The Basic School reinforced Eric's decision to join the Marine Corps. However, he was not to have an easy time of it because of an unusual gaffe during in-processing. While in his junior or Second class year at Annapolis, Eric had decided that he wanted to pursue the Force Recon branch of the Marine Corps. That's the Special Operations Marine fighting force *somewhat* similar to the Navy's SEALS, Army Delta Force, or Air Force Special Operations forces although *all* four services would quickly deny *any* alleged similarity. Suffice to explain, Force Recon Marines are a very, very tough bunch.

When he arrived at the Basic School in June 1995, Eric's in-processing included completing a Dream Sheet, a list of the top five choices for future duty assignments. Eric wrote Force Recon, not realizing that the group is so exclusive that they rarely accept untried volunteers. "Writing that on the form was sort of like Babe Ruth calling the shot," Eric said later. "I had no idea of the ramifications at the time," he continued. "There are only so many Marines, and there are so few platoon commanders in Force Recon. Ninety percent of the guys say they want to be infantry at first, and that number gets cut in half by the end of the Basic School," he explained. "Then *maybe* after completing *two or more years* of infantry in the field, one *might* apply to be in Force Recon," he continued. "I had *no idea* how hard it is, and *no idea* how bold my choice listing appeared," he explained sheepishly.

"So I was ordered to report to the Staff Platoon Commander on the very first day at the Basic School," he recalled. "He proceeded to chew my ass for thirty minutes, asking me 'Who do you think you are?' and 'Aren't the grunts [infantry] good enough for you?' as his voice got louder and louder, and mine became softer and softer. He yelled across the room to another Staff Platoon Commander and said, 'Hey, this Kapitulik thinks *he* wants to be Force Recon!' This is *three* days after I graduated from the Naval Academy, and I am *already* in trouble!" Eric explained ruefully.

At first, Eric was ill prepared for the military side of Marine Corps life because he had missed an important special Marine training program between his junior and senior year. Most midshipmen who chose the Marine Corps attend six weeks of rigorous training at Quantico, VA, called "Leatherneck." A combination of unfortunate sports injuries and academic summer school to repeat failed classes kept Eric from attending these programs. Although he quickly made up for lost time, some gaps were evident. He cited his lack of experience with the M-16 rifle as an example.

"My father taught me to shoot with a BB gun when I was a little kid, probably seven or eight years old," Eric recalled. "Then I progressed to a .22-caliber rifle and finally a 30-06 deer rifle," he explained. "But an M-16 is *not* a 30-06 deer rifle! I literally had *no idea* how to break down and assemble the M-16." Fortunately, his Basic School roommates were able to help. Michael T. Johannes was commissioned through the Naval ROTC scholarship program at my Alma Mater, the College of the Holy Cross, in Worcester, MA. After graduating in the top quarter of his class as a math major in 1995, Mike entered the U.S. Marine Corps and found himself linked alphabetically as one of Eric's three roommates at the Basic School.

"The very first day, they issued us our M-16s, and we eager Second Lieutenants immediately took 'em apart to clean them," Mike explained. "The three of us were working away when I looked over at Kap, and he was just sitting there, inspecting the rifle from every angle, trying to determine how to pull it apart. After giving him a start, and returning to my rifle, eventually reassembling it, I again looked over at Kap. He was staring at the twenty rifle parts he had managed to take apart and put down on the floor," he recalled.

"I asked, 'What's the matter?' and Kap replied, 'I have *no clue* what I'm doing with this thing. Can you help me?' So we did, but *not* without first offering a few choice comments about his previous training. Most of us were used to putting together the M-16 in less than a minute, but Kap was up to speed in less than a week, but we still had fun busting him about it," Mike laughed, adding seriously, "But you should know that this guy is a *charismatic* leader."

After successfully completing the Basic School in six months, the next day Eric checked in for the Infantry Officers Course where the staff's professionalism and instruction continued to impress the young lieutenant. "I loved the practical application of the instruction and the physical intensity of it," he said simply.

Finally, in the spring of 1996, Eric completed his training and reported for work at Camp Pendleton, CA. He was an infantry Rifle Platoon Commander in the Second Battalion, Fourth Marine, leading 36 troops and training for war. "I thought it was much better than I expected," he recalled. "You see all these stories about a new officer taking over and none of the guys are listening to him. That was *not* the case with my experience in the Marine Corps. My Platoon sergeant, Staff Sergeant George Sanchez, was very respectful, and we worked together." Eric added, "I think the Marine Corps prepares the enlisted Marines to respect their NCOs and officers," adding, "You don't have to *earn* their respect. It's a *given,* but it's also there to *lose.*" His duties ranged from personnel training to off-base community services in San Clemente. That assignment was followed by a move to lead one of the Battalion's 81-mm mortar platoons where he supervised 60 Marines and their weapons used for missions ranging from support for infantry platoons to coordinated close air support missions.

In a subtle forecast of his graduate school studies years later, Eric explained that he would brief his Marines regularly on financial matters. "You know Marines don't see a whole lot of money in their paychecks each month, but what they *do* see can be stretched with some good financial planning that includes savings," he remarked. "We worked on that, and I am happy that we did."

Two years after completing the Basic School, Eric was on board a ship, supporting a big amphibious landing in an exercise off the coast of Southern California when he saw the other former Staff Platoon Commander from the School across the room. That other SPC was now the operations officer of an Infantry Battalion. "I joined him for dinner in the wardroom, and his battalion commander sat down with us," Eric reported. "The former SPC proceeded to tell his commander about the exchange that first day at the Basic School and concluded, '*Now* look at him, sir, he's doing *exactly* what he set out to do!'"

In March 1998, Eric was named Force Reconnaissance Platoon Commander, Fifth Platoon, First Force Reconnaissance at Camp Pendleton, CA. During the next three years, he led twenty-man teams of covert operations specialists in successfully performing a variety of Special Forces-related missions. Training in the USA and overseas, the platoon worked in a range of classified missions, including special duty in the Middle East training Kuwaiti, Omani, and Qatari Special Forces units. The combat-ready teams completed high-altitude parachute jumps from 25,000 feet down to low releases at 1,200 feet above water and land. They also swam long-range dive missions with special air-pack equipment that eliminated telltale bubbles called LAR-V. Force Recon Marines could accomplish these challenging missions due to the strength and dedication of the team members who often swam five to ten kilometers (three to five miles) on the top of the water before swimming another three kilometers (half mile) *underwater.*

One training exercise on Thursday, December 9, 1999, changed the lives of Eric and his Marine Corps family forever in a fatal accident that resonated throughout the military. That clear and sunny day was blustery cold in Southern California. Eric and his team were on the aircraft carrier USS *Bon Homme Richard* (CV-31), in the Pacific, fifteen miles from Point Loma off the coast. They were working one of their final test missions before deploying to duty in the Persian Gulf. The assignment—called a Vessel Boarding, Search, and Seizure (VBSS)—is to approach, board, search, and seize a ship. It is a critical exercise to detect and intercept questionable transports on the high seas. Frequently used to stop illegal shipments of arms or drugs, the takedown exercise quickly puts Marines on a ship that has violated an embargo. A helicopter flies in low under the radar then pops up at the last minute and lands at the rear of a ship. In twenty seconds, a dozen men are on board, ready to capture the ship. The objective is to seize the forward radio room and the aft engine room. Eric and his team had practiced takedown missions and completed them successfully at least a dozen times, but danger on the high seas is always present.

That fateful day, Eric woke up and exercised with a quick lift of weights for an hour. While eating breakfast, he heard the intercom message to report to duty for the day's mission. His platoon sergeant, then Gunnery Sergeant Tom DeWitt from Illinois, heard the same announcement and assembled the platoon. "We checked ourselves and our equipment, went over our last-minute drills, including where everyone would sit in the helicopter that was scheduled to take us to our objective," he said calmly as he described his team on board the helicopter. "We reviewed the order in which we would fast-rope exit the helicopter when we reached the ship," he explained. "They had begun the exercise where they prepared to board probably thirty times and had completed the actual boarding at least a dozen times. We were ready to do our jobs."

This time, Eric and ten of his Marines were on board a CH-46 Sea Knight helicopter that approached the USNS *Pecos* (T-AO 197), a 677-foot refueling ship. The CH-46 included a four-man crew plus three men Eric called "cats and dogs" who were checking the exercise's progress. "We were getting ready to fast rope onto the ship so each of us stood up, carrying 50 to 70 pounds of equipment, and were ready to exit the helicopter down the rope."

The grainy video of the accident was frightening. So was the experience as Eric told the story. "Suddenly, we hit that ship *hard*," he told me. "The helicopter's landing gear snagged on a steel safety net at the rear edge of the ship, flipped over, and sank into the ocean. We were all knocked out and underwater without oxygen."

Eric was unconscious, and the impact of the crash broke his right leg at the fibula near his kneecap. The cold water of the sea slapped him awake as the helicopter was sinking sixty feet below the calm waters' surface. And the lack of oxygen was almost overwhelming.

"I remember waking up and thinking, I need air, and I don't want to die now," he explained later. "My training kicked in, and I really only thought about three things: one, getting oxygen; two, my Mother; and three, my Marines. I knew I could barely do anything for myself let alone the other Marines on board, so I just kept telling myself, 'You will not die! Hold your breadth.' Gunnery Sergeant DeWitt is another hero of mine. As a young Captain, hell, as a General, you couldn't ask for a better man than Gunny DeWitt." He recalled an experience of watching a training film on a team of soldiers being confronted with the possibility of giving up when faced with insurmountable odds. "He told me that would *never* be us," Eric recalled, "and I remembered that too." Then he added, "I can honestly say I *never* thought I was going to die. I just kept telling myself, 'You will not die! Hold your breadth.'"

Despite his compound leg fracture and equipment, Eric was able to kick his way to the top where the safety boats were ready to help rescue the downed men.

Six of his fellow Marines, including five men in his platoon, were killed in the accident—one of the worst in Marine Corps training. They were Marines Gunnery Sgt. James Paige Jr., Staff Sgt. William C. Dame, Staff Sgt. David E. Galloway, Staff Sgt. Vincent A. Sebasteanski, Staff Sgt.

Jeffrey R. Starling, Cpl. Mark M. Baca, and Navy Petty Officer First Class
Jay J. Asis.

They were all physically fit and well trained. They were just unlucky.
Only five of the eleven Marines from Eric's platoon would survive.

The six Marines who died left behind six children. They became the
next and possibly the most important project in Eric's young life. At the
same time, he was still charged with leading his platoon that was scheduled
to leave for the Persian Gulf in less than a month's time.

After their rescue, Eric and the other survivors were returned to the
Bon Homme Richard and, two days later, returned to Camp Pendleton.
With his leg in a cast, he visited the families of the deceased Marines. "Of
course, they had been notified right away," he explained. "But Gunnery
Sergeant DeWitt and I went to talk with each family for a while. That was
one of the hardest things I have ever done," he said slowly. Then he added,
"Having to go around to talk to the wives and children of my men and
talk about how their husbands and fathers died—those are the things in
my life that I consider to be *hard*. Everything else has been *challenging*,"
he emphasized.

The Marine Corps' Law Enforcement Foundation gave $20,000
education bonds to each child of the Marines who died in the accident.
Later Eric and the Force Recon Association created an account called
the Force Recon Scholarship Fund, which funds more scholarships and
other support programs. "We set up a special smaller fund within the
larger fund for a scholarship for each kid in their names," he explained.
"We're supporting the families of these men who were serving our country.
They were also serving me and our unit so, because of that, I still am very
much responsible for them."

I asked Eric if he was uncomfortable talking about the accident and
its aftermath, and he replied simply, "Sir, the *only* way we can raise money
for these kids is to talk about what happened." And he does raise money,
totaling more than $150,000 by 2008. How he does it is another story.

Soon after the accident and a rigorous rehabilitation program, Eric
deployed again to the Persian Gulf. When asked how he was able to recover
in a month from a broken leg, he replied, "I don't know, sir, and to be
honest with you, I don't know if it was that noteworthy. It's the Marine
Corps, and it's what's expected of you."

When Eric isn't working, he relaxed by playing sports. When he first got
out to Southern California and his first duty station in 1996, he managed
to play some club lacrosse. But he missed more competitive competition.
Some friends encouraged him to enter some shorter triathlons. Long
before the so-called "extreme sports" became popular at the beginning
of the 21st Century, intense athletes would compete in triathlons at three

distinct levels. The sprint includes a 0.75-km (0.46 mile) swim, a 22-km (13.75 mile) bike ride, and a 5-km (3.12 mile) run. The Olympic triathlon has a longer 1.5-km (0.93 mile) swim, a 40-km (25 mile) bike ride, and a 10-km (6.25 mile) run. The Ironman competition involves a 3.84-km (2.4 mile) swim, a 179.2-km (112 mile) cycle, and finishes with a marathon—a 41.6-km (26.2 mile) run.

Eric started with a Sprint triathlon in North Carolina in 1998 and, in just over a year, competed in the Ironman Florida in November of 1999. He placed 113th out of 1,545 competitors. Upon returning from the Persian Gulf in May 2001, he placed 174th out of 1667 in Oceanside, CA. A month later, he was 11th in the Armed Forces Eco-Challenge in Alaska sponsored by TAPS, the military's Tragedy Assistance Program for Survivors. In 2001, he was awarded the Perry Rendina Carpe Diem Award as the most motivational Ironman Triathlete of the year. In October 2001, he participated in the Ironman World Championships in Kona, HI; and in July 2002, he won the Janus Charity Challenge while participating in Ironman USA. That provided $10,000 more to the Force Recon Scholarship Fund. In July 2002, he was named Ironman USA in recognition of his achievements in the sport and in his volunteer work as he continues to compete globally.

In October of 2000, Eric was sent from the field back to a desk job at the Naval Academy to work in the admissions office. He managed the volunteer USNA admissions counselors, called the Blue and Gold officers, for the Western Region of the USA. He also reviewed applicants who were enlisted Marines and wanted to go to the academy. "I saw that a lot of the guys who applied to the academy were aware of the academy because they were working in front of computers in administrative jobs," he explained. "I wanted to try to get more guys who were out in the field in the infantry, and I was able to call up some of their commanders and recruit their people as future Marine officers." Next he worked on budgeting and special marketing, recruiting minority candidates. At the same time, he focused on his own future, which included leaving the Marine Corps.

"When I was back at the academy, I realized that I had pretty much accomplished the goals that I had set for myself at graduation, and that I was ready to move on to the next stage of my life," he explained. "I knew that this was the time in my life when I should go to graduate school, and I also knew that someday, I might want to go into politics." However," he added quickly, "leaving the Marine Corps, hands down, was the toughest decision of my life." I asked Eric why he was considering politics in his future, and he replied, "My Mom always told me if you want to change something, then get yourself to the position where you can change it. I see a lot of people who sit around and complain about our country but never do anything more than that. I say, 'If you want change something, go and change it. Don't sit around and talk about it!'"

Eric applied to the University of Chicago, which accepted the one-time self-described 'poor student' for its Masters of Business Administration (MBA) program to begin in the fall of 2001. At first, Eric hoped to study for both an MBA and a law degree. Even for an overachieving Marine Ironman, the combination proved daunting, and the university accepted him for their MBA program. Just before he began his studies, the attacks of September 11 challenged his decision, but he had already moved mentally to this next stage of his life.

I first caught up with Eric in 2004, in the library at the University of Chicago where he was studying for one of his business courses. I asked him how he reached that prestigious school. "I'm here because I've got very good recommendations," he explained. "It surely was not my whopping 2.42 GPA from the Naval Academy or my GMAT [Graduate Management Admission Test] scores. I did pretty well my first semester here," he said modestly. Then he explained that the University of Chicago had a "grade nondisclosure" policy that kept him in the dark about his official progress. "I'm sure we got ranked somewhere, but they don't ever publish it. I think I'm doing fine," he continued, "but I really don't know the details. All I can say is that I am putting all my energies into learning and studying. I'm motivated," he emphasized.

Eric continued his pace, combining his graduate studies with Ironman competitions, marathons for the children of his Marine families, and public speaking engagements to raise funds. On April 19, 2004, he ran the 26 miles and 385 yards of the 108th Boston Marathon, finishing 456th in a seven-minute mile pace for three hours, five minutes and twenty seconds. Usually a sub-three-hour marathoner, he was not pleased with the results. He returned to his parents' Connecticut home to relax and recover. However, that night, a phone call from a Chicago investment firm invited him to an interview for a summer job at 9:00 AM the next day in the Windy City. Eric said he rose at 4:00 AM, flew to Chicago, and made it on time for the interview. A woman at the firm looked at his resume and recognized the Ironman efforts, and he got the job. No one mentioned the previous day's Boston Marathon or his schedule.

He spent a few weeks in the summer of 2004 acclimating himself to the world of corporate finance and was asked to contrast it the Marine Corps. "I enjoyed it, and I learned a lot. I certainly learned that it's not *only* the Xs and Os of the finance industry," he replied. "But I learned that a lot of the things that I learned in the military, at the end of the day, are applicable to the finance industry. Can you read people? Can you lead people? Can you see advantages with this team of people? Although I might be behind the curve ball with some parts of the finance equation, I felt comfortable in other areas of working directly with people in my new chosen profession.

"It's sort of like when I first turned up at NAPS in uniform," he continued. "You can't follow everything, but every day, you pay attention and pickup something new and useful." He added, "The Naval Academy helped, the Marine Corps helped, and that combined with what I'm learning at the University of Chicago certainly helped me be the man who is the sum of his experiences." The University recognized his leadership skills and appointed him to their Discipline Committee at the end of 2004. "All of my friends teased me about that, but I guess it was a sign that I was maturing somewhat," he laughed.

In the spring of 2005, he went to the University of Cape Town in South Africa for a semester abroad. He also managed to keep up some of his outdoor adventures while he was in Africa, including Ironman South Africa and a climb of Mount Kilimanjaro in Tanzania. He described the seven-day climb as "fun." He returned to the USA in April and received his MBA on Sunday—June 19, 2005—along with 701 others. He didn't mention or even know his class rank but said, "I did manage to make the Dean's List one semester." He added, "I gave the letter to my Mother as a Mother's Day gift. She cried." A few days later, he took another mountain climbing holiday, this time, to Alaska and Mount McKinley. "It was colder than heck, and we carried a big pack" was the way he described the jaunt. "Twelve days up and two days down, but the guides and the experience were great," he added.

Captain Eric Kapitulik,
USMC, in 2003

*Eric completed the 2006
Johannesburg Marathon.*

Next Eric reported to Boston to go to work for the Goldman Sachs Group Inc., the global financial services firm. He joined the Private Wealth Management Division, bringing his drive and enthusiasm to yet another new task at that next stage of his life. However, after a year at Goldman Sachs, an acquaintance approached him about what looked like a great opportunity working for a company that provided medical and security evacuation help around the world. But his experience there led him to leave that enterprise, to reassess what he was doing, and to start his own company. In 2008, Eric established the Program LLC, an athletic and leadership development company. He leveraged his and his team members' experiences playing collegiate sports, military special operations backgrounds, and corporate leadership for special speeches, classes, and seminars. More information about the company is available on its web site, www.theprogramathletics.com.

But the saying is true—Once a Marine, always a Marine—and Eric stayed involved with his friends and classmates and the families of his men. Sometimes he telephones, and when his schedule permits, he visits them.

The ten-year reunion of the Class of 1995 was a joyful yet somber event as many classmates were at war in Iraq and Afghanistan and other hotspots throughout the world. Class President John Fleet, who was also ranked near the bottom and not commissioned despite numerous attempts for a medical waiver, reported, "Our class has lost more people in combat than any USNA class since the Vietnam War, and sadly, there may be more as well." Two of those lost were Navy SEAL (Sea, Land, Air) Lieutenant Commander Erik S. Kristensen of Washington DC, who died June 28,

2005, and U.S. Marine Corps Major Megan M. McClung of Coupeville, WA, who died December 6, 2006.

Later those losses included Eric's best friend—Major Douglas A. Zembiec, USMC—who was killed on May 11, 2007, in Baghdad. A much-decorated veteran on his fourth tour of duty in Iraq, Doug was called the "Lion of Fallujah" for his exemplary service during the siege in that city in the spring of 2004. "Doug's death hit all of us very hard," Eric explained, "and it was my honor and privilege to deliver the eulogy at his funeral. Of course, Doug's parents and his wife, Pam, and their daughter—Fallyn, my goddaughter—were right there in front at the Naval Academy Chapel." Eric spoke to the overflow crowd of one thousand that included generals and privates and civilians there to honor their friend and colleague. He told many stories about his friend, including this one about his leadership that was widely quoted.

"Soon after returning from Iraq in 2005, Doug's parents (Jo Ann and Don Zembiec) visited him at Camp Pendleton," Eric reported. "As they reached the entry gate, the Marine guard who was checking IDs saw Doug and the gentleman sitting with him. The guard asked if he were Doug's Father. After hearing the reply 'yes,' the young Marine looked at Mr. Zembiec and said, 'I was with your son in Fallujah. He was my Company Commander. If we had to go back in there, I would follow him with a *spoon*.'"

Then Eric added, "Today, I am the most privileged man in the world. Not only because I have the opportunity to tell you what he meant to me, but seeing the warriors who are assembled here today to honor him, I realize how lucky I was to call him my best friend, if only for seventeen very short years."

Eric quoted from Doug's journals with a credo that spoke for the kind of person he was:

> Be a man of Principle. Fight for what you believe in. Keep your word. Live with integrity. Be brave. Believe in something bigger than yourself. Serve your country. Teach. Mentor. Give something back to society. Lead from the front. Conquer your fears. Be a good friend. Be humble, but be self-confident. Appreciate your friends and family. Be a leader, not a follower. Be valorous on the field of battle. Take responsibility for your actions.

"No other quote could better exemplify everything that Doug believed, represented, and fought for," explained Eric. "And for good reason, after the quote, all that was written was 'what my father taught me.'"

After the funeral, Eric and several classmates gathered near the Yard in Annapolis at McGarvey's Saloon and Oyster Bar. "We wanted to do something special as a class and decided to Run to Honor in the 2007 Marine Corps Marathon in Arlington, VA, in October. I give all the credit to those folks who organized an amazing event." After several appropriate celebrations and memorials, and a USNA football game, more than one hundred members of the USNA Class of 1995, including Eric Kapitulik, ran the 26-mile course.

Going back to 1999 and the initial coverage of the helicopter crash off the California coast, some members of the news media have continued to write about Eric and the work he does on behalf of his Marine families. He reacted very modestly to the media attention he has received, deflecting it in a self-effacing way. However, he realized the notoriety helps raise funds for the families, so it's helpful. To contribute, visit the web site, www.theprogramathletics.com.

"Since December 9, 1999, I have gotten a lot of credit for doing what I do," he explained directly, "and some people even call me a hero. But that couldn't be further from the truth. Yes, I have been in pain, sometimes even extreme pain, while racing and trying to raise money for the college educations for my men's children. I have competed in several ultra distance endurance events to raise money." Then he emphasized, "But let's not forget that the mothers of these children have woken up *every single day* for the last nine plus years, made breakfast for their sons or daughter, packed their lunch for them, picked them up from school, cooked dinner, helped them with their homework, put them to bed at night, etcetera, etcetera, etcetera.

"I can tell you without reservation that *they* are doing a great job of it, and their kids are and will be great Americans," he continued. "You tell me," he asked, "who are the heroes in this?"

Then he concluded, "Although I do get a lot of credit for doing what I do, if I could have one wish, it would be for all of the Mothers to hear and receive every single bit of it, not me."

Chapter 19

Whose Footsteps?

Kim Reed Campbell, USAFA '97

Kim Reed was a fifth grader in 1985, at Vinci Park Elementary School in San Jose, CA, when she decided that she wanted to be an astronaut. She remembered learning about spaceflight and the people who flew in space, achieving their dreams. She also recalled the horror of watching the ill-fated *Challenger* Space Shuttle explode on January 28, 1986, taking the lives of seven astronauts—including high school teacher Christa McAuliffe. Fifteen years later, when Kim was asked if the dream still was there after the Space Shuttle *Columbia*'s explosion, she replied, "Yes, it's a tough week, but we'll move on." When asked if becoming an astronaut is still her dream, she replied quickly, "Oh, yeah!" Asked why, she cited the inspiration and sense of purpose exhibited by all members of the astronaut team.

Interviewing Kim and all the other people in this book involved numerous e-mails and telephone calls across time zones and continents. In Kim's case, scheduling conflicts were a bit more complicated by her life and her workplace.

She is a fighter pilot for the U.S. Air Force, a combat veteran with 66 missions in Afghanistan and 55 in Iraq, including a harrowing return from Baghdad flying her shot-up and damaged A-10 Warthog aircraft. Kim still wants to be an astronaut, but she has taken her combat experience to help develop better weapons systems for the venerable A-10.

Kim's father was an Air Force Academy graduate of the Class of 1970 who became a lawyer and public servant. Charles "Chuck" R. Reed, who was profiled in Chapter 11, was the Cadet Wing Commander and ranked first in Military Order of Merit in the Class of 1970. His daughter, Kim, recorded those very same accomplishments 27 years later in the Class of 1997.

That father-daughter achievement is unique among all U.S. service academy graduates, according to an informal survey of the alumni of all three academies.

Kim recalled her father's encouragement as he walked that fine line every parent encounters between support and push. She was born at Tripler Army Hospital in Honolulu, HI, on June 6, 1975, but spent most of her early life in Northern California. Her Mom, Paula, and Dad, Chuck, supported her when Kim wanted to join the Civil Air Patrol as a seventh grader at Piedmont Middle School. She thought that would help her reach her goal. The CAP also let her handle the controls of small single-engine Cessna aircraft, and she thought that was fun too. They taught her how to wear the uniform and introduced her to military discipline, and she was comfortable with that. Kim also attended space camp in Huntsville, AL, and also enjoyed those experiences.

She also wanted to *fly*. At a time when many fifteen-year-olds badger their parents to learn to *drive cars*, Kim was also asking for flying lessons to *fly planes*. Her persistence was rewarded with a sixteenth birthday present from Paula and Chuck that included flying lessons at the San Jose Municipal Airport in the heart of California's Silicon Valley. Asked for her reaction at the time, Kim replied, "Hey! It was *cool!* I was *flying!* And I was *sixteen!* I can't believe they let me learn how to fly then, but I was *sure happy* I was flying!"

Her Mom recalled that Kim "always loved to go fast." She added, "She had a little plastic red elephant on wheels when she was two years old, and she used to take that thing and *fly* down the sidewalk." Paula remembered that Kim always wanted to fly. "This was her *dream*," Mom said softly. "I couldn't think of anything better for her to be doing than what she wanted to do."

Readers may share my belief that the Reeds bring new meaning to the age-old statement that, as parents, we give our children "roots and wings."

At the same time, as a teenager, Kim figured out that the Air Force Academy was probably *the* path to take to reach her goals, so she worked hard in school. She was one of the top student athletes in her class at Piedmont Hills High School where she regularly made the honor roll. She would eventually graduate eighth out of 419 in the Class of 1993. She played both offense and defense for the Pirates' soccer team and ran track and cross-country. She also served as a member of the cheerleader squad for football and basketball games. While in high school, Kim accompanied her Mom and Dad for one of his reunions at the Air Force

Academy and remembered talking with cadets who made the place seem even *more* attractive.

During her senior year in high school, Kim obtained a nomination from her local U.S. Congressman, Don Edwards, and completed the necessary paperwork for her application. That process included interviews with local liaison officers, volunteer Air Force officers who assist the academy's evaluation process with detailed evaluations and formal written evaluations. Her father's 1970 Classmate, Lt.Col. Dana C. Arbaugh, was the Deputy Liaison Officer Commander for her area. Arbaugh wrote in his written evaluation—"highest recommendation for selection." Then he added prophetically in an underlined comment: *Kim Reed is a future Cadet Wing Commander.*

But the Air Force Academy Admissions Office disagreed. They sent her a rejection letter on April 23, 1993, citing keen competition among 12,000 applicants that year. Kim remembered that she was disappointed but still determined. She also applied for admission to the University of California-San Diego where she was awarded an Air Force ROTC scholarship. At the same time, both Lt.Col. Arbaugh and her parents encouraged her to continue to send the Academy regular updates on her progress throughout her senior year. She sent the Academy letters almost every week, and her diligence paid off. Kim was accepted on June 2, 1993, for the Class of 1997, due to report to Colorado Springs in four short weeks.

On June 30, 1993, Kim flew from San Jose to Colorado Springs with Tim Welter, a friend from Santa Rosa, CA. They were both met by her sponsor, Colonel Joseph G. Burke. He was one of Chuck's other classmates who was assigned to the Academy; and his son, Scott Burke, was to be one of Kim's new classmates. After a restless night, the three new cadets and their 1,161 classmates reported for the beginning of BCT.

Fortunately, Kim had continued to stay fit as she ran regularly, sometimes with her father, who had begun to offer more direct advice to the almost new cadet. "He helped me to get into shape, so running was fine," she recalled. "But I had no upper body strength, so he had installed a pull-up bar in the bathroom for me to practice pull-ups. That *wasn't* Dad *pushing* me," she emphasized. "That was Dad *helping* me." At first, as a high school senior, she said she couldn't do any of the pull-ups required as part of the academy's physical fitness test. But by the time she completed Basic Cadet Training, she could do ten. "BCT certainly wasn't fun, but my preparation helped," she reported. Chuck thought the whole basic training process has not changed very much, and Kim agreed with a few plusses and minuses for some new special rules thrown in.

During BCT, Kim discovered that her preparation, both from Civil Air Patrol and in physical conditioning, paid big dividends. "I knew the ranks and I had learned drill and I knew how to wear the uniform properly," she reported. "That helped me stay out of trouble. I could also memorize things because I'm blessed with a good memory." Then she almost "aced" the practice Physical Fitness Test, scoring 478 out of a possible 500 points. "That let me off the hook for other practice exercises," she explained. "If they know you're athletic, that makes it a bit easier."

One day after BCT, Kim was told to report to the Administration Office of the Academy's Superintendent. Thinking she might be in some kind of trouble, she hurried up to the office on the third floor of Harmon Hall, fearing the worst. She didn't know that the Superintendent's office shared that floor with the Admissions Department. Apparently, the woman who had been on the receiving end of Kim's regular weekly progress updates wanted to meet her. And she was glad she did, congratulating the new Basic Cadet in person.

Kim followed the new cadet's creed to stay alert and balanced, without appearing to be too good or too bad, while trying to blend in. Although a few friends knew about her father, she and her other classmates with parents who were Academy grads managed to stay anonymous during BCT. However, that changed abruptly later during her first year when the *Checkpoints*, the alumni magazine from the Academy's Association of Graduates, proudly carried a photo of Chuck and Kim as a father-daughter combination. Someone posted the magazine on her door in 35th Squadron, and the un-welcomed notoriety lasted for a few days. She recalled that it centered on the fact that the magazine, which most often publishes photos of grads in uniform, ran a picture of a smiling Kim Reed in her high school prom dress! "Everyone kind of gave me a hard time for *that*," she laughed. The article pointed out that her father was the Wing Commander in 1970 and asked the rhetorical question, "Is C4C Reed going to follow in her father's footsteps?"

However, by then, she was making her own mark in the Class of 1997, working successfully through a succession of leadership training posts. Then, as a two degree or junior, she transferred to the First Squadron, which had been her father's squadron almost three decades earlier.

"My Mom and Dad were always very supportive," she recalled. "I'm sure it was hard on both of them, especially my Mom. I don't remember my Dad telling me too many 'bad' stories until I actually got to the academy. It seemed like he didn't want to lead me one way or the other. But once I was a cadet, we could share stories, especially about some of the leadership issues we both experienced." She said that helped her focus on the right activities to work her way through the maze of boards and panels that determine leadership positions. Eventually, in her third year, she was named the Wing Sergeant Major, the highest-ranking three degree cadet position. She monitored the discipline, training, welfare, and morale of the lower three classes and assisted the First-Class Cadet Wing Commander in all duties.

During her final year, Kim was named the Cadet Wing Commander in the Fall Semester. As the highest ranking cadet at the Academy, she supervised all Cadet Wing activities, executed command-directed policies and instructions, and was responsible for over 4000 cadets. It was the same post held by her father and predicted by her Academy Liaison Officer when she was in high school.

I asked her Mother to react to Kim's Wing Commander position and linked it to her father's earlier cadet duties. "I think it's wonderful," said Paula. "When I first met Chuck, I just knew he was going to move up into leadership positions because that's the kind of person he was and is. Our daughter was class president, also involved in things, and is very driven. It's very much like father, like daughter—very committed and very driven but with a sense of concern for the people they're leading," she continued. "And I think that's what makes them such good leaders." Then she added, "And of course, I'm so proud of both of them, and my son included."

Kim recounted a range of good experiences in the top post, citing the interesting visitors she met as the senior academy cadet. These included the Secretary of the Air Force at the time, Secretary Dr. Sheila E. Widnall, and several senior general officers who would actually have considerable impact on her future.

Kim's senior-year physical exam included discovery of a minor heart problem by the Academy's medical team. Since a "minor heart problem" is an oxymoron in military and other medical circles, it threatened not only to keep her from flying but also from being commissioned as a Second Lieutenant. She swung into action to keep it in perspective and to prevent it from denying her future plans. She used her persuasive abilities to arrange all the necessary medical tests to prove the condition was not threatening.

Years later, she described her attitude philosophically, "If someone decided somewhere down the road that I should not fly for safety reasons, then I probably should not be flying, and I was ready to accept that. Fortunately, I was able to prove that medical condition was *not* threatening, and they went the other way." Eventually, she was the first pilot-qualified cadet to successfully negotiate the medical waiver for this condition. Later she would continue to go through special annual physical exams to check her heart with treadmill stress tests and an overnight monitor. The condition remained minor.

While she was undergoing these medical reviews, she was also balancing her post as the cadet commander while planning her future. As the Cadet Wing Commander in the Fall semester of her Firstie or senior year, she led the 40-cadet squadrons who made up the 4,125-person cadet wing in parades and other formations. These included five home games at Falcon Stadium to watch the Air Force team. The former high school cheerleader joined her fellow cadets in more than one roar as the Falcon team won three and lost two at home that year en route to a six and four record that included a thrilling overtime win at Notre Dame but losses to both West Point and Annapolis.

She said the toughest parts of her Wing Commander job were that sometimes, the cadet leader had to discipline peers. For example, she explained, "Half of our class skipped a Dean's call one day. And because it was so obvious, we had to take accountability, and I'm sure half of our class ended up marching tours. In the hierarchy of the four-class system, it was unusual to say the least to see hundreds of Firsties out marching tours." Kim concluded, "I had to be there on duty, so I had no choice to be involved in that action."

Academically, she started out studying astronautical engineering with a French minor but said she realized quickly that she couldn't do both while staying active in cadet leadership roles. So she switched to Space Operations and eventually graduated with a 3.7 cumulative grade average and a minor in French.

She was a female in a highly visible post, and I asked her about sex discrimination. Her reply was quick and direct: "I never had a single problem at the Academy dealing with anyone saying anything about me being female or different or anything like that. Other females might have had a problem, but I think I didn't because I was lucky that I had such a great relationship with those guys. They were my brothers, and I was never afraid to let them know if I was upset about anything they said or did that was out of line, right away. That has stayed with me over the years, and it still works well."

Kim returned to the Academy in 2003 and 2004 for several special programs designed to address the discrimination scandals that rocked the school and redirected its attention to assist female cadets. She remarked, "I continue to think that the cadets at the Academy are very strong. Yes, there are a few bad scenarios, but the cadets that I talked to are very committed and want the academy to be a good place with a good reputation."

During her first cadet year in 1993, Kim met Scott C. Campbell, an upstate New Yorker in her squadron who was in the Class of 1995—two years ahead of her. Although he would eventually become her husband, her first memory of him was not too pleasant. Scott was one of her first sergeants in basic training. "I think I disliked all of them at that time," she laughed later.

Scott said he remembered from his first impressions that Kim was a very smart, quiet, and confident Basic Cadet. "I remember that she did not get shaken very easily." And then, he added, "Those same adjectives describe her today."

After Scott graduated and went to pilot training, he and Kim reconnected, and he remembered that they started corresponding more frequently. Their long-distance friendship would continue for several years. They were together for special events, brief vacations, and occasional holidays, setting the pattern for an atypical relationship.

Scott grew up in Watervliet—just outside of Albany, NY—and moved to the very small town of Perth, which is just outside Amsterdam. He said he always wanted to be a fighter pilot and excelled at Broadalbin-Perth High School where he also played soccer and baseball. He majored in Business Management at the Academy, graduating 200th among 994 members of his Class of 1995 and then he went to Undergraduate Pilot Training (UPT) at Vance AFB in Enid, OK. Kim went to Scott's UPT graduation and pinned on his pilot's wings. Later Scott returned to the Academy for her graduation. Eventually, he would be assigned to bases in Arizona and North Carolina while the long-distance relationship continued to develop.

Kim remembered her graduation day on May 28, 1997, as a cloudy one but both busy and relaxing at the same time. She invited her political science, military arts, and science teacher, USAF Lt.Col. Donna Schutzius, to administer the oath of office. Her Dad, Chuck, pinned on her gold bars. Falcon Stadium was under remodeling construction so the Cadet Wing filed into the stands rather than onto the stadium floor. "That was a big deal at the time," she recalled later. "Somehow it doesn't seem so important now." The 797 grads in the Class of 1997 listened to Defense Secretary and former Maine U.S. Senator William S. Cohen praise them for joining the world's best Air Force. The low clouds restricted the Air Force Thunderbirds to a fly-by show, but all the grads still threw their hats in the air, and youngsters scurried about to claim their prizes.

Kim received the General George C. Marshall Scholarship sponsored by the British Government and was a distinguished graduate with several military, academic, and athletic awards. She was number one in Military Order of Merit and ranked 11th overall among her 796 classmates. Her friends from her first day as a Basic Cadet, Scott Burke and Tim Welter, also graduated. Tim later flew C-5 transports, and Scott worked as a medical administrator in the Air Force.

After graduation and a family vacation, Kim flew to London to use her scholarship for graduate studies as a guest of the British government. First she completed a Master's of Arts degree in International Security Studies at the University of Reading, about a half hour northwest of London. Her dissertation explored the use of U.S. military forces after the Cold War. In July 1998, she moved to Imperial College at the University of London for her Master's of Business Administration and specialized in Project Management.

When she learned that she needed an internship to complete the MBA program, Kim contacted the Johnson Space Center in Texas. "I called up NASA and said I was a First Lieutenant in the Air Force and offered them a free employee for two months." When NASA said yes to the free labor, Kim began to work in the agency's International Training and Integration Office.

Kim's lifelong dreams to work in the Space program soon became evident. When asked to describe her first time at NASA, she exclaimed, "*That* was an *awesome* experience! The people there were *terrific*, and I even got to fly and land the simulator for the Space Shuttle!" While in Texas, she met Eileen Collins, the first female pilot of a Space Shuttle and the first female Shuttle Commander. Collins, a U.S. Air Force Lieutenant Colonel at the time, commanded STS-93—the *Columbia* Space Shuttle. It flew from July 22-27, 1999, in a mission that deployed an advanced X-ray telescope. Kim also met several of NASA's international partners and learned about their cooperative efforts firsthand. She said the cooperation is super on the astronaut-to-astronaut level but gets complicated as the government agencies proceed up through the administrations, especially in the areas of budgets. Her thesis explored improving interaction and cooperation with NASA's international partners.

While she was in Houston that summer, Kim decided to take care of a few other projects in her spare time. She began flying lessons and managed to spend some more time with Scott, who was then stationed in North Carolina. As a result of her medical problems at the Air Force Academy, Kim had been unable to learn how to fly during her cadet days. So, armed with a medical waiver, she made arrangements to take civilian flying lessons at Ellington Field in Texas. After a few weeks of intense ground and flying school, she finally obtained her pilot's license. She returned to London and completed her thesis on September 10. A week later, she returned to California. Kim and Scott were married in the Sunnyvale Presbyterian Church on September 18, 1999. More than a dozen grads from Scott's and Kim's classes and the older generation from Chuck's class formed a strong USAFA contingent. Scott wore his formal Air Force mess dress uniform, and the bride wore her traditional white gown. Six of the military guests performed the requisite saber arch in an honor guard to salute the newlyweds, including four from Scott's class and two from Kim's.

The separations they experienced during their courtship and engagement would continue after they were married. Neither one of them dwelled on the subject; they almost dismissed it as a routine part of their relationship. I asked Kim's Mom, Paula, about it; and she replied, "They knew going into this marriage that it was going to be difficult. They just have this incredible bond and love for each other to sustain them while they're being separated. They have frequent contact with each other. It's very hard being separated because they want to be together."

Later Kim and Scott would learn they had unwittingly selected as the day for their wedding the birthday date of the U.S. Air Force in 1947—September 18. "Pure coincidence," she insisted with a laugh. Then the newlyweds headed for a Saint Lucia honeymoon before Kim reported to Columbus AFB in Mississippi to begin her Air Force Undergraduate Pilot Training. The Mississippi base was the closest available training base to Scott's assignment at Pope AFB, NC. During their spare time, the newly married couple would rendezvous in Atlanta about halfway between their Air Force assignments. "We have spent a lot of time in hotels halfway between the places we've been apart," Scott explained.

Despite some additional medical scares, Kim was able to successfully complete UPT and received the Air Force Association's top graduate leadership award. Next she was off to Davis-Monthan AFB in Tucson, AZ, for flight training with the A-10. The twin-engine A-10, officially called the Thunderbolt II but popularly labeled the Warthog or Hog for short, was the first Air Force jet aircraft specifically designed for close air support of ground forces. First build by the Fairchild Republic Company in 1975, the sometimes-maligned plane is a workhorse in the glamorous world of faster jets. With a top speed of 420 mph and a range of 800 miles from forward bases, the A-10 loiters near battle areas for extended periods and delivers bombs and missiles to support ground troops 24/7. It also provides aerial firepower during search and rescue missions. More than 300 aircraft were built and used by the regular active-duty Air Force, the Air Force Reserve, and the Air National Guard.

According to official Air Force descriptions, the A-10 carries special armor to strengthen it.

The pilots are protected by titanium armor that also protects parts of the flight-control system. The redundant primary structural sections allow the aircraft to enjoy better survivability during close air support than did previous aircraft. The aircraft can survive direct hits from armor-piercing and high explosive projectiles up to 23 mm. Their self-sealing fuel cells are protected by internal and external foam. Manual systems back up their redundant hydraulic flight-control systems. This permits pilots to fly and land when hydraulic power is lost. (USAF Air Combat Command Fact Sheet)

Kim would later say dryly, "It works as advertised."

Cadet Wing Commander Kim Reed

Kim and Scott posed with one of their Hogs.

After she completed A-10 training, Kim finally got an assignment together with Scott. They both flew A-10s in the 23rd Fighter Group at Pope AFB, near Fort Bragg and Fayetteville, NC. Although assigned to different flying squadrons, they began to enjoy a reasonably regular schedule. They began living together for the first time in January 2002, two and a quarter years after they were married. The couple bought a three-bedroom ranch in the suburbs and picked up dog and a cat. But their Air Force jobs still required considerable TDY (Temporary Duty) assignments, leading to some interesting separations for most of the year. When they were home, Kim said that sometimes they played golf though she laughed and said she's good for the first nine and then just wants to drive the cart and head off for a beer.

Both of them continued to fly training missions as the U.S. Air Force prepared for war.

On March 2, 2002, 172 days after the 9/11 attacks, U.S. and allied forces brought the fight to the Taliban and El Qaeda in Afghanistan. The Air Force deployed first Scott's squadron and then Kim's to the war zone for close air support and air rescue. Scott flew fourteen Operation Enduring Freedom missions, including four during Operation Anaconda—the U.S. Central Command's war effort combining all armed forces. He modestly avoided mentioning the fact that he was awarded three Distinguished Flying Crosses for his work in Anaconda. Kim added that bit of information to set the record straight.

Scott's unit spent four months in the war zone. When they were to be replaced by Kim's squadron, she was sent overseas as a member of the advance party. The two were reunited for a couple of days at a forward base where Scott's friends rigged a set of Christmas lights shaped like a heart in the window of his trailer. Kim described the war effort in terms of escorting ground troops and working with Special Forces. "We spent a lot of time holding [flying or loitering near battle], ready to provide close air support when called." However, she didn't drop any ordnance in her twenty missions. Several months later, the war in Iraq would provide a much different scenario for both Scott and Kim whose pilot call sign is Killer Chick. Scott Campbell uses the call sign Soup, named as a play on words for his last name. The second Iraq War began with major combat action on March 20, 2003, and Baghdad was liberated on April 9, 2003. As they supported Operation Iraqi Freedom, Scott worked with Special Forces and Kim flew 50 missions, including one that almost took her life.

According to her own description and official Air Force reports, Kim and her flight lead, Lt.Col. Richard Turner, had fired high-explosive rockets at targets in Baghdad on April 7, 2003. They were still over the hostile target area in Baghdad when Kim's A-10 was hit by enemy fire and became uncontrollable. "Right away, I noticed several caution warnings and I lost all hydraulics, so I completely lost control of the jet," she recalled in a calm voice later. "The Hog rolled left and pointed toward the ground, which was an uncomfortable feeling over Baghdad," she continued. "Plus the entire caution panel lit up, and the jet wasn't responding to any of my control inputs."

Kim said she tried several different procedures to get the jet under control, but none worked. At that point, she decided to put the jet into manual reversion. Although she was now flying the aircraft without hydraulics, it immediately began to respond to her controls. "The jet started climbing away from the ground, which was a good feeling because there is no way I wanted to eject over Baghdad," she added.

Lt.Col.Turner positioned his aircraft where he could view the damage and told Kim that the jet was flying "pretty good," and the damage had not affected flight-control surfaces or the (landing) gear. "I told her that if she could keep it flying, we would get out of Baghdad and might be able to make it back to the base," he recalled. Kim said Turner's calm demeanor and attention to detail were instrumental in her being able get the airplane home. Richard ranked in the middle of the USAFA Class of 1982.

"I could not have asked for a better flight lead," Kim explained enthusiastically. "He was very direct when he needed to be because all I could concentrate on was flying the *jet*," she exclaimed. "Then once we were out of the Baghdad area, he concentrated on the checklists—all the possibilities, all the things I needed to take into account," Kim continued. She said she and Turner discussed all her options, which ultimately came down to two: fly the aircraft to a safe area and eject or attempt to land the disabled plane.

Kim remembered thinking, *I can either try to land a jet that is broken, or I can eject, which I really didn't have any interest in doing, but I knew it was something that I had to consider.* Turner said that even though he could advise Kim, only one person could make the decision about whether to eject or attempt to land the aircraft. "She had a big decision to make," he said. "Before anyone else could throw their two-cents worth into the mix, I made sure that she knew that the decision to land or eject was hers and hers alone."

To Kim, the decision was clear. "The jet was performing exceptionally well," Kim said. "I had no doubt in my mind I was going to land that airplane. The jet worked as advertised," she repeated. "And that is a tribute to our maintainers and the guys who work on the jet. It's nice when things work as advertised," she added. After landing and getting the aircraft on the ground, her final task was getting it stopped and keeping it on the runway. "When you lose all the hydraulics, you don't have speed brakes, you don't have brakes, and you don't have steering," she explained patiently.

"One of the really cool things was that, when I did touch down, I heard several comments on the radio—and I don't know who it was—but I heard things like, 'Awesome job, great landing.' Things like that." She smiled. "I guess we all think we are invincible, and it won't happen to us," Kim said. "I hadn't been shot at—at all—in all of my other missions. This was the first," she said. "Thank God for the Warthog because it took some damage, but it got me home" (Haag 2003).

Her Mom and Dad remembered the 1:30 AM call from halfway around the world that woke them up at home in San Jose. "My first reaction was 'Oh, it's Kim, that's nice to hear from her.' Then she realized her daughter was 'all business,' telling her parents that she was safe and OK." Paula added, "Then my reaction was 'Oh, my god, I'm glad. I don't know what happened, but I'm awfully glad you're safe.'" Paula explained that Kim was not able to provide details and could only talk for a minute or maybe two at most. "When we hung up, Chuck and I turned to each other and said, 'We're *grateful*, but are we supposed to be able to go to *sleep* after *that?*'"

Despite the secrecy, Paula said she knew instantly that her daughter must have been hit, and that realization was followed quickly by the relief that she had survived the attack. The Reeds learned details two days later when Kim was able to send her parents an e-mail to alert them to the news coverage of the episode. "As we learned what had happened," Paula recalled, "there were tears shed and thanks given that she was OK. The more you know about these things, the more you realize the dangers that these young men and women face every day, and we can never forget that."

At the same time, during the first six weeks of the Iraq War, Scott was working for a special operations unit as their air planner in a classified location. "Normally, I would work from noon to six AM in eighteen-hour shifts," he explained. "So about the time she was probably taking off, I was just coming off my shift for the night and going to sleep. When I rolled in at midday, I walked into the operations center for another shift.

"There on my computer I read a note,

> Soup, your wife got hit over Baghdad.
> She was able to bring the jet home and land it and she's doing fine.
> Give her a call when you get a chance.

"It was left by one of our intel [intelligence] officers, a good buddy and classmate from the academy who was there with me," he continued to recall softly. "As I was making my way down to another room to give her a call, one of the Colonels that I worked for and had already gotten the news added, 'Yeah, yeah, glad to hear that your wife is doing fine.' Then a two-star [general] passed along the same thing, so a lot of people knew before I did."

Scott worked his way to a telephone and called into the weapons and intel mission planning shop at Al Jaber Air Base in Kuwait and was able to reach his wife. "I was able to talk with her and hear from her that she was all right. It was pretty *interesting*," he said, using that same, understated word his comrade-in-arms Jim Hayes—in Chapter 2 from West Point's Class of 1942—used to describe battles he witnessed in World War II.

Scott explained that his secondhand report from Kim, "in retrospect, was probably better because, from where I was sitting most days and nights, I was usually monitoring several classified conversations." Later he explained that the tapes of the exchanges between Kim and her wingman, Richard, included details about the Hog's condition that would have been more alarming if he had been listening to them live.

"I had spoken with Kim the day before and knew that she was scheduled to go up to Baghdad with Bino [Richard]. So based upon the time, I would have known it was her up there flying. When the chatter referred to 'she' or 'her,' there were only two people who that could have been," he continued. "In a way, I'm glad I didn't get to hear all the details of how she was coming back in manual reversion [without hydraulics]. Based on historical data in Desert Storm, a couple of guys tried to do it, and some were successful, and some packed it in. Certainly, that would have made me less comfortable than hearing about it after she had landed safely."

Two weeks later, Scott was in Kuwait where he was able to see Kim's aircraft. He also ran into another friend, the Al Jaber Air Base Chief of Safety Major Michael "Foot" D. Millen, who graduated 840th in the USAFA Class of 1990. Scott explained that Millen told him he was sent to the flight line to film Kim's attempted landing for historical purposes. "Foot told me later, after everything was good, that knowing the same historical data, he did not film the landing because he didn't want to have footage if she actually hit the ground and fire-balled it in."

In 2004, the U.S. Air Force had 3,233 fighter pilots on active duty. Men numbered 3,173; and 2,486 of them were married. Female fighter pilots numbered 60, and 33 of them were married. No one would offer an estimate of the number of Air Force fighter pilots who are married to each other, but Kim and Scott say they know several.

When asked about the uniqueness of her and her husband's job, Kim replied quietly, "Some people try to make a big story out of the two of us flying the A-10, but neither of us are big fans of talking to the media. However, we know it's important to the Air Force and to the A-10 community, so we are happy to be able to tell the story of this aircraft's success."

Despite its continuous service for three decades, the A-10 continues to function as a front-line combat aircraft. When describing its future, U.S. Air Force General Robert "Doc" H. Foglesong—then commander of U.S. Air Forces in Europe and former Air Force Vice Chief of Staff—remarked, "It does bring a capability that we're going to keep around for a significant period of time. It's going to depend, of course, on how long the airframe can last. There are certain points where it gets too expensive [to maintain] . . . But for right now, the A-10's got a lot of legs left on it, and we have just proven that." He added, "Airpower in the Iraq War just validated that that airplane has a mission that's very valuable to us" (*Air Force Magazine* 2004, 42).

Our nephew, U.S. Army Captain Michael W. Lynch, a combat veteran of conflicts in Bosnia with Operation Joint Endeavor and Iraq with Operation Iraqi Freedom offered this assessment. "The A-10s are the most coveted aircraft that you can ask for, flying low and slow and supporting us very effectively," he remarked. "The sound of their armament strikes fear into the hearts of the enemy. It's no exaggeration to say that all of us on the ground really appreciate the A-10s, which were built for ground attacks to support what the Army wants to accomplish."

Both Kim and Scott returned to the USA for more regular flying and continued training after their overseas adventures. In early 2004, Scott was transferred to Nellis AFB—eight miles northeast of Las Vegas, NV—where he was an instructor pilot at the USAF Weapon's School. For a while, Kim continued her duties in North Carolina. "We both just want to keep on flying the Hog," Scott explained. "For the time being, we're just taking things one assignment at a time."

When I caught up with Kim and Scott a few days before Christmas in 2004, they had actually been living under the same roof for two weeks. Kim flew west on leave before heading back to fly in the war zone. The two weeks' vacation was one of the few times in their relationship that happened. I asked during our interview, "And you're together for a while?" Kim replied, "Yes, that's very good." And Scott added, "For *just* two weeks."

Kim began 2005 back in the Middle East, flying her trusty Hog in support of troops chasing Al Qaeda in the hills of Afghanistan. She recorded 44 missions; some more memorable than others. She explained that some new equipment helped mission effectiveness. She also reported some humanitarian work looking for survivors of a flood when a dam burst in Afghanistan. And she recorded her one hundredth combat sortie.

After completing her Afghanistan assignment, Kim returned to Nevada. Nellis, known as the Home of the Fighter Pilot, opened in early 1941 as a gunnery school for the U.S. Army Air Corps. Its 11000 acres include the Air Warfare Center that helps train Air Force, Army, Navy, Marine Corps, and allied forces worldwide. Kim flew A-10s for the 422nd Test and Evaluation Squadron. Later, she worked on on the A-10C, a newer, upgraded Hog that included a digital cockpit configuration and more weapons capabilities.

Scott looked back at the ten years that he has known Kim and said, "She's extremely smart and well spoken. She's confident in what she does but hates when you point out the fact that she's a woman. She's a *fighter* pilot, *not* a *female* fighter pilot." He said emphatically, "She can't stand when that is made an issue over what she does and has done."

Kim hopes to keep flying her Hog and wants to accumulate enough experience to be eligible to apply for astronaut training. Her husband and her parents have no doubt that she will get what she wants. Dreams begin at an early age.

While updating this chapter prior to publication in 2008, I re-contacted Kim and Scott and learned of an important new development in their lives. Their son, Colin Reed Campbell, arrived August 16, 2008, on his Grandpa Reed's sixtieth birthday. Proud Grandpa reported "Mom, Dad, and baby are doing well" and added that Kim and Scott had been promoted to Major. Both were attending the advanced Command and General Staff College at Fort Leavenworth, KS.

Chapter 20

The Marine Captain

Jeremy J. Graczyk, USNA '99

Cellular telephones tether us and let us connect when our busy schedules keep us apart. Several friends of a friend had urged me to call Jeremy Graczyk, a USMC Captain who had graduated in the Class of 1999 from the U.S. Naval Academy and served with distinction in the War in Iraq. We exchanged e-mails, and I learned he was stationed in San Diego. I finally caught up with him on Veterans' Day in 2004 while he was on the highway, driving to Las Vegas.

"So where are you heading?" I asked after we connected.

"Sir, to the Marine Corps Ball at the Tropicana Hotel," he replied.

"And with a sweet young thing on your arm?" I shot back.

"Well, sir," he replied patiently, "I went to my Battalion's Ball *last* weekend with my girlfriend. *This* weekend, I am escorting the wife of one of my Marines who was killed three months ago. I am proud to be with her," he added, with a sentiment that spoke volumes about this combat-hardened Marine with maturity way beyond his then 27 years.

I had reached Jeremy by connecting with Jay Siembieda, a longtime friend and high school classmate of our youngest son, Jack. Jay had graduated from Ramsey High School in New Jersey and went to the Naval Academy where he graduated 396th among 926 in the Class of 1998. Later he flew H-46D Sea Knight helicopters off the USS *Wasp* (LHD 1), USNS *Sirius* (T-AFS 8), and USNS *Spica* (T-AFS 9) before a special assignment to the White House Military Office. I had contacted Jay when I was looking for a young Marine at the top of his Annapolis class to complete this book. Several e-mails and telephone calls later, I met up with this tough guy with a soft heart—Jeremy J. Graczyk, Captain, USMC.

Jeremy was born and raised in Southern New Hampshire in Atkinson, a small town of five or six thousand people a few miles northeast of the border from the larger Massachusetts burg of Haverhill, MA. His Dad, James F. Graczyk (pronounced "gray-sick"), is from Reading, PA. He was studying electrical engineering at Lehigh University in Allentown, PA, when he met Darlene Shoop from Shippensburg, PA. She was studying at the Albright Nursing School in Reading. They met on a blind date arranged by friends, fell in love, and were married on March 21, 1970, while Jim was completing his MSEE at Stanford University in Palo Alto, CA.

Later they settled in North Andover, NH, two hours north of Boston. Jim worked on software and hardware development for Bell Labs, and Darlene worked in hospital intensive care units and served as a nursing educator. Their daughter, Jennifer, was born on August 29, 1973; and their son, Jeremy, arrived on the same date four years later—often prompting the crack, "That's what happens when a nurse marries an engineer!" Jennifer completed a double major in business and Spanish at the University of New Hampshire and worked in the Information Technology field. She married mechanical engineer, Aaron Sakash, in 1998; and they have two sons, Aidan and Gabriele.

Tall and slim as a youngster, Jeremy played both soccer and basketball as he entered Timberlane Regional High School in 1990 just after the end of the First Gulf War. The public school in Plaistow, NH, serves four flatland communities in the seacoast suburbs of Southern New Hampshire. Jeremy was team captain and a swingman for the Owls' hoops team and also team captain and sweeper on the soccer team. His 175 pounds athletically filled his six-feet-two frame. He was also active in several organizations like the National Honor Society and Spanish Club.

Although very busy as a varsity athlete, in his senior year, Jeremy served as president of the school's student council. He excelled in the classroom and was valedictorian among the 168 members of his 1995 class. Fourth in the class was Christopher G. Comora of Danville, NH, who also received an appointment to the Naval Academy.

Hearing Jeremy and Chris describe other grads from Timberlane, it quickly became obvious that their high school is what the three service academies call a "feeder" school, a fine institution with an excellent track record of producing several graduates who enter the academies each year. In his graduation speech, Jeremy quoted from President Theodore Roosevelt nearly a century earlier.

> It is not the critic who counts, nor the man who points how the
> strong man stumbled or where the doer of deeds could have

done them better. The credit belongs to the man who is actually in the arena; whose face is marred by dust and sweat and blood; who strives valiantly . . . who knows the great enthusiasms, the great devotions, and spends himself in a worthy cause; who, at best, knows the triumph of high achievement; and who, at the worst, if he fails, at least fails while daring greatly, so that his place shall never be with those cold and timid souls who know neither victory nor defeat. (1910)

"I like to use that quote as an as an example of old school, pull-yourself-up-by-the-bootstraps rhetoric," Jeremy explained. "Sometimes it's too easy to make excuses for your actions, and I think the 'Man in the Arena' message is a good one."

When asked why he aspired to attend the Naval Academy, Jeremy first dismissed his youthful motivation with a laugh. "Probably too much GI Joe." Then he added with the serious perspective of a Gen-Xer a few years removed from the decision, "I was aware of the options for a good education and an opportunity to serve through one of my soccer teammates, Brian Sifferlan. His older brother, Eric, was three years ahead of me and went to Annapolis." Eric graduated among 946 members of the Class of 1996 and became a U.S. Navy pilot, flying H-60 helicopters.

During his Junior Year at Timberlane, Jeremy also attended the Naval Academy's Summer Seminar. "So I think I knew what I was getting in to," he remarked dryly. "Team sports and athletics were always important to me, and the Naval Academy was a great match," he explained. "I liked the combination of the whole-man education although, at first, I did think everyone there would be an All-American and expected to get my ass kicked." That healthy respect or concerned anticipation would serve him well. He quickly described the added dimension of the bonds with classmates that all of the academy grads mention as they talk about their experiences.

"If I walk away from the service tomorrow or I walk away twenty-five years from now, the one thing that I cherish the most is the friendships that I have developed through the Naval Academy and eventually the Marine Corps," he said quickly. When I told him virtually all the subjects in this book and virtually every grad that I have ever spoken with echoed those remarks, he replied, "It doesn't surprise me to hear you say that, and I cannot emphasize that enough."

Then he described his first day as a plebe. "I expected everyone to be six feet five, first in their class, and all everything," he recalled, forgetting that he was first in *his* class but only six feet two. "I consider myself a competitive person, and I am very wary of a kindler, gentler military because from the very beginning of my time at the Naval Academy, I wanted to be a SEAL or a Marine Infantry officer." Then he explained, "If you look at the Marine Corps' recruiting [effort], you don't see anything about 'get money to go to college' or other personal benefits. You see the opportunity to be one of the few and the proud. *That's* what I wanted from day one. I remember talking to my roommates about the fabric of America that we all saw among our classmates. I was definitely seeking a meritocracy," he recalled. When pressed, he replied, "My *biggest* shock was to see someone who was not prepared as an out-of-shape plebe."

Jeremy explained that his Dad did a lot of woodworking and mechanical projects when he was growing up. "One summer, I spent time working with him on a deck for a cottage for Lake Winnipesauke," he recalled. "I enjoy working with my hands and creating things. So I tried to figure out a niche in my studies at the Academy that would let me explore the way things work." Then he added, "I didn't see myself as a programmer but more of a 'hands-on' guy." He majored in systems engineering and minored in Spanish and said the academic load was what he expected. He took several computer sciences and programming courses. He continued his high school academic success, with a 4.0 grade point average in his Spring Semester of his plebe year.

"I figured out what I needed to do in class for my academics during my plebe year," he explained. "And I started playing rugby because it was a sport that I was attracted to and could work into my schedule and enjoy. I didn't blow off my academics by any means, but I balanced what I had to do within and outside the classroom with what I wanted to athletically." He continued to progress, once again illustrating what the admissions teams at all colleges will report—that the best predictor of future success is the student's past records. His senior project was building a walking robot for an international student competition in Montreal, Canada. An eight-man team designed, constructed, and operated the robot, which successfully performed its assigned tasks. He would end up with a 3.4 GPA and ranked in the top quarter of his class, with a systems engineering major and a minor in Spanish.

All three of the service academies play rugby as a club sport. The Naval Academy's Rugby Club, founded in 1963, is a member of the Mid-Atlantic Rugby Football Union and plays a range of U.S. and international teams. "We played approximately eleven games each year, in the Fall and Spring, on a schedule not unlike college football," Jeremy reported. "At first, I tried to 'walk on' to the soccer team [as a player not recruited], but that didn't work out and ended up being pretty fortuitous for me because rugby's been such a big part of my life. "At first, I played fly half, number 10 of the fifteen positions—similar to quarterback on a football team," he explained patiently. "It helped that I played soccer growing up because the tactical positions tend to kick a little more," he continued. "Then I played wing for while, but I really enjoyed playing, plus the friends and connections from rugby."

In both his junior and senior year, the Naval Academy's rugby team successfully reached the NCAA tournament's Final Four before losing to the University of California-Berkeley, a perennial powerhouse. Coincidentally, Jeremy would later play for the UC Berkeley head coach, Jack Clark, as a member of the All-Marine Corps Rugby Team. "At the academy, rugby provided a good outlet for me." He added, "It's a bit more physical and a good all-around combination of the athleticism I had experienced with soccer and basketball."

In his junior year, Jeremy was the Rugby Club's treasurer, keeping track of its funds. Then he served as Club President and co captain in his senior year. During Spring Break, the team flew to Ireland and played five matches against rugby teams there. "We had some great time both on and off the field or pitch as they say, and I still enjoy playing rugby from time to time, including going back to Annapolis as a grad to play in the alumni game each year. That's a lot of fun," he reminisced.

In his modesty, he neglected to mention that he was twice named to the NCAA All-American rugby team. His Mother told me that.

All of the service academies balance academics and athletics with leadership training. Cadets and midshipmen learn "followership" and then leadership through a series of ever-increasing responsibilities. Jeremy spent his first year in the 36th Company, and that was converted to the 30th Company with a reduction in the size of the Brigade from 4,400 to 4,000 midshipmen in 1994. All three academies downsized by ten percent during the administration of President William J. Clinton.

Rising through the ranks at Annapolis, Jeremy was assigned to the post of Brigade Adjutant in his "Firstie" year. Now officially labeled a "striper" because of the distinctive gold stripe on his uniform sleeve, Jeremy was a member of the battalion staff, participating in meetings and handling administrative tasks such as "writing the watch bill" (Navy jargon for the process of assigning tasks).

His was also the voice heard calling commands at all formations and parades. His voice seems soft when we were discussing this chapter, so I asked him if he's got a big mouth with a loud-enough voice to do that. He replied, "Apparently, I do. I was told I do. *Attention to Orders*," he said quietly, in a phrase that resonates with anyone who has ever marched in the disciplined ranks of the military.

"I have two good friends from that experience," Jeremy explained. "The Brigade Commander was Maurice "Mo" Uenuma, a Marine who was and is a great character." Uenuma would graduate in the top ten percent in the class and then served as an infantry officer and platoon commander. "The XO [Deputy Commander] was Jim Shroeder whose father was Retired Navy Commander John 'Fritz' Shroeder, a legendary Naval aviator who flew off the aircraft carrier USS *Oriskany* (CV-34) during the Vietnam War." Jeremy explained that the Senior Shroeder served in the same squadron as famous flight crew members John McCain and Jim Stockdale. Jim Shroeder ranked twelfth in the class with Jeremy and was recognized as a Trident Scholar. He went to flight school and received his MBA from the University of Minnesota before returning to flight duty.

"Although I'm not a complete knucklehead," Jeremy quickly clarified, "both of those guys were pretty serious and kind of straight arrows, and I like to think I provided some balance as the "token" rugby player on the Brigade staff. It was a good experience, and I have close friends from it still." When I commented that some people express prejudice about rugby players, Jeremy tossed it off with a laugh, "We kind of take that as a *compliment!*"

The Class of 1999 approached their graduation on May 26 with a sunny day and the usual smiles. Secretary of Defense William S. Cohen addressed the grads, and U.S. Marine Corps Commandant General Charles C. Krulak administered the Oath of Office to 158 Marines and 727 Ensigns, including Chris Camora, Jeremy's friend from high school. Krulak, who ranked 342nd among 927 grads in the Annapolis Class of 1964, was one of nine men who graduated from the Naval Academy and later served as Marine Corps' Commandant.

Jeremy's graduation photo

Captain Jeremy Graczyk, USMC

Jeremy's mother, Darlene, and his grandmother, Leora Shoop, pinned on his bars, and then the celebrations began with graduation parties and several weddings. After graduation, Jeremy and his high school friend, Chris Comora, flew to Washington State for what might seem to some a bit of an unusual vacation before going on active duty. Chris, who also ranked in the top third of the Class of 1999, was first assigned to Norfolk, VA, as a Surface Warfare Officer. He served on a destroyer, the USS *Arthur W. Radford* (DD-968), and a patrol ship, the USS *Shamal* (PC-13). Later he worked as a Barracks Officer for 600 Naval recruits in "boot camp" at the Recruit Training Command at the Great Lakes Training Center near Chicago.

Chris explained that he and Jeremy had started climbing together at the Academy. "We wanted to take one last fling at a real mountain before we went to work. So we flew west, to Washington State, and started up Mount Rainier. Chris recalled that they had practiced for a couple of days and then planned their climb from the base at Camp Shurman up through the Emmons-Winthrop Glacier Route. "We got up at midnight and started climbing," Chris recalled. "We had climbed pretty much nonstop for nine hours when we decided to take a break and rest. I woke up after an hour and was mumbling and not making much sense at 9000 feet of altitude," Chris continued. "Fortunately, the other guys helped me decide that we had better start back down before someone was hurt."

Next Jeremy and his Dad flew west and went fishing off Vancouver before he finally returned east to begin work as a new Marine Second Lieutenant. First he went back to the Naval Academy to teach close-order drill and physical fitness to the new crop of plebes who arrived for the

Class of 2003. "That was fun to be back at the academy after four years as an underclassman and now to be there as an adult, live in town, and enjoy life in Annapolis for the first time," he laughed. However, his brief holiday ended in September when he reported to the Marine Base at Quantico, VA, for the Basic School.

When asked why he chose infantry, this Annapolis grad echoes all the men I spoke with about that branch of the military, "That's where the action is," he explained patiently. "It's definitely the most intense in terms of leadership, and everything supports it. To me, the infantry is the quintessential Marine Corps. For me, I cannot imagine doing anything else in the Marine Corps."

After six months at the Basic School, Jeremy moved to the Infantry Officers School, also at Quantico in Virginia. He called it "one of the best schools I ever went to" as he relished the memory. "This was *pure* infantry. We were all guys in the field, all the time, in a warrior brotherhood," he recalled. "Our instructors were all experienced officers, and they were passing along what they had learned. This was another place where I had a strong peer group. Most guys there are pretty like-minded, aggressive, and excited about the work we were training for."

The U.S. Marine Corps, which often works on seaside beaches, operated its largest base at the edge of the Mojave Desert in Southern California. Twentynine Palms, the gateway to the Mojave and Joshua Tree National Park, has hosted the huge Marine training center since the Korean War. The scope of the base almost boggles the mind as the USMC Air Ground Combat Center includes the world's largest live-fire facility. Second Lieutenant Jeremy J. Graczyk arrived on August 18, 1999, and immediately began to work as a rifle platoon commander with India Company, Third Battalion, Seventh Marine Regiment.

"I was lucky to go right to work with the forty guys in my platoon and was supported by a lot of friends from the Academy and the Basic School," he recalled. "This is where I really began to appreciate the strength of our teamwork at all levels but especially the three sergeants who ran our squads. From my experience, the rank of sergeant is a pretty hallowed rank," he explained softly. "Those guys are first-rate."

Describing the environment at Twentynine Palms, Jeremy said, "There's not a lot of social life or other distractions there, so I did a lot of rock climbing in Joshua Tree and ran some dirt bikes in the desert during off-duty time."

After six month's training, he and his rifle platoon deployed to Okinawa, Japan, for additional training that took them to Asia and the South Pacific. He flew to Guam and then visited the Philippines and Thailand on board the USS *Frederick* (LST-1184). Jeremy and his Marines worked in the Philippines in the annual Balikatan exercises with Filipino Marines and in Thailand with Thai Marines in the Cobra Gold exercise. Six months later, Jeremy returned to Twentynine Palms for a new assignment in the Fall of 2000.

At that stage in their young careers, Marine First Lieutenants take two tracks in their development and training. Half begin to learn the intricacies of administration and staff jobs as executive officers in the three rifle companies or as headquarters officers. The others continue to develop their leadership skills with more responsibilities for more Marines. Heavy-weapons companies need platoon commanders, and Jeremy said he was "lucky enough to become the commander of the 81-mm Mortar Platoon with 80 men, the largest platoon in the Battalion."

He trained with his platoon for a year and said he remembered all of it, but especially that fateful day of September 11, 2001. "We were sitting on the Parade Deck at Twentynine Palms waiting on seven-ton trucks to take us out into the field when we heard the news," he recalled. When pressed, he recalled, "First we were concerned about several guys who had relatives and friends in New York, and then we were angry and frustrated about what was happening to other Americans while we were sitting in a training situation. We wanted to help and wondered what our new roles might be in this new conflict to counter the threat. To be honest, we were angry about what happened in the attack. As Marines, ultimately you signed up for one thing—to fight. We wanted to know when it would be our turn."

A year and three months later, Jeremy and his platoon joined Operation Iraqi Freedom as part of the allied force of 150,000 Soldiers, Sailors, Airmen, and Marines from the USA, the UK, and the other countries assigned to change the regime in Iraq. They boarded contract aircraft transports and flew from March AFB near Riverside, CA, directly to Kuwait International Airport. They quickly transferred to a contracted civilian bus for the long drive out into the regimental staging area, about thirty miles from the Iraqi border. He described January weather quite differently from home in New England or the Southern California desert. "This was a big, boring desert with sand as far as you could see," he recalled, "with weather into the forties at night and swings up into the eighties during the day." He and his Marines were living in big canvas tents, "which were nice for a Marine base." He added, "And we even had a little bit of a chow hall that served what someone described as mostly ground camel meat."

When I asked him about going off to war, Jeremy answered softly, "It's an epic event in your career," as he described leading 70 men as a 25-year-old First Lieutenant. "You talk about doing it in training, and often we heard from our sergeants, 'In combat, you'll do it this way.' And then, there you are, *doing* it. We were ready to do our part, but that old trite saying—'Be careful what you wish for when you hear guys saying, "I can't wait until we get some combat"'—is very real. The Marine Corps has that long, proud heritage of combat, and we were now in it."

All military folks use a shorthand series of numbers to describe their organizations in a code that belies quick understanding by outsiders. It's almost like hearing about an extended family clan with Aunts and Uncles and Cousins labeled with a confusing array of descriptors. However, Jeremy wasn't talking about a St. Patrick's Day Parade when he described his platoon's initial move into Iraq. They were among the first Marines to move across the border on the night of March 17, 2003.

"I remember listening to President Bush's address on a shortwave radio," he said, "and I thought, *We are the legions marching into war.*" Then he added a comment that stopped me in my tracks. He mentioned a comment from then MGen James N. Mattis, who commanded the First Marine Division during the initial attack, "General Mattis reminded us that the word 'infantry' derived from the same Latin roots as 'infant.' Those young guys right there on the front lines are fighting America's wars," he said simply. "Yes, there's artillery and planes dropping bombs, but you fall back on your training. When you stop, you dig a fighting trench. You've been trained and you're prepared and those preparations kick in. A lot of it is easier, and everything is simpler because you're ready." Then he added, with the respect that any officer who has been fortunate to work with experienced NCOs would recognize, "The *sergeants* are diligent tacticians and professionals going to work." He concluded his strong reverie, "*That's a hallowed rank in the Corps, and the sergeants never fail you.*"

One of those Marine Corps sergeants was Elia P. Fontecchio of Milford, MA. The two New Englanders met in California when Jeremy was assigned to command the 81-mm mortar platoon. Then Gunnery Sergeant Fontecchio joined the platoon six months later as his platoon sergeant. "I can't think of any relationship that's more critical than the relationship of a platoon commander and his platoon sergeant," Jeremy reported. Then the bachelor quickly added, "Like a marriage between a husband and a wife." Jeremy fondly recalled Fontecchio as one of the best. He had moved up the ranks to gunnery sergeant in less than a dozen years. "He was my platoon sergeant, and I just can't say enough good things about him," Jeremy said simply.

A Marine "Gunny," for Gunnery sergeant, is an almost mythical figure in the Marine Corps. Although all military officers rely on noncommissioned officers to do their jobs effectively, the Marine Gunny is special. Each one is charged with the overall well-being of a unit. These "jack-of-all-trades" are expected to combine training and experience with common sense and a strong no-nonsense personality to solve almost any problem, according to one of my Holy Cross classmates, a Vietnam-era Marine named R. J. Del Vecchio of Bridgeport, CT. Del added that the Gunnery Sergeant rank, E-7 on the military's pay scale, is where the largest number of senior NCOs exercise the broadest range of responsibilities in the Marine Corps.

In his 2007 book, *Why Marines Fight*, former Marine and bestselling author Jim Brady echoes that praise for sergeants. He quoted retired General James L. Jones Jr., USMC commandant from 1999-2003, "Sergeants run the Marine Corps." Then he explained, "Jones was attempting to tell me what he believed differentiates the Marine Corps from other military arms" (Brady 2007, 2).

Jeremy's mortar platoon rolled thru Safwan on the Iraq-Kuwait border at the beginning of the war. The hills on the horizon marked the only significant piece of terrain disturbing miles and miles of desert sand. "I have a pretty vivid memory of being up in the commander's hatch amphibious tracker [tank] literally rolling across the border, thinking, 'This is the real deal.'" He added, "It was certainly surreal looking at maps and talking on the radios to my guys and others at my higher headquarters. I remember not eating very much and not sleeping very much during the first forty-eight hours as we pushed very fast into Iraq."

When pressed for details, he added, "I remember talking to guys on the radio as we moved thru very little opposition from what was basically a third-world Army. The guys that I'm talking to are my peers. A short while earlier, we had enjoyed liberty while driving to Las Vegas or climbing in Joshua Tree." Then he added, "I don't even need to hear their call signs, I know their voices and who they are when we key up the radio. And these are guys you can trust, and that's pretty rewarding."

Jeremy credited all of his extensive training collectively and, when asked, singled out then Captain Dan Schmidt—his first weapons company commander. Schmidt was a USMC Reserve Lance Corporal during the First Gulf War. He was commissioned a USMC Second Lieutenant after graduating from the University of Illinois-Urbana. Jeremy said Dan created that environment of trust and relationship and was "by far, the best Marine I had ever been around." He added, "I remember when we're in the fight and under fire, and I knew I didn't need to ask permission to do the job that we had been trained for. I didn't hesitate. I knew this was the time to act because I had been prepared."

His unit moved into the town of Numenaya on the Euphrates River and then into Baghdad, where they fought soldiers and the Fedayeen wearing civilian clothes. They were several blocks away from the Marines in their sister battalion, the Third Battalion Fourth Marines, who ripped down Saddam Hussein's statue in the famed photo that was one of the early symbols of the war. After a few weeks in the capital with Security and Stability Operations, called SASO in the Marines' lexicon, they moved to Karbala and later Hindyah.

In the twists and turns that became more apparent as the War in Iraq evolved over the years, Jeremy explained, "Almost immediately, in Hindyah, we switched from fighting to fixing. We were helping farmers form a police force for the first time and going to town council meetings with the mayor." He continued, "We had a battalion of two thousand Marines, and we relied on college students as translators. I remember a businessman who was very helpful. He ran a watch and jewelry business—an ordinary guy. It was a hard transition after thirty years of a totalitarian regime and no concept of civic initiative. Even the eager good guys had difficulty as we tried to explain that a guy we caught looting a house was bad, but you can't keep his car because we caught him." He concluded, "I saw lots of friction based upon tribal affiliations and nepotism."

After six and a half months in Iraq, Jeremy flew back home in September 2003 for some liberty before he reported to his next assignment, the ultra intense world of Force Recon. When he told his parents about his new job, his Mother said she thought, "Oh, that's nice, he's going to be in *forest* reconnaissance." She laughed later at her naivety and proudly pointed out that Force Recon is an extremely challenging environment. Jeremy was assigned to the Fifth Platoon of First Force Recon at Camp Pendleton, an hour's drive north of San Diego. Again he was training and leading troops with help from the NCOs. He was named Platoon Commander and, in less than a year, was back in Western Iraq, putting that training to work in war.

Jeremy said he is often asked to contrast his first two tours in Iraq. "The first time we were there, we were liberating a country with the modern American military always fighting, going forward and the enemy fleeing," he explained. "The second time, we faced a more traditional insurgency, and there were aspects of the fight that were more frustrating." The results of that contrast showed up in casualties. "In our second tour, the sheer number of casualties we sustained put a tremendous psychological toll on the unit. However, I can't say that one was more serious than the other."

Among the units he was supporting was his old unit, the Third Battalion of the Seventh Marine Regiment that included his former Lance Corporal, now Gunnery Sergeant Elia P. Fontecchio as the Gunny for Kilo Company.

The Town of Al Qaim at the Western edge of Iraq is a wayside on the road to Syria. By August 2004, Gunnery Sergeant Fontecchio had been "in country" for more than six months. He was less than two weeks from heading home to reunite with his wife, Kinney, and their two-year-old son, Elia. Although he usually worked at the battalion's base camp, that fateful day Fontecchio decided to lend a hand on a patrol. As Fontecchio moved by, the enemy set off a concealed roadside bomb with enough power to destroy a tank. Fontecchio was seriously injured. A rescue helicopter was called quickly and took him almost immediately to the Forward Resuscitative Surgical System, the Iraq War's *M*A*S*H* unit. There surgeons poured eight liters of blood into his hemorrhaging body as they tried vainly for two hours to save his life. But the damage was too extensive. Fontecchio, 30, was the fifteenth fatal casualty of the 3/7, in the First Marine Division of the First Marine Expeditionary Force. His unit recorded more than 150 Purple Hearts for their combat wounds, among the highest casualty rates in Iraq.

"Through some unusual circumstances, I was in the field and actually heard radio reports of the attack because our unit was supporting the 3/7," Jeremy explained. "But it wasn't until later that I realized that it was Fontecchio who had been hit. That was a terrible loss," Jeremy said simply. "He was legitimately a great guy. He struck a really good balance between role model that the younger guys hoped to emulate. When you have a guy who can pull off leadership that the guys will follow him because they respect him, it's always a great thing."

After Jeremy completed his second tour in Iraq, he returned home once again. The extensive deployments of U.S. troops to Iraq and Afghanistan have been well documented. By the time he returned to the USA in September 2004, Jeremy had spent thirteen months out of the previous twenty months in Iraq.

When I first caught up with him in November 2004, Jeremy was in training and preparing to deploy still a third time to Iraq. He was commander of the Fifth Platoon with the Eleventh Marine Expeditionary Force and was scheduled to deploy again in January 2006. Listening to him matter-of-factly describe the methodical preparation to move to fight a war in an extended deployment reminds the reader or listener of how dedicated professionals approach their work.

He continued, "We spend a year in a workup with the company with six months' school phase and six months' green side [in the field] long-range patrolling. Next you do the reconnaissance workup, and then you lock on with a MEU [Marine Expeditionary Unit] to do a shooting package with close-quarters battle like the raids that people think of Force Recon doing." He explained, "Then you deploy for six months as a MEU. So it's almost like a two-year cycle."

In the midst of his training, Jeremy met up again with his high school and Annapolis classmate, Chris Comora. The two friends managed to spend some time skiing together during the Christmas holidays in New Hampshire.

Jeremy Graczyk has taken more than his share of lumps as a high school athlete, rugby fly half, sometime mountain climber, skier, and combat Marine. This lifelong skier reported a "pretty big crash" in January 2005 at Breckenridge, CO. "I knocked myself unconscious for five minutes, picked up a pretty good black eye, and broke my thumb," he reported. "Luckily, I was wearing a helmet," he explained sheepishly. He added, "Then I skied a bit more, crashed again, and tore my rotator cuff." That injury led to some physical therapy, but later, he reported that he was fully recovered.

In mid-August 2005, I reached Jeremy by cell phone, once again, after several e-mail exchanges. He was driving back to San Diego after a flight from Las Vegas, where he had attended a bachelor party for another Marine buddy. This time, however, he was driving by himself. I asked him for an update on Kinney Fontecchio, and he reported that his former Gunny's widow had purchased a home, and she and her son were supported by a strong community of friends in the Twentynine Palms area. "She was a Montessori teacher and is active in her church and is working things out," he remarked.

In April 2007, as part of what became known as the "surge," Jeremy deployed again to Iraq. He was commander of Bravo Company, First Battalion in the Fourth Marine Regiment, responsible for 180 combat Marines augmented at times by up to 75 other support troops. They were primarily providing security for Anah, a town of 30,000 people on the major east-west road that runs along the Euphrates River in Western Anbar province.

Jeremy's COIN or Counterinsurgency mission involved his Marine company plus engineers and U.S. Navy Emergency Ordnance Disposal teams as well as some U.S. Army soldiers from time to time. Their mission was to support local officials and police, working to create a secure, stable environment to help the local Iraqis transition to stability. Each day, Jeremy worked in what he called key-leader engagement with town officials such as the mayor and the local police force.

"Of my five deployments and four times in Iraq, this was by far, my most challenging and most rewarding," Jeremy explained upon his return. "That was largely a result of my direct association with the Iraqis, six or seven hours each day. I learned enough Arabic to get by with their passable English, eating what they ate, and conducting combined patrols side by side. For example, four of my Marines would go out with four Iraqis on tasks ranging from security patrols to stopping by the open market," he explained. "We would check to see where we could improve commerce and sometimes do raids to capture bad guys."

He spoke very highly of the partnership with the Iraqi security forces in the Western provinces. "We saw an evolution as we returned for more assignments," he explained. "In fact, I'm pretty sure that I fought *against* some of these guys two or three years ago. But now, the pendulum has swung. It's helped by the fact that they are all Sunni there and, so out of fairness probably, not quite as complicated [in religious conflicts] as other parts of the country. In fact, I would say the people I met with were more secular than is usually reported." Then he added, "They grew up there. These are their neighbors. They don't just speak Arabic, they speak *Iraqi*."

In an aside, Jeremy reminded me that the Marine Corps' counterinsurgency is one mission that they have done throughout their history. He cited places like China and Vietnam plus South American hotspots like Nicaragua, Haiti, and the Dominican Republic. "We are accustomed to working with the locals to find the bad guys in a cooperative way."

Then he continued, "People ask me, 'That must be hard?' And I respond, 'I signed up for this. It's what Marines do.' Plus we have all these support things going for us, like body armor, armored vehicles, and attack aircraft. And if needed, I can call in a med evac helicopter in minutes. We have all these things going for us, but it's still a very capable enemy."

Then he continued, "Compare that to my Iraqi counterparts. One man who I got to know very well is an Iraqi police captain with a wife and three kids. Three or four guys from his tribe spend every night on his roof with guns, protecting them, and that may continue for a long time," he said emphatically. "Quite frankly, that's the big difference. Ultimately, I have a lot of respect for these guys—my Iraqi counterparts. People are people. They are in a tough situation. They are concerned about their family and their children, and they have taken charge of their destiny. I consider many of them my friends, and I consider them patriots."

The Battalion redeployed back to Camp Pendleton in November 2007. "Although we lost two of our Marines in the Battalion, we were very fortunate that none of our Marines in our company were lost," he recalled. "[In my company], we had [combat wounds resulting in] seven Purple Hearts, mostly from roadside bombs of IEDs." Those are the Improvised Explosive Devices that account for so many casualties in the war.

In describing his Marines, Jeremy added a very specific comment. "Every Marine on their first enlistment in my company was in high school or graduated from high school after September 11," he noted. "They knew exactly what they were getting into when they joined the Marines.

They want to go fight, but most of the time, they're not shooting, which they would rather do." Then he recalled the description of warfare or flying as "thousands of hours of boredom punctuated by seconds of sheer terror." He added, "In a lot of ways, that's more challenging than attacking a specific target because you fight complacency all the time, and it's a real challenge to be alert and effective all the time. That takes a lot of discipline."

When he came back to the USA, Jeremy was able to enjoy reunions with his family including his octogenarian Shoop grandparents who journeyed from Pennsylvania to New Hampshire for the holidays. "I was also able to teach my four-year-old nephew, Aidan, to ski, and that was lots of fun," he recalled. Later ski vacations included time on the slopes with friends, both active and former Marines, in the Alpine mountains of Switzerland, Austria, and France. They also skied and snowboarded and climbed some more mountains in Southern California and Nevada. He enjoys the contrast of the heat and sand and the cold and snow.

"When you have time off, you gotta take advantage of it," he reminded us.

I asked Jeremy to contrast a typical Marine Corps' day in California with a typical day in Iraq, and he answered dryly, "I get asked that question a lot." He replied pointedly, "There was and is no real typical day."

The Marine Captain continues his training so he can continue to serve our country every day.

CHAPTER 21

Admissions, Athletics, and Alumni

During my research for this book, it should be no surprise that I learned quite a bit about the three academies, their students, and their graduates. I also heard some interesting stories about the admissions process to complement my own experience of the past two decades. And throughout my research, I kept reading and hearing about the heritage of the athletic programs at the three schools. Finally, many people have asked about the class ranks of famous academy graduates. This final chapter responds to those interests.

Admissions

Although I had been born and raised in an Air Force family and had served in the Air Force since 1964, I had never visited USAFA until 1982. That year, I flew out to Colorado Springs as a USAF Reserve Lieutenant Colonel for my orientation as an Air Force Academy Admissions Liaison Officer, or admissions counselor. Our two older sons, Kevin and Jim, came along, enticed to attend summer sports camps there while their Dad was in seminars, learning how to counsel applicants who are called candidates. A few years later, I was able to visit Annapolis and West Point.

Like all colleges and universities, the three service academies have very specific requirements for applicants. Of course, the military academies add a few admissions wrinkles that their civilian counterparts could not imagine. These include rigid medical and physical requirements as well as the added complication of obtaining a nomination from an elected official or other specified source. The usual sequence of events is, first, complete the application process; second, request and obtain a nomination; and third, receive an appointment.

All three academies have attractive and helpful web sites that provide information about each institution. USMA at West Point may be reached at www.usma.edu, USNA at Annapolis can be accessed at www.usna.edu, and USAFA at Colorado Springs connects at www.usafa.edu.

Each school also has admissions counselors throughout the world who help the applications and admissions process. We're called Admissions Liaison Officers at USAFA, Field Force Representatives at USMA, and Blue and Gold officers at USNA. Applicants to the service academies face extremely tough competition each year, and all of the college preparation guides list the three service academies in "most competitive" or "highly competitive" categories. During the 2002-2003 application cycle for the Class of 2007, for example, 14,101 people applied to the Naval Academy while only 1,228 entered as midshipmen.

Applicants must be successful high school graduates and at least 17 but not yet 23 years of age by July 1 of the year admitted; be a U.S. citizen at time of enrollment, although foreign students may be nominated by agreements between U.S. and other countries; and be unmarried and not be pregnant or have a legal obligation to support a child or children. They must complete either the Scholastic Aptitude Tests or the ACT Assessment and pass thorough medical and rigorous physical exams. Taking the SAT or ACT more than once or twice is not uncommon, and scores often improve each time the test is taken. All the academies take only the highest score in each category.

All three academies are quick to point out that prior-enlisted service provides another route to admissions. Soldiers, Sailors, Airmen, and Marines already in the military should check with their unit personnel departments to learn about their direct admission process. In 2003, the USNA's 1,228 new midshipmen for the Class of 2007 included 108 prior-enlisted personnel. USAFA's 1,287 new cadets in 2007 included 62 former enlisted while West Point's Class of 2011 entered with 1,305 members who included 227 prior enlisted.

As indicated in the web sites and catalogues, which are usually available in high school guidance departments, junior year is the best time to write letters to request nominations. As a minimum, applicants should send out four letters, although they can read exactly alike. Letters should be sent to their local district's U.S. Congressional Representative, both U.S. Senators and the Vice President of the United States. Applicants and their families should understand this is *not* a case of "who do you know?" It *is* the case of civilian control over America's military at the very beginning of officer development.

Congressional nominations are based upon applicants' qualifications and the results of an important interview with the military academy selection committee of the Congressional representative or Senator. It is *not* a political process in any way! Parents or friends do not need to know these political people, and that cannot be stressed enough. It is one of the worst misconceptions of the admissions process. Other categories of nominations are described in the academies' web sites and catalogues. These range from certain high school Junior ROTC units to sons and daughters of Medal of Honor recipients. Soldiers, Sailors, Airmen, and Marines and college or university ROTC cadets also qualify for special nominations. Often, 20 to 25 percent of each academy's entering class consists of students who graduated from high school one or two or more years earlier.

As soon as candidates receive information from the academy or nominating committee, they should act promptly. This is an extremely competitive process, and timing is critical. I always cautioned students and parents alike that the clock began running when the application was requested. As an Air Force Academy admissions officer since 1982, I have seen some hesitant applicants lose to more eager ones.

More than three-quarters of students entering the academies are usually in the top 20 percent of their graduating high school class. Admissions committees at the three schools also look carefully at athletics and leadership in extracurricular activities. More than 90 percent of all new cadets and midshipmen were varsity athletes in high school. West Point's Class of 2011 included 194 Eagle Scouts and Gold Award winners among 1,305 plebes. Cadet and midshipman ranks at all three academies are filled with students who captained teams, led clubs, edited yearbooks and newspapers, and directed high school choruses, bands, and plays.

Each of the service academies provides free tuition, dormitory rooms, and meals as well as medical and dental care. Cadets and midshipmen are also paid each month because, as is often noted, they are *in* the military service and their *job* is to attend the service academy. Cadets and midshipmen pay for their books, computers, uniforms, travel, and other incidentals. They pay taxes and are subject to all military rules and regulations.

Calling the academy a "free" education is a misnomer subject to misinterpretation by many observers. Cadets, midshipmen, and their families are quick to point out that military students *earn* their educations through active-duty service obligations. These are a minimum of eight years, including five years active duty and three in the reserve plus additional time for training such as Undergraduate Pilot Training or flight school, graduate school, and other special programs.

Cadets and midshipmen pay is set at 35 percent of the basic pay for second lieutenants and ensigns with less than two years of active duty.

Their first major expenditure as students is for personal computers. However, cadets and midshipmen also pay for newspapers, laundry, and haircuts, including that first infamous buzz cut on the first day. Cadets and midshipmen call their pay "magic money" since most of it is withheld to pay for their uniforms and other required purchases such as their PCs. Their monthly allowance is doled out in increments that increase each year. A significant jump at the beginning of the third year reflects two real situations: commitment and cars. When students return for their third or junior year, they reach a point of no return. If they leave the academy after that time, they incur considerable expense and the real possibility of active duty in the active-duty military's enlisted ranks. The timing also coincides with one of the first real liberties that cadets and midshipmen experience—the ability to purchase and own an automobile.

Sometimes the military services work in strange ways to bring new cadets and midshipmen to their academies. One graduate, Peter Karter of the West Point Class of 1947, described an unusual route to his plebe year during World War II. Unlike virtually all other volunteers who became cadets, Karter was literally *ordered* to attend West Point before he even knew about it!

Peter was born in Chicago on August 19, 1922, to parents who were Greek immigrants. His family returned to Greece when he was a child and lived above Sparta until they returned to the USA in 1930. Peter was raised in Kearny, NJ, and the U.S. Army noted his proficiency in Greek and English in 1943 when he was drafted. In fact, he reported he *almost* returned to Greece to work with the resistance there. However, confusion over the spelling of his surname, Karter, with others named Carter led to a few misplaced records and assignments. He was sent to England where his commander noted his prowess and nominated him to attend the USMA prep school, then located at Amherst College in Western Massachusetts.

"I was a Corporal, serving in an engineering battalion that was building an airfield in England," Peter explained. "One day, in early 1944, my company commander called me into his office and said, 'Karter, you've got to be up in Scotland tomorrow because you're going back to the States to go to West Point.' Then he told me he had put my name on a list of *possible* new cadets a few months earlier and hadn't bothered to tell me since he wasn't sure if *anything* would come of it. One day, the orders came in, and I was on my way. However, that was not a simple task during World War II, or for any war, for that matter."

Karter had to be transported during wartime from the European Theater of Operations to the USA to begin his studies. As a Corporal, he was low man on the priority list of any air transport travel. It was most unusual for an enlisted man to be flying across the Atlantic Ocean in those days, even one who had been ordered to attend the West Point Prep School.

Luckily, Peter met up with an Army Air Corps Colonel who was directing the Air Transport Command in Scotland. Also fortuitous was the fact that a senior leadership conference was just concluding, so a group of generals and their staffs were flying back to the USA from Scotland. The Colonel, who had graduated earlier from West Point, literally took the young soldier under his wing. He told him he was about to embark on a great adventure. He called in his aide and told him to reissue the enlisted man's orders with a higher priority. He also arranged for young Peter to enjoy a brief vacation at home before he began his studies.

The West Point Colonel's aide issued orders that read, "Proceed!" And so he did, to study engineering and graduate 13th among 310 men in his Class of 1947. After graduation, he served as a civil engineer in Kansas, Germany, and Korea. He also earned an MS degree in soils and foundation engineering from Harvard University. Later he worked for American Machine and Foundry and established Resource Recovery Systems, a recycling firm in Connecticut.

Athletics

Peter Karter and his classmates received their diplomas on June 2, 1947, from General Dwight D. Eisenhower, who returned to his Alma Mater for the ceremonies. First in the class was Robert Miller Montague Jr. from Hawaii. Montague would later retire as a Brigadier General and work in public service in the Special Olympics and Kennedy Foundation. Last in the class was Robert Maxwell Ehrlich of Illinois. He served in the U.S. Air Force and retired as a Lieutenant Colonel to become a realtor and rancher. Two of their other classmates were among the more famous graduates of the USMA, winning fame on the football field on the successful West Point teams during the 1940s. South Carolinian Felix Anthony Blanchard, known by the nickname Doc, was dubbed "Mr. Inside" because he liked to run *through* the lines between tackles. He won the Heisman Trophy as the nation's outstanding collegiate football player in 1945. He ranked 295th in the class. Blanchard would go on to a 25-year military career, primarily in athletics. He served as the Deputy Director of Athletics at USAFA and retired as a Brigadier General in 1971.

His classmate and teammate, Glenn Woodward Davis, won the 1946 Heisman as "Mr. Outside" because he ran successfully *around* the line. He ranked 304th in the class. After three years in the Army, Davis played professional football for the Los Angeles Rams, playing on the team that won the 1951 NFL championship before a knee injury cut his career short in 1952. Although never injured playing, Davis tore a knee ligament while filming a 1946 movie, *The Spirit of West Point.* That injury recurred in 1951 and eventually led to his retirement from football in 1952. He later worked for the *Los Angeles Times* newspaper as a special events director.

West Point, Annapolis, and more recently, the Air Force Academy, have included thousands of other graduates who achieved additional fame as athletes and in other fields. For example, Black Knight football's Peter M. Dawkins won the Heisman Trophy in 1958 and then graduated 10th among 498 classmates in 1959. He was a Rhodes Scholar and decorated for combat heroism in Vietnam. He later earned a PhD at Princeton University before another successful career in business on Wall Street.

Joe Bellino, Navy's All-American running back, graduated 754th among his 786 classmates in 1961. Navy quarterback Roger T. Staubach won the Heisman Trophy as a junior at USNA in 1963 and graduated 488th among his 802 classmates in 1975. He played his Hall-of-Fame career for the Dallas Cowboys of the National Football League and stayed in Texas as CEO of a Dallas-based commercial real estate firm. Among the other notable USNA grads to play professional football were the New York Giants' Phil McConkey, 462nd out of 934 grads in the Class of 1979, and the Los Angeles Raiders' Napoleon McCallum, one of the more famous Annapolis Anchors, who was last among his 1,042 classmates in 1985.

Another former Dallas Cowboy was Iowan Chad W. Hennings, who received the Outland Trophy as the NCAA's outstanding college lineman in 1987. He was also an academic All-American-ranked in the top 10 percent among his 1,074 classmates in the USAFA Class of 1988. He flew A-10 Warthogs fighter aircraft in the Air Force. After a successful NFL career, Chad formed three Texas-based companies, including Vitus Inc., a private equity firm specializing in technology. More recently, Washingtonian Bryce A. Fisher, a defensive end who was with the all-Western Athletic Conference during his successful career at USAFA, graduated in the middle of 963 in the Class of 1999. He later played in the NFL for the Buffalo Bills and St. Louis Rams. Another member of the NFL was Troy Calhoun, who ranked in the top quarter among 1,022 in the USAFA Class of 1989. He coordinated recruiting and junior varsity offense at USAFA before leaving active duty in 1995. He coached at Ohio University and Wake Forest and then moved to the NFL's Denver Broncos and Houston Texans. In January of 2007, he was named head football coach at USAFA, the first USAFA graduate to return to his Alma Mater as head football coach.

The Naval Academy's David M. Robinson ranked 543 as a mathematics major among 1,033 members of the Class of 1987. He was that year's

Collegiate Basketball Player of the year. After two years' active duty in the Navy, he joined the San Antonio Spurs in the National Basketball Association, playing until he retired in 2003. His coach for the Spurs team was Gregg Popovich, who graduated in the middle of his Class of 1970 at USAFA. Both are included in Jimmy Love's profile in Chapter 9. Robinson, nicknamed "the Admiral" for his powerful presence on and off the basketball court, played on the last amateur U.S. Olympics basketball team in 1988 and the first "Dream Team" to include professionals in 1992 and again in 1996. He concluded his Hall-of-Fame career in 2003. He also helped establish The Carver Academy with a $9 million pledge to build and operate an independent and culturally diverse school for San Antonio.

All of the academies require cadets and midshipmen to participate in athletic programs, either at the varsity, intramural, or club level. They have produced athletes who successfully competed within their academies and outside, including the international Olympics, throughout the years. Since the 1912 games in Stockholm, 88 Naval Academy grads have participated in sports ranging from rowing, yachting, and swimming to bobsledding, gymnastics, and track and field. West Point reports 85 Olympians, including many in horsemanship and riding. Fifth place in the 1912 Games' pentathlon, including 25-meter pistol, fencing, a 300-meter freestyle swim, five-kilometer steeplechase, and four-kilometer cross-country run was George S. Patton Jr. who had graduated 46th out of 103 in West Point's Class of 1909.

Among the many other Olympians, but the only one from USAFA, is Alonzo C. Babers, whose father was in the Air Force when he entered the Air Force Academy in 1979 from an air base in Germany. Babers graduated from USAFA in 1983 and ranked in the middle among 956 grads. He majored in management and was a championship sprinter. He competed in the 1984 Olympics in Los Angeles where he ran the 400 meters in 44.27 seconds to win the gold medal. Two days later, then Second Lieutenant Alonzo was part of the 4 X 400-meter relay team that also won the gold. A month later, he reported to Undergraduate Pilot Training at Laughlin AFB, TX, and spent the next six years flying C-141 and C-21 transport aircraft. In 1991, he joined the Air Force Reserve and later flew for United Airlines while serving as a USAFA Admissions Liaison Officer.

Sports at the academies and in other institutions lead to many legendary exploits both on and off fields or courts. And of course, the dedicated effort to succeed in athletics helps form people who can inspire and lead others. I was interested in one leadership story that has resonated for many years. It's a quote from World War II that some thought was attributed to West Point's General Douglas MacArthur. Others claimed it was General George Marshall, a graduate of Virginia Military Institute. In his classic 1970 book on military leadership, *Military Men,* Ward Just described a scene at West Point: "There is a plaque on a rock near the football stadium, a quotation attributed to George Catlett Marshall, '*I have a secret and dangerous mission. Send me a West Point football player*'" (Just 1970, 46).

Despite its stirring sentiment, the quote is not genuine. Historian Dr. Larry I. Bland—Director of the Marshall Papers for the General George C. Marshall Foundation at VMI in Lexington, VA—told me in 2005 that it simply is not true. "No one has been able to confirm that he ever said it," reported Dr. Bland, adding that several people have questioned a VMI grad praising a West Point footballer in that way. (Bland Interview)

Although many cadets in the early days of West Point were athletic, General Douglas MacArthur was responsible for expanding sports at the USMA during his tenure as Superintendent from 1919 to 1922. Author William Manchester explained in his extensive biography, *American Caesar,* that MacArthur "made intramural athletics compulsory for the whole corps . . . and urged congressmen to appoint gifted athletes to the academy, asking Washington to build a 50,000-seat stadium on the Hudson, and gave his football players special privileges during the autumn months" (Manchester 1978, 123).

MacArthur also composed this quatrain that is chiseled in a granite memorial at the entrance to Holleder Center, the West Point sports facility named for Army infantry Major Donald W. Holleder—a New York football player who graduated 443rd among 480 members of the Class of 1956, coached at USMA, and was killed in combat in the Vietnam War:

> Upon the fields of friendly strife
> Are sown the seeds
> That, upon other fields, on other days,
> Will bear the fruits of victory.

Retired VADM William P. Lawrence, who ranked eighth among 725 graduates of the USNA Class of 1951 and was Naval Academy superintendent from 1978 to 1981, once noted: "I think there is one characteristic of the American people that contributes immensely to the greatness of our country, and that's our dedication to excellence in every way of American life. And I think we attach a high degree of significance to excellence in physical fitness. Intercollegiate sports more or less represent the ultimate in excellence in amateur sports—that's one of the real values of intercollegiate athletics."

Many other observers—including my fellow USAFA Admission Liaison Officer, Lt.Col. Larry Griswold, USAF Ret. and a longtime advertising salesman at *Sports Illustrated* magazine—believe the service academies' athletic programs contribute greatly to their success and the pride that people have in these three institutions. The academies field teams in virtually all of the sports sponsored by the NCAA. Larry became friends with Fisher DeBerry, the legendary football coach at USAFA, several years ago. He told me they discussed the important balance of sports and academics and leadership that each of the service academies maintains to successfully produce lieutenants and ensigns. In his 2000 book, *For God and Country*, DeBerry wrote to confirm this point. "At the Academy, the greatest pride I get is when those guys throw their hats in the air at graduation, not when they cross the goal line on a football field" (DeBerry 2000, 88).

Alumni Class Rank

Those "hats off" have signaled important milestones for the more than 62,000 West Pointers, 73,000 Annapolis grads, and 38,000 USAFA grads. This final section includes some of the more notables.

Class rank was so ingrained among West Pointers that, 65 years after his graduation and a monumentally successful career, five-star General of the Army Omar N. Bradley lamented, "Had I not given so much time and effort to athletics, I believe I could easily have graduated about twentieth" (Bradley 1983, 34). This autobiographical comment came from a man who ranked 44th out of his 1915 Class of 164 that included enough general officers (59) to be known as "The Class the Stars Fell on." Many observers believe their success was helped by the combination of "right place" and "right time" since they graduated just prior to World War I and were senior career officers during World War II.

That West Point Class of 1915 also included Dwight D. Eisenhower, who ranked 61st, another five-star General of the Army who would serve as the 34th President of the United States. Four-star Generals include Joseph T. McNarney, who ranked 40th, and James A. Van Fleet, who ranked 92nd. Last in the Class of 1915 was Charles Curtis Herrick of Illinois. He served in the Infantry in the American Expeditionary Forces in the World War I and was discharged in 1922. He returned to active service and entered World War II as a Major. He served as a member of the War Department General Staff in 1942 and 1943 and retired in 1951 as a Colonel.

The other Army generals to wear five stars were World War II Chief of Staff and postwar Secretary of State George C. Marshall, the Army's Pacific Theater Commander Douglas MacArthur, and the Air Force founder Henry H. Arnold. Marshall graduated 15th among his 31 classmates in the Class of 1901 at the Virginia Military Institute. MacArthur was first in his West Point Class of 1903, and Arnold was 66th out of 111 classmates in 1907 at West Point.

Five-star Fleet Admirals in the U.S. Navy included William D. Leahy, Ernest J. King, William "Bull" F. Halsey, and Chester Nimitz. All were Annapolis grads. Leahy was 35th out of 47 in his Class of 1897, and King was fourth out of 67 in 1901. Halsey was 43rd among 62 in 1904, and Nimitz ranked seventh among 114 in the Class of 1905.

Others to hold the General of the Armies position were Civil War generals Ulysses S. Grant, William T. Sherman, Philip H. Sheridan, and World War I hero John J. Pershing. Grant ranked 21st out of 39 in the Class of 1843; Sherman was sixth out of 42 in 1840; Sheridan was 34th out of 52 in 1853; and Pershing was 30th out of 77 in the Class of 1886. All wore special insignia with four stars.

The Center of Military History reported that there were no other generals that held this position until 1976 when President Gerald Ford posthumously appointed George Washington as General of the Armies of the United States. President Ford noted at the time that Washington would rank first among all military officers.

Reviewing class rank among the senior military leaders throughout West Point's history revealed that only Generals Robert E. Lee and Douglas MacArthur ranked first or second in their respective classes. None of the senior generals ranked last although several were in the bottom half of their classes. That group includes Hap Arnold, the legendary father of the U.S. Air Force. Another famed U.S. Army Air Corps pioneer, General Carl Spaatz, graduated 56th among the 107 members West Point's Class of 1914.

Lee and MacArthur also served West Point as Superintendent. Lee's era covered 1852 to 1855, and MacArthur was Superintendent from 1919 to 1922. Lee was second in his West Point Class of 1829 and was one of the relatively few cadets to go though four years without a single demerit (Ambrose 1999, 157). His son, George Washington Curtis Lee, was first in his Class of 1854. Robert E. Lee was offered the opportunity to lead the Union Army before he accepted Confederate President Jefferson Davis's invitation to lead the Confederate States of America forces. MacArthur, of course, was one of the leading military figures of the 20th Century. More recently, the Superintendent from 1996 until his retirement in 2001 was Lt.Gen. Daniel W. Christman who ranked first in his West Point Class of 1965.

West Point's Class of 1846 included several famous grads among its 58 members, including Union Civil War General George B. McClellan (later Governor of New Jersey), and Thomas J. Jackson, the Lieutenant

General of the Confederate States of America (more popularly known as Stonewall Jackson). Last in that Class of 1846 was a man destined to be linked immortally with the Civil War. George Edward Pickett led Confederate soldiers in the fateful Pickett's Charge at Gettysburg on July 3, 1863. Although Pickett had been last among his 58 graduating classmates, another 52 men, who had enrolled as plebes in 1842, failed to complete their schooling.

The three academies have produced many grads who achieved fame outside of the military. In addition to the Naval Academy's Albert A. Michelson, the first American to receive a Nobel Prize (mentioned in Chapter 4), these include Thomas J. Rodman, Reuben Pomerantz, and Steve Rowe from West Point, for example. Rodman, seventh among 51 in the Class of 1841, perfected the design of weapons, enabling them to fire more-powerful ordnance over greater distances. Pomerantz, who ranked 378th among 875 grads in 1946, was later president of the Holiday Inn hotel chain. G. Steven Rowe, Attorney General of the State of Maine, was 571st among 862 in the Class of 1975. Another Mainer, the State's Adjutant General, Army MGen John "Bill" W. Libby, left West Point's Class of 1965 after his plebe year and was commissioned through Army ROTC at the University of Maine. He is one of countless former academy cadets and midshipmen who went on to successful military and civilian careers.

Air Force Academy grads famous outside the military included, for example, Harry J. Pearce, 40th among 499 in the Class of 1964, and the former Vice Chairman of General Motors Corporation. Richard T. Schlosberg III, 63rd of 517 in the Class of 1965, was publisher of the *Los Angeles Times* and former head of the David and Lucille Packard Foundation.

A review of the military service's Chiefs of Staff revealed that none of the senior generals ranked last although several were in the bottom half of their classes. That group includes Hap Arnold, who was 65th out of 110 classmates who graduated from West Point in 1907. Another was General Harold K. Johnson, who was 231st out of 346 grads in West Point's Class of 1933. General Carl E. Vuono, Chief of Staff from 1987 to 1991, who ranked 438th out of 545 members of West Point's Class of 1957. The Army Chief of Staff at the outset of the 21st Century was General Eric K. Shinseki, who ranked 332nd out of 595 peers as a classmate of Christman in 1965.

The only Chief of Naval Operations (CNO) to rank first in his class at the Naval Academy was Admiral Carlisle A. H. Trost of the Class of 1953, profiled in Chapter 5. Trost and General MacArthur are the only grads from the top of their respective academy classes to reach the top command of their military branch. Trost and virtually every CNO after World War II graduated from the Naval Academy. The two exceptions were Admiral Jeremy M. Boorda, who enlisted in the Navy in 1956 and was commissioned through Officer Candidate School (OCS) six years later. The second was the CNO at the change of millennia, Admiral Vern Clark, who graduated from Evangel College in Springfield, MO, in 1967 and was commissioned through OCS in 1968. Nearly all the 25 Annapolis grads who became CNO ranked in the top halves of their classes. Exceptions were early World War II Admiral Harold R. Stark, 29th of 50 in the Class of 1903, and postwar Admiral Louis E. Denfeld, 87th out of 156 in the Annapolis Class of 1912. Admiral James K. Holloway, who was CNO from 1974 to 1978, ranked 338th out of 615 members of his Class of 1943. Admiral Gary Roughead, who ranked 267th out of 888 in his USNA Class of 1973, was named 29th Chief of Naval Operations in September 2007.

Eleven men commanded the U.S. Marine Corps before the first Naval Academy grad reached that position in 1914. The first was World War I MGen George Barnett, who served as Commandant from 1914 to 1920 and ranked 28th among 72 grads in the Class of 1881. The next four Marine Corps Commandants were also grads. MGen John A. Lejeune, 13th out of 36 grads in 1888, served from 1920 to 1929. MGen Wendell Neville ranked 24th out of 34 in 1890 and served from 1929 to 1930. MGen Ben H. Fuller was also 24th in his 1889 class of 34 and served from 1930 to 1934. MGen John H. Russell, who ranked 33rd among his 40 classmates in 1892, served from 1934 to 1936. General Wallace M. Greene Jr. was Marine Corps Commandant from 1964 to 1967. He ranked 118th among his 402 Naval Academy classmates in 1930. General Robert E. Cushman Jr., Commandant from 1972 to 1975, was the highest-ranking Naval Academy graduate to serve as the top Marine. He was ninth in his 1935 class of 442. General Charles C. Krulak, who served from 1995 to 1999, was 342nd among 927 graduates of his Class of 1964. General Michael W. Hagee, who was named Commandant in January 2003, ranked 74th out of his 836 Annapolis classmates in 1968. Nine out of the 33 men who have been Marine Corps' Commandants were Naval Academy graduates.

Ten of the seventeen Chairmen of the Joint Chiefs of Staff have graduated from West Point or Annapolis, beginning with General of the Army Omar N. Bradley, who was the first to hold the position, from 1949 to 1953. Bradley was succeeded by Admiral Arthur W. Radford, who was 58th out of 177 in the Annapolis Class of 1916. The first Air Force General to hold the Joint Chief of Staff post was General Nathan F. Twining, who was 137th out of 283 in the West Point Class of 1919. The highest class rank among academy grads who reached the top U.S. military post was Army General Maxwell D. Taylor, Chairman from 1962 to 1964. He ranked fourth of 101 graduates in West Point's Class of 1922.

Admiral William J. Crowe Jr., who was Chairman from 1985 to 1989, ranked 80th in the Annapolis Class of 1947 that included President

Jimmy Carter. President Carter ranked ahead of him—59th out of the 821 graduates.a few other Chairmen of the Joint Chief of Staff have been graduates of Reserve Officer Training Corps programs at civilian universities. These ROTC grads include Army General Colin L. Powell—from 1989 to 1993—and the Chairman during the beginning of the Iraq War, Air Force General Richard B. Myers. Powell, Secretary of State during the administration of President George W. Bush, graduated from City College of New York. Myers graduated from Kansas State University. In 2005, Marine Corps General Peter Pace was named the first Marine to serve as Chairman of the Joint Chiefs. He was ranked 428th among 890 classmates in the Naval Academy's Class of 1967. He was succeeded in 2007 by Admiral Michael G. Mullen, ranked 610th among 836 members of the USNA Class of 1968.

Another of West Point's famous grads was the Third Army Commander in World War II, General George S. Patton Jr. Patton first attended Virginia Military Institute as a freshman "Rat" in the Class of 1907. Then he was appointed to the West Point Class of 1908 but failed freshman-year mathematics and rolled back to the Class of 1909. After completing three plebe summer experiences (one at VMI and two at West Point), Patton eventually graduated 46th out of 103 in West Point's Class of 1909. Little known about General Patton, according to military leadership expert and author Edgar F. Puryear Jr., is that he was dyslexic. Dyslexia, which was discovered near the end of the 19th Century about the time Patton was born, disturbs reading ability. As a result of his condition, Puryear believes Patton actually memorized his material. (Puryear Interview.) Vietnam War General William C. Westmoreland was 112th out of 275 West Point graduates in 1936.

At the Naval Academy, Navy aviator veteran, Vietnam War POW, Arizona U.S. Senator, and 2008 Republican presidential candidate John Sidney McCain III was sixth from the bottom among 900 grads in the Class of 1958. His father, Admiral John Sidney McCain Jr., graduated 18th from the bottom of his 1931 class of 423 men. His grandfather, Admiral John Sidney McCain, was 79th out of 116 or 37th from the bottom of the Class of 1906. His son, John Sidney McCain IV, was a member of the Annapolis Class of 2009.

From Abrams to Zumwalt, senior U.S. military officers have been consistent in their career achievements mostly unrelated to their academic pedigrees or class rank. General Creighton W. Abrams, who was Army Chief of Staff during the Vietnam War, ranked 185th out of 275 members of West Point's Class of 1936 that also included Westmoreland. Admiral Elmo Russell Zumwalt Jr. was 33rd out of his 615 classmates in the Naval Academy's Class of 1943 that graduated in 1942. He was Chief of Naval

Operations from 1970 to 1974. General Alexander M. Haig Jr.—President Richard Nixon's chief of staff, NATO Commander, and Secretary of State for President Ronald Reagan—ranked 213th among 310 graduates in West Point's Class of 1947.

General Wesley K. Clark, a Rhodes Scholar who was ranked first in his West Point Class of 1966 and later served as NATO commander, tried to follow in the footsteps of Presidents Grant, Eisenhower, and Carter but was not successful in his bid for the presidency in 2004. An earlier unsuccessful presidential candidate, in 1992, was Texas billionaire H. Ross Perot, who ranked in the middle—453rd in the Naval Academy's Class of 1953. His running mate was retired Navy VADM James Bond Stockdale, a Naval aviator who was awarded the Congressional Medal of Honor for his gallantry as a Prisoner of War during the Vietnam War. Stockdale ranked 129th among 821 grads in the Naval Academy's Class of 1947.

Virginia U.S. Senator James H. Webb Jr.—U.S. Marine Corps Vietnam veteran, bestselling author, and former Secretary of the Navy—ranked 314th among 836 in 1968 at Annapolis. Rhode Island U.S. Senator John "Jack" F. Reed ranked 16th among 729 classmates in West Point's Class of 1971. Lt.Gen. David H. Petraeus, named commander of U.S. forces in Iraq in 2007, was ranked 39th among 833 graduates in his West Point Class of 1974. Montel B. Williams, the motivational speaker and television personality, ranked 864th among 947 grads of the Naval Academy's Class of 1980. New Mexico U.S. Representative Heather Ann Wilson, the first female veteran in the U.S. Congress, ranked 56th among 842 graduates of the Air Force Academy Class of 1982.

Dr. Larry Bland, curator for the General George C. Marshall Foundation, told the story of Marshall's Chief of Staff, General Malin Craig and his West Point classmate, David L. Stone. Craig ranked 33rd in the Class of 1898, and Stone was at the bottom of their class of 59 graduates. In the 1930s, Craig wrote to then MGen Stone when the latter was the Commanding General of the Army's Third Division at Fort Lewis, WA. Stone was experiencing some difficulty with a subordinate, and Craig told him "that he was peculiarly in a position to counteract this lowered morale by throwing out his chest and making the statement, which everybody knows is correct, that he himself managed to scrape through no. 59 in a class of 59 at West Point; that he had never been to any school in his life; and that he was, as everybody could see, a Major General in good standing." (Bland Interview and Marshall 1981, 516.)

After all, he had started out with all of his classmates with the same date of rank.

Acknowledgments

M any fine people helped me in the research, writing, and publishing of this book, a project more than two decades in the making. The text cited scores of generous contributors and there were lots of others who also must be acknowledged here. And while I appreciate all of your help, please be sure that we recognize that any inaccuracies are mine. Thanks again to all of you.

Airmen: Jim Arpe, George Bumiller, Dom DeAngelo, Jim FX Doyle, Michael Emerson, Larry Griswold, Steve Hatt, Bill Hall, Kevin Hoppin, Joe Liro, John Lowden, Bill McCarron, Jim Moore, Tom Morrill, and John Wetterau.

Marines: Skip Bartlett, Jim Brady, Bill Bushnell, R. J. Del Vecchio, Mike Hoppin, Bob Love, Jim O'Brien, John Ripley, and Jim Webb.

Sailors: John Butler, Frank Cleary, Moe and Charlie Cragin, Tom DeBow, Dan Doyle, Mick Hocker, John James, Kevin Lynch, Doug MacVane, Sandy Mendelsohn, Jeff Metzel, Mike Murray, Dick Norris, Ted Rippert, Phil Ryan, and Jay Siembedia.

Soldiers: Chris Arney, John Baker, Patricia Buel, Adam Cote, Steve Daffron, Peter Deane, Charlie Forshee, Joe Gancie, Ned Gerrity, Jim Hayman, Jim Heigle, Bill Hinderer, Mike Hoffman, George Knapp, Bill Kowal, Tom Lydon, Mike Lynch, Tom Lynch, John McKinney, Dan Murphy, Butch O'Neill, Bill Raymond, Marie Watson, and Dan Weadock.

Air Force Academy: Nancy Bogenreef, Laurent Fox, Rich Fullerton, Troy Garnhart, Gary Howe, Betsy Muenger, Tad Oelstrom, Steve Orie, Uriah Orland, Dick Rauschkolb, Duane Reed, Jim Shaw, Mark Wells, Johnny Whitaker, and Ruth Whitaker.

Naval Academy: Marge Bem, Jim Cheevers, Dave Church, Jennifer Erickson, Deborah Goode, Beverly Lyle, Terry Murray, John Ryan, Scott Strasemeier, Tom Trueblood, and George Watt.

West Point: Bob Beretta, Patricia Brown, Dan Christman, Frank DeMarco, Kelly Gorreck, Steve Grove, Andrea Hamburger, Seth Hudgins, Julian Olejniczak, and Joe Tombrello.

Others: Victor Berger, Juan Cappello, Peg Collins, Jerry Crotty, Tom Fieldsend, Jim Gallagher, Wayne Gronlund, Jean Gulliver, Karen Houppert, Mike Hughes, Mary Jervis, Andy Lawrence, Steve Little, Dan Lynch, Peter Lysy, Joe Malichio, Eleanor Lincoln Morse, Bill Powers, Mark Savolis, Vaughan Stanley, Cynthia Thayer, Jim Trelease, Jamal Thomas, Ed Wakin, Priscilla Webster, and Steve Yesenosky.

And Family: My wife, Barbara, and our children: Patti, Kevin, Jim, and Jack. Their partners: Bill, Sue, Kerry, and Janna. And our grandchildren: Garrett, Owen, Emily, and Mira. Plus the roots provided by my Mother and Father, Christina Victory and John Edward Hoppin, and my brothers: Michael, Dennis, John, and Franc.

References

Air Force Magazine. *Springboard for Airpower.* Journal of the Air Force Association, March, 2004.

Ambrose, Stephen E. *To America.* Simon & Schuster. 2002.

Ambrose, Stephen E. *Citizen Soldiers.* Simon & Schuster. 1997.

Ambrose, Stephen E. *D-Day, June 6, 1944: the climactic battle of World War II.* Simon & Schuster. 1994.

Ambrose, Stephen E. *Duty, Honor, Country.* The John Hopkins University Press. 1999.

Arny, Chris. *West Point's Scientific 200: Celebration of the Bicentennial.* Palmetto Bookworks. 2002.

Atkinson, Rick. *The Long Grey Line.* Simon & Schuster. 1989.

Banning, Kendall. *ANNAPOLIS TODAY.* United States Naval Institute. 1957.

Barkalow, Carol and Raab, Andrea. *In The Men's House.* Poseidon Press. 1990.

Beauchamp, Al. *Green Among the Blue.* Vantage Press. 1969

Bonn, Keith E. *When the Odds Were Even.* Presidio Press. 1994.

Brady, James. *The Marines of Autumn.* St. Martin's Press. 2000.

Brady, James. *Why Marines Fight.* St. Martin's Press. 2007.

Bradley, James. *Flags of Our Fathers.* Bantam Books. 2000.

Bradley, Omar and Blair, Clay. *A General's Life.* Simon and Schuster. 1983.

Brokaw, Tom. *The Greatest Generation.* Random House. 1998.

Bruegmann, Robert. *Modernism at Mid-Century: The Architecture of the United States Air Force Academy.* The University of Chicago Press. 1994.

Carew, Walter R. Jr. *Men of Spirit Men of Sports.* Ambassador Books. 1999.

Carlisle, Rodney P. and Monetta, Dominick J. *Brandy, Our Man in Acapulco.* University of North Texas Press. 1999.

Cassidy, Susan. *The Brat Journal.* Nomad Publishing. 1997.

Clark, Wesley K. *Waging Modern War.* Public Affairs. 2001.

Class of 1899 Centennial Edition: Register of Graduates and Former Cadets.
Association of Graduates, USMA 1999

Cooper, Henry S.F. Jr. *Before Lift-Off.* The Johns Hopkins University Press.
1987.

Coram, Robert. *Boyd.* Little, Brown and Company. 2002.

Crane, John and Kieley, James F. *United States Naval Academy: The First
Hundred Years.* McGraw-Hill Book Company, Inc. 1945.

Cullum Memorial Edition: Register of Graduates and Former Cadets. Association
of Graduates, USMA. 1980

DeBerry, Fisher and Schaller, Bob. *For God and Country.* Cross Training
Pub. 2000.

Eisenhower, David. *Eisenhower At War 1943-1945.* Random House. 1986.

Eisenhower, Dwight D. *At Ease.* Avon Books. 1967.

Fagan, George V. *The Air Force Academy: An Illustrated History.* Johnson
Books. 1988.

Fair, Charles. *From The Jaws of Victory.* Simon and Schuster. 1971

Feinstein, John. *A Civil War: Army vs. Navy.* Little, Brown and Company.
1996.

Feinstein, John. *The Last Amateurs.* Little, Brown and Company. 2000.

Freeman, Douglas Southall. *R. E. Lee A Biography.* Charles Scribner's Sons.
1934.

Garrett, Sheryl and Hoppin, Sue. *A Family's Guide to the Military for Dummies.*
Wiley Publishing, Inc. 2008.

Haag, SSgt Jason, *AFPN Release.* 332nd Air Expeditionary Wing Public
Affairs, Langley AFB, VA. April 12, 2003.

Halberstam, David. *One Very Hot Day.* Houghton Miflin Company. 1967.

Halberstam, David. *The Best and the Brightest.* Random House. 1972.

Halberstam, David. *The Fifties.* Fawcett Books. 1993.

Harahan, J. P. *On-Site Inspections Under the INF Treaty.* U.S. Gov. Printing
Office. 1993.

Horn, Miriam. *Rebels in White Gloves.* Random House. 1999.

Houppert, Karen. *Home Fires Burning.* Ballentine Books. 2005.

Janowitz, Morris. *The Professional Soldier.* The Free Press. 1960.

Just, Ward. *Military Men.* Alfred A. Knopf. 1970.

Kirshner, Ralph. *The Class of 1861.* Southern Illinois University Press.
1999.

Landis, L. C. *The Story of the U.S. Air Force Academy.* Rinehart & Company.
1960.

Lipsky, David. *Absolutely American.* Houghton Mifflin. 2003.

Lowden, John L. *Silent Wings at War.* Smithsonian Institution Press. 1992.

Manchester, William. *American Caesar.* Little, Brown and Company. 1978.

Maraniss, David. *When Pride Still Mattered.* Touchstone. Simon & Schuster. 2000.

Marshall, George C. *The Papers, Volume 1.* Johns Hopkins University Press. 1981.

Marshall, S.L.A. *Pork Chop Hill.* William Morrow and Company. 1956.

McCain, John. *Faith of My Fathers.* Random House. 1999.

McConnell, Malcolm. *Into The Mouth of the Cat.* W.W. Norton & Company, Inc. 1985.

Moore, Harold G. and Galloway, Joseph. *We Were Soldiers Once . . . And Young.* HarperTorch. 1992.

Murphy, Bill Jr. *In A Time of War.* Henry Holt. 2008.

National Aeronautics and Space Administration. *Astronaut Fact Book.* September 2000.

Powell, Colin. *My American Journey.* Random House. 1995.

Puryear, Edgar F. Jr. *George S. Brown.* Presidio Press. 1983.

Puryear, Edgar F. Jr. *19 STARS—A Study in Military Character and Leadership.* Presidio Press. 1994.

Puryear, Edgar F. Jr. *American Generalship.* Presidio Press. 2000.

Robbins, James S. *Last In Their Class.* Encounter Books. 2006.

Ruggero, Ed. *Duty First.* HarperCollins. 2001.

Register of Alumni, United States Naval Academy Alumni Association. 1845-1993.

Register of Graduates, Association of Graduates, U.S. Air Force Academy. 1999.

Schaeffer, Frank and John. *Keeping Faith.* Carroll & Graf Publishers. 2003.

Shapiro, Fred R. *The Yale Book of Quotations.* Yale University Press. 2006.

Skelnar, Larry. *To Hell With Honor.* University of Oklahoma Press. 2000.

Stiehm, Judith Hicks. *Bring Me Men and Women.* University of California Press. 1981.

Taylor, Robert L. and Rosenbach, William E. Editors, *Military Leadership: In Pursuit of Excellence.* Westview Press. 1984.

Tannenbaum, Abraham J. *Gifted Children.* Macmillan Publishing Company. 1983.

Thomas, Emory M. *Robert E. Lee.* W.W. Norton & Company. 1995.

Timberg, Robert. *The Nightingale's Song.* Simon & Schuster Inc. 1995.

Westmoreland, General William C. *A Soldier Reports.* Doubleday & Company, Inc. 1976.

Yellin, Emily. *Our Mothers' War.* Free Press. 2004.

Index

7703031R0

Made in the USA
Lexington, KY
09 December 2010